Population Economics

Research on population economics deals with some of the most pertinent issues of our time and, as such, is of interest to academics and policymakers alike. Like the Journal of Population Economics, the book series "Population Economics" addresses a wide range of theoretical and empirical topics related to all areas of the economics of population, household, and human resources. Books in the series comprise work that closely examines special topics related to population economics, incorporating the most recent developments in the field and the latest research methodologies. Micro-level investigations include topics related to individual, household or family behavior, such as migration, aging, household formation, marriage, divorce, fertility choices, labor supply, health, and risky behavior. Macro-level inquiries examine topics such as economic growth with exogenous or endogenous population evolution, population policy, savings and pensions, social security, housing, and healthcare. These and other topics related to the relationship between population dynamics and public choice, economic approaches to human biology, and the impact of population on income and wealth distributions have important individual, social, and institutional consequences, and their scientific examination informs both economic theory and public policy.

All books in this series are peer-reviewed.

Nadir Altinok · Claude Diebolt

Edumetrics

Measuring Human Capital for the 21st Century

Springer

Nadir Altinok
BETA/CNRS
University of Lorraine
Nancy Cedex, France

Claude Diebolt
BETA/CNRS
University of Strasbourg
Strasbourg Cedex, France

With Contribution by
Romain Diebolt
Southampton Business School
University of Southampton
Southampton, UK

ISSN 1431-6978
Population Economics
ISBN 978-3-032-13276-5 ISBN 978-3-032-13277-2 (eBook)
https://doi.org/10.1007/978-3-032-13277-2

This Springer imprint is published by the registered company Springer Nature Switzerland AG
The registered company address is: Gewerbestrasse 11, 6330 Cham, Switzerland

Acknowledgments We would like to express our deepest gratitude to all those who have accompanied us on the journey that led to *Edumetrics*. This book is not only the fruit of research and collaboration, but also of shared trust, patience and encouragement.

Our warmest thanks go to UMR BETA/CNRS, whose intellectual environment and unwavering support have been indispensable throughout this project. We are equally grateful to the Association Française de Cliométrie, which has continually nurtured the spirit of curiosity and rigor that animates our work. We also extend our sincere appreciation to Professor Klaus F. Zimmermann, whose commitment to the dissemination of knowledge has enabled this book to find its place in the *Population Economics* series and within the global scientific community.

A very special word of thanks goes to Niko Chtouris and to Springer Verlag—without your guidance, kindness and faith in this endeavor, *Edumetrics* would never have become the "living book" it is today.

We would also like to express our heartfelt appreciation to all those who have generously shared their time, expertise and encouragement throughout the development of this work. Our sincere thanks go to Noam Angrist (Youth Impact / What Works Hub for Global Education), Manos Antoninis (Director, UNESCO Global Education Monitoring Report), Paul Atherton (Founder & CEO, AI for Education), Abdurrahman Aydemir (Professor of Economics, Sabancı University), Jean-Marc Bernard (La Chouette LLC, Georgetown University), Nihan Köseleci-Blanchy (Economist, European Investment Bank), İpek Coşkun Armağan (General Coordinator, Enstitü Sosyal), Luis Crouch (Emeritus Senior Economist, RTI International), Deon Filmer (Director, Development Research Group, World Bank), Amber Gove (Strategic Advisor, Gove Consulting LLC), Montserrat Gomendio (Chancellor, Universidad Nebrija; former Head, OECD Centre for Skills), Rick Hanushek (Paul and Jean Hanna Senior Fellow, Hoover Institution, Stanford University), Geeta Kingdon (Emeritus Professor of Education Economics, University College London), Patrick Montjouridès (Senior Policy Analyst, UNESCO Global Education Monitoring Report), Silvia Montoya (Director, UNESCO Institute for Statistics), Harry Patrinos (Head of the Department of Education Reform and 21st Century Endowed Chair in Education Policy, University of Arkansas), Dan Wagner (Professor of Education, University of Pennsylvania) and Ludger Woessmann (Professor of Economics, University of Munich and Director, ifo Center for the Economics of Education).

Their pioneering contributions to education policy and research have been a constant source of inspiration and intellectual guidance. We are profoundly grateful for their insights, generosity and enduring commitment to advancing education for all.

With humility and respect, we dedicate these pages not only to measurement, but also to the conviction that through education, we learn not merely to know—but to become.

Competing Interests The authors have no competing interests to declare that are relevant to the content of this manuscript.

Contents

Chapter 1
From Standard Human Capital Theory to Edumetrics: An Introduction

Abstract This chapter introduces *Edumetrics* as a data-driven framework for measuring human capital in the twenty-first century, inspired by Lord Kelvin's principle that improvement begins with measurement. Positioned at the intersection of economics, education and the social sciences, it argues that quantifying learning outcomes is not only possible but essential to scientific progress and sound policy. The book situates edumetrics within the tradition of human capital theory while emphasizing its interdisciplinary scope and methodological innovations. By harmonizing international learning assessments since 1970, edumetrics makes it possible to trace long-term trends in both quality and equity worldwide, revealing their economic implications. Ultimately, it reframes the education–growth nexus by shifting the focus from schooling years to actual skills, offering new evidence for the design of more effective and equitable policies.

The starting point of this book, *Edumetrics: Measuring Human Capital for the twenty-first Century*, is the celebrated 1889 statement by William Thomson, Lord Kelvin:

"I often say that when you can measure what you are speaking about, and express it in numbers, you know something about it; but when you cannot measure it, when you cannot express it in numbers, your knowledge is of a meagre and unsatisfactory kind: it may be the beginning of knowledge, but you have scarcely, in your thoughts, advanced to the stage of science, whatever the matter may be" (Thomson, 1889, pp. 73–74).

Kelvin's principle stands as the cornerstone of edumetrics, recasting educational research as a genuinely data-driven discipline. Closely aligned with the tradition of cliometrics (Diebolt, 2016; Diebolt & Haupert, 2024), in this book our approach is resolutely interdisciplinary, bridging the sciences and the humanities. We contend that the quantification of qualitative educational processes is not merely possible but indispensable. Measurement is the foundation upon which scientific progress is built; edumetrics embraces this principle by establishing itself as a vital framework for measuring human capital—both quantitatively and qualitatively—for the twenty-first century.

N. Altinok and C. Diebolt, *Edumetrics*, Population Economics,
https://doi.org/10.1007/978-3-032-13277-2_1

Ultimately, one cannot improve what one cannot measure. This conviction gives edumetrics its dual character: it is not only a research program but also a lens with far-reaching implications for educational and economic policy.

Many countries today, perhaps more than ever before, face another dual challenge: how to remain competitive internationally while maintaining genuine equity within their populations. Education is at the heart of this challenge. As a major factor in productivity and, therefore, economic growth, the expectations placed on schools are enormous and regularly give rise to demands to reduce or even eliminate inequalities so that everyone can continue to find their place in society in the future.

Historically, it was the Coleman Report of 1966 that highlighted questions about the nature, sources and causes of educational inequality. While education systems in developed countries have succeeded in enrolling almost all of their young people in school, the major issues now relate more to analyzing forms of "qualitative democratization". Furthermore, the issue of educational inequality raises questions about how to measure educational achievement.

This book on Edumetrics—i.e. the quantitative study of variables related to learning through education, based on the seminal work in psychometrics by Carver (1974)—aims to contribute to the debate by tracing the long-term evolution of all dimensions in the academic skills of students since 1970.

Carver's seminal 1974 work proposes a fundamental distinction in the field of educational and psychological measurement. The author identifies the existence of two dimensions inherent in any test: the psychometric dimension, focused on measuring stable differences between individuals, and the edumetric dimension, centered on measuring the gains or progress achieved by an individual as a result of learning. Contrary to the widespread view that norm-referenced and criterion-referenced tests are mutually exclusive, Carver demonstrates that both dimensions coexist within any instrument, yet methodological choices made during test design tend to privilege one dimension over the other.

Psychometric tests aim to discriminate among individuals, for example by measuring general aptitudes or personality traits, whereas edumetric tests seek to detect and quantify internal changes, such as the acquisition of new skills or knowledge. This distinction manifests itself at every stage of test development and evaluation. In terms of objectives, a psychometric test is designed to predict or compare performance across individuals, while an edumetric test focuses on assessing a specific learning outcome. In item selection, the psychometric approach favors items with a success rate close to 50 percent, thereby maximizing variance and inter-individual discrimination, whereas the edumetric approach seeks items that are most sensitive to progression as measured between a pre-learning and a post-learning situation. With respect to validity, the psychometric perspective relies on correlations with a stable external criterion, while the edumetric approach requires the ability to faithfully capture an expected gain. In psychometrics, reliability denotes the stability of discriminations between individuals from one administration to another, whereas in edumetrics it refers to the consistency of gains measured within the same individual. Score interpretation also differs: the psychometric approach depends on norms and inter-individual comparisons, whereas the edumetric approach is referenced to an objective or criterion independent of group performance.

To illustrate this analytical framework, Carver applies it to the *Sequential Tests of Educational Progress* (STEP)—Reading Test. Although the stated aim of the test—measuring reading comprehension and interpretation—aligns more closely with edumetric purposes, its design, item selection, validity and reliability evaluation, and score interpretation are all dominated by psychometric principles. This methodological inconsistency limits the instrument's capacity to measure actual learning effectively. In the discussion of his 1974 article, Carver critiques the inappropriate use of psychometric models for evaluating educational effects, which often leads to underestimating the impact of programs or schools. He notes that education, which inherently involves an intervention or treatment, naturally calls for an edumetric approach, one more closely aligned with scientific experimentation. The example of the Coleman Report (1966) illustrates the risks of using tests designed to discriminate stable aptitudes in contexts where the aim is to measure the effects of instruction: the observed differences may reflect pre-existing disparities between individuals rather than the effectiveness of schools.

In sum, Carver argues that measuring inter-individual differences and measuring intra-individual gains each requires instruments specifically designed for their respective purposes. He maintains that the future of educational measurement depends on the development and evaluation of tests that address both dimensions simultaneously, thereby equipping researchers and practitioners with tools truly suited to their objectives. He calls for the methodological advancement of edumetrics—still in its infancy—to close a major gap in the measurement of learning and educational growth. It is precisely in this regard that the ambition of our work resides.

1.1 Positioning within the Existing Literature

It is mainly since the 1960s that significant efforts toward systematic theorization (Blaug, 1968-1969), with decisive contributions from Schultz (1961), Becker (1964), Mincer (1974) and others, have emerged and given rise to human capital theory. The modern father of this theory is widely regarded as Theodore Schultz (Nobel Prize, 1979), who estimated the stock of human capital in the United States in 1900 and 1957 and its contribution to the country's economic growth. However, despite his pioneering work, Schultz never explicitly developed the theory underlying his research. Another American economist, Gary Becker (Nobel Prize, 1992), seeking to examine the relationship between economic growth and educational development through an analysis of income statistics by level of education, formulated a theory of human investment. Despite differences in context and approach between Becker and his predecessors, he arrived at virtually the same conclusions, which were very similar to those of neoclassical capital theory. His approach sought to explain the decisions of individuals and businesses to invest in education (formal and informal, as well as in health, information, workers' living conditions, etc.) by the expected additional income. Once the momentum generated by this seminal work had passed, research on this topic slowed down in the 1970s. However, the persistence of economic difficulties and new questions about the drivers of growth contributed to a revival of the economic analysis of education in the mid-1980s. Education is studied in all its forms (formal education, on-the-job training, etc.), and research has been extended to all aspects of human resource development.

Originally, human capital theory (Goldin, 2024) viewed education spending as an investment, seeking to specify the demand for it and understand its impact on economic growth. Education spending was seen as an efficiency factor that raised productivity and determined the level and distribution of individual earnings. This analysis has been subject to various criticisms (e.g., the filter model), which have led to new avenues of research. Efforts have thus been made to study the supply of education, the internal efficiency of the education system, the optimal financing of the training system, the links between education and health, and economic analyses of the family. Since the 1980s, there has also been interest in constructing growth models (Lucas, 1988; Romer, 1986) that attempt to better represent the various aspects of the links between education and economic growth. Indeed, we must not forget that the influence of an individual's education on economic activity can be transmitted directly through the individual themselves, through their descendants (legacy effects) or through other individuals (externalities). Economic activity can also affect the education system, or the type and level of education. The very diversity of all this work makes any exhaustive approach difficult.

1.2 Methodology

The economics of education aims to study the internal relationships between educational variables, as well as the external relationships between education and its environment. Its purpose is to facilitate an understanding of the economic aspects of the creation and use of qualifications within a society. In this perspective, it is systematically confronted with other disciplines that may, to some extent, be complementary to or in competition with it (history, sociology, psychology, etc.). Its main fields of application are the study of the relationships between education and employment, education and the economy, education and income distribution, and so on (Diebolt, Hippe, Jaoul-Grammare, 2017).

Work on growth theories, for example, is of great interest to public authorities, emphasizing in particular the role of education and training as key long-term determinants of a nation's economic performance. The question of the effectiveness of education is becoming a purely economic issue, in addition to its social, ethical, ideological and pedagogical aspects—not to mention its long-recognized budgetary implications. Internal efficiency raises questions about the pedagogical, systemic and financial determinants of academic results. External efficiency concerns the links between education and the quality of human capital through its effects on productivity, remuneration and the return on investment in training. However, despite being the subject of numerous studies and proposals, the efficiency of education—both external and internal—remains a mystery in terms of its content and determinants.

The informed researcher can only be amused by the trends in the search for knowledge. We discover the importance of a concept or a particular approach to problems. The public becomes enthusiastic about these new ideas. But very quickly, the dogma of their infallibility falls apart. The difficult questions remain unanswered. It is also legitimate to ask these kinds of questions about the economics of education. Even today, it is still primarily a body of doctrines that recommends a methodological approach to problems. In any case, we believe that future efforts should focus on comparative methodology, one potential application of which is international comparison.

In this book, we will assume that any international comparison at the global level aims to highlight the effect of the national context on the research subjects observed in order to measure their degree of generality according to the theoretical model and the hypotheses that we will seek to verify empirically. That said, we do not aim to offer a critical or epistemological analysis of what the economics of education is or should be. However, it is clear that advances in knowledge become evident as soon as we take a comparative, long-term perspective.

These perspectives are, of course, of various kinds. The emergence of new concepts sharpens our analytical skills. The formulation of new hypotheses gives more content and structure to our view of phenomena. The definition of new mathematical models provides frameworks for studying the predictive consequences of our knowledge. At the same time, in addition to a strong trend toward the development of all forms of experimentation, we find that the nature of discussions among education economists has remained remarkably—if not paradoxically— unchanged throughout the twentieth century and even today.

In fact, the complexity of the phenomena, the nature of the data that can be collected, and the actual potential of econometric methods make it difficult to advance knowledge and, therefore, to make discoveries in the purest sense of the term. With regard to data, for example, we believe that any new dataset is too limited, taken in isolation, to enable discovery, but that the accumulation of observations gradually changes the evidence available to us and, subsequently, the scientific knowledge we can derive from it.

Having reached this conclusion, the question posed by this book is not to compare the economics of education with other human and social sciences concerned with education. In particular, we would have to acknowledge that the economics of education is undoubtedly unique in giving such a major role to logical deductions based on specified a priori assumptions. However, when it comes to scientific discoveries, we suspect that the situation in other humanities and social sciences is not very different from that in the economics of education. Of course, a historian may discover an ancient manuscript, or an anthropologist a tribe, but such cases are rare and, above all, their main interest lies not in the manuscript or the tribe, but in the new material they provide for scientific research in education.

Perhaps this material will offer little that is new and the discovery will be negligible. Perhaps, on the contrary, it will contain the necessary confirmation or imply a revision of previously accepted ideas, in which case the discovery will be regarded as crucial. Overall, most of our current knowledge of the economics of education comes, in our view, from the gradual accumulation of statistically or institutionally stylized factual elements, which remains insufficiently historical and comparative.

1.3 Expected Results

This book aims to trace the long-term evolution of all dimensions in student academic skills worldwide since 1970 and to estimate, through causal analysis using counterfactual methods, the past, present and future effects of the quality of education on economic growth worldwide and in certain countries selected as experimental laboratories.

Indeed, while the role of education in economic growth seems to be one of the most widely accepted truths among economists, it was the subject of considerable debate at the turn of the 2000s. Since then, a series of reports aimed at policymakers (driven by new economic research, particularly in line with so-called neo-Schumpeterian approaches) have highlighted the need to mobilize our education systems—particularly higher education—in order to maintain our competitiveness and growth. The echo of more critical empirical work on the relationship between education and growth has been such that a re-examination of these findings is undoubtedly worthwhile. This is all the more so given that skepticism about this relationship has also been echoed in works aimed more at the general public (e.g., Alison Wolf, 2002, in *Myths about Education and Growth*). If we examine the history of economic thought (and economic history), it turns out that these debates are not new. In fact, as Blaug (1985) points out, we can see that phases of optimism and skepticism about the link between education and growth have alternated over time.

In short, the relationship between education and growth is far from clear. Several empirical strategies have been developed to test theoretical questions and assess the extent to which increasing human capital is central to growth. Problems with data quality and measurement have led to much debate and, for the most part, to a wave of skepticism about the future.

Our book continues this line of inquiry and aims to offer new insights into the subject.

Edumetrics is not just a new label for well-known statistics. Its novelty lies in the way it transforms scattered educational indicators into a coherent measurement system that is comparable across time and space, and that can be directly linked to macroeconomic outcomes. For instance, while PISA or TIMSS provide snapshots of student performance every three to five years, *edumetrics* reconstructs long-run series of learning inequalities at the country level since the 1970s, harmonized and corrected for methodological shifts. This allows us to answer questions that were previously inaccessible: How much of a country's growth acceleration can be attributed to narrowing learning gaps? What is the economic cost of an additional year in which disadvantaged students fall further behind? By grounding the measurement of human capital in robust, long-term and comparable learning outcomes rather than in crude proxies such as years of schooling, *edumetrics* renews the very foundations of the human capital-growth debate.

The second chapter, *"A Review of International and Regional Achievement Tests in the Long-Run"*, will provide a comprehensive overview of international and regional assessments over the past six decades.

The third chapter, *"Learning-Adjusted Years of Schooling Worldwide"*, demonstrates that analyzing education involves more than measuring years of schooling—quality matters. This study aims to produce better data on schooling with a focus on learning outcomes. It presents the largest dataset to date on learning outcomes, years of schooling and learning-adjusted years of schooling (LAYS), with internationally comparable data spanning 1970 to 2020. The quantity dimension is measured by years of schooling, while the quality dimension is derived from linking standardized, psychometrically robust international achievement tests and hybrid assessments. The dataset covers more than 120 countries between 1970 and 2020. Several findings stand out: a global convergence in both learning outcomes and enrollment occurred from 1970 until around 1990, after which divergence reappeared. Since 2000, very few countries have recorded improvements in schooling quality, while in most countries learning outcomes have remained stable.

The fourth chapter, *"Mapping Educational Inequality Worldwide"*, addresses the fact that while research increasingly emphasizes the quality of education systems, the analysis of inequalities in educational attainment remains comparatively underexplored. We present a new database offering an international and temporal perspective on educational inequalities, drawing on the wealth of student achievement surveys. This multidimensional database measures the equity of education systems through several indicators. Cross-country and longitudinal comparability is achieved through a rigorous methodology that incorporates the principle of anchoring via multiple-country participation in various surveys. Covering approximately 100 countries over nearly half a century (1970–2020), the database reveals that the international average score over the last fifty years has been 420 points—well below the OECD average of 500 points in PISA. Around 66% of students achieve at least the minimum competency threshold, with wide disparities between countries. Fewer than 6% reach the advanced threshold, although some countries surpass 30%.

The fifth chapter, *"The Price of Inequality: Fifty Years of Education and Growth in France"*, uses original data to trace the long-term evolution of inequalities in the academic skills of French students from 1970 to 2020. Drawing on France's results in international achievement surveys, we provide an original analysis of inequalities in educational attainment. We estimate the economic cost of these inequalities, concluding that French economic growth could have been 0.5% higher had an effective equity policy been implemented since the late 1970s. This constitutes the first cliometric study—drawing on a unique edumetric database and counterfactual methods—devoted to the structural and spatial dynamics of educational inequality in France and globally.

The sixth chapter, *"The Price of Progress: Access, Quality, and Equity in the Turkish Education System"*, shows that Türkiye has experienced rapid growth in primary and secondary completion rates over the past two decades. Secondary completion rates rose from less than 60% in 2000 to nearly 90% in 2023. We investigate the extent to which this expansion in school access has affected educational quality. To do so, we use the new global schooling quality database from Altinok and Diebolt (*Cliometrica*, 2024), which provides comparable data for more than 130 countries between 1970 and 2020. In addition to the quality dimension, we examine equity issues. Using a counterfactual approach, we compare Türkiye's relative performance with that of the most similar developing countries. While Türkiye remains one of the OECD countries facing the greatest challenges in ensuring access and retention in formal education, we find that the recent democratization of education has not led to a decline in quality. On the contrary, alongside expanded access, Türkiye has recorded notable improvements in quality indicators, especially in mathematics and reading. Nonetheless, as in France and Germany, significant inequalities in access, completion and skill levels persist and are likely to remain among the country's most pressing education policy challenges in the years ahead.

The seventh chapter, *"Conclusion—What Edumetrics Still Has to Teach Us"*, synthesizes the main findings and discusses their implications for education and human capital policy in the twenty-first century.

The book also includes an Online Appendix, which contains the publication of a unique database in this field.

References

Becker, G. (1964). *Human Capital. A Theoretical and Empirical Analysis with Special Reference to Education*, New York, Columbia University Press.

Blaug M. (1968–1969). *Economics of Education*, 2 Volumes, Harmondsworth, Penguin Books.

Blaug M. (1985). Where are we Now in the Economics of Education?, *Economics of Education Review*, *4*(1), 17–28.

Carver R.P. (1974). Two Dimensions of Tests: Psychometric and Edumetric, *American Psychologist*, *29*(7), 512–518.

Coleman J.S (1966). *Equality of Educational Opportunity*, Washington, US Department of Health, Education, and Welfare, Office of Education.

Diebolt, C. (2016). Cliometrica after 10 years: Definition and Principles of Cliometric Research. *Cliometrica, 10*(1), 1–4.

Diebolt C., Haupert M. Eds. (2024). *Handbook of Cliometrics*, 3rd Edition, 3 Volumes, Berlin, Springer Nature.

Diebolt C., Hippe R., Jaoul-Grammare M. (2017). *Bildungsökonomie. Eine Einführung aus historischer Perspektive*, Wiesbaden, Springer Gabler.

Goldin C. (2024). Human Capital, in: Diebolt C., Haupert M. (Eds.), *Handbook of Cliometrics*, Vol. 1. Berlin, Springer Nature, 353–384.

Lucas, R. (1988). On the Mechanics of Economic Development. *Journal of Monetary Economics, 22*(1), pp. 3–42.

Mincer J. (1974). *Schooling, Experience and Earnings*, New York, Columbia University Press.

Romer P. (1986). Increasing Returns and Long-Run Growth, *Journal of Political Economy*, *94*(5), 1002–1037.

Schultz T. (1961). Investment in Human Capital, *American Economic Review*, *51*(1), 1–17.

Thomson, W. (Lord Kelvin) (1889). Electrical Units of Measurement [A Lecture delivered at the Institution of Civil Engineers on May 3, 1883; being one of a series of Six Lectures on "The Practical Applications of Electricity."], in: Thomson, W. (Sir), (Ed.), *Nature Series. Popular Lectures and Addresses*, Vol. 1, New York, Macmillan & Co., 73–74.

Wolf A. (2002). *Does Education Matter? Myths about Education and Growth.* London, Penguin Books.

Chapter 2
A Review of International and Regional Achievement Tests in the Long-Run

Abstract This chapter provides an overview of the main instruments used to assess learning achievement and adult skills. It addresses the central methodological challenge of distinguishing between performance and competence, emphasizing that any assessment can only observe performance in a specific context and must then draw inferences about the underlying competences.

2.1 A Typology of Achievement and Competence Tests

In this chapter, assessments of student and adult knowledge are classified into five broad categories according to their geographical scope, purpose and object of analysis. These categories include national, regional, international, hybrid and adult skills assessments, each with specific objectives and methodological approaches.

To date, there are several sets of surveys covering almost 140 countries. Assessing the quality of education by measuring achievement and skills raises a central methodological issue: the differentiation between performance and competence. It is essential to remember that any assessment is, by its very nature, reductive. Indeed, it consists in observing an individual's performance in a specific context, in order to deduce inferences concerning his or her underlying skills (Mislevy, 1992).

Assessments of pupils' or adults' knowledge can be grouped into five main categories, according to their geographical scope, purpose and object of analysis.

- **National Student Achievement Tests (NSATs)** aim to measure knowledge and/or skills from a national perspective. They are generally aligned with the curriculum in force in each country. For example, Chile's *Sistema de Medición de la Calidad de la Educación* (SIMCE) survey is administered annually to the entire school population. The levels assessed (grades 4, 6, 8 or 10) vary from year to year. These tests, based on the national curriculum, play an essential role in steering the education system, particularly in the allocation of public funding (Agencia de Calidad de la Educación, 2025). Results are published very early on to inform families about the performance of public and private schools. Subsidies can be modulated according to school ranking, in a system resembling a quasi-market

N. Altinok and C. Diebolt, *Edumetrics*, Population Economics,
https://doi.org/10.1007/978-3-032-13277-2_2

(Vegas & Petrow, 2007a). For a comparative analysis of national assessments and public examinations, see (Greaney & Kellaghan, 2008).

- **Regional Student Achievement Tests (RSATs)** bring together several countries that share a geographical, linguistic or cultural proximity. Their aim is to produce harmonized assessment tools, adapted to regional specificities, while enabling comparisons between countries. Among the best-known RSATs are SACMEQ (Southern and Eastern Africa Consortium for Monitoring Education Quality), PASEC (Programme d'analyse des systèmes éducatifs de la CONFEMEN) and LLECE (Latin American Laboratory for the Assessment of Education Quality).
- **International Student Achievement Tests (ISATs)** adopt a comparative perspective on a global scale. These surveys are gradually being opened up to countries on all continents and at all economic levels. Their main objective is to compare education systems via international rankings (often called *league tables*), based on global quality standards. Major surveys include PISA (Programme for International Student Assessment), PIRLS (Progress in International Reading Literacy Study) and TIMSS (Trends in International Mathematics and Science Study).
- **Hybrid Student Achievement Tests (HSATs)** are not explicitly aimed at international comparison, although they are not strictly regional. For example, the EGRA (Early Grade Reading Assessment) survey, launched in 2007, assesses the reading and writing skills of primary school pupils, but each country organizes the tests independently, with no harmonized international timetable, unlike PIRLS or TIMSS. Other similar assessments include EGMA (Early Grade Mathematics Assessment), SSME (Snapshot of School Management Effectiveness) and MLA (Monitoring Learning Achievement). The latter was originally intended for international comparison, but the high variability of items between survey cycles limits its comparability.
- **International assessments of adult skills (Adult Competences Achievement Tests, ACATs)** differ from the above in that they are aimed exclusively at the adult population, and focus on measuring skills rather than academic knowledge. The main surveys are IALS (International Adult Literacy Survey), ALL (Adult Literacy and Life Skills Survey) and PIAAC (Programme for the International Assessment of Adult Competencies), carried out mainly in developed countries. However, projects such as UNESCO's LAMP (Literacy Assessment and Monitoring Programme) and the World Bank's STEP (Skills Toward Employability and Productivity) aim to extend adult skills assessment to developing countries. These projects are designed to assess the effectiveness of education systems in training individuals to be competent in professional contexts, in line with the macroeconomic challenges of productivity and competitiveness.

This typology of assessments reveals markedly different purposes, depending on the level at which they are implemented. The main aim of national assessments is to measure the effectiveness of the education system in terms of how well pupils have assimilated the curriculum at the level tested. They thus provide an indicator of the quality of teaching, understood as compliance with curricular expectations. In regional assessments, the participating countries often share certain common features—be it a language of instruction or elements of the curriculum. In such cases, the test is built around the highest common denominator between the national curricula,[1] enabling both standardization and contextual relevance. International assessments, on the other hand, do not have such clear anchor points. They are based on a comparative rationale in highly heterogeneous areas, from both linguistic and curricular points of view. In this context, the measurement of learning outcomes cannot be based on a single reference program. As a result, these surveys tend to focus on the assessment of so-called transversal or "macro-competencies", presumed to be independent of the teaching context. The aim is no longer simply to verify the acquisition of specific knowledge, but to assess students' ability to mobilize transferable skills, considered essential for their integration into adult life. This shift in purpose—from curricular validation to preparation for working life—raises a still open debate on the nature of the learning to be assessed and the objectives assigned to international surveys. As Vrignaud (2006) points out, the central question is how to define the quality of education in a globalized context.

Below, we present national surveys and their nature, while focusing on a few concrete examples.

2.2 National Surveys

This section describes standardized student assessments, which are becoming increasingly important in national education systems. They are designed and administered by the central education authority to provide a unified assessment framework, aimed at supporting teaching, improving the quality of education and steering the education system.

2.2.1 Presentation

Standardized student assessments are playing an increasingly important role in national education systems, both as instruments for steering quality and as structural diagnostic tools. The main purpose of nationally standardized surveys or tests is to provide a unified assessment framework, designed and administered by the central educational authority—or, in decentralized systems, by the entity in charge of the education sector. The standardization of these assessments thus reflects the institutional organization specific to each education system.

The question of the level of initiative—centralized, decentralized or deconcentrated—is particularly significant. In many European countries, where the principle

[1] For example, the programs for sub-Saharan Africa—SACMEQ for the southern English-speaking zone and PASEC for the French-speaking zone—have relatively found this denominator based on the monitoring of basic reading/writing and mathematical skills.

of subsidiarity prevails, education is traditionally managed at local or regional level. This reflects a logic of proximity in public policies, particularly for basic education, which is often placed under the responsibility of the most decentralized entities.

However, this institutional architecture has been partially reconfigured over the last few decades, under the influence of the dissemination and media impact of international assessments, in particular PISA. These surveys have helped redefine the level perceived as optimal for guaranteeing the quality and equity of learning. A significant example is that of the Swiss Confederation: since the popular vote of May 21, 2006, constitutional provisions on education stipulate that the Confederation and the cantons, while respecting their respective competences, have a joint responsibility to ensure the quality and coherence of the Swiss education system (Article 61a, Swiss Constitution) (Swiss Confederation, 2000). Although the obligation to provide the means is still the responsibility of the cantons (subsidiarity principle), the requirement to achieve results applies nationwide, particularly in terms of the uniform acquisition of basic skills.

In the United States, the *No Child Left Behind* Act (NCLB) was passed amid concerns about the loss of the American educational advantage, particularly in basic math, compared to Asian countries. The purpose of this legislation was to verify whether the states' educational initiatives were capable of ensuring both quality and homogeneity in the acquisition of fundamental skills across the entire population. Generally speaking, international assessments have led to an intensification of national assessments. The former implicitly impose a standard of average performance, accompanied by controls on the dispersion of results around this average. As a result, national education systems are increasingly called upon to produce results that comply with a dual imperative: efficiency (meeting expected standards) and equity (limiting differences between groups of pupils).

Student assessment, particularly in its international dimension, is a complex system, mobilizing a wide range of tools and methods. Although these systems are often steered by external bodies, the evaluation or research departments of ministries of education also play an active role. In a national context, forms of evaluation are more varied: they can be internal or external, formative or summative, with a notable diversity of instruments mobilized. Despite the heterogeneity of approaches, linked to the specificities of education systems, assessment of learning outcomes is now an integral part of the educational structure in most countries. Its aim is to support teaching and improve the quality of education.

As a result of this integration, student assessment is often governed by regulations and official guidelines. Assessment tools are generally aligned with national curricula, textbooks and teaching practices. These normative frameworks set the aims of assessment: to verify whether pedagogical objectives are being achieved, while analyzing inequalities in results according to pupils, regions or social contexts.

In this context, national assessment is closely linked to continuous assessment. This encompasses daily observation of learning, grading of homework, class participation and student production. It is akin to formative assessment, integrated into teaching practices, with the aim of adjusting learning processes in real time. This assessment, conducted throughout the year, provides direct feedback to teachers and students alike, and can be used for decisions such as promotion, guidance or support.

In many developing countries, the culture of assessment has been gradually built up from the structuring and coherence of learning assessment systems. Schools can supplement continuous assessment with standardized national tests, based on centralized protocols. The purpose of these tests is to guarantee the comparability of performance, to detect learning difficulties and to situate pupils' results at different levels: class, school, region or nation.

In countries with longer experience of standardized tests, educational policies have been developed to better articulate formative and summative national assessments, with a view to complementing each other. This is notably the case in France. Since 2017, the French Ministry of Education has organized national assessments of French and mathematical achievement for pupils in CP, CE1 and 6e every autumn, extended in 2023 to CM1 and 4(e) classes (Ministère de l'Education Nationale, 2023). In addition, since 2003, the DEPP (Direction de l'évaluation, de la prospective et de la performance) has been conducting national assessment cycles at key points in the curriculum, with rotating subject tests (reading, modern languages, history-geography, experimental sciences, mathematics). The back-to-school tests provide teachers with precise benchmarks for adapting their teaching methods and offer families individual feedback on their children's strengths and weaknesses (Ministère de l'Education Nationale, 2025).

In countries with a long tradition of national assessments—notably in Europe—there is a marked tendency to use these tests as pedagogical references. These assessments are used to identify students' individual needs and adapt teaching practices accordingly, reinforcing their role in improving the learning process.

Standardized national assessments are also becoming central instruments for steering education systems. A gradual convergence is taking place between these centralized systems and internal assessments or self-evaluations carried out at school level. This cross-fertilization reflects an articulation between top-down logics (centralized steering and evaluation) and bottom-up dynamics (local formative evaluation initiatives). This combination aims to improve educational quality both from the top down and from the bottom up.

However, two critical issues could influence these dynamics:

- On the one hand, the growing use of the results of these evaluations to assess the performance of schools—and even teachers—raises questions about the aims of the system.
- On the other hand, certain reservations have been voiced by parents' groups, concerned about the potential effects of these assessments on student orientation and selection. There is a risk that excessive use of these tests will reinforce pre-existing inequalities, if it leads to social sorting mechanisms in schools.

In a context of liberalization and competition between schools, national assessments are also used to measure school quality and guide intervention policies. Two contrasting models illustrate this trend:

- In Sweden, the 1992 reform—introducing freedom of school choice with direct subsidies to families—was implemented without any prior benchmarking of schools. Johan Wennström, in a study published in 2020, points out that this pioneering reform was not accompanied by structures designed to regulate competition between schools on the basis of quality criteria, leading to perverse effects such as grade inflation (Wennström, 2020).
- Conversely, the *Grant Maintained Schools* reform in the UK (1988) was based on assessments of prior learning to incorporate a measure of the school's "added value", taking into account the socio-economic background of the pupils. These results were used to adjust public funding (Harlen, 2007). This concept of "added value" emerged later, in the form of Contextual Value Added (CVA), used in the 2000s to assess school progress by taking into account students' socio-economic background, before being gradually abandoned (Ray et al., 2009).

According to the summary provided by Eurydice (2009), national evaluations are systematically used in the external evaluation of schools in Hungary, Lithuania, Sweden, Slovenia and Romania. In other countries—such as Belgium, Bulgaria, Estonia, Iceland, Latvia, the Netherlands, Portugal, the United Kingdom and once again Slovenia—these evaluations make a partial contribution to school evaluation, complementing other sources.

National tests are generally organized under the authority of a central or national body, with the exception of the federal configurations mentioned above. These assessments are administered under conditions that are as homogeneous as possible for all the students concerned. This study does not include tests designed to detect developmental disorders, nor those specifically designed for certain specialized streams or minority populations. Similarly, digital tools (NTIC) designed to support teachers in their continuous assessment practices or in measuring the impact of their teaching are not covered here.

The analyses presented relate to ISCED 1 (primary) and ISCED 2 (lower secondary) levels of education. All national tests—whether formative or summative—are taken into account, whether exhaustive (covering an entire cohort) or based on representative samples.

Like international surveys, national tests can be grouped into three main functional categories:

(1) Summative tests (or "learning assessments") are designed to assess learning achievement at the end of the school year or at the end of an educational cycle. These tests have direct implications for the student's career path, such as the awarding of certificates, career guidance decisions, access to a school or promotion to the next grade. They are instruments of certification and selection.
(2) Steering tests are mainly used to assess the performance of schools or the education system as a whole. These assessments provide indicators for measuring results against targets, identifying discrepancies and considering corrective measures. In this way, the results can feed into political decisions on school restructuring or curriculum adaptation.

(3) Finally, formative tests are designed to support the individual learning process. They make it possible to identify students' specific needs, set up differentiated pedagogical follow-up and adjust teaching practices. This form of assessment is closely linked to the classroom context, and is integrated into local pedagogical dynamics.

Assessment systems mobilize a variety of observation and measurement methods. In international surveys, interviews or contextualized tests are frequently used, while in national assessments, the end-of-school-period test remains the dominant model.

However, other approaches are developing, notably the value-added measure, which aims to assess student progress between two points in time, generally between the beginning and end of the school year. This method makes it possible to link students' achievements to the teaching resources they have used, by assessing their progress rather than their absolute level. A variant of this approach, combining summative assessment and longitudinal monitoring, consists in observing progress over an entire school cycle: in this case, cohort monitoring surveys are used to analyze cumulative effects over several years.

However, this method has certain methodological limitations, particularly when it comes to attributing the effects observed. Indeed, while biases are relatively low at the individual level, they are more pronounced when it comes to estimating the teacher effect or the school effect. As Rothstein (2010) points out, the progress of a group of pupils in year t is strongly influenced by the characteristics of the teachers who taught the group in previous years, making it problematic to attribute added value to a single teacher.

Furthermore, there is a tendency in national assessments to target specific moments in the school curriculum, rather than long periods, reflecting a desire to enhance the precision and relevance of measurements. As part of a formative assessment approach, these systems find a natural extension in day-to-day teaching practices. The teacher continuously assesses student participation, written and oral production, homework and tests, with a view to fine-tuning teaching. This integrated assessment aims to regulate the learning process in real time.

Historically, in European education, curriculum-linked instructions have been put in place to standardize the homework and assessments offered to students. In Northern European countries, in particular, teaching teams are often given greater responsibility: not only for designing assessments, but also for ensuring harmonized practices between classes. Vaniscotte (1996) points out that some Nordic systems, which have not developed a centralized inspectorate, have been more inclined to standardize assessment methods locally, thus reinforcing the coherence of practices within schools.

Finally, an important dimension is the degree of independence of the assessment system. In many countries, particularly those with decentralized education structures, certification of learning achievement is entrusted to autonomous agencies, separate from the ministries of education. Initially responsible for organizing national examinations, these authorities have gradually extended their scope of intervention to include large-scale assessment functions.

2.2.2 The Pioneering Example of the United States

The aim of this section is to outline the main features of student assessment systems in the United States. In the United States, the culture of school assessment is rooted in a meritocratic logic. Created in 1926, the Scholastic Aptitude Test (SAT) was conceived as a tool for democratizing access to higher education, through a standardized ranking of high school students. This national test, administered mainly in the form of multiple-choice questionnaires (MCQs), enabled universities to select students on supposedly objective criteria. As Goastellec (2003) points out, the SAT meets a need for competition between schools in a highly differentiated context, but is not strictly speaking an instrument for evaluating the education system.

The first attempts to assess students' basic learning achievements date back to the 1930s. Under the impetus of Ralph Tyler, a conceptual framework for assessment began to be developed, but soon came up against resistance from the federated states, anxious to preserve their constitutionally guaranteed educational autonomy. The National Assessment of Educational Progress (NAEP), officially launched in 1964 under the Johnson administration, was the first structured nationwide assessment initiative. The program is designed to measure student achievement in core subjects (English, mathematics, science, history-geography, civics), based on a representative sample from each state. In this way, it provides a longitudinal view of the progress of school generations over time.

Despite tensions between federal and local authorities, a gradual consensus has built up around NAEP, supported by education authorities, teachers' unions and parents' associations. This stabilization has helped to make NAEP a shared frame of reference for education policy.

Among the major studies based on NAEP, the Equality of Educational Opportunity Survey (EEOS), directed by James Coleman in 1966, revealed that inequalities present at the start of the school system persisted on leaving, and even increased for certain minority groups. The report also highlighted the fact that schools have sometimes concentrated the best-performing students, thereby limiting the system's ability to reduce social inequalities (Coleman, 1966).

Since the implementation of NAEP, now known as the Nation's Report Card, the United States has strengthened its capacity to produce longitudinal tracking data on students throughout their compulsory education. This assessment infrastructure, although centralized in its design, is still administered locally to respect the principle of devolution.

Finally, the Hawkins-Stafford Act of 1988 established the National Assessment Governing Board (NAGB), an independent body responsible for defining NAEP policy: it selects the areas to be assessed, draws up sampling plans, validates the measurement instruments, oversees their use and supervises data analysis. This evaluation model, which reconciles local autonomy with a federal framework, continues to evolve under the influence of successive reforms, notably the No Child Left Behind (NCLB) Act which, while reinforcing the use of results for accountability purposes, has revived certain criticisms of federal centralization.

Since the late 1960s, the National Assessment of Educational Progress (NAEP) has regularly assessed representative samples of American students aged 9, 13 and 17. Since 1983, a cohort tracking approach has been integrated, making it possible to cross-reference the age and grade levels of students. The system is based on several priority subject areas, such as reading, mathematics, science and writing, assessed at regular four—to five-year intervals. Other disciplines are integrated on a more spaced-out cycle, every six to 8 years.

The NAEP sampling plan is designed to guarantee statistical representativeness of the federated states, types of establishment (public, private) and the main socio-demographic categories, notably ethnic minorities. This rigorous model has been hailed by numerous researchers, including Gipps & Murphy (1994), who emphasize its potential for international use.

As early as the 1970s, the OECD drew on the NAEP model to develop instruments for cross-national comparison, complementing the surveys carried out by the IEA. However, it was not until some 15 years later that the idea of an assessment focused on acquired skills, rather than on the strict assimilation of national curricula, took shape with the creation of the Program for International Student Assessment (PISA).

2.2.3 The Expansion of National Surveys of Pupil Achievement

The development of national surveys has provided ministers of education with an accurate description of overall levels of school performance, particularly in key areas. These surveys also make it easier to compare results between different sub-groups, such as boys and girls, ethnic groups, rural and urban populations, or public and private schools. The aim is to track the evolution of student learning over time, thus enabling a diagnostic aspect. This diagnosis can, in theory, support the evaluation of possible modifications to school programs. An emblematic example is the American No Child Left Behind (NCLB) law, implemented since 2000, where these surveys help identify vulnerable groups and provide indicators on the achievement of assimilation goals and standards.

Regional and international surveys, such as PISA, seek to establish assessment tools acceptable to all participating countries. However, they often fail to explain the variability of performance within countries. For example, two federal countries, Canada and Switzerland, over-sample in PISA to enable sub-national analysis of results, used to adjust educational policies to territorial realities.

National surveys generally offer a better understanding of disparities within countries, thanks to broader sampling and test content that is better adapted to the specific features of the national education system. Their main objective is to describe the level of pupil acquisition according to a curriculum defined by the Ministries of Education or the relevant authorities. These surveys may cover the entire school population, or only a fraction selected according to representativeness criteria. They are often accompanied by questionnaires for teachers, parents or school heads, to help contextualize the results.

A major synthesis work was initiated by Encinas-Martin (2007) for UNESCO, completed by Benavot & Tanner (2008), constituting to date the most extensive database on national assessments. These data come mainly from:

- Government websites, international agencies and platforms dedicated to evaluations.
- A questionnaire sent to national experts to confirm and comment on the presence of assessments.
- Online reports and documents, used on a more limited basis.
- Commissions launched by the Education for All Global Monitoring Report program, which studied certain national assessments.
- A World Bank report on evaluations in Latin America (Vegas & Petrow, 2007b).

In addition, since 2010, the International Bureau of Education has been endeavoring to include the presence of national assessments in questionnaires sent to countries, although this information is still incomplete.

Some interesting results from Benavot & Tanner (2008) are worth highlighting:

- The number of countries having conducted a national assessment has increased since the early 1990s. Over the period 1995–1999, only 65 countries carried out such an assessment, while this figure rose to 111 countries over the period 2000–2006.
- What's more, it is mainly the countries of North America and Western Europe that have carried out the most national assessments (77% of them over the 2000–2006 period), compared with almost 36% of sub-Saharan African countries.
- Nearly 8 out of 10 developed countries carried out such an assessment over the 2000–2006 period, compared with around half of developing countries. However, there has been a recent surge in the participation of developing countries in national surveys.
- The proportion of national assessments has increased in all regions, and particularly in the Arab countries, where it has risen from 15% to 55% of countries.
- The domains most often tested were mathematics (93% of cases) and language (92% of cases). Nearly a third of countries also tested science, two-fifths social sciences (38%) and one-fifth foreign languages (21%).
- National assessments focus more on grades 4–6 than on grades 1–3 or 7–9. Between 2000 and 2006, 84 countries conducted at least one survey in grades 4–6, compared with only 55 countries for grades 1–3 and 54 countries for grades 7–9.

Certain characteristics are frequently observed in national surveys of pupil achievement (ENAE):

- **Areas assessed**: Reading and mathematics are the areas most often tested. In recent years, the sciences have become more widespread. Other areas, such as foreign languages and civics, are assessed less systematically.

- **Target school levels**: ENAEs mainly concern compulsory schooling, in particular elementary school. Sometimes, they also cover secondary school. However, no grade is systematically assessed everywhere. There are two main reasons for this:
- The varying length of primary and secondary schooling in different countries.
- Lack of international coordination to harmonize assessment practices. The grades assessed are often chosen without clear scientific criteria, often under pressure from international donors. However, there is some convergence around grade 3 or 4 in primary school, focusing on fundamental literacy and numeracy skills. Another key assessment corresponds to the end of primary school, often carried out via the secondary exploitation of secondary school entrance exams.
- **Test frequency**: This varies widely. Some countries carry out annual assessments, others sporadically, often depending on the availability of international funding. Sometimes, the assessment focuses on a specific skill (reading, arithmetic, etc.) each year in the rapid cycle. Longitudinal assessments, which track performance over time, are rare. Only a few countries, such as Chile and Mexico, use this approach on a regular basis. On the other hand, trend analysis of the results of national examinations at the end of primary school is more common, especially in countries with a high level of educational decentralization, where this examination serves as an indicator of the homogeneity of results.
- **Responsible institution**: Testing may be coordinated by the Ministry of Education, an independent government agency, a research center or a donor. This diversity can influence the scope and impact of the assessment. With the growing interest of donors in the quality of education, countries are encouraged to carry out these evaluations, but delegation to third parties can limit their political impact.
- **Voluntary or compulsory**: A school's participation may be voluntary or compulsory. When participation is voluntary, the refusal of certain schools may bias the results. In addition, the "high stakes" or "low stakes" nature of the assessment influences its acceptance: low-stakes assessments are generally better accepted, while those used to steer the education system may meet with resistance from teachers and families.

Most industrialized countries began conducting national assessments several decades ago. The real development of NAEs in developing countries dates back to the 1990s, particularly in Latin America, where they have been used to analyze educational reforms (Rojas & Esquivel, 1998). Today, this region is the most advanced in terms of national evaluation among developing countries. In Asia, ENAEs are often still at an experimental stage, in the absence of a coordinated regional survey. In parallel, the Arab countries are in an intermediate position, with their recent participation in international assessments highlighting the need for national assessments. Finally, in sub-Saharan Africa, national assessments have been little developed over the last 10 years, mainly under pressure from the World Bank and other donors. The heterogeneous nature of the public evaluated reflects this still experimental character.

2.3 International Surveys of Pupil Achievement

This section presents surveys that adopt a worldwide comparative perspective, such as TIMSS, PIRLS and PISA. Their main aim is to compare education systems via international rankings, based on global quality standards and assessing skills rather than the strict assimilation of national curricula.

2.3.1 The TIMSS Survey

The first initiative to measure learning achievement on an individualized, internationally comparable basis was undertaken in the early 1960s by the International Association for the Evaluation of Educational Achievement (IEA). This organization has conducted a number of multi-year surveys in a variety of fields such as mathematics, science and reading, but also in less traditional areas such as pre-primary education (14 countries between 1988 and 1995) or computers in schools (20 countries between 1988 and 1992). While current international assessments focus mainly on skills in reading, mathematics and science, the IEA's first surveys also covered citizenship (1968–1973, 1994–2002, survey planned for 2009 with at least 39 participating countries) or foreign language teaching (1968–1973 survey in ten European countries, attempt between 1993 and 1995 on four European languages, abandoned for lack of funding).

Firstly, it is possible to present the surveys that evaluate mathematics and science. The first survey to assess mathematics took place between 1963 and 1967 (The First International Mathematics Study), involving 12 developed countries (Australia, Belgium, England, Finland, France, the Federal Republic of Germany, Israel, Japan, the Netherlands, Scotland, Sweden and the USA). The students assessed were aged 13 or in their final year of secondary school (Husen, 1967). The survey evaluating science was conducted over a longer period (1968–1972) and focused on biology, chemistry and physics. The population evaluated was aged 1 to 14, or in the final year of secondary school. A total of 19 education systems were evaluated (Australia, Flemish Belgium, French-speaking Belgium, Chile, England, Federal Republic of Germany, Finland, France, Hungary, India, Iran, Italy, Netherlands, New Zealand, Scotland, Sweden, Thailand and USA). A summary of the main results of this survey can be found in Walker et al. (1976).

The Second International Mathematics Study took place between 1977 and 1981, and involved 13-year-olds and students in their final year of secondary school (Burstein, 1992). Nineteen education systems were evaluated, including 2 African countries (Nigeria and Swaziland). The Second International Science Study was carried out in the early 1980s. This involved 23 education systems, including 3 African countries (Ghana, Nigeria and Zimbabwe) and 5 developing countries (China, Papua New Guinea, Philippines, Poland and Thailand).

However, it is the TIMSS (Third International Mathematics and Science Study) cycle, launched in the 1990s, that has established itself as the benchmark program for comparative assessment in mathematics and science. TIMSS aims to measure student performance while analyzing the associated educational contexts. This dual approach has made it possible to integrate pedagogical and systemic dimensions into the analysis of results. Since its first edition in 1995, which covered 45 education systems on three levels[2] (grades 3/4, 7/8 and end of secondary), TIMSS has gone through several waves, including that of 1999 (38 systems at grade 8) and that of 2023, in which some 72 education systems, including 64 countries, took part. Test content covers several sub-domains: numbers, algebra, geometry for mathematics; life sciences, physical sciences, history of science for science, with specific weightings according to cycles.

The assessment of student learning in TIMSS is based on a common reference framework of knowledge defined to be relevant to all participating countries. To construct the questionnaires, several hundred items were analyzed to check their conformity with the curricula of the different nations, thus guaranteeing a reasonable level of comparability. Particular attention was paid to ensuring maximum standardization of items, even though some of them may not be explicitly included in the national curricula of all countries.

In addition to assessment tests in mathematics and science, various contextual questionnaires are administered to various players in the education system. A student questionnaire collects data on personal and family characteristics (motivation, access to resources, parents' professions, etc.). A teacher questionnaire collects information on the classroom (size, material resources), teaching practices (correction time, pedagogical interaction), as well as initial and in-service training. The school principal answers a questionnaire on school organization, grouping arrangements and available resources. Finally, a questionnaire for ministerial authorities documents the official curricula, their implementation and the assessment systems in place.

For the first edition of TIMSS in 1994–1995, three school populations were assessed: Population 1, made up of pupils aged around 9 (grades 3 and 4); Population 2, grouping pupils aged 13 (grades 7 and 8); and Population 3, corresponding to pupils at the end of secondary school, subdivided into two sub-groups: those taking a general test and those specializing in mathematics or physics. However, Population 3 was gradually excluded from subsequent cycles, with assessments now focusing on the first two populations. Since 1995, eight TIMSS cycles have been carried out (1995, 1999, 2003, 2007, 2011, 2015, 2019 and 2023), with the next edition scheduled for 2027.

[2] In some cases, certain Canadian provinces or US federal states have participated in IEA surveys. For the sake of simplicity, we do not include these regions in the calculation of the number of countries participating in the surveys.

2.3.2 The PIRLS Survey

The first international assessments in the field of reading were carried out by the IEA between 1968 and 1972 through *The Study of Reading Comprehension* survey, involving 15 education systems, including three developing countries (Chile, India and Iran). This study, targeting pupils aged 10, 14 and at the end of secondary school, highlighted the difficulties associated with standardized measurement of reading comprehension skills, given the linguistic specificities of each country. Analyses of this survey can be found in Thorndike (1973) and Walker et al. (1976).

A second initiative, *The Reading Literacy Study* (1985–1994), aimed to develop valid measurement tools that could be generalized to all participating countries. Conducted between 1990 and 1991, it involved two populations (9- and 14-year-old pupils) in 32 education systems, including several developing countries (among them: Botswana, Nigeria, Zimbabwe, Indonesia, Philippines, Thailand, Trinidad & Tobago, Venezuela).

However, it is the PIRLS survey (*Progress in International Reading Literacy Study*), also carried out by the IEA, that has become the benchmark for reading assessment at primary level. Conducted in 2001, 2006, 2011, 2016 and 2021, PIRLS assesses the skills of Grade 4 pupils (aged 9 or so) according to two reading purposes: literary reading (focused on imagination and narration) and informative reading (focused on comprehension of logically or chronologically organized content).

Four cognitive processes are assessed: identifying explicit information, making inferences, interpreting and integrating ideas, and critically examining the content and form of texts. The assessment uses a rolling booklet method (ten booklets, one per student), enabling broad coverage of skills while reducing individual load. Advanced psychometric techniques are then used to produce comparable scores. Instruments include multiple-choice and open-ended questions. Context-sensitive questionnaires are also administered to students, teachers and principals. To take account of students' age, the questionnaire on individual and family characteristics is sent to parents. The next edition of PIRLS is scheduled for 2026, with the announced participation of 61 education systems, including 55 countries and 6 regional entities.

2.3.3 The PISA Survey

The Organisation for Economic Co-operation and Development (OECD) launched the Programme *for* International *Student Assessment* (PISA) in 1997 to meet a growing need for internationally comparable data on student performance. The fundamental principle underlying the survey is based on the notion of "literacy", i.e. the ability of students to mobilize their knowledge to solve concrete problems, extrapolate from what they have learned and apply their skills to new situations, beyond the simple restitution of school knowledge. Assessment is thus part of a lifelong learning approach, and has been carried out cyclically, every 3 years since 2000. It focuses on three main areas: reading, mathematics and science, each of which is prioritized in turn according to the cycle.

Unlike IEA surveys (such as TIMSS or PIRLS), PISA assesses 15-year-old students, regardless of their school level, to measure the extent to which they have acquired the knowledge and skills essential for their future adult life. In 2000, the focus was on reading, in 2003 on mathematics and in 2006 on science. The cycle is repeated every 9 years thereafter. The program is based on five key principles: an orientation toward educational policies, a competency-based assessment, relevance to lifelong learning, regular periodicity and broad geographical coverage. PISA 2006 already involved 57 countries, with nearly 350,000 students representing millions of 15-year-olds worldwide.

The two-hour tests include multiple-choice and open-ended questions, organized around units contextualized in everyday situations (texts, graphs, concrete problems, etc.). Students also complete a questionnaire on their family background, attitudes to learning and school habits. Headteachers are asked about the characteristics of their schools. In 2006, some countries also distributed a questionnaire to parents, gathering information on their commitment to education and their views on science. An option on the use of digital technologies was also offered to 39 countries.

The skills assessed are precisely defined in each domain. In reading, they involve locating information, interpreting texts and reflecting on their content. In mathematics, there are three levels of complexity: reproduction (simple operations), connection (solving direct problems) and reflection (mobilizing mathematical thought). In science, students must be able to identify scientific questions, explain phenomena rationally and use factual evidence.

Since 2000, the number of participating countries has risen steadily: 32 in 2000, 41 in 2003, 57 in 2006, 65 in 2009, 72 in 2015, 79 in 2018, then 81 in 2022 (despite the postponement caused by the COVID-19 pandemic). More and more developing countries have joined the scheme, thanks to the technical and financial support of international partners. Countries such as Vietnam, Peru, Indonesia, Morocco and Colombia are now regular participants, extending the comparative scope of the global assessment beyond the most advanced economies.

The next PISA survey is scheduled for spring 2025 and will bring together over 90 countries and education systems, including several developing countries such as Kenya, Morocco and Peru. This cycle will focus on science as a core domain, and will introduce an innovative new domain: *Learning in the Digital World*, aimed at measuring students' skills in digital learning environments. The results of this survey will be published in December 2026, and should provide an up-to-date, in-depth overview of the state of young people's skills around the world, in a rapidly changing educational context.

2.3.4 *Past Surveys Not Renewed*

A number of international assessments, although important in the past, are no longer in operation. These include the Monitoring Learning Achievement (MLA) surveys, specifically carried out in developing countries, and the International Assessment of Educational Progress (IAEP), which aimed for a broader comparative approach. These schemes have contributed to methodological reflection on the assessment of learning achievement in international contexts, but have not been pursued over the long term. At the same time, other, more recent projects are being developed, such as the AHELO (*Assessment of Higher Education Learning Outcomes*) survey, which aims to assess students' skills in higher education, tackling a stage as yet little explored by major comparative surveys.

The IAEP survey, in particular, was designed on the basis of the experience of the National Assessment of Educational Progress (NAEP), the main measure of educational achievement in the United States since the 1970s. Two IAEP series were carried out: the first in 1988, covering six countries, assessed 13-year-olds in mathematics and science, and the second in 1991, covering 19 countries, with assessments for two age groups—9 and 13—again in these same two areas. While the methodology employed enabled comparisons to be made on the basis of solid empirical evidence, it was also criticized for being too firmly rooted in US curricula and pedagogical expectations. The tests were largely based on American standards, which limited their relevance and fairness for other education systems. This lack of adaptation to local realities led to a questioning of the international validity of the results, and the survey was therefore not pursued. On the other hand, this observation helped to reinforce the legitimacy and methodology of assessments developed by the IEA, such as TIMSS and PIRLS, which are perceived as being better contextualized and more sensitive to the diversity of national educational frameworks.

The MLA (Monitoring Learning Achievement) program, launched as part of a joint project between UNESCO and UNICEF, aims to assess fundamental learning achievements in a wide variety of national contexts, while transferring to participating countries the capacity to analyze and steer educational policies (Chinapah et al., 2000). Over forty countries have been involved in this initiative, with the aim of identifying the factors that facilitate or hinder learning at elementary school, and proposing improvements adapted to local realities. Data is collected at the end of the basic learning cycle, i.e. between grades 3 and 6, depending on the education system. The more recent MLA II project has extended the evaluation to the beginning of secondary school (grade 8), reinforcing the coverage of educational cycles.

Unlike the PASEC and SACMEQ surveys, which focused exclusively on academic knowledge, MLA integrates broader dimensions, including questions of practical knowledge and prevention, and allows countries to add specific items according to their priorities. A total of 72 countries took part in the various phases of the program, although not all data are published. However, a separate report on MLA I has been produced for 11 African countries: Botswana, Madagascar, Malawi, Mali,

Mauritius, Morocco, Niger, Senegal, Tunisia, Uganda and Zambia (Chinapah et al., 2000), illustrating the desire to capitalize on results to feed into educational policies.

Despite its ambition, the program has been widely criticized. Questions were raised about the quality of sampling procedures, the administration of questionnaires and the comparability of items between countries. These methodological limitations affected the scope of the comparative analyses. However, in several contexts, notably in South Asia, the MLA initiative has been a trigger for the development of national evaluation systems, encouraging a culture of educational quality measurement in environments hitherto unfamiliar with this type of approach.

The *Assessment of Higher Education Learning Outcomes* (AHELO) is an OECD initiative designed to measure, from a comparative perspective, the skills acquired by students at the end of their university education. At a time when higher education represents a growing strategic investment for governments and individuals alike, it is essential to have reliable instruments for assessing the quality and relevance of learning on a global scale. Today, some 135 million students are enrolled in one of the world's 17,000 higher education institutions, but there is no standardized mechanism for comparing the effectiveness of university systems internationally.

In response to this shortcoming, the OECD launched a feasibility study for the AHELO project. The aim of this project was to explore the extent to which it would be possible to design a scientifically rigorous and operationally realistic transnational assessment of learning outcomes. The aim was to assess the real quality of university education, not just through graduation rates or the reputation of institutions, but through analysis of the skills actually mastered by students at the end of their course.

Despite clear interest from a number of countries, and the completion of a pilot phase between 2010 and 2012 in 17 countries, the AHELO initiative has not been implemented on a large scale. Methodological obstacles, political resistance and differences of opinion on how to fairly assess highly heterogeneous training courses led to the gradual abandonment of the project. As a result, AHELO remains today an unfinished experiment, which nevertheless paved the way for international reflection on the evaluation of higher education.

2.4 Regional Surveys of Student Achievement

This section describes assessments that bring together several countries sharing geographical, linguistic or cultural proximity, such as SACMEQ, PASEC and LLECE. Their aim is to produce harmonized assessment tools, adapted to regional specificities, while enabling comparisons between participating countries. There are three major regional surveys, covering Latin America and Africa.

2.4.1 The SACMEQ Survey

The SACMEQ (Southern and Eastern Africa Consortium for Monitoring Educational Quality) consortium has its origins in a large-scale national survey of primary education quality carried out in Zimbabwe in 1991, supported by the International Institute for Educational Planning (IIEP) (Ross & Postlethwaite, 1991). Eager to build on this success inspired by the IEA model, several Ministers of Education in East and Southern Africa expressed an interest in participating in a joint evaluation. In July 2004, planners from seven countries met in Paris to found the Southern Africa Consortium for Monitoring Educational Quality (SACMEQ). Today, 15 member ministries participate: Botswana, Kenya, Lesotho, Malawi, Mauritius, Mozambique, Namibia, Seychelles, South Africa, Eswatini (formerly Swaziland), Tanzania mainland, Tanzania (Zanzibar), Uganda, Zambia and Zimbabwe.

The first cycle, SACMEQ I, took place between 1995 and 1999, involving seven countries assessing the reading level of grade 6 pupils: Kenya, Malawi, Mauritius, Namibia, Tanzania (Zanzibar), Zambia and Zimbabwe. Although mainly national studies, they shared common elements (questions, instruments, populations, sampling and analyses) ensuring an international dimension. A report was published for each country.

The second cycle (SACMEQ II), between 2000 and 2002, brought together 14 countries and one territory (Zanzibar), extending the assessment to mathematics and reading for the same grade 6 students. The participating countries were: Botswana, Kenya, Lesotho, Malawi, Mauritius, Mozambique, Namibia, Seychelles, South Africa, Swaziland, Tanzania mainland, Zanzibar, Uganda and Zambia. Some SACMEQ II items were taken from the TIMSS survey to ensure international comparability. Questionnaires also collected data on educational resources, school conditions and socio-economic background via student questionnaires. SACMEQ II also incorporated elements from previous surveys, including the Zimbabwe survey, SACMEQ I, TIMSS and the IEA Reading Literacy study.

The third phase, SACMEQ III, carried out in September 2007, covered the same countries as the previous cycle. This phase innovated by integrating questions on HIV-AIDS education into the questionnaires for pupils, teachers and principals, reflecting an adaptation to major local issues. The SACMEQ protocol, while demanding in terms of sampling, excluded small schools (fewer than 15 pupils in the grade), which could lead to bias in some countries.

The fourth cycle, SACMEQ IV, took place between 2013 and 2017, with the participation of 14 education systems from the region: Botswana, Kenya, Lesotho, Malawi, Mauritius, Mozambique, Namibia, Seychelles, South Africa, Eswatini, Tanzania Mainland, Tanzania (Zanzibar), Uganda, Zambia and Zimbabwe. This phase continued the assessment of grade 6 pupils in reading and mathematics, as well as deepening the analysis of school conditions, school management and knowledge of HIV/AIDS. These data have enabled a better understanding of the factors influencing educational quality, and have guided regional policies.

More recently, SEACMEQ V has been launched from 2021 to continue monitoring performance in reading and mathematics, while integrating new themes adapted to current challenges, such as digital education and twenty-first-century skills.[3] Several countries have begun collecting data, but the official results have not yet been published. This continuity illustrates the importance of SACMEQ as a regional tool for monitoring educational quality in Southern and Eastern Africa. However, the project has experienced delays, with only results from the Seychelles available to date.

2.4.2 The PASEC Survey

The PASEC evaluation was carried out in two distinct phases. From the early 1990s, the first phase of PASEC consisted of national assessments, while attempting to preserve certain items in common. After 2014, a standardized assessment replaced national tests repeated at various intervals.

2.4.3 The Former PASEC Tests

There are three types of assessment carried out by PASEC:

- **Diagnostic assessment**, which measures students' achievements over the course of a school year, while identifying factors that promote or hinder learning. Nearly fifteen such assessments have been carried out or are in progress.
- **Thematic** evaluations are based on the same principles as diagnostic evaluations, but target a specific topic, such as teacher training or the recruitment of contract teachers. Four thematic evaluations have been carried out. Sampling no longer concerns students, but the categories of teachers studied.
- **Cohort follow-up**, which follows the same group of students for five consecutive years, assessing their learning each year. Two complete follow-ups have been carried out.

The PASEC survey is designed to assess grade 2 and grade 5 pupils at the beginning and end of the year. For example, the grade 5 mathematics test includes items on number properties and simple calculations (addition, subtraction), as well as problem solving using addition, subtraction, multiplication and division. Other questions assess knowledge of decimals, fractions and basic notions of geometry.

[3] Since 2020, SACMEQ has become SEACMEQ under the name "The Southern And Eastern Africa Consortium for Monitoring Education Quality", and now has 16 members: Angola, Botswana, Kenya, Lesotho, Malawi, Mauritius, Mozambique, Namibia, Seychelles, Eswatini, South Africa, Tanzania, Zanzibar, Uganda, Zambia and Zimbabwe.

The database covers primary school performance in mathematics and French. In CP2 and CM1, between 2000 and 2500 pupils per country, in around a hundred schools, as well as their teachers and principals, were surveyed in eleven countries. The protocol features two assessments of learning achievement during the year, one at the beginning and one at the end, making PASEC the only international survey to measure "added value" (CONFEMEN, 2004).

Several countries have participated in successive phases of PASEC:

- PASEC I: Djibouti (1993/94), Congo (1993/94), Mali (1994/95).
- Phase II: Central African Republic (1994/95), Senegal (1995).
- PASEC III: Burkina Faso (1995/96), Cameroon (1995/96), Ivory Coast (1995/96).
- PASEC IV: Burkina Faso (1996/98), Côte d'Ivoire (1996/98), Senegal (1996/2000), Madagascar (1997/98), Chad (2000/01).
- PASEC V: Togo (2000/01).
- PASEC VI: Guinea (2003/04), Mali (2001/02), Niger (2001/02).
- PASEC VII: Benin (2004/05), Cameroon (2004/05), Mauritania (2003/04), Madagascar (2005/06), Mauritius (2006), Chad (2003/04).
- PASEC VIII: Congo (2006/07), Senegal (2006/07), Burkina Faso (2006/07).
- PASEC IX: Burundi (2009/10), Côte d'Ivoire (2008/09), Comoros (2009/10), Lebanon (2009/10).
- PASEC X first phase: Chad, Togo, Democratic Republic of Congo (2009/10).
- PASEC X second phase: Vietnam, Cambodia, Laos (2011/12).
- PASEC XI: three new countries in 2011/12 and four more in 2012/13.

It should be noted that the surveys in Senegal (1995/2000), Côte d'Ivoire (1995/98) and part of Burkina Faso (1995/98) were cohort follow-ups, while the others were diagnostic assessments. Finally, the results of the first four assessments are difficult to access, as they were not always conducted under comparable conditions.

2.4.4 New PASEC Tests

In 2014, PASEC conducted a new series of assessments, for the first time simultaneously in 10 countries: Benin, Burkina Faso, Burundi, Cameroon, Chad, Congo, Côte d'Ivoire, Niger, Senegal and Togo. PASEC's methodology is based on measuring fundamental skills in language of instruction and mathematics, at the start and end of primary school, among a representative sample of pupils in each country. The evaluation also collected extensive data on students, classes, schools, communities and educational policies, in order to analyze resource allocation, school practices and their relationship with performance.

Tests are administered in the official language of instruction. Where this language differs from French, such as Kirundi in Burundi at the start of schooling or English in English-speaking Cameroon, the tests have been translated and adapted to the linguistic contexts, while maintaining the same level of difficulty between versions.

This work has been validated by the countries and a specialized external body. In most countries, the language of instruction is not the students' mother tongue and is little used on a day-to-day basis (this is the case for French in Benin, Burkina Faso, French-speaking Cameroon, Congo, Côte d'Ivoire, Niger, Senegal, Chad and Togo, and for English in English-speaking Cameroon). In Burundi, the language of instruction and assessment at the start of schooling, Kirundi, is widely used.

The Grade 2 tests, taken at the start of schooling, assess initial learning in the language of instruction and mathematics, providing an initial assessment of fundamental skills. They are designed to detect major learning difficulties at an early stage, before they worsen and lead to school failure. Total duration is around thirty minutes per subject. According to the curricula, the priority objective in reading is for pupils to be able to read fluently and independently by the end of primary school. This implies rapid deciphering of familiar words, as well as good oral comprehension and vocabulary to grasp simple sentences and texts. At the start of primary school, all pupils are expected to read and understand a short, familiar message. The test assesses listening comprehension, familiarity with the written word and reading-decoding, as well as reading comprehension. In mathematics, the aim is to support the development of knowledge in numbers, calculation, problem-solving, geometry and measurement. The test measures basic skills in arithmetic, geometry, space and measurement, with exercises including an example followed by questions.

In grade 6, tests assess knowledge and skills in reading and mathematics. These skills must enable pupils to understand, learn and adapt to everyday situations, and are a prerequisite for successful continuation in post-primary education. The tests consist of multiple-choice questions, with a maximum duration of 2 hours per subject. At the end of the cycle, assessment focuses on comprehension of informative texts and documents, with less emphasis on literary texts. The decoding of isolated words and sentences plays a lesser role. The tests do not cover written production, oral comprehension or expression, or specific linguistic tools (spelling, grammar, conjugation). In mathematics, assessment focuses on arithmetic, geometry and measurement, with the aim of helping students to integrate mathematical concepts, link them together and reason. Performance is measured through knowledge, understanding and application of formulas, and to a lesser extent, the ability to reason about problems.

A large volume of contextual data was collected to describe educational environments and understand the impact of home and school environments on performance. These data come from students, teachers, principals and ministries, both at the beginning and end of schooling. The questionnaires for teachers and principals are identical at both points in time, while the one for pupils at the start of schooling has been greatly simplified. Pupil information was collected via an individual questionnaire, administered in the language of instruction and/or mother tongue, to facilitate comprehension. At the end of primary school, more data is available on pupils than at the beginning.

The second wave of the PASEC test took place in 2019, with 15 participating countries, compared with 10 in the first wave: Benin, Burkina Faso, Burundi, Cameroon, Chad, Congo, Côte d'Ivoire, Democratic Republic of Congo, Gabon, Guinea, Madagascar, Mali, Niger, Senegal and Togo. This second wave revealed overall trends, including a moderate improvement in mathematical skills in several countries, while performance in reading remained stable or declined slightly in some cases. Disparities between urban and rural areas persist, as do inequalities linked to gender and students' socio-economic background. These results underline the need to adapt education policies to reduce disparities and improve basic learning outcomes, notably by strengthening teacher training and access to educational resources.

In 2024, PASEC launched the third major international assessment, PASEC2024, involving 21 African countries: Benin, Burkina Faso, Burundi, Cameroon, Congo, Côte d'Ivoire, Gabon, Guinea, Guinea-Bissau, Democratic Republic of Congo, Mali, Niger, Central African Republic, Senegal, Chad, Togo, Djibouti, São Tomé and Principe, Mozambique and Nigeria. This assessment introduced several methodological innovations. For the first time, it included tablet-based tests, particularly for grade 2 students, in order to modernize data collection tools. In addition, a survey was conducted among the parents of all students tested, providing information on the students' family background. The evaluation also included questions on dimensions such as global citizenship, the security crisis, the health crisis, well-being at school and a taste for learning. In addition, special attention was paid to the inclusion of students with disabilities, with items adapted to ensure their participation. Data collection involved a sample of over 654,000 respondents, including pupils, teachers, head teachers and parents, in the 21 participating countries.[4] The aim of this vast mobilization is to provide reliable and comparable data to assess student achievement in reading and mathematics, and thus guide educational policies in Africa.

2.4.5 The LLECE Survey

The Latin American Laboratory for Assessment of the Quality of Education (LLECE) is a network of national education systems in Latin America and the Caribbean. Created in 1994, it is coordinated by UNESCO's Regional Office for Latin America and the Caribbean. Its fundamental objective is to provide reliable data on student performance levels and the contextual factors associated with these performances, with a view to informing educational policy decisions within the region.

The LLECE approach is based on a series of central questions: What do students know? At what level do they learn? What skills are they developing? When and under what conditions does this learning take place? Finally, the survey seeks to measure learning inequalities between rural and urban areas. These issues are at the heart of the first analyses developed by Casassus et al. (1998), and continue to guide the methodological structure of the program.

As part of the LLECE evaluations, representative samples were drawn up in each country, comprising around 4000 grade 3 pupils (aged 8–9) and grade 4 pupils (aged 9–10). In all, over 50,000 pupils were involved, in at least 100 classes per country.

[4] Source: PASEC website: https://pasec.confemen.org/actualite/evaluation-internationale-pasec2024-vision-et-principaux-contenus/ (Accessed August 6, 2025)

The second assessment, carried out in 2006 and also known as SERCE, measured student performance in mathematics, breaking this domain down into five components: numeration, geometry, measurement, information-based skills and variation (UNESCO-OREALC, 2008). This structure is reminiscent of that adopted by TIMSS, several items of which inspired the LLECE tests for grade 4. The items are constructed according to the correspondence between school curricula and students' actual achievements, placing greater emphasis on academic knowledge than on life skills (unlike the PISA approach). Contextual questionnaires were also administered to students, teachers and school principals, to gather data on the home and school environment. Analysis of the results often emphasizes the disparities between urban and rural areas.

Unlike the 1995 TIMSS survey, which also assessed two adjacent grades (grades 3 and 4),[5] LLECE I did not allow the same students to be tracked over time, as they were different in each grade tested. For SERCE, the levels assessed were grade 3 and grade 6, providing a broader perspective on attainment at the end of primary school (UNESCO-OREALC, 2008).

The SERCE assessment was carried out in 13 Latin American countries: Argentina, Bolivia, Brazil, Chile, Colombia, Costa Rica, Cuba, Dominican Republic, Honduras, Mexico, Paraguay, Peru and Venezuela. However, only 11 countries are included in the official report (Casassus et al., 1998). What's more, for six of these countries, a science assessment was included, in addition to reading and mathematics.

In 2013, LLECE implemented its third assessment, known as TERCE. It involved around 3200 schools and over 134,000 students, with an average of 250 schools and 9000 students tested per country. Although sample sizes varied from country to country, they were always representative of pupils in grades 3 and 6. One of TERCE's major objectives was to ensure comparability with the results obtained under SERCE. To this end, the domains assessed remained identical, with the exception of writing, which could not be compared.

The TERCE results enabled us to measure the progress made between 2006 and 2013. The majority of participating countries saw their pupils improve their performance in the disciplines assessed. Nevertheless, in four of the fifteen countries evaluated, a decline in results was observed over the period.

As in the previous test, the ERCE 2019 assessment, covered two core school levels: the 3[e] grade and the 6[e] grade of primary school but included 16 Latin American and Caribbean countries (Argentina, Brazil, Colombia, Costa Rica, Cuba, Dominican Republic, Ecuador, El Salvador, Guatemala, Honduras, Mexico, Nicaragua, Panama, Paraguay, Peru and Uruguay). More than 160,000 students in around 4000 representative schools took part in the assessment, covering reading, written production, mathematics and, at 6[e] grade, science. For the first time, a module dedicated to socio-emotional skills (empathy, openness to diversity, academic self-regulation) was included in the study. The results show that around 40% of 3[e] grade students

[5] In contrast to TIMSS, the LLECE 2—SERCE survey assesses pupils in grades 3 and 6, whereas in TIMSS only pupils in grade 4 at primary level are assessed (pupils in grade 8 are at secondary level).

and 60% of 6^{e} grade students do not reach the minimum expected competencies in reading and math, a rate that has not decreased since 2013, and has even declined in some countries. Only Brazil, Peru and the Dominican Republic show significant progress since the previous adjudicative wave (Flotts et al., 2015). In reading in 3^{e} grade, over 55% of students exceed Level I, while in 6^{e} grade only 31% reach Level III, supposed to represent appropriate mastery of text. In mathematics, just over 52% of 3^{e} grade students are at least at Level II, but only 17% in 6^{e} grade reach Level III, revealing a widespread weakness in advanced mathematical reasoning.

Complementing the previous surveys, the Regional Comparative and Explanatory Study (ERCE, 2025), a fifth cycle piloted by LLECE, is scheduled for 2025 and will focus on the learning achievements of pupils in grades 3 and 6 across 19 member countries in Latin America and the Caribbean, with the addition of delegations from Spain and Portugal (UNESCO, 2024). This new edition will mobilize some 190,000 students from almost 5000 schools, to ensure solid representation on a regional scale.

2.5 Hybrid Surveys

This section introduces assessments that are not explicitly aimed at international comparison and are not strictly regional, such as EGRA, EGMA and SSME. They are often system diagnostic tools, based on examples, designed to inform ministries and donors about systemic needs for instructional improvement, without being high accountability tools. We will call them “hybrid surveys” (Wagner, 2011).

2.5.1 The EGRA Survey

Ministries of education and development professionals at the World Bank, the US Agency for International Development (USAID) and other institutions have called for the creation of simple, effective and inexpensive analyses of student learning performance (Abadzi, 2006; Chabbott, 2006; Evaluation Gap Working Group, 2006; World Bank, 2006). In response to this demand, the development of an assessment of basic reading skills (EGRA) has begun. The fundamental aim of this assessment was to test pupils’ first steps in learning to read: recognizing the letters of the alphabet, reading simple words and understanding sentences and paragraphs.

The development of EGRA began in 2006, when USAID called on RTI International to develop an instrument for assessing fundamental reading skills, as part of the EdData II project. The aim was to analyze the extent to which children in the early years of elementary school acquire reading skills, and to subsequently generate effective policies to improve performance in this essential learning skill. RTI has developed a protocol for an individual oral assessment of students’ basic reading skills.

A workshop was organized in November 2006 by USAID, the World Bank and RTI to test the different tools that could be used. The first tests took place in Senegal (in French and Wolof) in 2007, and in Gambia (in English). USAID also supported an application in Nicaragua (in Spanish). Other evaluations piloted by national governments, USAID missions and non-governmental organizations (NGOs) have taken place in South Africa, Kenya, Haiti, Afghanistan and Bangladesh.

The EGRA assessment was developed for several reasons. Firstly, it is directly linked to research into reading acquisition and cognitive development. The importance of the fundamental nature of skills has been emphasized in the literature in this field. In particular, Stanovich (1986) points to the existence of a "Matthew effect" in reading acquisition.[6] This effect means that if solid fundamental skills are not acquired at an early age, the gap in learning performance widens between pupils. Another reason relates to the simplicity of the analysis for stakeholders (ministries, teachers, parents). The evaluation carried out in Peru highlights the importance of the results of a simple reading and math assessment, administered to 330,000 children in 10,000 villages using entirely volunteer staff. The initiative was coordinated by the Indian NGO Pratham, the UK Department for International Development (DFID) and the World Bank. The test has sparked an important dialogue about school quality and student learning.

The EGRA instrument is designed to be an example-based "system diagnostic" analysis. Its purpose is to document student performance in basic reading skills in order to inform ministries and donors about systemic needs to improve instruction (Gove & Cvelich, 2011). As such, EGRA is not intended for direct use by teachers, nor is it designed to be a high-accountability analysis used to make investment decisions or to determine the transition of students from one primary grade to the next.

Several features of EGRA underline the limited scope of this assessment, compared with the PASEC, SACMEQ or LLECE tests. Firstly, EGRA cannot be used as a tool for high accountability. It is only a diagnostic tool for departmental staff. Secondly, EGRA is not suited to international comparisons. In particular, differences between language structures and acquisition rates reduce the chances of direct comparisons. Whatever the language, all children who learn to read progress from the non-reading level (unable to read words), through the partial reader level (can read some items but not others) to the proficient reader level (can read all or most items). The progression through these levels varies between languages. In languages with more complex orthographies, this process can take several years (2 years or more), as is the case with English. In contrast, regular, transparent languages such as Italian, Finnish and Greek require just 1 year of instruction for students to reach a comparable level (Seymour et al., 2003). And within a single language, comparisons are just as difficult. Differences in dialect and vocabulary from one locality to another can be significant. To date, some 54 countries have completed the EGRA evaluation.

[6] The expression "Matthew Effect" comes from a situation that appears in a biblical parable in the Gospel of Saint Matthew: "For to him who has, more will be given, and he will have plenty. But to him who has not, even that which he has will be taken away" (25:29). This effect refers to the idea that "the rich get richer and the poor get poorer".

2.5.2 EGMA and SSME Surveys

The EGMA (Early Grade Mathematics Assessment), developed on the basis of the EGRA approach, aims to measure students' fundamental mathematical skills in the first years of compulsory schooling (grades 1 to 3). Funded by the United States Agency for International Development (USAID), this system was designed to meet a diagnostic need in mathematics learning at an early stage of schooling. After an in-depth analysis of school curricula, USAID experts identified a convergence of mathematics expectations in most countries at the early grades. Skills such as recognizing and using Arabic numbers, comparing quantities and classifying objects appear to be essential and universally present in primary school curricula.

The EGMA assessment is therefore an oral test, administered individually, designed to detect any gaps in basic mathematical skills. It is a valuable tool for policymakers and educational authorities wishing to assess the level of their primary education system. Unlike conventional national and international assessments, which focus mainly on grades 3 and above, EGMA fills a gap by providing a structured assessment above this threshold.

A pilot study was carried out in July 2009 in the Malindi region of Kenya, to test the feasibility and relevance of this tool. The results confirmed the assessment's ability to identify students' strengths and weaknesses. The test, which lasts an average of 15 minutes per pupil, comprises seven types of tasks: number identification, quantitative discrimination, identification of missing numbers, solving stated problems, operations (addition/subtraction), pattern recognition and extension of logical sequences. A professional examiner accompanies each student and establishes a final grade. Given the more universal nature of mathematical concepts compared with those of reading, some EGMA items could be comparable between countries. However, this assessment is still in the experimental stage, and the exact number of participating countries remains undetermined. Early candidates include Kenya, South Africa and Jamaica.

In parallel with the EGRA and EGMA assessments, USAID has launched the Snapshot of School Management Effectiveness (SSME) initiative. The aim is to provide a rigorous, multidimensional snapshot of school management practices within a country or region. The data thus collected is intended to inform education managers—at local, regional and national levels—about actual practices in classrooms and schools, in order to identify levers for improving school performance.

The SSME methodology is based on a mixed-methods approach, combining direct observations, questionnaires addressed to pupils, and interviews with parents, teachers and headteachers. This format has the advantage of being inexpensive, while providing usable data. Pilot studies carried out in 2007 in Jamaica and Peru demonstrated the feasibility of the tool, as well as its ability to discriminate between effective schools and those requiring specific adjustments. Since then, MCHS modules have been implemented in over 10 countries in Africa, Latin America and Asia, often in conjunction with the EGRA and EGMA surveys. Countries that have already completed an MCHW assessment include Peru, Jamaica, Liberia, Senegal and Ethiopia, while others are currently undergoing assessment, such as Kenya, Uganda, Mali, Honduras, Guatemala and Nepal.

2.6 Surveys of Adult Populations

This section focuses on adult skills assessments, which differ from the previous ones in that they are aimed exclusively at this population and focus on measuring skills rather than academic knowledge. Surveys such as IALS, ALL, PIAAC, LAMP and STEP aim to assess the operationality of knowledge acquired in adult life, in relation to the macroeconomic issues of productivity and competitiveness.

Back in the 2000s, Education For All goal no. 6 stipulated: "improving all aspects of the quality of education and ensuring excellence of all so that recognized and measurable learning outcomes are achieved by all, especially in literacy, numeracy and essential life skills". This objective was reiterated with the Sustainable Development Goals in 2010. In addition to the goal of quality education, this also refers to the need for sustainable learning that enables autonomy and initiative in everyday life. In recent years, particularly for sub-Saharan African countries, the question of basic skills acquired and, more specifically, their measurement has been re-examined. An indirect indicator of the quality of education is based on the measurement of the non-obsolescence of learning, i.e. the probability that an individual enrolled in basic education will retain these skills into adulthood. Traditionally, UNESCO has published statistics on the adult literate population.[7] These statistics, based mainly on self-reporting by individuals in censuses, have often been criticized for their fragility. The MICS and EDS-DHS surveys, initiated by USAID, UNICEF and WHO and available in almost all developing countries, often in several waves since 2000, use simple tests to measure the literacy levels of the populations surveyed. This makes it possible to compare survey levels, school completion statistics and the UNESCO source of literate populations. A study by the Pôle de Dakar (2007) shows the extent of the discrepancies between these three measures, which may constitute an indirect measure of the quality of education received.

A broad reconsideration of the link between knowledge acquired during initial training and its operationality in adult life has been spurred by the OECD's literacy surveys. The *International Adult Literacy Survey* (IALS) was the first assessment of adult skills. It is the result of collaboration between the OECD, Statistics Canada, the US National Center for Education Statistics and the US Education Testing Service. The IALS was administered to nationally representative samples of adults between the ages of 16 and 65. The survey was carried out in three cycles between 1994

[7] Widely used in previous UNESCO yearbooks, the results of this indicator were questionable, as some countries showed significant rates of progress over the average period, while the young population's access to education stagnated.

and 1998. The 1994 cycle included nine countries—Canada (English—and French-speaking populations), France,[8] Germany, Ireland, the Netherlands, Poland, Sweden, Switzerland (Germanic and French-speaking), and the USA. Five new countries or territories administered IALS instruments in 1996: Australia, the Flemish Community of Belgium, Great Britain, New Zealand and Northern Ireland. Nine other countries or regions took part in the third wave in 1998: Chile, Czech Republic, Denmark, Finland, Hungary, Italy, Norway, Slovenia and Italian-speaking Switzerland. A final report was published in 2000, summarizing the main results of the IALS survey (OECD and Statistics Canada, 1997).

IALS is based on the notion of literacy. Literacy is defined as a specific ability and mode of behavior: "*the ability to understand and use written information in everyday life, at home, at work and in the community, to achieve personal goals and to extend one's knowledge and abilities*" (OECD and Statistics Canada, 2000). More specifically, three aspects of literacy were tested:

- Prose literacy—the knowledge and skills needed to understand and use information in prose texts, such as editorials, news, brochures and instruction manuals.
- Schematic text comprehension—the knowledge and skills required to locate and use information presented in a variety of formats, such as job applications, pay slips, transportation schedules, etc.
- Comprehension of texts with quantitative content—knowledge and skills required to apply arithmetic operations, separately or successively, to numbers contained in printed matter, for example to establish the balance of a cheque account, calculate a tip or fill in an order form.

The survey also employed a methodology developed by ETS to measure literacy ability on a scale ranging from 0 to 500 points. Five levels of literacy were defined to enable detailed analyses of performance. Since the end of IALS, China, Japan, Malaysia, Portugal, Vanuatu and the province of Ontario have also collected data using instruments inspired by IALS. Experience has shown that the IALS analyses are more difficult to compare, because unlike the outcome of initial education, there is also the context of use of these skills in adult life, with its cultural biases, Guerin-Pace and Blum (1999).

An extension of the IALS survey, the *Adult Literacy and Life Skills Survey* (ALL), took place in 2003. The ALL survey is a "large-scale joint study conducted by governments, national statistical agencies, research institutions and multilateral organizations" that provides internationally comparable measures in four domains: prose and document literacy (representing the two literacy domains), numeracy and problem solving (OECD and Statistics Canada, 2005). More specifically, development and management of the ALL survey was coordinated by Statistics Canada and ETS in collaboration with the U.S. Department of Education's National Center for Education

[8] France's participation was subsequently cancelled just before the results were released; this is described by Guerin-Pace and Blum (1999), p 274.

Statistics (NCES), the OECD and the UNESCO Institute for Statistics (UIS). Participating countries include Bermuda, Canada, Italy, Switzerland, the United States and the Mexican state of Nuevo Leon.

The ALL survey, which was carried out in the first half of 2003, required all participating countries to collect data from a nationally representative sample of at least 3000 respondents aged 16 to 65 for each language surveyed. As was the case with IALS, the 2003 ALL survey conceptualizes skills along a continuum that indicates the extent to which adults use information to function in society and the economy. Skills in each area are measured on a continuous scale. Each competency scale ranges from zero to a theoretical maximum of 500 points. A person whose knowledge places him or her at a given step on the scale has an 80% probability of succeeding at a task involving that same level of difficulty.

The Program for the International Assessment of Adult Competencies (PIAAC) is a project whose first wave took place between 2011 and 2012, with 24 participating countries. An extension of the ALL and IALS assessments, its aim is to assess the level and distribution of adult skills from an international perspective. It focuses on the cognitive faculties and professional skills that are essentially required to participate successfully in the economy and society of the twenty-first century.

The main skill measured is literacy in the information age. Four skill areas are assessed—problem solving in a technology-intensive environment, literacy, numeracy and mastery of fundamental knowledge. The major innovation of PIAAC is the collection of information from respondents on how they use basic professional skills in their jobs. This makes it possible to use the data obtained to study differences between countries in the use of these skills, and to identify the existence and nature of skills deficits.

The first wave of PIAAC (2011–2012) revealed significant disparities in adult literacy, numeracy and problem-solving skills in digital environments across the 24 participating countries. On average, around 20% of adults had literacy and numeracy skills deemed insufficient to function effectively in modern society. The results showed that skills decline with age, and that level of education is a key factor influencing performance. This survey underlined the importance of lifelong learning policies to improve adults' essential skills (OECD, 2013).

Following the first wave of PIAAC (2011–2012), two further cycles were conducted to assess the evolution of adult skills. The second round began in 2014 with data collection between April 2014 and March 2015, involving nine countries: Chile, Greece, Indonesia (Jakarta), Israel, Lithuania, New Zealand, Singapore, Slovenia and Turkey. The third and final round of this cycle took place in 2017, with the participation of six additional countries: Ecuador, Hungary, Kazakhstan, Mexico, Peru and the United States. The results showed notable variations between countries, with gaps in performance in literacy, numeracy and problem-solving in technological environments. For example, Mexico showed lower proficiency levels than the OECD average, while countries like Finland continued to perform above average (OECD, 2016, 2019).

The third cycle of PIAAC was launched in 2023, with the participation of 31 countries, including Austria, Belgium (Flemish region), Canada, Chile, Croatia,

Czech Republic, Denmark, Estonia, Finland, France, Germany, Hungary, Ireland, Israel, Italy, Japan, Korea, Latvia, Lithuania, Netherlands, New Zealand, Norway, Poland, Portugal, Singapore, Slovakia, Spain, Sweden, Switzerland, United Kingdom (England) and United States. This edition introduced a new dimension, adaptive problem solving, aimed at assessing adults' ability to solve complex problems in dynamic contexts. The results revealed significant differences between countries, with the top three performers being Finland, Japan and Norway, while the bottom three were Chile, Poland and Portugal. The data collected enabled analysis of changes in adult skills over time, providing valuable insight into trends in literacy, numeracy and adaptive problem-solving. This longitudinal analysis is essential for informing educational policies and skills development strategies on an international scale (OECD, 2024).

Participation in adult learning is stagnating in many OECD countries, although ambitions to widen access are shared. On average, 40% of adults participate in training each year, with rates ranging from 58% in Finland and Norway to just 13% in Korea. English-speaking and Nordic countries have the highest rates. However, participation is declining in several countries, notably Korea and Israel, while Ireland and Estonia are recording an increase thanks to job-related non-formal learning.

Gaps between socio-economic groups are tending to narrow, mainly due to a sharper decline among men, high-income earners and highly skilled workers. This phenomenon underlines a general decline in participation, underscoring the need for targeted policies to remove structural barriers. Formal education plays a reduced role, with only 8% of adults enrolled in formal programs, compared with 37% in work-related non-formal training. Some countries, such as Finland, Norway and the USA, manage to maintain high rates of both types of learning, thanks to robust and well-developed systems (OECD, 2025).

As the PIAAC assessment is organized by the OECD, only developed countries or a few middle-income countries can participate. To enable developing countries to assess literacy skills, the UNESCO Institute for Statistics has developed the Literacy Assessment and Monitoring Programme (LAMP) to provide policymakers, donors and other parties with the information required to effectively plan and implement literacy programs. The skills measured by LAMP are the abilities required to cope with everyday situations. These include:

- texts of a continuous nature structured into sentences and paragraphs;
- texts of a discontinuous nature organized in tables, diagrams or graphs;
- the use of numbers and basic mathematical concepts such as shape, dimension and volume.

The advantage of LAMP is that it meets the needs of countries at all levels of development, has been validated since 2009 in nine languages belonging to five language families, and can produce data that can be compared across time, country and culture. The program has been tested in 10 countries: Afghanistan, El Salvador, Jordan, Laos, Mongolia, Morocco, Niger, Palestine, Paraguay and Viet Nam. It gathered data on the distribution of literacy and numeracy skills, providing valuable information for policymakers and development agencies. Unfortunately, the program was not continued and came to a halt after the first pilot phase.

In parallel, the World Bank's STEP (Skills Toward Employability and Productivity) survey aims to measure the skills of adults in developing countries, focusing on cognitive, socio-emotional and technical skills. Launched in the mid-2000s, STEP collects representative data on the skills required for employability and economic productivity. The survey provides crucial insight into the skills gaps in the working population, helping decision-makers to guide education and vocational training policies. STEP contributes to a better understanding of the link between skills, employment and economic growth in a variety of contexts.

The STEP survey has been carried out in over 17 countries,[9] mainly in Africa, Asia and Latin America, since 2006. Among the first participating countries are Tanzania (2006), Vietnam (2006), Peru (2008) and Kenya (2009). STEP reveals significant gaps in cognitive and socio-emotional skills between countries, often linked to unequal access to education and training. The results show that, in several contexts, low mastery of basic skills limits employability and productivity, underlining the need for targeted investment in training to strengthen human capital and boost economic development (Pierre et al., 2014).

Table 2.1 summarizes all existing assessments to date, with the organization overseeing the assessment, the abbreviation commonly used, the areas assessed, the number of participating countries and the grade tested. Sometimes, the number of countries varies within the same assessment, as some provinces have taken part in the survey or some countries have participated several times in different waves. In addition, information on students' grades should be treated with caution, since in some surveys, the method of selecting students is based on their age rather than their grade alone.

2.7 Conclusion

This paper provides a comprehensive overview of the ways in which adults' educational achievements and skills are assessed, highlighting a central methodological issue: the differentiation between observed performance and underlying competence. It categorizes these assessments into five major families, each with distinct purposes and scopes.

National assessments (ENAE), designed by the central education authority, aim to measure knowledge aligned with national curricula, playing a crucial role in steering and improving the quality of education, while revealing disparities within countries. Their development is often influenced by international surveys.

[9] Albania, Armenia, Azerbaijan, Bolivia, Bosnia & Herzegovina, Colombia, Georgia, Ghana, Kenya, Kosovo, Lao PDR, Macedonia, Serbia, Sri Lanka, Ukraine, Vietnam, and the Yunnan Province in China.

Table 2.1 Student and adult learning assessments since 1959

Year	*Organization*	*Abbreviation*	*Subject*	*No. of countries*	*Grade*
1959–1960	IEA	Pilot study	Mathematics Reading Science	12 12 12	7,8 7,8 7,8
1964	IEA	FIMS	Mathematics	12	7, FS
1970–71	IEA	SRC	Reading	15	4,8, FS.
1970–72	IEA	FISS	Sciences	19	4,8, FS.
1980–82	IEA	SIMS	Mathematics	19	8, FS
1983–1984	IEA	SISS	Sciences	23	4,8, FS
1988, 1990–91	NCES	IAEP	Mathematics Sciences	6, 19	7–8 / 4,7–8
1990–1991	IEA	RLS	Reading	32	3–4,7–8
1995,1999,2003,2007,2011, 2015, 2019, 2023	IEA	TIMSS	Mathematics Science	45 / 38 / 48 / 66 / 65 / 70	3–4.7–8, FS / 8 / 4.8 / 4.8 / 4.8
1992–97	UNESCO	MLA	Mathematics Science Reading	72 72 72	6,8 6,8 6,8
1997, 2006, 2013, 2019	UNESCO/ OREALC	ELCE	Mathematics Reading Science	11, 13	3,4 / 3,6
1999, 2002,2007, 2020	UNESCO/ IIEP	SACMEQ	Reading Mathematics	7 / 15 / 15 / 15	6 6
1993–2011, 2014, 2019	CONFEMEN	PASEC	Mathematics Reading	22 / 10 / 14 / 21	2,5 2,5
2001,2006,2011, 2016, 2021	IEA	PIRLS	Reading	35 / 42 / 56 / 50 / 57	4
2011	IEA	prePIRLS	Reading	6	2,3
2000,2003,2006,2009, 2012, 2015, 2018, 2022, 2025	OECD	PISA	Mathematics Science Reading	43 / 41 / 57 / 65 / 65 / 72 / 79 / 81 / ~90	8, 9, 10
2013	OECD	AHELO	Economics Sciences General	17	University
2006–2020	USAID	EGRA	Reading	70+	1–5
2009–2020	USAID	EGMA	Mathematics	14	1–5
2007–2020	USAID	SSME	Management	11	Primary
1994–1998	OECD / stat Canada / NCES / ETS	IALS	Literacy	23	Adult population

(continued)

Table 2.1 (continued)

Year	*Organization*	*Abbreviation*	*Subject*	*No. of countries*	*Grade*
2003	OECD / stat Canada / NCES / ETS	ALL	Literacy	6	Adult population
2011, 2012, 2023	OECD	PIAAC	Literacy	24 / 9 / 39	Adult population
2009-	UIS UNESCO	LAMP	Literacy	8	Adult population

Note "FS" means the last year of secondary school

On a supranational scale, international assessments (IALS) such as PISA, TIMSS and PIRLS are distinguished by their global comparative perspective, seeking to rank education systems and assess so-called transversal or "macro-competencies", beyond national curricular knowledge alone. At the same time, regional surveys (ERAE) such as SACMEQ, PASEC and LLECE bring together countries that share geographical or cultural similarities, developing harmonized tools adapted to regional specificities to enable targeted comparisons.

Hybrid assessments (EHAE), such as EGRA and EGMA, are positioned differently; they do not aim for strict international comparisons, but act as systemic diagnostic tools for fundamental skills, informing ministries and donors of the need to improve instruction.

Finally, Adult Population Surveys (APS), including IALS, ALL, PIAAC, LAMP and STEP, focus on measuring acquired skills and their operationality in adult life. They assess the ability of individuals to use written and digital information, numeracy and problem-solving in professional contexts, highlighting the link between skills and the macroeconomic issues of productivity and competitiveness.

In short, all these systems, varied in scope and objectives, collectively contribute to measuring and analyzing the quality of lifelong education and skills, providing essential data to inform educational policies and adapt systems to contemporary challenges, despite the inevitable methodological limitations inherent in any evaluation.

References

Abadzi, H. (2006). *Efficient learning for the poor: Insights from the frontier of cognitive neuroscience*. World Bank Publications.

Agencia de Calidad de la Educación (2025). *Resultados Educativos* 2024. https://s3.us-east-1.amazonaws.com/archivos.agenciaeducacion.cl/Simce+PPT+EERR+Nacional+2024+-+P%C3%BAblica.pdf

Benavot, A., & Tanner, E. (2008). The growth of national learning assessments in the world, 1995-2006. *Background paper for the education for all global monitoring. Report.*

Burstein, L. (1992). *The IEA study of mathematics III: Student growth and classroom processes.* Elsevier.

Casassus, J., Froemel, J. E., Palafox, J. C., & Cusato, S. (1998). *First international comparative study of language, mathematics, and associated factors in third and fourth grade.* Latin American Laboratory for Evaluation of the Quality of Education.

Chabbott, C. (2006). Carrot soup, magic bullets, and scientific research for education and development. *Comparative Education Review, 51*(1), 71–94.

Chinapah, V., H'ddigui, E. L. M., Kanjee, A., Falayajo, W., Fomba, C. O., Hamissou, O., Rafalimanana, A., & Byomugisha, A. (2000). With Africa for Africa. Towards quality education for all. *1999 MLA Project*. ERIC.

Coleman, J. S. (1966). *Equality of educational opportunity* (Vol. 1). US Department of Health, Education, and Welfare, Office of Education.

Swiss Confederation (2000, January 1). *Constitution de la Suisse.* https://www.fedlex.admin.ch/eli/cc/1999/404/fr

CONFEMEN. (2004). *Synthèse de rapport—Les enseignants contractuels et la qualité de l'enseignement de base I au Niger: quel bilan.* https://pasec.confemen.org/wp-content/uploads/sites/2/2022/11/2004-Niger.pdf

Encinas-Martin, M. (2007). A Global Survey of Educational Evaluation: International, Regional, and National Assessments of Student Learning. *Paper Commissioned for the EFA Global Monitoring Report*.

Eurydice. (2009). *Standardized Pupil Assessments in Europe: Objectives, Organization and Use of Results.* https://op.europa.eu/fr/publication-detail/-/publication/dac32463-5f05-4782-898b-dd399e66efc6

Evaluation Gap Working Group (2006). *When Will we Ever Learn? Improving Lives through Impact* Evaluation. https://www.cgdev.org/sites/default/files/7973_file_WillWeEverLearn.pdf

Flotts, M. P., Manzi, J., Jiménez, D., Abarzúa, A., Cayuman, C., & García, M. J. (2015). Informe de resultados TERCE: logros de aprendizaje. *OREALC.*. https://unesdoc.unesco.org/notice?id=p::usmarcdef_0000243532

Gipps, C. V., & Murphy, P. (1994). *A fair test? Assessment, achievement and equity.* Open University Press.

Goastellec, G. (2003). The SAT and access to higher education: Recruiting America's elites in question. *Sociologie Du Travail, 45*(4), 473–490.

Gove, A., & Cvelich, P. (2011). Early reading: Igniting education for all. A report by the early grade learning community of practice. *RTI International.*

Greaney, V., & Kellaghan, T. (2008). *Assessing national achievement levels in education* (Vol. 1). World Bank Publications.

Harlen, W. (2007). The impact of summative assessment on children, teaching, and the curriculum. In *QualitÄt von Grundschulunterricht: entwickeln, erfassen und bewerten* (pp. 51–65). Springer.

Husen, T. (1967). *A comparison of twelve countries: International study of achievement in mathematics* (Vol. 1). Almquist & Wiksell.

Ministère de l'Education Nationale, de l'Enseignement supérieur et de la R. (2023, November). *Évaluations nationales de septembre 2023 en CP, CE1, CM1, 6e ET 4e.* https://www.education.gouv.fr/evaluations-nationales-de-septembre-2023-en-cp-ce1-cm1-6e-et-4e-379971

Ministère de l'Education Nationale, de l'Enseignement supérieur et de la R. (2025, February). *L'évaluation globale du système éducatif.* https://www.education.gouv.fr/l-evaluation-globale-du-systeme-educatif-12215

Mislevy, R. J. (1992). Linking educational assessments: Concepts, issues, methods, and prospects.

OECD. (2013). OECD Skills Outlook 2013. *OECD.* https://doi.org/10.1787/9789264204256-en

OECD. (2016). *Skills matter: Further results from the survey of adult skills* (OECD publishing). *OECD.* https://doi.org/10.1787/9789264258051-en

OECD. (2019). *Skills matter: Additional results from the survey of adult skills* (OECD publishing). *OECD.* https://doi.org/10.1787/1f029d8f-en

OECD. (2024). Do adults have the skills they need to thrive in a changing world? Vol. *OECD Skills Studies* (OECD Publishing). OECD. doi:https://doi.org/10.1787/b263dc5d-en.
OECD. (2025). Trends in adult learning. *OECD Publishing.* https://doi.org/10.1787/ec0624a6-en
Pierre, G., Puerta, M. L. S., Valerio, A., & Rajadel, T. (2014). STEP skills measurement surveys. *Methodological Note. The World Bank.*
Ray, A., McCormack, T., & Evans, H. (2009). Value added in English schools. *Education Finance and Policy, 4*(4), 415–438.
Rojas, C., & Esquivel, J. M. (1998). Los sistemas de medición del logro académico en Latinoamérica. *LCSHD Paper Series, Washington DC: World Bank, LAC Regional Office.*
Ross, K. N., & Postlethwaite, T. N. (1991). *Indicators of the quality of education: A study of Zimbabwean primary schools.* Ministry of Education and Culture.
Rothstein, J. (2010). Teacher quality in educational production: Tracking, decay, and student achievement. *The Quarterly Journal of Economics, 125*(1), 175–214.
Stanovich, K. E. (1986). Matthew effects in Reading: Some consequences of individual differences in the acquisition of literacy. *Reading Research Quarterly*, 360–407.
Thorndike, R. L. (1973). *Reading Comprehension Education in Fifteen Countries: An Empirical Study* (I. I. I. International Studies in Evaluation, Ed.). Almqvist and Wiksell.
UNESCO. (2024, December 9). *UNESCO to commemorate 30 years of the LLECE Laboratory and initiate coordination for the implementation of the 2025 ERCE regional learning* study. https://www.unesco.org/en/articles/unesco-commemorate-30-years-llece-laboratory-and-initiate-coordination-implementation-2025-erce
UNESCO-OREALC. (2008). *Student Achievement in Latin America and the Caribbean, Results of the Second Regional Comparative and Explanatory Study (SERCE).* https://unesdoc.unesco.org/ark:/48223/pf0000161045
Vaniscotte, F. (1996). *Les écoles de l'Europe—systèmes éducatifs et dimension européenne* (INRP).
Vegas, E., & Petrow, J. (2007a). *Raising student learning in Latin America: The challenge for the 21st century.* World Bank Publications.
Vegas, E., & Petrow, J. (2007b). *Raising student learning in Latin America: The challenge for the 21st century.* World Bank Publications.
Vrignaud, P. (2006). La mesure de la littéracie dans PISA: la méthodologie est la réponse, mais quelle était la question? *Revue Française de Pédagogie. Recherches En Éducation, 157*, 27–41.
Wagner, D. A. (2011). *Smaller, quicker, cheaper: Improving learning assessments for developing countries.* UNESCO, International Institute for Educational Planning.
Walker, D. A., Arnold, A. C., & Wolf, R. M. (1976). The IEA six subject survey: an emprical study of education in twenty-one countries. *International Studies in Evaluation; IX.*
Wennström, J. (2020). Marketized education: How regulatory failure undermined the Swedish school system. *Journal of Education Policy, 35*(5), 665–691. https://doi.org/10.1080/02680939.2019.1608472
World Bank, T. (2006). *From schooling access to learning outcomes, an unfinished agenda: an evaluation of World Bank support to primary education.* World Bank Publications.

Chapter 3
Learning-Adjusted Years of Schooling Worldwide

Abstract This chapter introduces the most comprehensive dataset to date on global education, encompassing both schooling years and learning outcomes. By integrating these two dimensions, we develop the Learning-Adjusted Years of Schooling (LAYS), a measure that reflects not just quantity but quality. Covering more than 120 countries from 1970 to 2020, our panel dataset harmonizes international and regional achievement tests into comparable indicators. The results highlight sharp discrepancies between years spent in school and actual learning, exposing persistent inefficiencies and inequalities across education systems. Ultimately, the project provides policymakers and researchers with robust tools to evaluate human capital, design more effective reforms, and connect education more directly to long-term economic growth.

> It is the lack of relevant data more than the lack of relevant theory that is often the greater problem in research. In this way, cliometricians have made some of the greatest contributions to the fields of economics and history by discovering and compiling new data sets that can then be used by future researchers to better understand the evolution and growth of economies over time. The accumulation of the data is in itself monumental in many respects, but its usefulness has been expanded by the rapid growth of computing power. The ability to handle "big data" is not a cliometric issue by itself, but the construction of significant, important historical data sets, which can then be analyzed using the latest econometric techniques and computer programs, is very much a contribution of cliometrics. The marriage of cliometrics and big data is a natural one, and has been exploited by economic historians in new and creative ways.[1]

[1] Diebolt C. (27 February, 2020a). "Building a bridge between theoretical models and history", Springer Nature Interview: https://www.springernature.com/gp/researchers/the-source/blog/blogposts-life in research/claude-diebolt/17744496. See also (Diebolt, 2016; Diebolt & Haupert, 2019a, 2019b, 2020, 2021, 2022a, 2022b; Diebolt et al., 2019).

This chapter was first published in modified form as Cliometrics of Learning-Adjusted Years of Schooling: Evidence from a New Dataset, *Cliometrica*, 18 (3), 2024, pp. 691–764.

N. Altinok and C. Diebolt, *Edumetrics*, Population Economics,
https://doi.org/10.1007/978-3-032-13277-2_3

3.1 Introduction

This chapter summarizes the last decade of our scientific collaboration. We present a new data set on two dimensions of schooling, namely learning outcomes and years of schooling. Moreover, by combining the two dimensions, we propose a new measure for learning-adjusted years of schooling (LAYS). Compared to previous research, our dataset is novel in several ways. We combine several of the advantages of existing datasets in order to obtain a unique dataset offering multiple improvements, from the methodological point of view but also in terms of country and time coverage. First, we propose the first real panel dataset with 5-year intervals between 1970 and 2020 for more than 120 countries and for both dimensions of schooling (i.e. quality and quantity). To our knowledge, this is the largest existing dataset covering both dimensions of schooling. Second, our dataset aggregates all existing learning achievement tests in order to obtain comparable scores across countries, while most previous papers propose separate scores for each dimension. These scores are computed with a parsimonious methodology which combines multiple improvements derived from previous papers. For instance, we first focus on the actual results of student achievement tests, and only then do we use imputation methods for predicting results in a multiple dimension analysis (i.e. skill, year, grade, level of schooling). In a second step, additional data on schooling and literacy are used for the multiple imputation process. This makes our data close to the original results of achievement tests, but it also provides real panel data over time. Therefore, the data are more extensive than those in previous datasets and go back as far as 1970 for a large number of countries.

Schooling is not the same as learning (Filmer et al., 2020; Kraay, 2018). We need better and more extensive data on education (Kraay, 2018). Most governments devote a significant share of their budgets to education. Total public expenditure on education accounted for 10.7% of total government expenditure in OECD countries in 2018 (OECD, 2021). The proportion varies across countries, from less than 7% in Greece to 17% in Chile. In the meantime, schools are often too low quality to generate human capital. Shortfalls in quality persist for many reasons (World Bank, 2018). First, pursuing good policies may not have positive impacts for policy actors. Second, the bureaucracies tasked with implementing policies often lack the capacity or the incentive to do so effectively. For instance, a recent study conducted by the World Bank in seven countries in sub-Saharan Africa found that, on average, 3 in 10 fourth-grade teachers had not mastered the language curriculum they were teaching (Bold et al., 2017).

Better measurements of schooling highlight the political and bureaucratic failures that lead to the poor quality of schools. Information is thus an essential step which encourages citizens to demand more from their leaders and service providers (World Bank, 2018). In addition, a good measurement is essential to developing research and analysis to inform policies that improve human capital. Measures that only capture school quantity neglect the differences in the learning outcomes achieved (Hanushek & Woessmann, 2012). Indeed, we cannot reasonably accept that one year of schooling in Singapore or Japan results in the same increase in skills as one year of schooling in a low-income country where education spending is lower, schools are less efficient, and quality of teaching is *ceteris paribus* weaker. This intuition is confirmed by numerous empirical studies (ASER, 2021; Uwezo, 2014).

In parallel, several papers have proposed to contribute to the literature on learning outcomes. To our knowledge, the first paper to attempt to assess learning outcomes in an international setting is the work of J. Lee and Barro (2001). These authors used direct results from International Student Achievement Tests (ISATs) without any specific methodology for adjusting potential differences between all the series. Another method of anchoring was used by Hanushek and Kimko (2000). These authors adjusted ISATs between 1964 and 1995 using results from the National Assessment of Educational Progress (NAEP).[2] Their methodology is only based on United States scores, and the data are limited to the period 1964–1995. A research paper by Hanushek and Woessmann (2012) aimed at correcting some of these imperfections by using an approach that assumes stability over time of the variance of quality of student achievement in a restricted number of OECD countries. The authors suggest two criteria for a group of countries to serve as a standardization benchmark for performance variation over time. First, the countries have to be member states of the relatively homogenous and economically advanced group of OECD countries over the whole period of ISAT observations. Second, the countries should already have seen a substantial enrollment in secondary education in 1964. The authors suggest 13 countries that meet both of these measures of stability, named the "OECD Standardization Group" (OSG) of countries.[3] Hanushek and Woessmann (2015) (hereafter HW) assume that cross-country variations among the OSG countries have not varied substantially since 1964. On this assumption, they build new indicators of student achievements and educational quality.

In a series of other papers, alternative datasets are proposed to augment HW's sample by incorporating data on reading assessments and information from other sources, such as Regional Student Achievements Tests (RSATs) for countries that do not participate in ISATs (Altinok & Murseli, 2007; Altinok et al., 2014, 2018; Angrist et al., 2013). The main idea of this alternative methodology is to calculate an "exchange rate" that can be used to adjust differences in difficulty and grading scales among different achievement tests. Our paper follows this path, with several improvements.

In their paper, Altinok et al. (2018) provide panel data with, for most countries, several observations that correspond to "Harmonized Learning Outcomes" (HLO).[4]

[2] NAEP is the largest nationally representative system of continuing assessments in the United States. Since 1969, NAEP has been a common measure of student achievement across the country in mathematics, reading, science and many other subjects. More information about NAEP can be obtained in National Academies of Sciences & Medicine (2017).

[3] The OSG countries are Austria, Belgium, Canada, Denmark, France, Germany, Iceland, Japan, Norway, Sweden, Switzerland, the United Kingdom, and the United States.

[4] In addition to this paper, other analyses are conducted, with roughly the same methodology (Altinok & Murseli, 2007; Altinok et al., 2014, 2018; Angrist et al., 2013; Patrinos & Angrist, 2018). In this latter paper, the methodology is somewhat different since the standardization procedure is based on a regression of the form $y_i = a + bx_i + \varepsilon_i$. The equation is estimated using data for all

Using only learning outcomes may not be sufficient, since the stock of human capital is not the same across countries. By combining both quantity and quality of schooling, LAYS avoids the weaknesses of using either of these measures alone. Unlike the years of schooling measure alone, it keeps a focus on quality; and unlike the quality measure alone, it encourages schooling for all children, whether or not they will perform highly in achievement tests. A similar analysis is conducted by Glawe and Wagner (2022). These authors propose a new LAYS database over the period 1995–2015, using the World Bank (2018) methodology. Glawe and Wagner (2022) find that the average number of learning-adjusted years of schooling (LAYS) for the cohort of the population aged 25–29 is much lower than that of unadjusted years, which is around 9, ranging from 3 (for Morocco) to 15 (for South Korea). On average, mean school years are reduced by about 2.3 years when the quality of schooling is taken into account. One drawback of the study by Filmer et al. (2020) is the restriction of the data within a cross-country dimension. These authors compute average scores for the most recent years. While Glawe and Wagner (2022) innovate by providing a panel dataset on both quantity and quality of schooling, both the number of countries (35) and the time span (1995–2015) are very low.

An alternative analysis on the measure of human capital was conducted by Lim et al. (2018). These authors combine both education and health indicators in order to obtain a panel database on human capital for 195 countries between 1990 and 2016. Lim et al. (2018) estimate educational attainment using 2522 censuses and household surveys, while they base learning estimates on 1894 tests among school-age children. In the first step, the authors use the same methodology as Altinok et al. (2014), but they add different features. For instance, national assessments were included, such as the US National Assessment of Education Progress[5] and the India National Achievement Survey (Sreekanth, 2015), along with representative studies measuring intelligence quotient (IQ) in school-aged children (Dunn, 1959; Raven, 1936; Wechsler, 1949).[6] Another novelty is the methodology used to estimate test scores for all countries, years and ages (5-year age groups from 5 to 19 years), where the authors used an imputation methodology—spatiotemporal Gaussian process regression—with per capita mean years of education as a predictor (Gakidou et al., 2010; Lim et al., 2018; Vos et al., 2017).[7] This imputation methodology was quite new in education and resulted in a full panel dataset between 1990 and 2016.

---

countries that took part in both assessments and is then used to make an estimation of Y for those countries that only participated in X. According to Kolen & Brennan (2014), this anchoring is close to linear equating.

[5] Institute for Education Sciences National Center for Education Statistics. National Assessment of Educational Progress- overview. https://nces.ed.gov/nationsreportcard/about/ (accessed August 12, 2025).

[6] IQ data included the Wechsler Intelligence Scale for Children (Wechsler, 1949), the Raven's Standard Progressive Matrices (Raven, 1936), and the Peabody Picture Vocabulary test (Dunn, 1959).

[7] This method is strengthened across time, space, and age, incorporates both data and model uncertainty, and produces a full-time series of estimates for all geographies with the use of covariate relationships and spatial and temporal patterns in residuals (Lim et al., 2018).

In our paper, we propose to extend the data on learning outcomes in order to provide broader information on three complementary indicators, namely years of schooling, learning outcomes and LAYS, from 1970 to 2020. To this end, we combine the advantages of various existing methodologies. First, we follow the initial anchoring methodology presented in Altinok et al. (2018) to obtain a global dataset on learning outcomes for most countries. Second, we use an imputation methodology, quite similar to the one used in (Lim et al., 2018), in order to obtain a panel dataset for both dimensions of schooling—quality and quantity—between 1970 and 2020. In addition to this, our paper extends the Filmer et al. (2020) dataset on LAYS by combining both our learning-outcomes measures and the most recent data on years of schooling. In this way, our project seeks to fill two major gaps: to obtain a large panel database on learning outcomes and years of schooling over a 50-year period using alternative imputation techniques, but also to provide an alternative way to measure years of schooling by combining years of schooling with learning outcomes.

In Sect. 3.2, we focus on student achievement tests and methodology. The final database is then presented with several analyses based on trends and the potential impact of learning on economic growth. We then highlight the potential limitations of the study and conclude with new perspectives.

3.2 Data and Methodology

This section briefly describes the achievement tests we used to construct the dataset on learning achievement and additional data related to quantity of education, such as years of schooling.

The first set of achievement tests consists of international assessments which are already standardized; the second are regional standardized achievement tests; and the third are hybrid achievement tests. Each test covers different numbers of countries, from 10 to 81 for the Programme for International Student Assessment (PISA) conducted in 2022. By combining these assessments and making them comparable we are able to include 167 countries or territories covering almost the entire global population. It should be noted that although this is the largest dataset on learning and years of schooling, there are still availability issues. The main issue with data availability is related to learning achievement data. Indeed, data for learning outcomes is available at about 6.8 different points in time on average. For about 55 localities no data are available, but these localities are mostly islands with low populations.[8] For more than two-thirds of the countries, comparable data are obtained for almost all years between 1970 and 2020. For fewer than twenty countries/localities, only 1 observation is available.

[8] However, we failed to collect comparable data for the following countries with significant populations: Central African Republic, Comoros, Equatorial Guinea, Eritrea, Guinea, North Korea, Libyan Arab Jamahiriya, South Sudan, Sri Lanka, Suriname, Turkmenistan and Uzbekistan.

In addition to learning outcomes, we also provide data for years of schooling. Data from Barro and Lee (2013) are used in their latest version (i.e. September 2021). A multiple imputation procedure is conducted to extent this dataset to 2020 and to cover more countries. As expected, data availability is much greater for the quantity of schooling. Indeed, data for years of schooling are provided for more than 200 countries or territories with an average of 10 different points in time. Meanwhile, data are lacking for only 19 countries and territories. Most of them are islands with very low populations.

Our final database includes mean scores for all 167 countries and territories from 1970 to 2020.[9] Compared to previous datasets, our methodology allows us to extend the database over a 50-year interval. Cognitive skills are disaggregated by subject (mathematics, reading and science), schooling level (primary and secondary) and gender (male and female). Since data for years of schooling are disaggregated by schooling level and gender, our Learning-Adjusted Years of Schooling are also available for each schooling level and each gender. Below, we briefly present the methodology used to anchor these in order to provide a global snapshot of learning outcomes over the world.

3.2.1 A Snapshot of Learning Achievement Tests

The best way to evaluate learning outcomes is to focus on student learning achievement tests. A variety of tests have been conducted in recent years. Student achievement tests come in two varieties. The first one focuses on curricula and measures the academic achievement level of students at different grades of primary and/or secondary schools. The second set of tests focuses on students' command of the basic and applied skills that can be identified with a broad concept of literacy, instead an academic achievement in the strict sense.

We identify eight international achievement tests in which more than 160 countries have participated. These groups can be divided into three sub-groups. As well as well-known international assessments, a growing number of regional assessments across different regions have been observed since the 1990s. Moreover, some hybrid tests, which are not focused on a single region, have been conducted over the last two decades. Detailed information on these assessments is provided in Table 3.11. Only a short presentation of the various existing learning assessments is given below.

The *International Association for the Evaluation of Educational Achievement* (IEA) was the first body to measure individual learning achievement for international comparative purposes in the early 1960s. The surveys include the highly regarded "Trends in International Mathematics and Science Study" (TIMSS) and "Progress in International Reading Literacy Study" (PIRLS). The TIMSS test aims at evaluating

---

[9] Data for 2020 is extrapolated by using the latest results, provided mostly in either 2018 or 2019. In that sense, the potential effects of Covid-19 on learning achievement are not included in our analysis.

skills of students in grades 4 and 8[10] in mathematics and science, while PIRLS is based on a reading test in grade 4. Several rounds of TIMSS and PIRLS have been conducted to date.[11] Another well-known international assessment is PISA (Programme for International Student Assessment). The Organization for Economic Co-operation and Development (OECD) launched its PISA in 1997. More generally, PISA has assessed the skills of 15-year-olds every three years since 2000 in countries that together account for almost 90% of the global economy—i.e. the majority of world GDP. Seven rounds of PISA are available to date (2000, 2003, 2006, 2009, 2012, 2015, 2018 & 2022).[12]

Three major regional assessments have been conducted in Africa and Latin America. The *Southern and Eastern Africa Consortium for Monitoring Educational Quality* (SACMEQ) emerged from a very extensive national investigation of the quality of primary education in 15 African countries in 1995–1999, 2000–2002 and 2007.[13] Following a different approach, surveys under the *Programme d'Analyse des Systèmes Educatifs* (Program of Analysis of Education Systems, PASEC) of the Conference of Ministers of Education of French-Speaking Countries (CONFEMEN) have been conducted in the French-speaking countries of sub-Saharan Africa since 1993. PASEC was transformed and standardized in 2012 and two more recent rounds have since been conducted (2014 and 2019). Finally, the network of national education systems in Latin American and Caribbean countries, known as the *Latin American Laboratory for Assessment of the Quality of Education* (LLECE), was established in 1994 and is coordinated by the UNESCO Regional Bureau for Education in Latin America and the Caribbean. Assessments conducted by the LLECE focused on learning achievements in reading, mathematics and science[14] in grades 3 and 4[15]

[10] A grade consists of a specific stage of instruction in initial education usually covered during an academic year. Students in the same grade are usually of similar age. It is also referred to as a "class", "cohort" or "year" (Glossary of UIS website available at: http://glossary.uis.unesco.org/glossary/en/home).

[11] TIMSS was conducted in 1995, 1999, 2003, 2007, 2011, 2015, 2019 and 2023. PIRLS was conducted in 2001, 2006, 2011, 2016 and 2021. In our current version (version 1.1), we failed to include PIRLS 2021 & TIMSS 2023 due to the unavailability of results.

[12] Two other international assessments are available. Drawing on the experience of the National Assessment of Educational Progress (NAEP), the International Assessment of Educational Progress (IAEP) comprises two surveys first conducted in 1988 and 1991. Under a joint UNESCO and UNICEF project, learning achievements have been assessed as part of the *Monitoring Learning Achievement* (MLA) program on a vast geographical scale in more than 72 countries (Chinapah et al., 2000). This program of assessment is flexible and ranges from early childhood to basic and secondary education to nonformal adult literacy. However, not all the data have been published. Supplementing national reports, a separate report on MLA I was drafted for 11 African countries (Botswana, Madagascar, Malawi, Mali, Morocco, Mauritius, Niger, Senegal, Tunisia, Uganda and Zambia; see Chinapah et al. (2000)). As the microdata from IAEP and MLA are not available, we preferred not to include these assessments in our database.

[13] A fourth round of SACMEQ was conducted in 2012–2014. However, the results were not officially released, due to methodological issues.

[14] Science skill was included only after the second round.

[15] A grade is a stage of instruction usually equivalent to one complete year. Hence, grade 3 represents the third year of compulsory schooling—i.e., of primary education in most countries.

in 13 countries of the subcontinent in 1998, and for grade 3 and 6 pupils in 2006, 2013 and 2019.

Hybrid assessments can be considered as a mix of international and regional achievement tests. Wagner (2011) argues that EGRA represent a hybrid type of assessment. The Early Grade Reading Assessment (EGRA) is an individually administered oral assessment of the most basic foundation skills for literacy acquisition in early grades. The assessment lasts for about 15 min per child. We compile and include data on the proportion of pupils with a 0-score in the "Oral Reading Fluency" test provided in almost all EGRA tests. We believe this is the best comparable measure since it is not related to language complexity, which may differ across countries. Similarly to EGRA, ASER is a quick oral assessment on early grades. It has been conducted in rural localities of several countries, including India and Pakistan. We thus include results from ASER studies in both Pakistan and India for multiple rounds in order to obtain comparable results over time, although these studies began quite recently.[16]

All achievement tests undertaken and the main information concerning them are summarized in Table 3.12. The methodology used to adjust them in order to yield comparable indicators is presented below.

3.2.2 Methodology

As presented in Sect. 3.1, several previous studies have proposed a dataset on learning outcomes and/or LAYS. While some can be considered as "orthodox" papers, others use novel ways of predicting results and covering more countries and years. These "heterodox" studies suffer, however, from robustness and validity issues since most of the data provided are not based on original results. Our priority is to focus on original data based on student achievement tests, as "orthodox" papers have done. Next, we use additional data on literacy, adult learning outcomes and other proxies to improve data availability, similarly to "heterodox" papers. Therefore, our analysis can be considered as being midway between a conservative and a statistical approach. In order to obtain quality-adjusted years of schooling, we follow a four-step process. First, we compile and impute proxies for learning outcomes and years of schooling in order to obtain a large panel dataset on education variables between 1970 and 2020. Second, we compile and anchor all the student achievement tests presented in the previous section. Third, we use the global dataset on education variables compiled in step 1 to fill in missing values for our standardized measure for learning outcomes. We use a multiple imputation technique. Last, we combine quantity and quality of schooling and obtain a panel dataset on learning-adjusted years of schooling. Since

[16] ASER conducted its first study in 2005 in India, while Pakistan began in 2012. As these studies were only conducted in rural areas, we have been unable to extrapolate the results for the entire country and therefore considered them as representative of the whole.

we have disaggregated data for each gender, our dataset includes comparable data for both male and female populations. Below we present the details of the methodology.

Step 1. Preparation of background data for quantity of education. In order to obtain comparable data for a large number of countries, we employ a multiple imputation technique on several proxies of learning outcomes, but also variables which evaluate quantity of schooling. Four sets of variables are included in the "quantity dataset": proxies of quality of schooling with available data from 1970 to 2020; other variables without large data availability; variables related to quantity of schooling and the new literacy rates provided by Le Nestour et al. (2022). The list of all variables is provided in Table 3.14 and the correlation matrix can be found in Table 3.15. In particular, data for years of schooling are updated throughout this imputation process. Indeed, Barro and Lee (2013) propose a global dataset on years of schooling over the period 1950–2015 in their latest update (i.e. the version of September 2021). Data are not available for all countries and for 2020. Multiple imputation has been shown to reduce bias and increase efficiency compared to listwise deletion. We use the "Amelia II" program within R Statistics in order to obtain an imputation of the missing values. Amelia II imputes missing values using a bootstrapping approach called the EMB (expectation–maximization with bootstrapping) algorithm (Honaker et al., 2011). Multiple imputation involves imputing m values for each missing cell in a data matrix and creating m "completed" datasets. In order to obtain more precise predictions, we perform multiple imputation in several steps. Across these completed datasets, the observed values are the same, but the missing values are filled in with a sample of values from the predictive distribution of the missing data (Honaker et al., 2011). The imputation model in Amelia assumes that the complete data are multivariate normal. If we denote the $(n \times k)$ dataset as D (with observed part D^{obs} and unobserved part D^{mis}), then this assumption is

$$D \sim \mathcal{N}_k(\mu, \Sigma), \tag{3.1}$$

which states that D has a multivariate normal distribution with mean vector μ and covariance matrix Σ. The essential problem of imputation is that we only observe D^{obs}, not the entirety of D. Amelia assumes that the data are *missing at random* (MAR). This assumption means that the pattern of missingness only depends on the observed data D^{obs}, not the unobserved data D^{mis}. In order to make the MAR assumption more plausible, additional variables can be included in the dataset D. This auxiliary information is useful when it helps predict the value of the missing data. In Fig. 3.13, we present a schematic diagram of our approach to multiple imputations with the EMB algorithm.

Within each step, 10 different imputations are conducted. Results are obtained by computing the average value of each variable across these different imputations. Ultimately, we obtain a global dataset on 18 education variables which are considered important to both quantity and quality of schooling (see Table 3.14, for the list of all variables).

Step 2. Equating achievement tests. Various methodologies can be used for linking or equating assessments. Equating is a statistical process that is used to adjust scores on tests so that scores can be used interchangeably (Kolen & Brennan, 2014). The purpose of equating is to adjust for difficulty among assessments that are built to be similar. In our case, the assessments are not directly comparable since their difficulty and content may differ. The method to link achievement tests is quite similar to the one used in previous papers (Altinok & Diebolt, 2024; Altinok & Murseli, 2007; Altinok et al., 2018; Patrinos & Angrist, 2018). We present below the general methodology, while a more detailed description can be found in Altinok et al. (2018). When building globally comparable education quality estimates, we rely on classical test theory (Holland & Hoskens, 2003). Specifically, we use pseudo-linear linking (hereafter, the "exchange rate" approach) and equipercentile linking.

We examine the same population between two tests to determine the relationship between *Reference Test X* and *Anchored Test Y*. To this end, we compare the same countries which took an ISAT and an RSAT at the same point in time. Since ISATs and RSATs are psychometrically robust, sample-based tests designed to be nationally representative, they represent the same underlying population at the country level. Thus, by comparing *doubloon* countries which participate in both tests being linked, we can index difficulty and scales across tests by using the "exchange rate". Table 3.15 provides the list of countries that overlap in assessments. This enables the inclusion of Regional Standardized Achievement Tests (RSATs) from Latin America and sub-Saharan Africa, and thus an international comparison. This is a significant addition, since many developing countries have participated in RSATs (LLECE, SERCE, PASEC and SACMEQ) and HSATs (EGRA, ASER), but rarely or never in ISATs (PISA, TIMMS, PIRLS). The transformation of regional scores into an internationally comparable value is more accurate the more *doubloon* countries are available. If our index relies on just one *doubloon* country (if it is the only country participating in both surveys), it is ambitious to convert all other regional scores using this quotient. Student achievement tests are computed as averages taken over different achievement tests administered in the same year or nearby years, after adjusting their results for differences in difficulty. In parallel, following the approach of Hanushek and Kimko (2000), the adjustment of early international student achievement tests is done with the anchoring of each test to the results of the NAEP.[17]

The standardization process is mainly based on the average scores obtained in each test by the set of countries that participate in both of them in order to calculate an "exchange rate" that can be used to anchor all tests with each other, regardless of the difficulty and the grades. That is, given two tests X and Y, the score of country i in test X, x_i, is converted to the scale of test Y using

$$y_i = x_i \times e \tag{3.2}$$

with

[17] Since the U.S. participated in NAEP and various international achievement tests at every interval. We adjust old IEA studies by trend on NAEP results. We only include the NAEP adjustment for scores before the 1990s since standardized ISATs began to be conducted consistently from the 1990s onwards and are therefore comparable over time. This equating relative to the NAEP results was first used in Hanushek & Kimko (2000).

$$e = \frac{\mu(y)}{\mu(x)} = \frac{\frac{1}{n}\sum_{i \in X \cap Y} y_i}{\frac{1}{n}\sum_{i \in X \cap Y} x_i} \quad (3.3)$$

where the average scores for the two assessments, $\mu(x)$ and $\mu(y)$, are calculated over the n countries that have taken part in both of them.[18] By using the results of countries taking part in several achievement tests at the same time, we obtain "exchange rates" between achievement tests. Our reference tests are mostly TIMSS and PISA tests. All other tests are linked to these reference tests. Following the original idea of Angrist et al. (2021), we construct the exchange rate over the entire sample, and not only over two tests. For instance, while in previous papers authors used only data for PISA 2003 and TIMSS 2003 for the adjustment of PISA data, we now use all possible combinations between PISA and TIMSS. This approach improves the likelihood of capturing test-specific rather than country-specific differences. When fixing the exchange rate, we assume that the relationship between tests remains constant across rounds. For instance, in previous versions, only countries which simultaneously took part in both TIMSS 2003 and PISA 2003 in mathematics were chosen for the computation of the exchange rate. In this paper, all achievement tests which have been conducted at roughly the same time are included in the computation of the exchange rate.[19] This assumption allows us to keep the largest number of countries participating in a given pair of tests linked to each other. As indicated in Angrist et al. (2021), one advantage of this approach is that it means that any changes in test scores over the interval are due to actual progress in learning rather than changes in equating functions between tests. Every new round of tests allows the inclusion of more estimates by enabling the construction of a more robust equating procedure. We discuss this point in Sect. 3.4.

Step 3. Grouping and predicting scores. The result of step 2 is a global database of learning outcomes, at different levels (primary, lower secondary), different skills (mathematics, sciences and reading) and different years (between 1970 and 2020). Table 3.17 provides the data available for each dimension. As in previous papers, one disadvantage of the available data is the lack of a comparable dataset across skills and levels. Data are missing for several years and countries (Table 3.18). Indeed, while data for 1970 are more focused on secondary schools and developed economies, most African countries do not have an evaluation of the performance of lower secondary schools. By using this multidimensional dataset, we employ a multiple imputation process in order to take into account all this information and to obtain a global dataset on learning outcomes. We proceed to a parsimonious imputation approach in order to get as close as possible to the original results, and with less biased estimations too.

[18] The list of countries used for the equating process is presented in Table 3.15.

[19] For instance, in order to convert PISA scores on the TIMSS scale on mathematics, we use all available combinations across the two assessments: TIMSS 2003/PISA 2003, TIMSS 2007/PISA 2006, TIMSS 2011/PISA 2012, TIMSS 2015/PISA 2015, TIMSS 2019/PISA 2018. The adjustment process for PISA 2000 is based separately with TIMSS 1999 since data from the OECD are not fully comparable between PISA 2000 and PISA 2003 for both math and science.

We adapt the imputation procedure in order to obtain the most complete data but also to avoid bias due to prediction. Since most achievement tests were conducted after 1995, we first restrict our imputation procedure to the panel dataset over the years 1995–2020. After having imputed data for this restricted subsample, we use the Amelia package to predict a larger timespan, namely 1980–2020. We follow a multi-step procedure to fill in the missing values. The main idea of our methodology is to first focus on the portion of the data with few missing values, and then use the new imputed data to improve the multiple imputation method for countries and years with few observations. Learning outcomes scores recorded over time within a cross-sectional unit are observed to vary smoothly over time. In such cases, knowing the observed values of observations that are close in time to any missing value may greatly help the imputation of such values. We therefore use this option in Amelia in order to build a general model of patterns within variables across time by creating a sequence of polynomials of the time index with a second-order level. These polynomials can be interacted with the cross-section unit to allow the patterns over time to vary between cross-sectional units. We believe that this is a reasonable setting since we do not think that all countries have the same patterns over time in all skills and levels. We therefore impute with trends specific to each country by using a specific option available in Amelia ("intercs"). An additional way of handling time-series information is to include lags and leads of the variables of interest. Since the measure of learning outcomes we are using can be considered as a "global stock of human capital", using *lags* and *leads* may increase the accuracy of the EMB multiple-imputation procedure.

Step 4. Adjusting years of schooling with learning outcomes. The learning-adjusted years of schooling (LAYS) are obtained by using Eq. (3.4). Filmer et al. (2020) propose combining HLOs with data on years of schooling to construct learning-adjusted years of schooling (LAYS).

In that way, LAYS for country i are calculated as

$$LAYS_i = S_i \times Q_i^b \tag{3.4}$$

where S_i is the average number of years of schooling of the population cohort and Q_i^b a measure of achievement, relative to a benchmark level b. In their work, this benchmark corresponds to the best performing country or to a maximum benchmark such as 625 points, i.e. the threshold level for reaching the Advanced International Benchmark set by TIMSS.[20] Filmer et al. (2020) define the measure of relative learning as

$$Q_i^b = \frac{L_i}{L_b} \tag{3.5}$$

[20] The Trends on International Mathematics and Science Study (TIMSS) is an assessment conducted by the IEA.

where L_i and L_b are the measures of average learning-per-year in countries i and b respectively. L can be thought of as a measure of the learning "productivity" of schooling in each country, while Q is a relative productivity (i.e. productivity in country i relative to that in country b). We define our benchmark as 700 points, which is the upper bound threshold of the highest benchmark in the PISA test.

3.3 Results

3.3.1 *The Database*

In this section, we present the coverage and detail of the database. Table 3.2 presents coverage for country-year observations by region for LAYS and both quantity and quality schooling. The database includes 1,506 observations for LAYS, 1547 observations for quality of schooling and 2,250 observations for quantity of schooling. The disaggregation of the schooling quality data by schooling level, subject taught and year are shown in Table 3.3. Most data come from reading scores with 1,466 country-year observations, followed by math scores with 1323, and lastly by science scores with 1104. Data for primary schools are more available (1,369 versus 1,019 for secondary level). Data relative to years of schooling are available for most countries. This shows that our availability of LAYS variables depends mostly on the qualitative dimension of schooling. Across all years, 1,506 observations are provided for the quality-adjusted years of schooling variable, which represents almost two-thirds of observations for years of schooling. Despite the methodology used to expand the data for most countries and years, missing values are problematic, especially for years before 1990 (Table 3.17). Indeed, data are missing for learning achievement for about 43% of countries between 1970 and 1985, while this rate drops to approximately 35% between 1985 and 2020. The expansion of the data using multiple imputation results in more comparable data for the period 1970–1990, since about 70% of the dataset on learning outcomes is predicted for these years (Table 3.18). Thanks to the expansion of learning achievement tests since 2000, only one-third of the dataset is imputed in 2005, and less than 10% in 2010 and 2015 (Table 3.18).

Our LAYS indicator is available for most countries around the world, and especially for sub-Saharan African countries with approximately 370 observations (Table 3.2). On average, LAYS are equal to 4.63 years. The highest level of LAYS is found in East Asia and Pacific with 11.75 years, while South Asian countries have the lowest value (approximately 1.9 years). In comparison with standard years of schooling, LAYS provides a slightly different picture. Figure 3.1 provides a decom position of LAYS with its quantitative dimension. The adjustment from traditional years of schooling to LAYS leads to a lower value for all regions. For instance, while Latin American countries have on average 9 years of schooling, the adjustment for quality of schooling tends to reduce this level by about 3 years. This represents a reduction of approximately 40%. This transformation is greatest for sub-Saharan

Table 3.1 Review of existing datasets on learning outcomes

Authors	Nature	Countries	Period	Panel data	Methodology—advantages/limits
Hanushek and Kimko (2000)	LO	50	1965–2000	No	Score adjustment is mainly based on the results of the USA on NAEP. No panel data available, imputation of scores for about 20 countries. No disaggregation of data, nor specific benchmarks
Lee and Barro (2001)	LO	58	1965–1991	Yes	No specific adjustment of scores across tests. Data not available. Inclusion of achievement tests with severe biases like IAEP or MLA. Data not available
Coulombe and Tremblay (2006)	LIT	14	1960–95	Yes	Use disaggregated results by age group in order to construct synthetic time series of scores using IALS data
Altinok and Murseli (2007)	LO	104	1965–2003	No	Adjustment similar to Hanushek and Kimko (2000) for most tests, extension made with regional tests with an adjustment based on an "exchange rate" across tests. Panel dimension is not really present. Disaggregation across gender is available. No measure of benchmarks
Hanushek and Woessmann (2012)	LO	77	1965–2007	No	Methodology partly similar to Hanushek and Kimko (2000) with an approach based on the cross-country variance in mean scores across a group of 13 advanced OECD countries
Angrist et al. (2013)	LO	128	1970–2010	Yes	The methodology is quite similar to Altinok and Murseli (2007). No disaggregation of data, nor specific benchmarks. Data hosted by the World Bank

(continued)

Table 3.1 (continued)

Authors	Nature	Countries	Period	Panel data	Methodology—advantages/limits
Altinok et al. (2014)	LO	151	1965–2012	Yes	The methodology is quite similar to Altinok and Murseli (2007). Provides a panel dataset for a low number of countries between 1965 and 2012. Disaggregation across gender and type of location available. Three different benchmarks available (minimum, medium and advanced)
Feenstra et al. (2015)	LAYS	145	1950–2019	Yes	Use a combination of different sources of data relative to years of schooling with additional data on rates of return. Rates of return are from Psacharapoulos (1994) and follow the implementation of Caselli (2005). Data from years of schooling are from Barro and Lee (2013), De la Fuente and Doménech (2006), Cohen and Soto (2007) and Cohen and Laker (2013)
Kaarsen (2017)	LAYS	78	1995–2011	No	Author uses results from TIMSS achievement test for years 1995, 1999, 2003, 2007 and 2011. Kaarsen (2017) estimates the quality of education by assuming that the test score is determined by a production function
Lim et al. (2018)	LO	186	1990–2016	Yes	The methodology uses the same approach as Altinok and Murseli (2007) but adds a prediction of scores in order to obtain a full panel dataset between 1990 and 2016. Disaggregation for each gender available. No data for benchmark

(continued)

Table 3.1 (continued)

Authors	Nature	Countries	Period	Panel data	Methodology—advantages/limits
Altinok et al. (2018)	LO	131	1965–2015	Yes	The methodology uses the same approach as Altinok et al. (2014), adds more countries (like India and China) and more disaggregation between subsamples, like gender or type of location. A larger panel dataset is provided between 1970 and 2015 than the one presented in Altinok et al. (2014) and Angrist et al. (2013)
Schwerdt and Wiederhold (2019)	LIT	31	1970–2014	Yes	Use disaggregated data by age group in order to construct synthetic time series of scores, as has been done by Coulombe and Tremblay (2006). Authors use results from PIAAC and IALS for the estimation of adult literacy across time. Not real panel data. Disaggregation across gender and type of location available. Five different benchmarks available
Filmer et al. (2020)	LAYS	174	2015–20	No	Use learning outcomes from TIMSS and PISA assessments and years of schooling from Barro and Lee (2017) to construct a hybrid indicator for education, namely the Learning-Adjusted Years of Schooling for about 174 countries. Only two years available (2015 and 2020). No disaggregation of data, nor specific benchmarks

(continued)

Table 3.1 (continued)

Authors	Nature	Countries	Period	Panel data	Methodology—advantages/limits
Angrist et al. (2021)	LO	163	2000–16	Yes	The methodology is similar to the approach of Altinok et al. (2014). The adjustment used is linear, instead of the "exchange rate" used previously. Comparability over time compromised with the use of linear methodology for adjustment. No real panel data provided. Disaggregation for each gender provided. No data for benchmark
Le Nestour et al. (2022)	LIT	58	1961–2004	Yes	Use disaggregated data from demographic surveys (DHS and MICS) by age group and schooling level in order to construct synthetic time series of literacy scores for populations with 5 years of schooling. Disaggregation for each gender available. No data for benchmark
Glawe and Wagner (2022)	LAYS	33	1995–2015	Yes	Authors mainly use original TIMSS data for learning outcomes and extended Cohen and Leker (2014) for years of schooling. The database includes almost exclusively either OECD countries or oil countries. Moreover, data are not available and no specific discussion about comparability over time. No disaggregation of data, nor specific benchmarks
Our data: Altinok (2022)	LO + LAYS	165	1970–2020	Yes	Use a hybrid approach by first focusing on original results from learning student achievement tests and then using an imputation methodology in order to expand the dataset to almost all countries in the world, over a 50-year period (1970–2020)

Table 3.2 Summary statistics

	Obs	Mean	SD	Min	Max	P10	P90
LAYS							
World	1506	4.63	2.56	0.14	11.75	1.34	8.42
East Asia and Pacific	230	5.34	2.52	0.81	11.75	2.21	9.06
Europe and Central Asia	415	7.01	1.63	1.67	10.27	4.97	8.98
Latin America and the Caribbean	221	4.09	1.53	0.62	7.87	2.07	5.96
Middle East and North Africa	195	3.95	1.97	0.44	9.49	1.53	6.53
North America	22	8.9	0.97	6.86	10.02	7.62	9.97
South Asia	51	1.86	1.02	0.25	4.31	0.72	3.35
Sub-Saharan Africa	372	2.35	1.28	0.14	5.81	0.65	3.96
Learning outcomes							
World	1547	420.3	75.94	249.46	599.19	324.82	524.49
East Asia and Pacific	231	461.68	68.79	325.81	599.19	372.18	556.11
Europe and Central Asia	455	491.51	36.84	372.58	560.03	439.96	534.37
Latin America and the Caribbean	221	403.07	33.25	327.78	519.26	367.52	445.95
Middle East and North Africa	195	398.91	44.71	249.46	504.11	351.99	454.82
North America	22	519.98	11.23	501.99	536.56	504.52	535.53
South Asia	51	364.66	10.41	336.62	388.91	353.62	377.45
Sub-Saharan Africa	372	330.69	30.71	254.13	407.89	290.16	371.22
Years of schooling							
World	2250	7.41	2.88	0.07	14.35	3.1	11.11
East Asia and Pacific	373	7.98	2.6	1.38	13.91	4.24	11.4
Europe and Central Asia	594	9.43	1.89	2.58	13.76	7.09	11.87
Latin America and the Caribbean	429	7.58	2.02	1.22	11.64	4.57	9.99
Middle East and North Africa	231	6.52	2.87	0.07	14.35	2.55	10.06

(continued)

Table 3.2 (continued)

	Obs	Mean	SD	Min	Max	P10	P90
North America	33	10.1	3.2	2.07	13.3	5.13	13.1
South Asia	88	4.86	2.79	0.52	11.58	1.63	9.24
Sub-Saharan Africa	502	5.12	2.55	0.09	10.74	1.44	8.41

Note Obs = number of observations, SD = standard deviation, Min = Minimum, Max = Maximum, P10 = Percentile 10, P90 = Percentile 90

Africa (48%), while it is lowest for North America (13%). This adjustment is carried out for a selection of countries across all regions (Fig. 3.2). In a country like Mauritius, years of schooling decrease from 10 to less than 6 when quality of schooling is taken into account. The difference is even larger for countries like Chad (from 8 to 4 learning-adjusted years of schooling).

Figure 3.3 presents our measure of schooling quality, while Fig. 3.4 focuses on the LAYS indicator for 168 countries and territories for the year 2015. A few clear trends emerge when our results are compared across regions. As expected, developed economies have a higher quantity and quality of schooling than developing economies; sub-Saharan Africa and South Asia lag behind all other regions. It is interesting to highlight the highest and lowest performers across regions. Table 3.4 provides a ranking of countries within regions for the three indicators (quality of schooling, quantity of schooling and LAYS). Some countries perform very well in both dimensions of schooling, such as Singapore, while others like Estonia rank differently. In Asia, the top-performing countries are Singapore, South Korea and Japan in all indicators. The US and Canada perform quite highly in years of schooling, although the quality of schooling is intermediate. In Latin America, the top performers are Cuba, Trinidad and Tobago and Chile, while countries like Honduras and Haiti perform the worst. Israel, Malta and the UAE are the highest performing in the MENA region, whereas countries like Morocco or Yemen have the lowest performance. In sub-Saharan Africa, Botswana, Mauritius and South Africa perform the best, while Niger is ranked 148th, the lowest rank in the world for 2015.

3.3.2 Comparison with Alternative Measures

In addition to our measure, alternative indicators have been proposed for learning outcomes and LAYS. First, we compare our indicator of quality of schooling with other leading measures of human capital (Table 3.5). Our database complements alternative measures of human capital. Figure 3.4 shows direct comparisons to learning data used in growth regressions by Hanushek and Woessmann (2012). Strong and significant correlations are found (0.9074), indicating high consistency.

Table 3.3 Country-year observations by year

Year	LAYS	Years of sch	%	Total	Reading	Math	Science	Primary	Secon	P + M	P + R	P + S	S + M	S + S	S + R
1970	119	204	58	122	116	105	87	109	81	83	62	103	78	81	61
1975	124	205	60	127	121	106	87	114	81	84	60	109	78	81	61
1980	125	205	61	128	123	108	87	116	83	84	60	111	81	81	61
1985	125	205	61	128	123	107	89	116	83	84	61	111	79	83	61
1990	146	204	72	150	142	128	107	133	100	97	73	125	98	100	78
1995	147	205	72	151	143	130	107	133	100	102	75	125	98	100	78
2000	145	204	71	149	141	127	107	131	100	97	72	123	97	100	78
2005	143	205	70	147	138	127	107	129	100	97	72	119	97	100	78
2010	146	205	71	150	142	127	108	131	101	97	72	123	98	101	79
2015	149	204	73	153	147	128	108	134	101	97	72	126	98	101	81
2020	137	204	67	142	130	130	110	123	105	97	72	115	102	105	78
Total	1506	2250	67	1547	1466	1323	1104	1369	1035	1019	751	1290	1004	1033	794

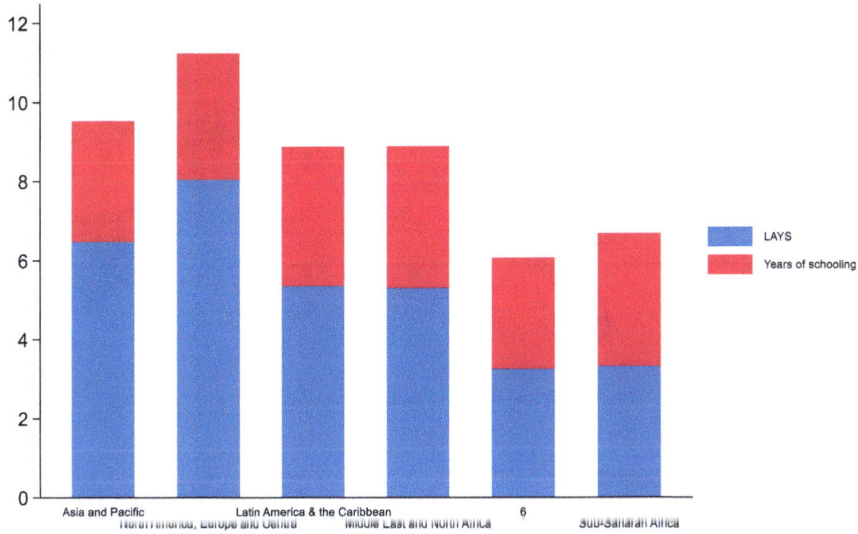

Fig. 3.1 Average years of schooling of the cohort of 15–64-year-olds, unadjusted and adjusted for learning (using the LAYS adjustment)

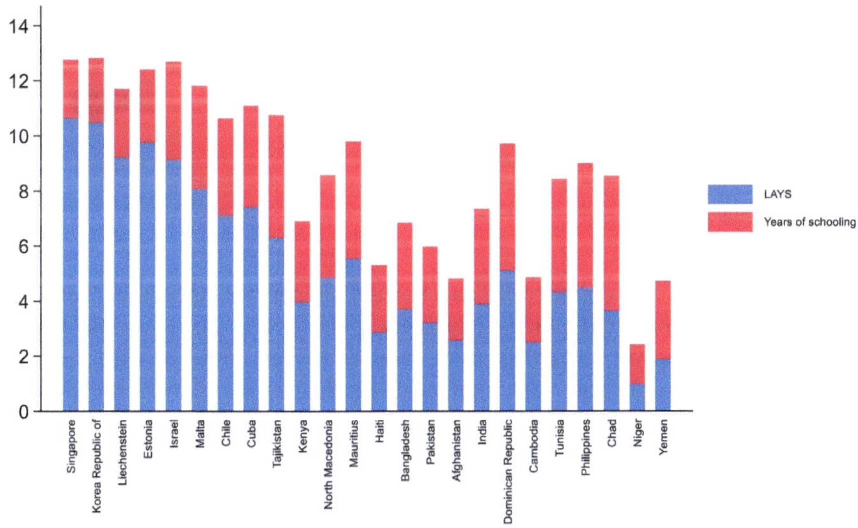

Fig. 3.2 Average years of schooling of the cohort of 15–64-year-olds, unadjusted and adjusted for learning (using the LAYS adjustment), Selection of countries

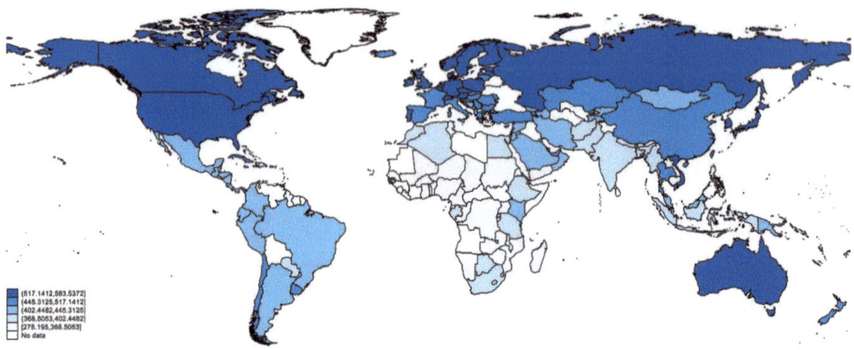

Fig. 3.3 Learning outcomes, both education levels, all skills, 2015

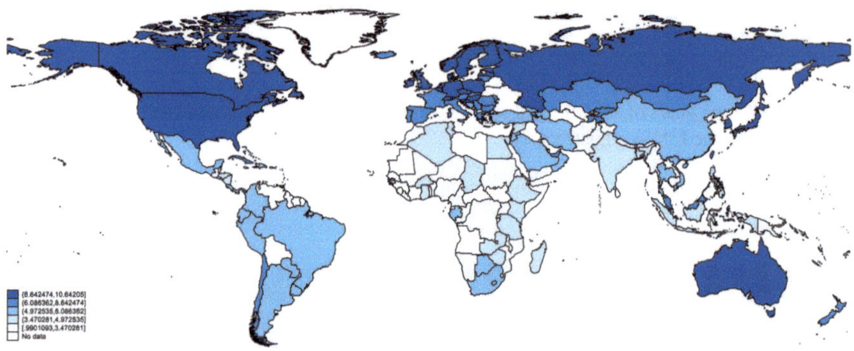

Fig. 3.4 Learning-adjusted years of schooling, 2015

In Table 3.5, we also compare our data to learning outcomes from other datasets, such as the Harmonized Learning Outcomes, published in 2021, or the dataset published by Altinok et al. (2018). Both datasets are very similar to the methodology used in our paper and show high consistency, since correlations are close to 0.90. Another dataset, published by Lim et al. (2018), confirms the high accuracy of our data in comparably measuring learning outcomes in a panel dataset. Lim et al. (2018) propose a panel dataset on learning outcomes between 1990 and 2010.

In the second part of Table 3.5, we also compare our LAYS indicators with the one provided by the World Bank. Correlation is again very high for the year 2020. The World Bank does not provide a panel dataset on LAYS, but one for only two different years. We therefore use only our values for 2020 in the comparison. Figure 3.5 offers a quick overview of the high consistency of our results with those provided by the World Bank. Correlation is equal to 0.88, indicating that the two datasets overlap very well for 2020.

Correlation is just as high as for other alternative datasets. In all cases, these comparisons indicate that even as we expand both country and period coverage,

Table 3.4 Ranking of countries for each region and around the world, 2015

Ranking	EAP	W	Western countries	W	LAC	W	MENA	W	SSA	W
Learning outcomes										
1	Singapore	1	Liechenstein	6	Chile	49	Israel	39	Kenya	89
2	Korea, Rep	2	Estonia	7	Cuba	50	Malta	47	Mauritius	95
3	Japan	3	Finland	8	Trinidad &T	56	Bahrain	54	Rwanda	97
Years of schooling										
1	Korea, Rep	6	USA	1	Trinidad &T	42	Israel	10	Botswana	56
2	Japan	7	Czech Rep	2	Cuba	46	Malta	26	South Africa	58
3	Singapore	8	Canada	3	Chile	54	UAE	31	Mauritius	64
Learning-Adjusted Years of Schooling										
1	Singapore	1	USA	5	Cuba	48	Israel	20	Botswana	70
2	Korea, Rep	2	Canada	6	Trinidad &T	50	Malta	35	Mauritius	81
3	Japan	3	UK	8	Chile	53	UAE	45	South Africa	83

Notes Ranking is presented within regions in rows and for the world in columns "W". For instance, Singapore is ranked first in learning outcomes in both the World and within the East Asia and Pacific region. Korea is ranked second for learning outcomes, 6th for years of schooling and 2nd for LAYS. Countries from South Asia are not shown since there are only five countries in this area. Western countries include North America, Europe and Central Asia. Full results are provided in Table 3.12

Table 3.5 Relationship with alternative learning human capital measures

	Pearson Coefficient	p-value	Observations
Correlation with quality of schooling			
Harmonized Learning Outcomes—HLO (2021)	0.9064	< .001	429
Altinok, Angrist, Patrinos—AAP (2018)	0.8713	< .001	564
Lim et al.—IHME (2018)	0.9255	< .001	857
Hanushek and Woessmann—HW (2012)	0.8926	< .001	77
Correlation with LAYS			
LAYS, Human Capital Index, World Bank, 2020	0.888	< .001	134

Notes IHME = Institute for Health Metrics and Evaluation, University of Washington. See Lim et al. (2018) for more information. Comparisons are made using average scores across subjects and schooling levels for HLO and IHME. Average across subjects, schooling levels and years are used for the comparison HW scores

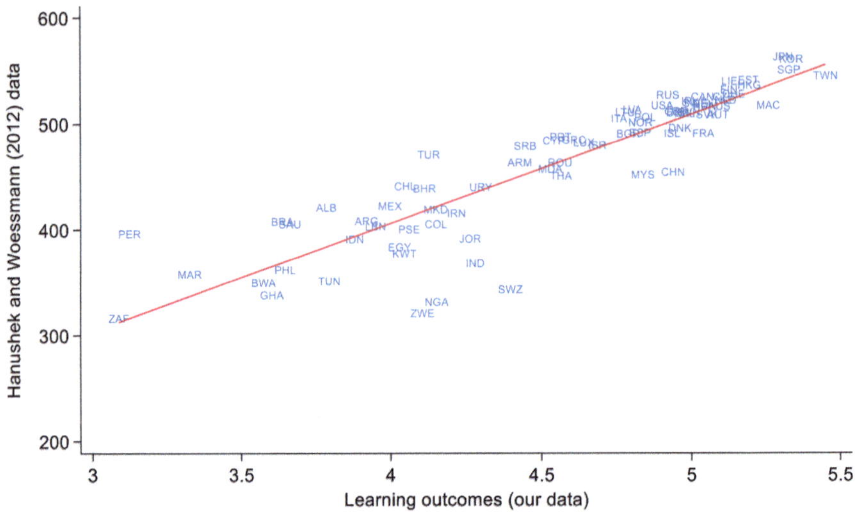

Fig. 3.5 Comparison to Hanushek and Woessmann (2012). *Note* Hanushek and Woessmann (2012) provide estimates of comparable learning measures of human capital, based on an expansion of the original work done by Hanushek and Kimko (2000). We compare these measures for the set of countries included in their growth regressions. Since their measures deal with means for the period 1970–2010, we use the global average for our indicator for the period 1970–2020

we maintain high levels of consistency with alternative measures where there is an overlap.

3.3.3 *Conditional Convergence of Schooling Indicators Over Time*

Since comparable data are available for more than 100 countries for both quantity and quality of schooling, we can compare LAYS trends over time between 1970 and 2020. In addition, it is also important to test for the stability of learning outcomes over time. To gauge the degree of stability of country performance over time, we estimate country-specific trends as follows. Given an educational indicator, x, let

$$\Delta x_n = \frac{x_n - x_{n-1}}{t_n - t_{n-1}} \tag{3.6}$$

be its average annual variation between observations $n - 1$ and n, dated at t_{n-1} and t_n respectively. It has become common to gauge improvements in education outcomes over time in terms of a fraction of a standard deviation in test scores. The method can use the standard deviation of a particular year, generally the start or end of a series for a particular unit such as a country (UNESCO Institute of Statistics, 2019b). We therefore adapt Eq. (3.6) in order to express the variation according to the standard deviation of the start of each series:

$$\Delta x_{n/SD} = \frac{x_n - x_{n-1}}{(t_n - t_{n-1}) \times \sigma_x}. \tag{3.7}$$

Hanushek et al. (2017) use a projection analysis of learning outcomes and attempt to answer the question, "how fast does any [education] reform achieve its results". These authors assume that an improvement of 0.5 standard deviations over a long period is possible, in the context of an "aggressive reform plan". A standard deviation here is the standard deviation of student scores across many countries in almost all achievement tests, such as PISA or TIMSS. In TIMSS and other tests, the standard deviation is set equal to 100 points, based on actual standard deviations among countries participating in the initial year of the test. In addition to the study of Hanushek and Woessmann (2007), Mourshed et al. (2010) use trends from twelve countries or regions to arrive at an improvement of 0.115 standard deviations in ten years, or 0.012 per year. Gustafsson (2014) finds that a feasible policy target could be premised on a test score improvement of 0.06 standard deviations a year. This figure is obtained from trends seen in several testing programs in the years 2000 to 2009, and specifically the trends of fast-improving countries. More recently, UNESCO Institute of Statistics (2019a) studied historical trends from PIRLS, PISA and LLECE and found annual improvements in learning outcomes of between 0.01 and 0.06 standard deviations a year.

In experimental studies, improvements appear to be larger than 0.06 standard deviation, and are quite often as high as 0.2 of a standard deviation following an intervention of one or two years (McEwan, 2015). This represents a larger improvement than the findings from the study of UNESCO Institute of Statistics (2019a). One reason for this difference is the fact that results from experimental research are difficult to replicate successfully across an entire system. For instance, while teachers' unions may not oppose a small research intervention, they might want to alter or even stop the same intervention when expanded (UNESCO Institute of Statistics, 2019a).

The results provided in Table 3.6 show that the increase in learning outcomes is somewhat lower than that seen in previous findings. Indeed, we find an average improvement of about 0.08 standard deviation for a decade if we aggregate data for all countries. However, the improvement is greatest in Latin America and MENA countries, whereas it is lowest in East Asia and Pacific and South Asia. When we use both quantity and quality of schooling, improvements in LAYS are quite similar to improvements in years of schooling. On average, countries improved the level of LAYS by about 0.27 standard deviations (per decade) between 1970 and 2020. Again, this improvement is highest in MENA and East Asia and Pacific.

We can test for a potential convergence of each indicator over time. Since some specific policies can improve learning outcomes or enrollment over a short-term period, we conduct a separate analysis between short-term (20 years, between 2000 and 2020) and long-term (50 years, between 1970 and 2020) trends. Comparisons between the two periods can highlight some specific recent improvements or declines.

Table 3.6 Trends of Schooling Indicators (1970–2020 and 2000–2020)

	Initial level (2000)			20 Year Trends (annual improvement in SD)		
Region	Quality	Quantity	LAYS	Quality	Quantity	LAYS
East Asia and Pacific	451.5	8.3	5.4247	−0.0002	0.0226	0.0254
N. America, Europe and Central	488.2	10.0	7.2713	0.0026	0.0224	0.0194
Latin America & the Caribbean	405.0	8.0	4.5769	0.0040	0.0228	0.0245
Middle East and North Africa	400.8	7.1	4.2572	0.0065	0.0479	0.0334
South Asia	367.5	5.3	2.1313	0.0052	0.0535	0.0324
Sub-Saharan Africa	332.6	5.4	2.4552	0.0069	0.0332	0.0226
Total	422.1	7.8	4.9557	0.0039	0.0288	0.0239
	Initial level (1970)			50-Year Trends (annual improvement in SD)		
Region	Quality	Quantity	LAYS	Quality	Quantity	LAYS
East Asia and Pacific	436.5	6.2	3.6888	0.0039	0.0228	0.0314
N. America, Europe and Central	475.2	7.3	5.6245	0.0044	0.0266	0.0273
Latin America & the Caribbean	386.8	5.9	2.8656	0.0057	0.0229	0.0295
Middle East and North Africa	375.7	3.6	2.1752	0.0081	0.0419	0.0346
South Asia	358.6	2.6	0.6415	0.0040	0.0383	0.0272
Sub-Saharan Africa	312.3	3.1	1.2982	0.0072	0.0277	0.0205
Total	404.9	5.4	3.3423	0.0056	0.0275	0.0275

Developing countries tend to have more scope for rapid improvements, given their distance from what one might think of as natural ceilings for cognitive skills or LAYS (Gustafsson, 2014). While a convergence of years of schooling occurs across countries over a 50-year period, results are more contrasted for learning outcomes and LAYS (Fig. 3.6). As we can see in the bottom-right part of Fig. 3.6, an inverted-U shape is obtained when we compare initial level of LAYS and trends. This may be explained by differences between the economic levels of countries. Figures 3.7 and 3.8 distinguish between OECD21[21] and developing countries. While a clear convergence is found for OECD21 countries (Fig. 3.7, R squared equal to 0.55), results are more contrasted for developing countries. Indeed, some countries grow quickly because they have low initial level of LAYS, like Botswana or Peru. However, a significant number of countries seem to be trapped in slow improvements, despite an initial low level. This is especially the case of several sub-Saharan African countries (for example, Mali, Senegal or Burundi). Conversely, a number of countries with an already high initial level increase their performance on LAYS. This is the case of the Russian Federation, Kazakhstan or Armenia. Some countries appear clearly to be low performers. For instance, France seems to be far from the convergence of

[21] The list of OECD 21 countries is provided in Table 3.7.

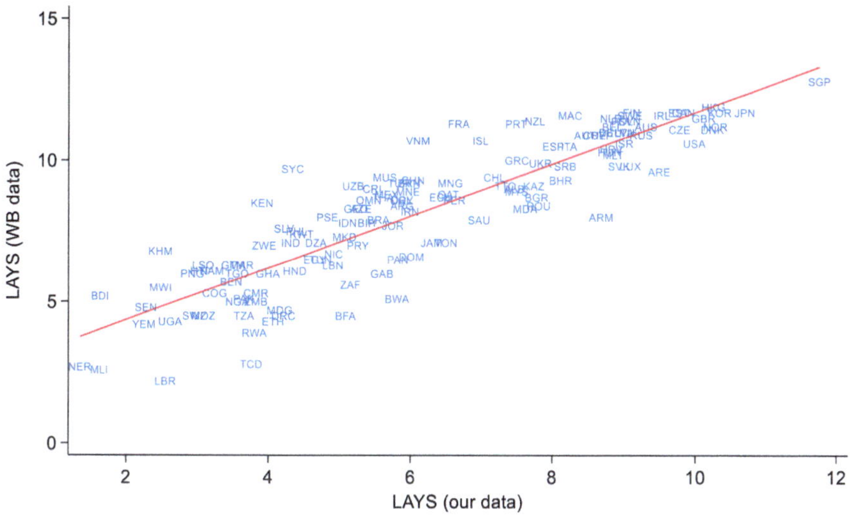

Fig. 3.6 Comparison to LAYS from the World Bank HCI project, year 2020

countries, since its improvement is lower than other countries such as Italy or Spain. On the contrary, Japan and the USA show larger improvements than expected.

We can thus obtain two main findings from the trends analysis. First, there is no global convergence across countries over time for learning outcomes. Results for years of schooling are more contrasted. Some countries seem to be in a trap while others perform better than expected where convergence is the case. Indeed, we find an inverse U-shaped relationship between LAYS and trends, indicating that specific outliers can be identified. In the meantime, convergence seems to occur within the OECD 21 countries in the long-run and for both quantity and quality of schooling (Fig. 3.7). Countries with low initial learning outcomes see a higher increase than others (such as Norway or Portugal). Results for LAYS are quite similar to those for learning outcomes and years of schoolings. More work should be done on this topic of convergence, but current results seem to confirm a possible conditional convergence, though not an absolute convergence among countries. Some initial factors such as quality of institutions may be an important condition for school expansion, both in quality and quantity (Glawe & Wagner, 2022).

The second most important result concerns the potential stability of learning outcomes over time. We believe that country performance is not stable in the long run, a hypothesis put forward in Hanushek and Kimko (2000) and Hanushek and Woessmann (2015). Short-term trends are higher for some countries than long-term trends, indicating that specific policies have been successful in the short run. For instance, countries like Portugal or Denmark experienced a significant increase in their learning outcomes over time. For developing countries, results are more contrasted because they have had to increase attainment levels in both primary and secondary schools since 1970. Therefore, a stagnation of learning outcomes cannot be considered as

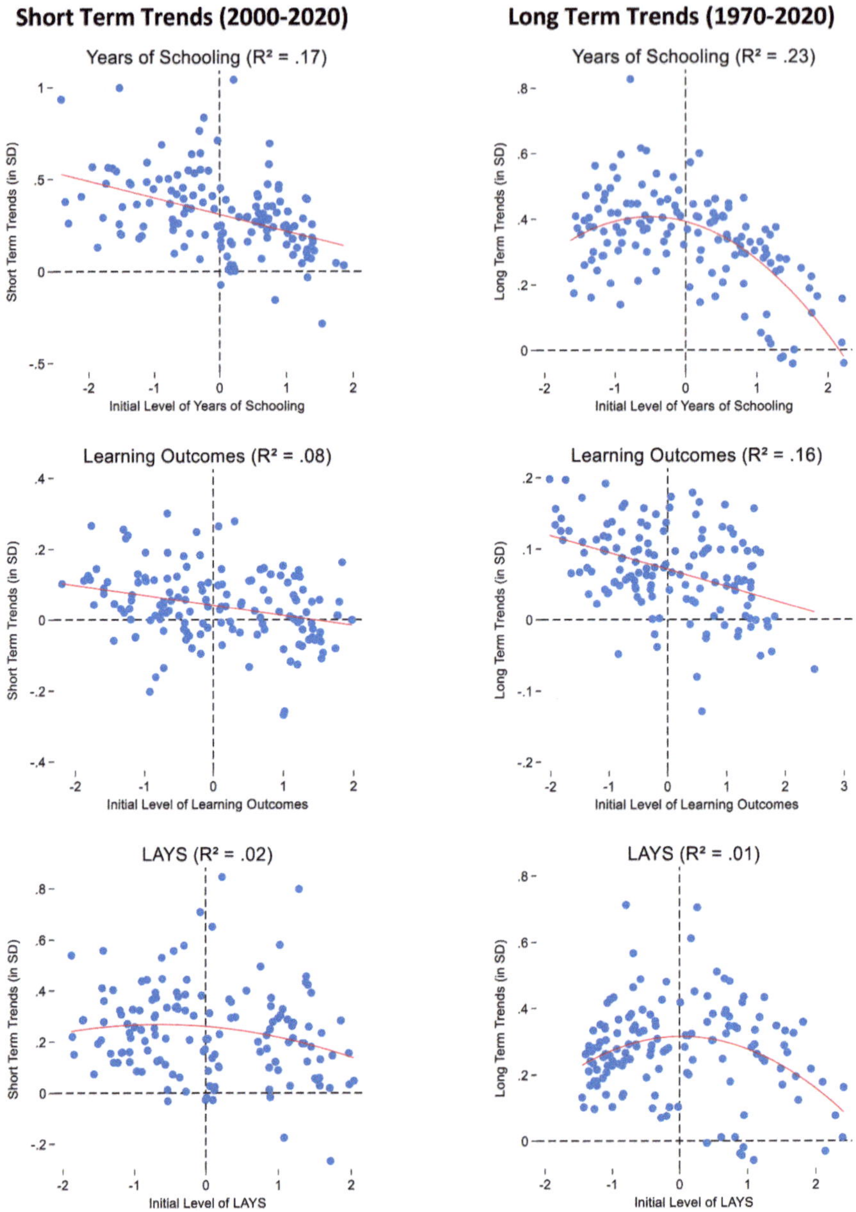

Fig. 3.7 Global trends on education indicators—All countries

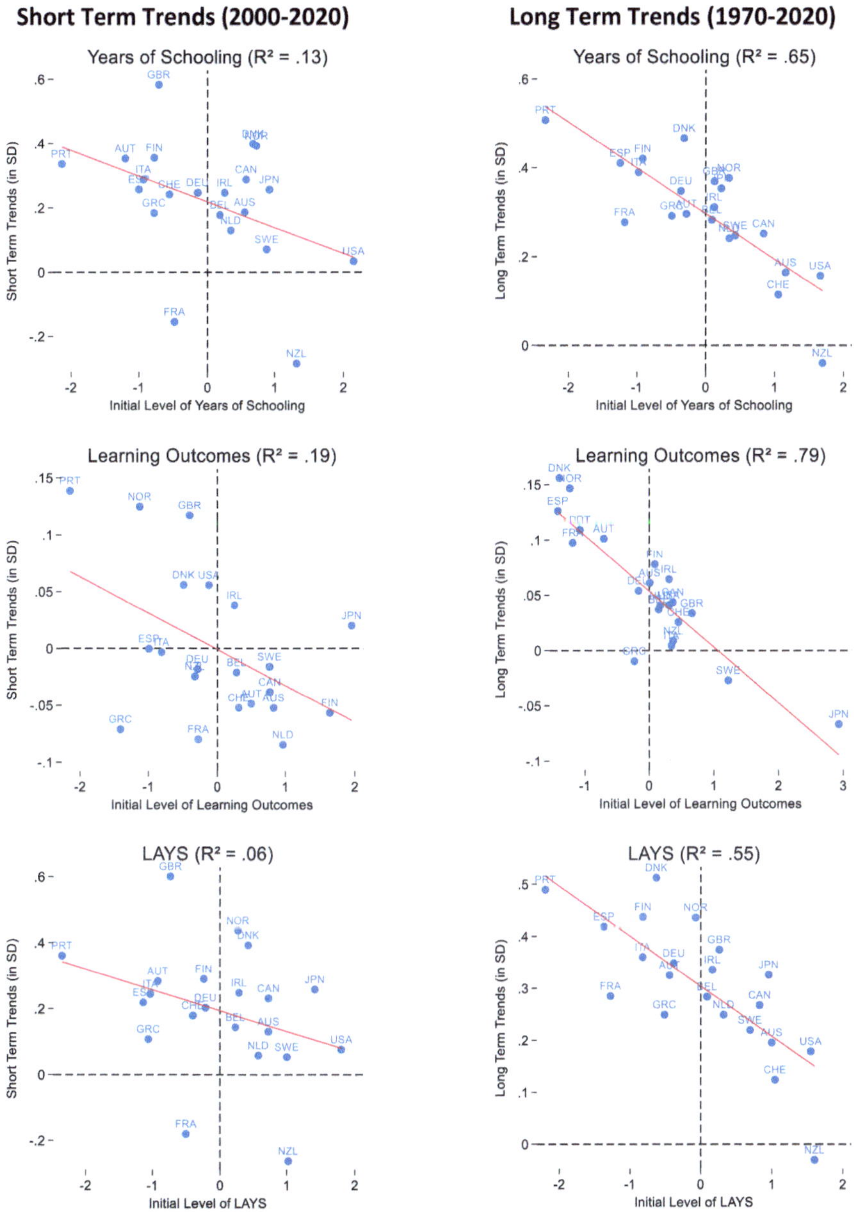

Fig. 3.8 Global trends on education indicators—OECD 21 Countries

a bad performance, if enrollment increased in the given country at the same time. In Fig. 3.8, some of the high-performing countries are Albania, Peru, Turkey and Vietnam. These countries increased the level of learning outcomes to a high level (i.e. higher than 0.1 standard deviation per decade). It should be noted that although 0.1 SD may seem to be a low performance, it indicates growth of about 1 point each year and thus 10 points for a decade. Over a 50-year period, this means that the performance of the given country increased by about 50 points, i.e. half of a standard deviation. Therefore, an increase of 0.13 SD in Norway can be translated as a global increase of 65 PISA-equivalent score points. Conversely, the slowdown found in France in the short-term trends is greater than it would seem. Indeed, the negative trend of about −0.075 SD is equivalent to a decrease of 15 PISA-equivalent score points in only 20 years. Given the fact that a year of schooling is roughly equivalent to 15–20 points on the PISA scale (Avvisati, 2021), this would mean that France experienced a dramatic decrease in learning outcomes between 2000 and 2020, equivalent to a loss of about 1 year of schooling.

The ranking analysis in Table 3.7 confirms our rejection of the hypothesis of the stability of learning outcomes. If learning outcomes were stable, the ranking of OECD 21 countries should be similar across years. This is only the case for Japan, while the average range of the ranking is equal to 8, which is quite close to half of 21, the number of countries. Our findings thus confirm the results of De la Fuente and Doménech (2021). We have fairly clear indications of sharp positive or negative trend rises, raising increasing doubts about the validity of the constant quality assumption for learning outcomes in the long run that has often been used in the growth literature.

3.3.4 The Importance of Schooling for Economic Growth

We wonder to what extent schooling variables are associated with economic growth. Since our database includes a large number of countries, we are able to run a regression analysis with about 101 countries. A prior analysis was conducted by Hanushek and Woessmann (2012) with 50 countries. The study of Altinok and Aydemir (2017) used the dataset from Altinok et al. (2014) in order to extend the number of countries to 84 countries. Our database thus has the largest number of developing countries that can potentially benefit the most from schooling accumulation. Although the recent work of Angrist et al. (2021) includes a large number of countries, their time interval is restricted to 2000–2010, while our dataset covers the period 1970–2020.

The full sample of countries for which we have data for all variables is 126. We exclude countries for which more than 25% of GDP is derived from rents from natural resources, such as the Democratic Republic of the Congo or Venezuela.[22]

We use a simple growth model based on the intuition of Nelson and Phelps (1966): a country's growth rate (g) is a function of the skills of workers (H) and other factors

[22] We also exclude from our regression some African countries for which data availability is poor for learning outcomes, such as Madagascar or Burkina Faso.

Table 3.7 Ranking for Learning Outcomes, OECD21 countries

	1970	1980	1990	2000	2010	2020	Average rank	Range max—min rank
Japan	1	1	1	1	1	1	1	0
Ireland	8	13	11	10	12	2	9.3	11
Finland	12	6	2	2	2	3	4.5	10
United Kingdom	3	16	20	12	8	4	10.5	17
Canada	6	4	5	5	5	5	5	2
USA	9	8	12	11	10	6	9.3	6
Australia	13	9	10	6	9	7	9	7
Sweden	2	11	7	4	15	8	7.8	13
Switzerland	4	2	8	8	3	9	5.7	7
Norway	19	15	13	19	19	10	15.8	9
Denmark	20	21	19	16	11	11	16.3	10
Netherlands	10	3	6	3	4	12	6.3	9
Austria	16	17	3	7	14	13	11.7	14
Belgium	11	5	4	9	6	14	8.2	10
Germany	14	12	9	14	7	15	11.8	8
New Zealand	5	7	14	13	13	16	11.3	11
Portugal	17	18	21	21	16	17	18.3	5
Italy	7	10	15	17	17	18	14	11
Spain	21	19	17	18	21	19	19.2	4
France	18	20	16	15	18	20	17.8	5
Greece	15	14	18	20	20	21	18	7

(X). These factors include initial levels of income and the investment rate.[23] Skills are often referred to simply as the workers' human capital stock. Our specification assumes that H is a one-dimensional index and that growth rates are linear in these inputs:

$$g = \gamma H + \beta X + \varepsilon. \tag{3.8}$$

Thus, in our model, it is the *level* of cognitive skills which explains the *variation* in economic output (i.e. GDP per capita).[24] The most important specification issue in

[23] We include the log of initial GDP per capita in 1970 or the nearest year, and the log of the gross fixed capital formation expressed as a % of GDP. Our explanatory variables are included as the average value across the period 1970–2020.

[24] It should be noted that the form of this relationship has been the subject of considerable debate. Our model can be considered as fitting with both basic endogenous growth models such as that of Lucas (1988) and Aghion et al. (1998) and neoclassical growth models such as that of Mankiw et al. (1992).

this framework is the nature of the skills (H) and where they might come from. In the educational production function literature (Hanushek, 2002), skills are explained by many factors such as family inputs (F), the quantity and quality of inputs provided by schools (qS), individual ability (A) and other relevant factors (Z) which include labor market experience, health and other specific characteristics:

$$H = \alpha F + \beta(qS) + \gamma A + \delta Z + \nu. \tag{3.9}$$

Human capital, however, is a latent variable that cannot be directly observed. Therefore, we need a correct measure of human capital in order to test its impact on economic growth. The main existing theoretical and empirical work on growth begins by taking the quantity of schooling of workers (S) as a direct measure of H. Following Hanushek and Kimko (2000), we focus on the cognitive skills component of human capital and evaluate H with our learning outcomes variable. In addition to this, we also test the relationship between *LAYS* and economic growth.

Figure 3.9 presents an added-variable plot of the relation between the average value of each schooling variable and economic growth over the period 1970–2020 (conditional on initial per capita income). Added-variable plots depict the association between two variables after the influences of other control variables (in our case the initial per capita income) are taken out (see also (Hanushek & Woessmann, 2008)). The plots indicate a positive association between each schooling component and economic growth. We further explore this relationship in our regression model (Table 3.8).

In columns (1)–(4), we include all countries in the sample, while in columns (5)–(8) we restrict the estimation to OECD countries and then to non-OECD countries (columns (09)–(12)). In all estimations, we include the initial level of GDP per capita and the average value of physical capital over the period 1970–2020. The negative coefficient associated with the initial level of GDP per capita supports the hypothesis of income convergence postulated by neoclassical growth theory. The relationship between standard years of schooling and economic growth is positive and significant (column 1). We further include only learning outcomes (column 2) or those in association with years of schooling (column 3). All estimations support the hypothesis that education is positively and significantly associated with economic growth over the period 1970–2020. In addition, we test the relationship between the LAYS indicator and economic growth (column 4). Results show a positive and significant effect. Although LAYS may capture important aspects of both quantity and quality of schooling, it seems that the explanatory power of the model with LAYS is lower than that of the model with schooling variables included separately (column (4) versus column (3) respectively).

One possible robustness test of this relationship is a focus on OECD countries (columns 5 to 8). The results show that both schooling variables seem to be positively correlated with economic growth, although years of schooling is not significant at the 10% level when learning outcomes are included in the model (column 7). Developing countries may benefit more from investment in education. The results tend to confirm

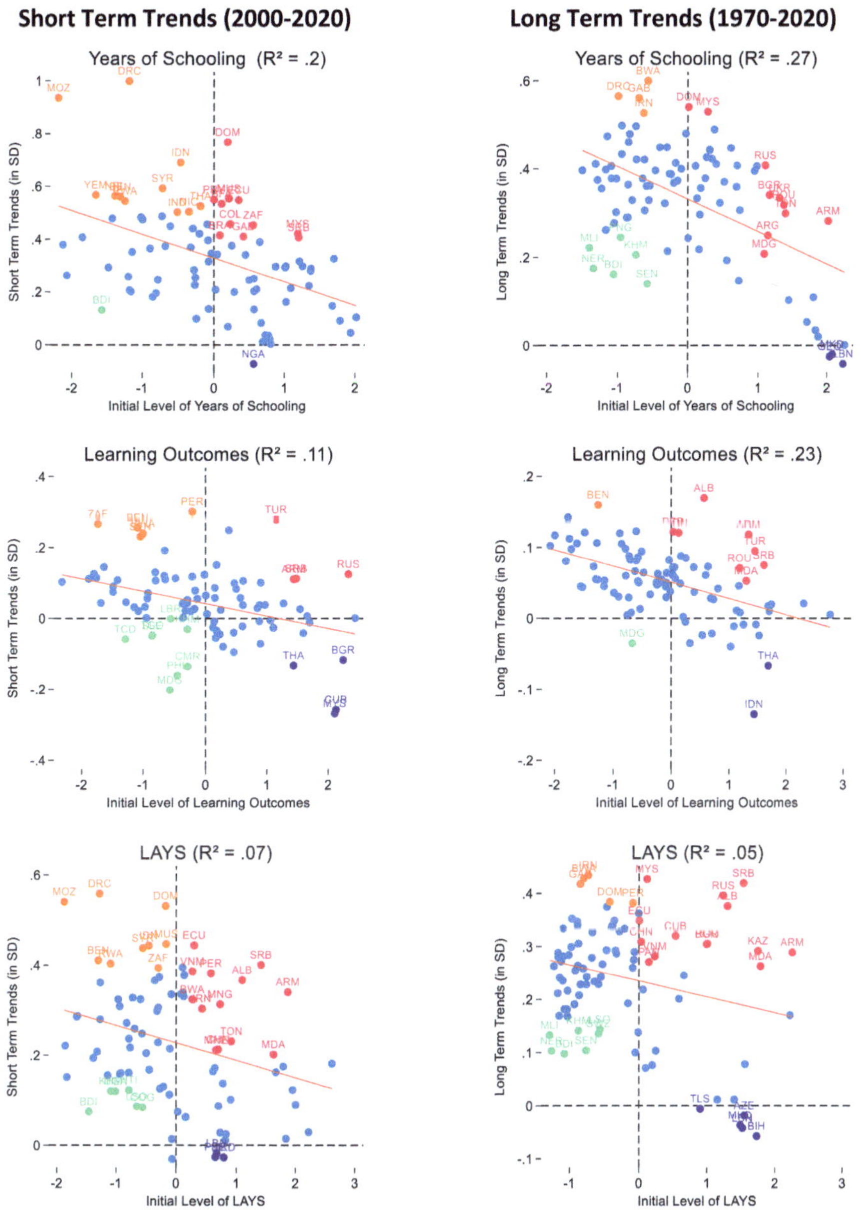

Fig. 3.9 Global trends on education indicators—Developing Countries

Table 3.8 Regression of GDP per capita growth 1970–2020 on education variables, mean values

	(1)	(2)	(3)	(4)	(5)	(6)	(7)	(8)	(9)	(10)	(11)	(12)
	All countries				OECD countries				Non-OECD countries			
Initial GDP pc	−0.528***	−0.499***	−0.589***	−0.572***	−0.586***	−0.573***	−0.598***	−0.595***	−0.538***	−0.464***	−0.569***	−0.578***
	(0.064)	(0.060)	(0.051)	(0.050)	(0.119)	(0.105)	(0.112)	(0.113)	(0.073)	(0.089)	(0.068)	(0.061)
Years of Schooling	0.229***		0.118***		0.078**		0.032		0.264***		0.159***	
	(0.027)		(0.034)		(0.028)		(0.028)		(0.035)		(0.036)	
Quality of Schooling		0.838***	0.599***			0.538***	0.434***			0.991***	0.723***	
		(0.098)	(0.125)			(0.119)	(0.130)			(0.131)	(0.152)	
LAYS				0.293***				0.103***				0.414***
				(0.027)				(0.032)				(0.039)
Physical Capital	0.444	0.500*	0.331	0.403	0.861*	0.105	0.168	0.612	0.379	0.540**	0.275	0.288
	(0.288)	(0.257)	(0.236)	(0.254)	(0.469)	(0.452)	(0.468)	(0.444)	(0.312)	(0.265)	(0.234)	(0.250)
R-squared	0.508	0.586	0.643	0.575	0.634	0.668	0.674	0.649	0.539	0.611	0.704	0.67
Observations	100	100	100	100	32	32	32	32	68	68	68	68

*** $p < 0.01$, **$p < 0.05$, * $p < 0.1$

this hypothesis (columns 9 to 12) with higher values for the coefficients associated with schooling variables.

While the results are robust across various specifications and subsamples, reverse causality and endogeneity bias may potentially be driving the results. Reverse causality would arise if higher economic growth enables countries to develop better education systems that yield higher test performances. The presence of other factors, such as institutions or access to natural resources, which affect growth and are also correlated with cognitive skills, will lead to an endogeneity bias in our estimations. One way to address reverse causality bias is the use of initial values for our schooling variables (Table 3.20). The results remain quite similar across different specifications. Obviously, a more detailed analysis of the impact of schooling on economic growth should be conducted with this new dataset. For instance, an estimation with a system GMM estimator, as proposed by Arellano and Bover (1995) and Blundell and Bond (1998), may help to correct endogeneity bias.

3.4 Limitations of the Study

The database obtained using the methodology presented in the previous section may include multiple estimation biases, since some assumptions may not be valid. Below we briefly discuss the potential limitations of our study. Further discussion on these limitations can be found in Altinok (2017) and Altinok et al. (2018). In order to validate our anchoring methodology based on "exchange rates", we make some assumptions to keep the results of countries' student achievement tests intact. These assumptions are mainly based on the fact that we suppose that the populations tested and instruments used are similar across assessments. More generally, we can consider at least four strong differences between achievement tests which may explain why comparability between these assessments should be treated with caution.

A. Differences in score distributions across assessments. First, although achievement tests are meant to be representative of studies of the whole population, there is no reason why the original distributions of scores in each assessment should coincide among themselves. For instance, it may be possible for the distribution of scores in the anchored test for a doubloon country to be different from the distribution of scores of the same country in the reference test. When we use the "exchange rates" methodology (also called "pseudo-linear linking"), we are assuming that the distribution of scores across assessments is similar. Each assessment uses its own psychometric methodology and hence the items included within each test are different for each assessment. This means that the degree of difficulty of items may also differ and thus the distribution of scores may not be exactly the same between assessments. For instance, the items included in the SACMEQ study may be easier than those in TIMSS and therefore the distribution of scores may be more positively skewed for TIMSS results and negatively skewed for SACMEQ results. This difference may lead to different results for countries that took part in several assessments simultaneously. In order to verify the accuracy of this assumption, we compared the normality of score distributions for each assessment by focusing on "doubloon countries" (Table 3.8).[25] In theory, the distributions of scores for these countries should be similar in order to proceed to pseudo-linear linking. We computed four different measures to test this normality (mean, standard deviation, skewness and kurtosis). The mean is usually used to test the central tendency for quantitative variables, while the standard deviation (SD) is the most widely used measure of dispersion. Normality is generally evaluated with two additional statistics that are known as skewness and kurtosis. Skewness is a measure of whether a distribution trails off in one direction or another.[26] Kurtosis measures the thickness of the tails of a distribution.[27] As shown in Table 3.9, there are some differences between anchored and reference assessments (respectively Assessment 1 and Assessment 2). For instance, while the skewness is positive and close to 1 in SACMEQ, it is close to 0.2 in the TIMSS assessment. The kurtosis comparison allows us to measure the thickness of the tails of a distribution. If our adjusting methodology does not take into account the variability of the distribution across assessments, the kurtosis may be similar for all countries used as "doubloon countries". If we focus again on SACMEQ countries, it appears that kurtosis is very different as compared to the TIMSS assessment. Indeed, while kurtosis is close to a normal distribution in TIMSS, its value is higher than 5 in the SACMEQ assessment, indicating that the main scores are concentrated in the middle and thus fail to capture very high and very low skill levels. However, the comparison between other anchors does not show very strong differences and hence allows us to adopt a linking approach based on "exchange rates". In general, we find that our methodology is well suited to all assessments with the exception of SSA studies, such as earlier PASEC assessments and the SACMEQ study. One potential solution to this issue is to use either equipercentile or presmoothed equipercentile linking methods which take into account the distribution of results from each assessment. Instead of using only mean scores, these linking methodologies match each percentile from anchored and reference tests and thus provide a one-to-one percentile matching which avoids the potential difference in the distribution of scores. We preferred to use the presmoothed equipercentile approach for the adjustment of benchmarks, but not for mean scores. Indeed, although this adjustment takes into account the distribution of scores, it does not keep original scores from achievement tests intact. A method which uses percentiles may convert specific thresholds better, but not trends over time based on mean scores. This is why we prefer to use the "exchange rate" approach to compute the adjusted mean scores and the presmoothed equipercentile methodology for benchmarks. In addition, the "exchange rate" methodology allows to preserve cross-country and over-time differences within international and regional student achievement tests, as shown in Fig. 3.11.

[25] We use the methodology provided in Altinok (2017) for the robustness section.

[26] A normal distribution has skewness of 0. If the skewness is greater than 0, the distribution is negatively skewed.

[27] A normal distribution will have a kurtosis of 3.00. A value less than 3.00 means that the tails are too thick (hence, too flat in the middle), and a value of greater value than 3.00 means that the tails are too thin (hence, too peaked in the middle).

Table 3.9 Comparison of main statistics between assessments for the restricted doubloon countries samples

Assessment 1	Nb of countries	Mean	SD	Skewness	Kurtosis	Assessment 2	Mean	SD	Skewness	Kurtosis
ELCE, math	4	707.61	120.39	0.26	3.89	TIMSS, math	395.39	98.80	−0.07	2.89
ELCE, science	4	718.14	117.10	0.20	3.44	TIMSS, science	437.96	93.43	−0.24	3.02
ELCE, reading	3	739.58	101.82	0.27	3.16	PIRLS, reading	475.79	79.87	−0.10	2.76
SACMEQ II, math	2	496.97	96.77	0.84	5.09	TIMSS 2003, grade 8, math	304.23	102.70	0.22	2.86
SACMEQ III, reading	1	497.87	115.04	0.57	2.92	PIRLS 2006, reading	295.32	123.46	0.52	3.23
PISA 2000, math	21	485.76	110.92	−0.30	2.91	TIMSS 1999 math	505.07	100.21	−0.28	3.10
PISA 2000, science	21	488.90	104.20	−0.12	2.73	TIMSS 1999 science	510.65	97.09	−0.24	3.22
PISA, math	45	471.03	105.48	0.00	2.75	TIMSS, math	496.04	104.01	−0.10	2.94
PISA, science	42	473.15	103.73	0.01	2.65	TIMSS, science	504.40	98.50	−0.44	3.33
PASEC II math	1	540.02	125.09	−0.19	2.16	SACMEQ III, math	619.20	135.90	0.24	2.62
PASEC II, reading	1	566.67	131.40	−0.47	2.03	SACMEQ III, reading	570.87	120.17	0.05	2.28

B. Estimation bias may also occur when tested populations differ across assessments used for the linking. The most evident difference can be obtained between PISA and other assessments. While PISA is an assessment based on the age of the student, the other tests focus on the grade tested. This distinction can lead to strong differences in countries where repetition and/ or drop-out rates are high. The focus on a single grade may exclude a proportion of students who repeated classes, while assessments based on the age of students may include these groups. Since we consider that populations are similar and comparable across assessments, this difference may lead to estimation bias. Wu (2010) showed that differences between TIMSS and PISA are not significantly large and comparisons can be made. It is possible to assess to what extent our results may be distorted by this difference by comparing results between TIMSS and PISA for countries that took part in both assessments. In Table 3.10, we compare the original results for countries that took part in both PISA and TIMSS assessments, in both math and science. We ran a linear regression to test to what extent results in PISA can explain student performances in the TIMSS assessment. Dummy variables were included for both skills and years to control for potential external factors related to these variables. We computed the mean grade tested in each doubloon country and each assessment. Therefore, only countries which took part at both assessments in roughly the same year were included. This yielded about 300 observations in our estimations. In column 1, we regressed the PISA results on the TIMSS results. While the R squared is very high (approximately 0.8), we find that the PISA results are underestimated compared to the TIMSS results, regardless of the grade difference. The most interesting test is to control for grade difference and hence to test to what extent this grade difference may impact the results of the linking process. When we include both dummies for grade difference (column 2), the overall difference between PISA and TIMSS remains quite similar. However, the dummy for a 2-year difference is not significant, which means that the differences found between PISA and TIMSS are not fully due to grade differences. Despite the fact that a significant and very high amplitude effect is found on the 3-year difference in grades tested, this concerns only two countries (Malta and New Zealand). The correlation is very high, suggesting that the anchoring between the two assessments may be considered as valid. However, for specific countries, we observe diverging results. This is especially the case for the Russian Federation and Kazakhstan, where TIMSS results appear to be overestimated. When estimations are done separately for samples with 2 years of difference (column 3) or 3 years (column 4), the results remain quite similar. In order to find which countries diverge between PISA and TIMSS, in Fig. 3.10 we plotted the residuals obtained by using the specification in column 2. For a small number of countries, we detect significant differences between PISA and TIMSS scores. This is the case of South Korea, Bulgaria and Kazakhstan, where student performance appears to be higher in TIMSS than in PISA. Conversely, we find the opposite results for Qatar, Norway and the Netherlands. For most countries, the difference is lower than 40 points in residuals, suggesting that the comparison between the two assessments is valid (Fig. 3.12).

Table 3.10 Effect of PISA results on TIMSS scores for doubloon countries

	(1)	(2)	(3)	(4)
	Mean scores			
PISA results	0.919***	0.939***	2.060***	2.145***
	(0.052)	(0.049)	(0.136)	(0.131)
Difference in grades				
2 years		−6.633		−3.729
		(5.612)		(2.547)
3 years		−38.189***		−17.122***
		(9.228)		(3.167)
Skills dummies	Yes	Yes	Yes	Yes
Years dummies	Yes	Yes	Yes	Yes
R-squared	0.800	0.815	0.714	0.739
Observations	304	304	304	304

*** $p < 0.01$, ** $p < 0.05$, * $p < 0.1$

Notes Cluster-robust standard errors provided in brackets. Clusters are countries. Difference in grades is calculated by the rounded mean grade in PISA and the actual grade in TIMSS. Hence, a difference of two years means that the mean grade tested in PISA is grade 10 while the grade tested in TIMSS is always grade 8. Both mathematics and science scores are included. All years are taken into account (2000, 2003, 2006, 2011, 2015 and 2018). When years of implementation are close, we group assessments. For instance, PISA 2018 results are compared with TIMSS 2019 results

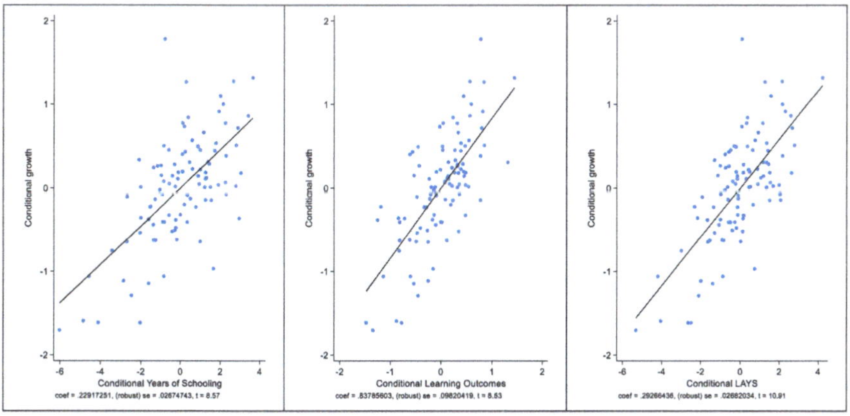

Fig. 3.10 Added variable plot. *Data source* see main text. *Notes* Added-variable plot of a regression of per capita (real) GDP growth on the average schooling variable over the period 1970–2020 (conditional on the initial per capita income)

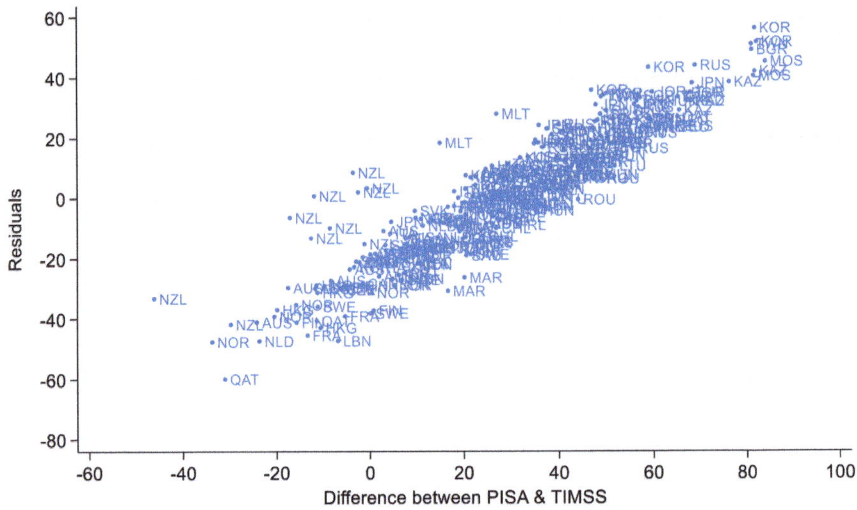

Fig. 3.11 Comparison of original scores between PISA and TIMSS assessments. *Note* Both mathematics and science skills are included. All available years are included (1999–2000, 2003, 2006–2007, 2011, 2015 and 2018–19). We group TIMSS and PISA results for similar years or when there is only one year difference. Hence, we directly compare TIMSS 1999 and PISA 2000 results. Results from PISA 2009 were not included. Residuals are obtained from Table 3.8, column (2)

C. The content tested may also vary among assessments. While in assessments such as PISA and PASEC III, items are more focused on competency skills, in all the other tests, items are mostly based on the common curricula of the countries. This distinction may lead to significant differences in countries that are more based on content knowledge rather than competence knowledge. This is especially true of most developing countries but may also include some developed economies. It is possible to test for this difference by focusing on countries that took part simultaneously in TIMSS and PISA assessments with approximately the same grade. Although grades are not exactly the same, we selected countries that took part in both assessments and where the mean grade tested in PISA was grade 9. This represents a lower number of countries than the number of doubloon countries. It is clear that our estimations are not robust since other factors may explain the differences found between the two results, but this analysis presents at least some robustness which is often lacking in previous studies. The results are provided in columns 7 and 8 of Table 3.9. If we focus on the mean scores, PISA scores are significantly different to TIMSS scores by about 0.8 score points, which is very low. As expected, the restriction to countries where the difference between grades tested is the lowest reduces the difference between PISA and TIMSS scores. When the estimation is made for countries with higher grade differences, the coefficient is higher, but still with a small amplitude (column 8). We can then conclude that characteristics directly related to assessments may not bias the estimation results, at least when we compare the TIMSS and PISA assessments. For the other assessments, since we do not have enough doubloon countries, the

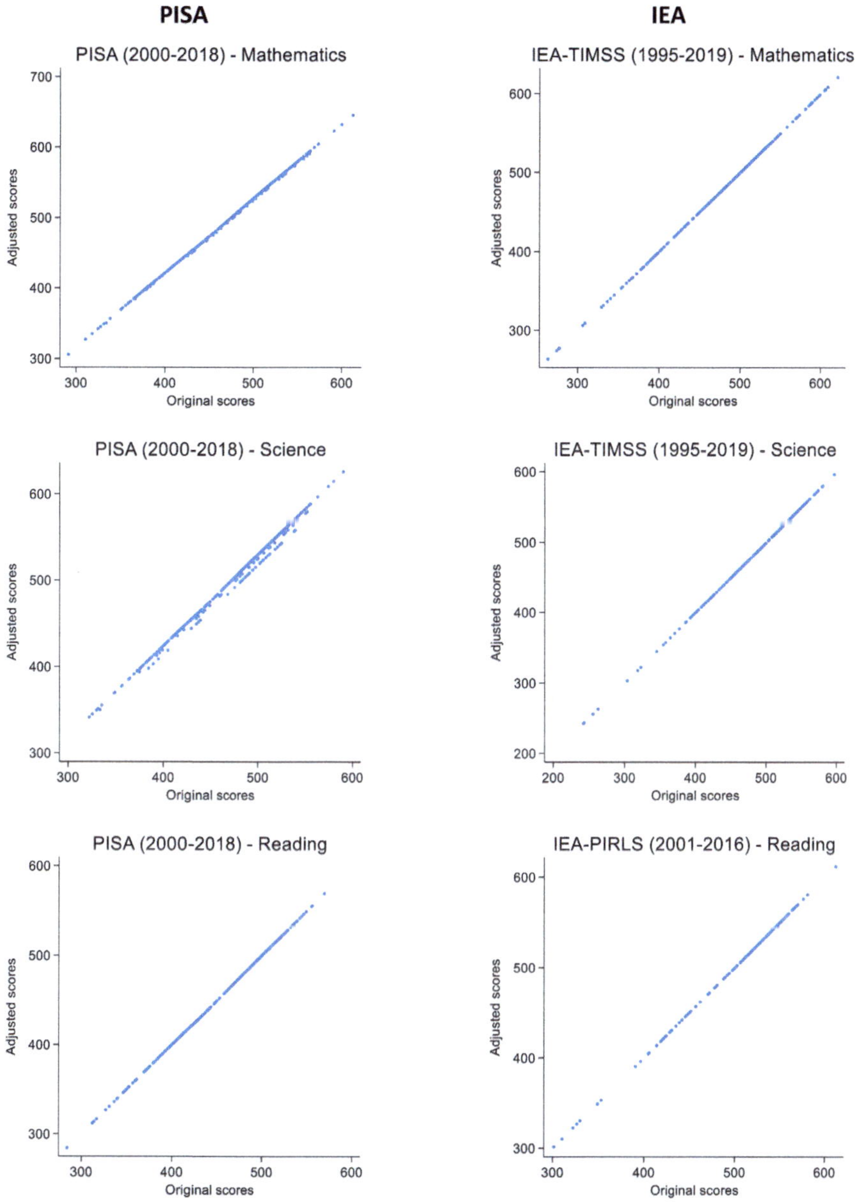

Fig. 3.12 Comparison between original and adjusted scores for PISA and IEA assessments

estimations cannot be performed. But we can reasonably assume that the differences are greater since the education systems of these countries are still developing and thus any difference between assessments may lead to performance divergences across them.

D. Hypothesis of absence of country-specific factors. Our methodology supposes that linking equations computed for the doubloon countries are mainly due to the differences between assessments and are independent of country-specific factors. We thus consider these coefficients as "exchange rates". For instance, when we anchor SACMEQ and PIRLS assessments using South Africa as a doubloon country, we are assuming that the differences in score distribution are only due to the specific characteristics of these two assessments and are independent of the education system in South Africa. Obviously, by using only one or two doubloon countries, our methodology includes a severe estimation bias, since within-country specific factors may explain differences found between anchored and reference assessments. When the number of doubloon countries is high, this bias may be lowered. Since we adapted our methodology in this paper in order to include all assessments for the computation of the "exchange rate", the bias relative to potential unobserved country-fixed effects may be significantly reduced. Moreover, Altinok (2017) tested this validity hypothesis by comparing linking equations between different rounds of these assessments. This analysis gives us two main results: first, it is important to highlight that country-specific factors are included in the linking process. These are not fully explained by the achievement tests themselves. This means that our estimation strategy is biased due to these country-specific factors. The second main result relates to the number of doubloon countries. The increase in these countries is very sharp in order to reduce the bias related to country-specific factors in the linking process. This is why we adapted our methodology in the current paper by increasing the number of countries in the computation of "exchange rates".

E. Limitations relative to multiple imputation process. Since our dataset is obtained by using a specific multiple imputation process (Honaker et al., 2011), it adds some estimation error in the mean scores obtained from regional and international student achievement tests. In order to minimize such estimation bias, we carefully chose the explanatory variables which may explain the most with the quality of schooling. These variables are presented in Table 3.14. In addition, results from the correlations across all the variables suggest strong association with our measure of schooling quality and these potential proxies (Table 3.15). The variables used for the imputation process can be divided into three different categories (Table 3.14). While some variables are strongly correlated with learning outcomes, they suffer from large missing values. An example of such variable can be the proportion of qualified teachers. The second group of variables are less correlated with learning outcomes, but they also have less missing values. For instance, one proxy of such group of variables can be the repetition rate of a given level of education. Lastly, some other variables can be used for the imputation process, although they are more based on school enrollment. One example is completion rates. All these variables were used into the imputation process and provided a quite important source of new estimations for our learning-adjusted year of schooling dataset (the proportion of imputed values is presented in Table 3.18).

3.5 Conclusion

We need better and more complete data to measure both quality and quantity of schooling. The purpose of this paper is to propose a new and more complete dataset on education. This dataset is not only based on learning outcomes, but also on the main measures surrounding the quantity of schooling. Based on previous works, our aim is to provide several improvements.

Three groups of datasets currently exist. First, "orthodox" papers focus only on achievement tests without making any adjustments. Although the dataset included in such a group may be considered as robust, it has the main disadvantage of being available only for recent years and mostly for developed economies. Another group of studies uses specific potential adjustments and thus extends the coverage of countries and the timespan. These studies have the main advantage of providing both better data and more data. A last group of studies, which we consider as "heterodox", take the risk of introducing several imputation methods. The main advantage of such studies is that they provide the largest datasets and thus cover almost all countries and several decades. However, since they are based on specific methods of prediction, the initial aim of providing better data with better coverage can be called into question.

In this paper, we propose to combine all these three groups of papers in order to keep the original scores intact as much as possible, but also to expand the coverage of countries and the timespan. By using the results from original student achievement tests, our dataset retains the main advantages of the "orthodox" papers. In addition, we expand this dataset using modern imputation methods through literacy studies and other proxies which can be correlated with learning outcomes.

We thus obtain a dataset with a panel dimension in terms of both quantity and quality of schooling for a large number of countries (i.e. more than 120) and over a 50 year span (i.e. between 1970 and 2020). While our dataset provides mean scores for learning outcomes as previous works have already proposed, we combine these with years of schooling in order to obtain a new indicator called "learning-adjusted years of schooling" (LAYS). Previous papers have already proposed a measure such as this (Filmer et al., 2020). Our main innovation is to obtain a panel dataset for a large number of countries. This dataset may be useful for further works which include the educational dimension in their analysis. Alongside the traditional dimension related to years of schooling, it is also important to include the potential differences related to quality of schooling.

As highlighted in the paper, our dataset is not perfect. Several biases can be found. Probably the greatest drawback of our work is the lack of quality of higher education. Indeed, student achievement tests are only conducted in primary and secondary schools, while innovation processes and sources of growth can be identified in the

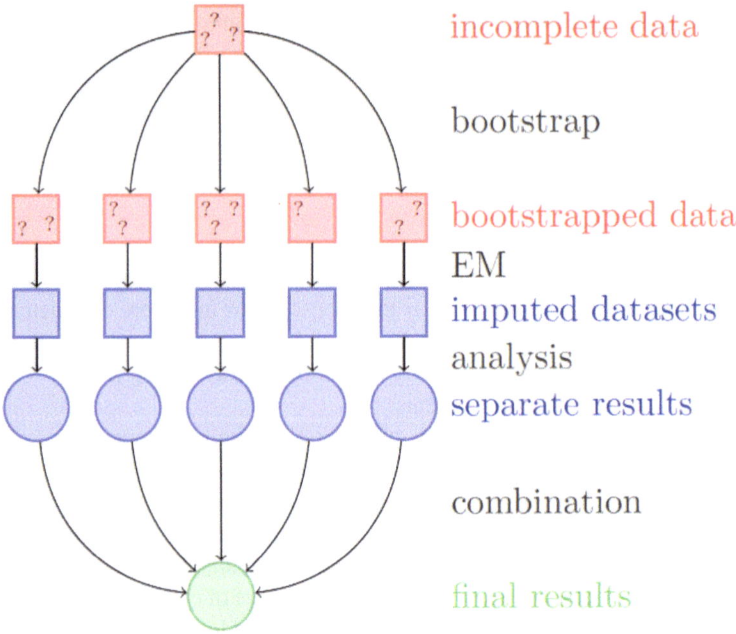

Fig. 3.13 A schematic approach to multiple imputation with the EMB algorithm. *Source* Honaker et al. (2011)

quality of higher education for developed countries. Recent works have attempted to include higher education in the human capital dimension (Demirgüç-Kunt & Torre, 2022). One possible extension of our work would be to include this level in the dataset on LAYS. This is our ambition for the years to come.

Data sources As described in the text. Note: Dependent variable: Growth of GDP per capita (1970–2020). Robust standard errors are in parentheses. Education variables are computed as the mean value across 1970–2020.

Below, we describe the student achievement tests which can be compared globally and over time. We divide the assessments into three main groups: The first consists of international assessments; the second contains regional assessments while the third is a hybrid assessment. A detailed summary of these assessments is provided in Table 3.11

3.5.1 International Standardized Achievement Tests (ISATs)

The Early ISATs (1960 to mid-1990s): **FIMS, FISS, SIMS, SISS, SRC, RLS, MLA and IAEP.** The *International Association for the Evaluation of Educational Achievement* (IEA) was the first body to measure individual learning achievements for international comparison. Tests began in the early 1960s. These tests were precursors of

Table 3.11 Review of Student Achievement Tests

No	*Year*	*Organization*	*Abbr*	*Subject*	*Countries or Areas*	*Grade*	*Included*
1	1959–60	IEA	Pilot Study	M,S,R	12	7/8	
2	1964	IEA	FIMS	M	12	7/FS	■
3	1970–71	IEA	SRC	R	15	4/8/ FS	
4	1970–72	IEA	FISS	S	19	4/8/ FS	■
5	1980–82	IEA	SIMS	M	19	8/FS	■
6	1983–84	IEA	SISS	S	23	4/8/ FS	■
7	1988/ 1990–91	NCES	IAEP	M,S	6–19	4/7–8	
8	1990–91	IEA	RLS	R	32	3–4/ 7–8	■
9	1995/ 1999/ 2003/ 2007/ 2011/ 2015/2019	IEA	TIMSS	M,S	45–38–26–48–66–65–64	3–4/ 7–8/ FS	■
10	1992–97	UNESCO	MLA	M,S,R	72	6–8	
11	1997/ 2006/ 2013/2019	UNESCO	LLECE	M,S,R	13–16–15–16	3–6	■
12	1999/ 2002/2007	UNESCO	SACMEQ	M,R	7–15–16	6 6	■
13	2000/ 2010/ 2014/2019	CONFEMEN	PASEC	M,R	22–22–10–14	2/5 then 3–6	■
14	2001/ 2006/ 2011/2016	IEA	PIRLS	R	35–41–55–50	4	■
15	2000/ 2003/ 2006/ 2009/ 2012/ 2015/ 2018/2022	OECD	PISA	M,S,R	43–41–57–74–65–71–79–81	Age 15	■
16	2010/ 2015/2019	USAID/RTI	EGRA	R	29–40–5	1 to 6	■
17	2008–2019	ASER	ASER	R	2	1 to 6	■

Note For the meaning of abbreviations, please consult Sect. 3.2. Only assessments for which there is information in the "Survey Series" column are included in our dataset. Subjects: M = math; S = science; R = reading

Table 3.12 Countries with comparable data for the EGRA/ASER tests

Country	Years available	Grades	Source
Afghanistan	2016	2;3;4;5	Raw Data
Bangladesh	2014;2015;2016	2;3	Raw Data
Cambodia	2018;2019	1;2	EGRA Barometer
DRC	2010;2012;2013;2015	2;3;4;5;6	Raw Data
Egypt	2009;2013;2014	2;3;4	Raw Data
El Salvador	2017	2;3	EGRA Barometer
Ethiopia	2010;2013;2014	2;3;4	Raw Data
Gambia	2007	1;2;3	Raw Data
Ghana	2013;2015	2	Raw Data
Guyana	2008	2;3;4	Raw Data
Haiti	2009;2014	1;2;3	Raw Data
Honduras	2008	2;3;4	Raw Data
India	2008–2014;2016;2018	1;2;3;4;5;6	ASER India
Indonesia	2012;2013;2014	2;3	Raw Data
Iraq	2012	2;3	Raw Data
Jordan	2012;2014	2;3	Raw Data
Kenya	2009;2012;2013;2016	1;2;3	EGRA Barometer (for 2016)
Kiribati	2016	1;2;3	Raw Data
Kyrgyzstan	2016;2017	2;4	Raw Data
Lao PDR	2012	3;4;5	Raw Data
Liberia	2011;2015	1;2;3	Raw Data
Macedonia	2015;2016	2;3	Raw Data
Malawi	2011;2012	2;4	Raw Data
Mali	2009;2011;2015	2;3;4	Raw Data
Mexico	2014;2015;2016	1;2;3;4;5;6	Raw Data
Morocco	2011	2;3	Raw Data
Mozambique	2013; 2016	1;2;3;4;5;6	Raw Data; EGRA Barometer (for 2013)
Myanmar	2014;2015	1;2;3	Raw Data
Nepal	2014;2016;2018	1;2;3;4;5;6	Raw Data
Nicaragua	2008;2009	1;2;3;4	Raw Data
State of Palestine	2014	2	Raw Data
Pakistan	2012–2016;2018;2019	1;2;3;4;5;6	ASER Pakistan
Papua New Guinea	2011;2012;2013	1;2;3;4	Raw Data
Philippines	2013;2014;2015;2019	1;2;3	Raw Data; EGRA Barometer (for 2019)
Rwanda	2011;2015;2016	4;6	Raw Data

(continued)

Table 3.12 (continued)

Country	Years available	Grades	Source
Samoa	2017	1;2;3	Official Report
Senegal	2009	3	Raw Data
Sierra Leone	2014	2;4	Raw Data
Solomon Islands	2017	1;2;3	Official Report
Somalia	2013	2;3;4	EGRA Barometer
South Africa	2013	5	EGRA Barometer
South Sudan	2017;2018	3	Official Report
Sudan	2016	3	Raw Data
Tajikistan	2017	2;4	Raw Data
Tanzania	2013;2017	2	Raw Data
Timor-Leste	2009;2011	1;2;3	Raw Data
Tonga	2009;2014	1;2;3	Raw Data
Tuvalu	2016	1;2;3	Raw Data
Uganda	2009;2013;2014;2017	1;2;3	Raw Data
Vanuatu	2010	1;2;3	Raw Data
Yemen	2011	2;3	Raw Data
Zambia	2011;2014;2015	2;3	Raw Data; EGRA Barometer (for 2015)

their more current counterparts: *Trends in International Mathematics and Science Study* (TIMSS) and *Progress in International Reading Literacy Study* (PIRLS). The precursors of TIMSS included: pilot studies in 1960, the First International Mathematics Study (FIMS) in 1964, the First International Science Study (FISS) in 1970, the Second International Mathematics Study (SIMS) in 1980–1982, the Second International Mathematics Study (SISS) from 1982 to 1986, and the *International Assessment of Educational Progress* (IAEP) conducted in 1988 and 1991. Precursors of PIRLS included: Study of Reading Comprehension Study (SRC) in 1970, and the Reading Literacy Study (RLS) in 1990–1991. According to the test developers, the earlier studies served as a model for the later studies (Campbell & Mullis, 2001; Elley, 1994). Data sources are based on major reports and raw data (Bloom & (DHEW), 1969; Burstein, 1992; Comber & Keeves, 1973; Foshay et al., 1962; Garden, 1987; International Association for the Evaluation of Educational Achievement, 1988; Keeves & A, 1992; Livingstone, 1986; Peaker, 1975; Robitaille & Garden, 1989; Thorndike, 1973; Walker et al., 1976; Westbury & Travers, 1990).

An additional early international assessment—a joint UNESCO and UNICEF project called the *Monitoring Learning Achievement* (MLA) program—covers more than 72 countries and ranges from early childhood, basic and secondary education to non-formal adult literacy (Chinapah et al., 2000). A series of results reports exist for MLA I across 11 African countries of interest (Botswana, Madagascar, Malawi, Mali, Morocco, Mauritius, Niger, Senegal, Tunisia, Uganda and Zambia). However, much of the data has not been published. Since microdata is sparse or often unavailable for the MLA and IAEP data, we prefer not to include these series in our dataset.

The Modern ISATs (mid 1990s onward): In the mid-1990s, standardized, psychometrically robust and relatively consistent ISATs emerged. Below we describe the major ISATs which we used to construct our database.

TIMSS. The Trends in International Mathematics and Science Study (TIMSS) is one of the main survey series conducted by the IEA. Six TIMSS rounds have been held to date in Math and Science subjects covering grades 4 and 8. The first, conducted in 1995, covered 45 national educational systems and three groups of students.[28] The second round covered 38 educational systems in 1999, examining pupils from secondary education (grade 8). The third round covered 50 educational systems in 2003, focusing on both primary and secondary education (grades 4 and 8). In 2007, the fourth survey covered grades 4 and 8 and more than 66 educational systems. In 2011, the survey covered 77 educational systems across grades 4 and 8. The fourth round was performed in 2015 and covered 63 countries/areas. The latest round was closed in 2019 and covered 64 countries/areas.

PIRLS. The other dominant IEA survey is the Progress in International Reading Literacy Study (PIRLS). Four rounds of PIRLS have been held to date: in 2001, 2006, 2011 and 2016. The PIRLS tests pupils from primary schools in grade 4 in reading proficiency.[29] In 2006, PIRLS included 41 countries/areas, two of which were African countries (Morocco and South Africa), 4 lower-middle-income countries (Georgia, Indonesia, Moldova, Morocco) and 8 upper-middle-income countries (Bulgaria, Islamic Republic of Iran, Lithuania, Macedonia, Federal Yugoslavian Republic, Romania, Russian Federation, South Africa). The third round of PIRLS was carried out with TIMSS in 2011 and included 60 countries/areas. In 2016, PIRLS was also conducted and included 50 countries/areas.

In our database, we use all recent IEA studies across two subjects (mathematics and reading/literacy). We use results from official reports (Martin et al., 2007, 2012; I. Mullis et al., 2020; Mullis et al., 2000, 2003, 2004, 2008, 2016, 2017, 2012a, 2012b, 2012a, 2012b, 2012c, 2016a, 2016b; Olson et al., 2008) and raw data provided by the IEA Repository website: https://www.iea.nl/data-tools/repository.

PISA. The Organization for Economic Co-operation and Development (OECD) launched the Program for International Student Assessment (PISA) in 1997 to provide comparable data on student performance. PISA emphasizes an extended concept of "literacy" and places the emphasis on lifelong learning. Literacy is considered more broadly because PISA studies are concerned with pupils' capacity to extrapolate from what they have learnt and apply their knowledge to novel settings. Since 2000, PISA has assessed the skills of 15-year-old pupils every three years.

---

[28] IEA assessments define populations relative to specific grades, while PISA assessments focus on the age of pupils. In IEA studies, three different groups of pupils were generally assessed: pupils from grade 4, grade 8 and from the last grade of secondary education. In 1995, two adjacent grades were tested in both primary (3–4) and secondary schools (7–8). In order to obtain comparable trends, we restricted the sample to grades 4 and 8. Some Canadian provinces and states in the United States of America have occasionally taken part in the IEA surveys.

[29] Similar to TIMSS, pupils from Grade 4 are chosen.

PISA concentrates on three subjects: mathematics, science and literacy. In 2000, PISA had a focus, in the form of extensive domain items, on literacy; in 2003, on mathematical skills; and in 2006 on scientific skills. The framework for evaluation remains the same across time to ensure comparability.[30] A main distinction between PISA and IEA surveys is that PISA assesses 15-year-old pupils, regardless of grade level, while IEA assessments assess grades 4 and 8. The number of countries taking part at PISA is growing over time. In 2000, 43 countries/areas participated while in 2022, 81 countries/areas participated. Data can be retrieved from OECD website. Main results can also be found in official reports (OECD, 2004, 2007, 2010b, 2013, 2016, 2019, 2023; Schleicher, 2019).

3.5.2 Regional Standardized Achievement Tests (RSATs)

In addition to the above international assessments, three major regional assessments have been conducted in Africa and Latin America and the Caribbean.

SACMEQ. *The Southern and Eastern Africa Consortium for Monitoring Educational Quality* (SACMEQ) grew out of a national investigation into the quality of primary education in Zimbabwe in 1991. It was supported by the UNESCO International Institute for Educational Planning (IIEP) (Ross and Postlethwaite, 1991). Several education ministers in Southern and Eastern African countries expressed an interest in a similar study. Planners from seven countries met in Paris in July 2004 and established SACMEQ. The current 16 SACMEQ education members are: Angola,[31] Botswana, Kenya, Lesotho, Malawi, Mauritius, Mozambique, Namibia, Seychelles, the Republic of South Africa, Swaziland, the United Republic of Tanzania, United Republic of Tanzania (Zanzibar), Uganda, Zambia and Zimbabwe.

The first SACMEQ round took place between 1995 and 1999. SACMEQ I covered seven different countries and assessed performances in reading at grade 6. The participating countries were Kenya, Malawi, Mauritius, Namibia, United Republic of Tanzania (Zanzibar), Zambia and Zimbabwe. The studies shared common features (research issues, instruments, target populations, sampling and analytical procedures). A separate report was prepared for each country.

SACMEQ II surveyed grade 6 pupils from 2000 to 2004 in 14 countries: Botswana, Kenya, Lesotho, Mauritius, Malawi, Mozambique, Namibia, Seychelles, South Africa, Swaziland, Tanzania (Mainland), Tanzania (Zanzibar), Uganda and Zambia. Notably, SACMEQ II also collected information on pupils' socio-economic status as well as educational inputs, the educational environment and issues relating to equitable allocation of human and material resources. SACMEQ II also included overlapping items with a series of other surveys for international comparison, namely the

[30] As explained in the PISA 2006 technical report, this is only the case for reading between 2000 and 2009, for mathematics between 2003 and 2009 and for science between 2006 and 2009. See OECD (2010a) for more details.

[31] Angola is a recent member of SACMEQ, but has not implemented any survey projects yet.

Indicators of the Quality of Education (Zimbabwe) study, TIMSS and the 1985–94 IEA *Reading Literacy Study.*

The third SACMEQ round (SACMEQ III) spanned 2006–2011 and covered the same countries as SACMEQ II plus Zimbabwe. SACMEQ III also assessed the achievement of grade 6 pupils. The latest round of SACMEQ (SACMEQ IV) began in 2013 in 15 countries, but results have not been published. We therefore included only the first three rounds of SACMEQ in our database.

PASEC. The "Programme d'Analyse des Systèmes Éducatifs" (PASEC or "Program of Analysis of Education Systems") was launched by the Conference of Ministers of Education of French-Speaking Countries (CONFEMEN). These surveys are conducted in French-speaking countries in sub-Saharan Africa in primary school (grade 2 and 5) for Mathematics and French. Each round includes ten countries. PASEC I ran from 1996 to 2003; PASEC II from 2004 to 2010 and PASEC III was conducted in 2014.

However, in contrast with other assessments, PASEC has not always been conducted simultaneously across countries and participation has varied considerably since 1994.[32] Moreover, data from the first four assessments are not available.[33] PASEC was modified significantly in 2014, rendering results hard to compare with previous PASEC items. While 10 countries took part at PASEC 2014, this number increased up to 14 in 2019,[34] in the second round.

LLECE. The network of national education systems in Latin American and Caribbean countries, known as the Latin American Laboratory for Assessment of the Quality of Education (LLECE), was formed in 1994 and is coordinated by the UNESCO Regional Bureau for Education in Latin America and the Caribbean. The main aim of this survey is to garner information on pupil performance and performance-related factors likely to guide politicians in educational policymaking.

Assessments conducted by the LLECE focus on achievements in reading and mathematics. The first round was conducted in 1998 across grades 3 and 4 in 13 countries (Casassus et al., 1998). These countries include: Argentina, Bolivia, Brazil, Chile, Columbia, Costa Rica, Cuba, Dominican Republic, Honduras, Mexico, Paraguay, Peru and Venezuela (Casassus et al., 1998). The second round of the LLECE survey was initiated in 2006 in the same countries as LLECE I. In round two, called the Second Regional Comparative and Explanatory Study (SERCE), pupils

---

[32] The following is a list of participating countries in chronological order: Djibouti (1994), Congo (1994), Mali (1995), Central African Republic (1995), Senegal (1996), Burkina Faso (1996), Cameroon (1996), Côte d'Ivoire (1996), Madagascar (1997), Guinea (2000), Togo (2001), Mali (2001), Niger (2001), Chad (2004), Mauritania (2004), Guinea (2004), Benin (2005), Cameroon (2005), Madagascar (2006), Mauritius (2006), Congo (2007), Senegal (2007), Burkina Faso (2007), Burundi (2009), Ivory Coast (2009), Comoros (2009), Lebanon (2009), Togo (2010), DRC (2010), Chad (2010). Additional countries took a slightly different test between 2010 and 2011 (Lao PDR, Mali, Cambodia and Vietnam).

[33] The first four assessments were mainly pilot studies and the purpose was not to disseminate results.

[34] In 2014, the following countries participated to the PASEC study: Benin, Burkina Faso, Burundi, Cameroun, Congo, Côte d'Ivoire, Niger, Senegal, Chad, and Togo. In addition to 2014 participating countries, Guinea, Gabon, Mali and Madagascar joined the PASEC initiative in 2019.

were tested in grade 3 and grade 6 (Treviño & OREALC, 2014). The Third Regional Comparative and Explanatory Study (TERCE) was done in 2013 across grades 3 and 6 and included 15 Latin American and Caribbean countries (Flotts et al., 2015; Treviño et al., 2015). The fourth and latest round to date was conducted in 2019 and included 16 countries, with Cuba the new country compared to the third round. Our analysis will include all LLECE results, since these assessments are mostly similar and cover comparable grades (UNESCO/UNICEF & OREALC/UNESCO, 2021).

3.5.3 *Hybrid Standardized Achievement Tests (RSATs)*

In addition to traditional international and regional student achievement tests, we also include some "hybrid tests" following the terminology of Wagner (2017).

Hybrid assessments can be considered as a mix of international and regional achievement tests. Wagner (2011) argues that EGRA represents a hybrid type of assessment. The Early Grade Reading Assessment (EGRA) is an individually administered oral assessment of the most basic foundation skills for literacy acquisition in early grades. The assessment requires about 15 min per child. It was designed as an inexpensive and simple diagnostic of individual student progress in reading. EGRA includes up to thirteen subtasks, such as "oral reading fluency", "vocabulary", "diction" and "reading comprehension". We compile and include data from the proportion of pupils with a 0-score in the "Oral Reading Fluency" test provided in almost all EGRA tests. We believe this is the best comparable measure since it is not related to the complexity of languages, which may differ across countries. Although EGRA has not been conducted in rounds as PISA or TIMSS have, we consider three different rounds of EGRA in years 2010, 2015 and 2019. The number of countries with comparable data is respectively 29, 40 and 5. The list of countries with data for EGRA is presented in Table 3.11. Similarly to EGRA, the Annual Status of Education Report (ASER) is a quick oral assessment of early grades. It has been conducted in several countries, including India and Pakistan. ASER is the largest annual household survey carried out among citizens of India to understand whether children are enrolled in school and whether they are learning. The main advantage of ASER is that it reaches a representative sample of children from every rural district in India. Since 2006, the ASER sample size has included 30 villages per district and more than 700,000 children surveyed. Table 3.12 presents the coverage of ASER over time for India. One potential advantage of ASER is the possibility to obtain results which are provided in each state within Pakistan and India. Moreover, since EGRA and ASER tests are quite similar, we were able to match scores for both tests and include results in our analysis. Data for EGRA have been mainly extracted from raw data.[35] When data were not available, we used results from the EGRA

[35] We are very grateful to Luis Crouch and Jennifer Ryan for their support with the EGRA datasets.

Table 3.13 ASER India coverage over time

	2008	2009	2010	2011	2012	2013	2014	2016	2018
No. of districts covered	489	557	569	577	580	567	564	568	550
No. of villages covered	9,593	15,841	16,131	16,303	16,484	16,149	16,159	16,243	15,941
No. of households surveyed	192,517	322,425	320,719	337,315	331,791	333,042	328,141	331,49	325,827
No. of children surveyed (total)	330,101	762,252	723,969	703,047	679,271	655,81	631,137	595,139	566,661
Children aged 3–5		148,054	125,416	119,322	119,238	124,349	116,618	112,773	107,392
Children aged 6–14	330,101	521,116	529,889	509,188	478,901	455,769	439,168	411,519	390,838
Children aged 15–16		93,082	68,664	74,537	81,132	75,692	75,351	70,847	68,431
No. of schools observed	8,306		14,066		14,748	14,24	14,373	14,662	14,724

Source ASER India website. Link: http://img.asercentre.org/docs/domains2005-2018.pdf. Accessed 13/08/2025

Barometer, available at https://earlygradereadingbarometer.org/. Results for ASER India and ASER Pakistan were downloaded from their respective websites.[36]

Table 3.13 summarizes the availability and details of the various international and regional assessments listed above (Tables 3.16 and 3.19).

3.6 Appendix: Presentation of Linking Methodologies

Various methodologies can be used for linking or equating assessments. Equating is a statistical process that is used to adjust scores on tests so that the scores can be used interchangeably (Kolen & Brennan, 2014). The purpose of equating is to adjust for difficulty among assessments that are built to be similar. In our case, the assessments are not directly comparable since difficulty and content may differ. Instead, we use a similar approach to equating, known as *scaling to achieve comparability* according

[36] ASER India: http://www.asercentre.org/. ASER Pakistan: http://www.aserpakistan.org/. We are very grateful to Preeti Mnchanda, Wilima Wadhwa and Sahar Saeed for their support during the analysis of raw data for ASER India and ASER Pakistan surveys.

Table 3.14 Source and definition of variables

Variable	Source	Definition
Group 1—Proxies for learning outcomes with large missing values		
% of teachers who are female	EdStats / UIS	Number of female teachers at the primary level expressed as a percentage of the total number of teachers (male and female) at the primary level in a given school year
% of qualified teachers	EdStats / UIS	Percentage of teachers by level of education taught (pre-primary, primary, lower secondary and upper secondary education) who have at least the minimum academic qualifications required for teaching their subjects at the relevant level in a given country, in a given academic year. A high value indicates that students are being taught by teachers who are academically well qualified in the subjects they teach
% of trained teachers	EdStats	Trained teachers in primary/secondary/tertiary education are the percentage of primary/secondary/tertiary school teachers who have received the minimum organized teacher training (pre-service or in-service) required for teaching in a given country
Group 2—Proxies for learning outcomes with few missing values		
Repetition rate	EdStats	Number of repeaters in a given grade in a given school year, expressed as a percentage of enrollment in that grade the previous school year. Divide the number of repeaters in a given grade in school year t + 1 by the number of pupils from the same cohort enrolled in the same grade in the previous school year t
Pupil-teacher ratio	EdStats/UIS	Primary school pupil-teacher ratio is the average number of pupils per teacher in primary school
Government expenditure per student (% of GDP per capita)	WDI/UIS	Government expenditure per student is the average general government expenditure (current, capital and transfers) per student in the given level of education, expressed as a percentage of GDP per capita

(continued)

Table 3.14 (continued)

Variable	Source	Definition
Government expenditure on education, total (% of government expenditure)	EdStats	Total general (local, regional and central) government expenditure on education (current, capital and transfers), expressed as a percentage of total general government expenditure on all sectors (including health, education, social services, etc.). It includes expenditure funded by transfers from international sources to government. Public education expenditure includes spending by local/municipal, regional and national governments (excluding household contributions) on educational institutions (both public and private), education administration and subsidies for private entities (students/households and other private entities). In some instances, data on total public expenditure on education refers only to the ministry of education and can exclude other ministries that spend a part of their budget on educational activities. The indicator is calculated by dividing total public expenditure on education incurred by all government agencies/departments by total government expenditure and multiplying by 100
Government expenditure on education, total (% of GDP)	EdStats	Total general (local, regional and central) government expenditure on education (current, capital and transfers), expressed as a percentage of GDP. It includes expenditure funded by transfers from international sources to government. Divide total government expenditure for a given level of education (e.g., primary, secondary or all levels combined) by GDP, and multiply by 100. A higher percentage of GDP spent on education shows a higher government priority for education, but also a higher capacity of the government to raise revenues for public spending, in relation to the size of the country's economy. When interpreting this indicator, however, one should keep in mind that in some countries, the private sector and/or households may fund a higher proportion of total funding for education, thus making government expenditure appear lower than in other countries

(continued)

Table 3.14 (continued)

Variable	Source	Definition
Group 3—Variables related to school enrollment		
Completion rate (%)	EdStats	The number of persons in the relevant age group who have completed the last grade of the given level of education is expressed as a percentage of the total population (in the survey sample) of the same age group. The primary completion rate is the percentage of a cohort of children or young people aged 3–5 years above the intended age for the last grade of primary education who have completed that grade. The intended age for the last grade of primary education is the age at which pupils would enter the grade if they had started school at the official primary entrance age, had studied full-time and had progressed without repeating or skipping a grade. For example, if the official age of entry into primary education is 6 years, and if primary education has 6 grades, the intended age for the last grade of primary education is 11 years. In this case, 14–16 years ($11 + 3 = 14$ and $11 + 5 = 16$) would be the reference age group for calculation of the primary completion rate
Gross enrollment ratio (%)	EdStats	Total enrollment in primary education, regardless of age, expressed as a percentage of the population of official primary education age. GER can exceed 100% due to the inclusion of over-aged and under-aged students because of early or late school entrance and grade repetition
Survival rate to the last grade of primary education (%)	EdStats	Percentage of a cohort of students enrolled in the first grade of primary education in a given school year who are expected to reach the last grade of primary education, regardless of repetition. Divide the total number of students belonging to a school-cohort who reached each successive grade of primary education by the number of students in the school-cohort, i.e. those originally enrolled in the first grade of primary education, and multiply the result by 100. The survival rate is calculated on the basis of the reconstructed cohort method, which uses data on enrollment and repeaters for two consecutive years

(continued)

Table 3.14 (continued)

Variable	Source	Definition
Total net enrollment rate (%)	EdStats	Total number of students of the official age group for primary education who are enrolled in any level of education, expressed as a percentage of the corresponding population. Divide the total number of students in the official school age range for primary education who are enrolled in any level of education by the population of the same age group and multiply the result by 100. The difference between the total NER and the adjusted NER provides a measure of the proportion of children in the official relevant school age group who are enrolled in levels of education below the one intended for their age. The difference between the total NER and the adjusted NER for primary education is due to enrollment in pre-primary education. The total NER should be based on total enrollment of the official relevant school age group in any level of education for all types of schools and education institutions, including public, private and all other institutions that provide organized educational programs
Out-of-school rate for each age group (%)	EdStats	Children in the official primary school age range who are not enrolled in either primary or secondary schools Total number of lower secondary school age adolescents who are not enrolled in lower secondary education
Adjusted net enrollment rate (%)	WDI	Adjusted net enrollment is the number of pupils of the school-age group for primary education, enrolled in either primary or secondary education, expressed as a percentage of the total population in that age group
Enrollment rate (%)	J. -W. Lee and Lee (2016)	Primary/Secondary/Tertiary adjusted enrollment ratio (original names: "pri", "sec", "ter")
Average years of schooling, 15–64 age group	Barro and Lee (2013)	Average years of total schooling, 15 + , total is the average years of education completed among people over age 15
GDP per capita	WDI	GDP per capita is gross domestic product divided by midyear population. GDP is the sum of gross value added by all resident producers in the economy plus any product taxes and minus any subsidies not included in the value of the products. It is calculated without making deductions for depreciation of fabricated assets or for depletion and degradation of natural resources. Data are in constant 2015 U.S. dollars

(continued)

Table 3.14 (continued)

Variable	Source	Definition
Group 4—Alternative measure for learning outcomes		
Literacy data for developing countries	Le Nestour et al. (2022)	Literacy rate for an adult with a given level of schooling (here, 5 years of schooling). Estimation based on repeated cross-sections from the Demographic Health Surveys (DHS) run by USAID and Multiple Indicator Cluster Surveys (MICS) run by UNICEF. Note: Results are disaggregated for women and men. We have imputed results for both genders and then computed the mean literacy rate by supposing similar weights across genders

to the *Standards for Educational and Psychological Testing* (AERA NCME, 1999). This is also known as *linking* in the terminology of Holland and Dorans (2006), Linn (1993) and Mislevy (1992). As explained by Kolen and Brennan (2014), similar statistical procedures are used in linking and equating, although their purposes are different. In this paper, we use the term *linking* instead of *equating* since the tests we link are purposefully built to be different. Notably, we do not link using Item Response Theory (IRT)—the technique used to generate scores for each respective international and regional assessment. IRT models the probability of a given pupil answering a given test item correctly as a function of pupil- and item-specific characteristics. While this methodology is used *within* each of the international and regional tests we use, to use it *across* ISATs and RSATs would require an overlap in test items.[37] This is not true for a significant enough number of tests and time intervals to create a globally comparable panel dataset. Moreover, even when there is an overlap, for IRT to be reliable there must be a large enough instance of item-specific overlap. When this overlap is small, standard maximum likelihood estimates will reflect both true variance and measurement error, overstating the variance in the test score distribution. Das and Zajonc (2010) elaborate on the various challenges of estimating IRT parameters with limited item-specific overlap.

In building globally comparable education quality estimates, we rely on classical test theory (Holland & Hoskens, 2003). Specifically, we use pseudo-linear linking and equipercentile linking. Below we describe each, starting from a foundation of mean linking.

Suppose that a population of pupils, sampled from target population T, takes two different assessments X and Y. Here, we suppose that any differences in the score distributions on X and Y can be attributed entirely to the assessments themselves, since group ability is assumed to be constant.

[37] Sandefur (2016) equates SACMEQ and TIMSS results with IRT methods. Sandefur (2016) measures the DIF as the distance between the item-characteristic curve (ICC) for the reference population and actual responses for the focal group, an approach first proposed by Raju (1988). The resulting DIF is high, casting doubt on the IRT approach in a context with limited item overlap.

Table 3.15 Correlation matrix

Primary level—mathematics

		1	2	3	4	5	6	7	8	9	10
Learning outcomes—pri—math	1	–									
Years of schooling	2	0.8010*	–								
GDP per capita	3	0.6608*	0.3769*	-							
Pupil-teacher ratio, primary	4	– 0.6601*	– 0.5972*	– 0.4687*	–						
Survival rate, primary education	5	0.6523*	0.6635*	0.3118*	– 0.6550*	–					
Adult literacy score	6	0.5062*	0.7543*	0.5664*	– 0.5051*	0.3981*	–				
Adult numeracy score	7	0.5685*	0.6972*	0.5306*	– 0.5769*	0.4208*	0.9609*	–			
Lim et al. data, secondary	8	0.9510*	0.7156*	0.5100*	– 0.6153*	0.6077*	0.8001*	0.7714*	–		
Primary enrollment rate	9	0.2214*	0.7009*	0.2155*	– 0.4028*	0.4999*	0.3926*	0.3578*	0.4016*	–	
Gov. expenditure on pri. ed. as % of GDP	10	– 0.4376*	– 0.0434*	– 0.1528*	0.0551*	– 0.0118	0.1240*	0.0984*	– 0.2271*	0.0648*	–

(continued)

Table 3.15 (continued)

Primary level—reading		1	2	3	4	5	6	7	8	9	10
Learning outcomes—pri—read	1	–									
Years of schooling	2	0.8177*	–								
GDP per capita	3	0.6445*	0.3769*	–							
Pupil-teacher ratio, primary	4	– 0.7728*	– 0.5969*	– 0.4690*	–						
Survival rate, primary education	5	0.7010*	0.6635*	0.3118*	– 0.6544*	–					
Adult literacy score	6	0.7141*	0.7543*	0.5664*	– 0.4994*	0.3981*	–				
Adult numeracy score	7	0.6247*	0.6972*	0.5306*	– 0.5723*	0.4208*	0.9609*	–			
Lim et al. data, secondary	8	0.8918*	0.7156*	0.5100*	– 0.6155*	0.6077*	0.8001*	0.7714*	–		
Primary enrollment rate	9	0.2870*	0.7009*	0.2155*	– 0.4017*	0.4999*	0.3926*	0.3578*	0.4016*	–	
Gov. expenditure on pri. ed. as % of GDP	10	– 0.2907*	– 0.0434*	– 0.1545*	0.0574*	– 0.0137	0.1341*	0.1057*	– 0.2302*	0.0663*	–

(continued)

Table 3.15 (continued)

Primary level—science

		1	2	3	4	5	6	7	8	9	10
Learning outcomes—primary—science	1	–									
Years of schooling	2	0.6995*	–								
GDP per capita	3	0.5202*	0.3769*	–							
Pupil-teacher ratio, primary	4	– 0.4731*	– 0.5972*	– 0.4687*	–						
Survival rate, primary education	5	0.5007*	0.6635*	0.3118*	– 0.6550*	–					
Adult literacy score	6	0.4315*	0.7543*	0.5664*	– 0.5051*	0.3981*	–				
Adult numeracy score	7	0.3819*	0.6972*	0.5306*	– 0.5769*	0.4208*	0.9609*	–			
Lim et al. data, secondary	8	0.9026*	0.7156*	0.5100*	– 0.6153*	0.6077*	0.8001*	0.7714*	–		
Primary enrollment rate	9	0.1484*	0.7009*	0.2155*	– 0.4028*	0.4999*	0.3926*	0.3578*	0.4016*	–	
Gov. expenditure on pri. ed. as % of GDP	10	– 0.3345*	– 0.0434*	– 0.1528*	0.0551*	– 0.0118	0.1240*	0.0984*	– 0.2271*	0.0648*	–

(continued)

Table 3.15 (continued)

Secondary level—mathematics

		1	2	3	4	5	6	7	8	9	10
Learning outcomes—sec—math	1	–									
Years of schooling	2	0.5950*	–								
GDP per capita	3	0.5690*	0.3769*	–							
Secondary enrollment rate	4	0.4377*	0.8319*	0.3707*	–						
Total net enrollment rate, lower secondary	5	0.3831*	0.7465*	0.3411*	0.7563*	–					
Lower secondary completion rate	6	0.1439*	0.7301*	0.3382*	0.7587*	0.8359*	–				
Adult literacy score	7	0.7340*	0.7543*	0.5664*	0.7417*	0.6776*	0.3611*	–			
Adult numeracy score	8	0.7442*	0.6972*	0.5306*	0.6814*	0.6617*	0.3688*	0.9609*	–		
Lim et al. data, secondary	9	0.9355*	0.7156*	0.5100*	0.6751*	0.5866*	0.6024*	0.8001*	0.7714*	–	
Gov. expenditure on sec. ed. as % of GDP	10	0.1569*	0.3230*	0.0628*	0.2741*	0.3674*	0.3140*	0.5260*	0.5594*	0.2398*	–

(continued)

Table 3.15 (continued)

Secondary level—reading

		1	2	3	4	5	6	7	8	9	10
Learning outcomes—sec—reading	1	–									
Years of schooling	2	0.6141*	–								
GDP per capita	3	0.5717*	0.3769*	–							
Secondary enrollment rate	4	0.5461*	0.8319*	0.3707*	–						
Total net enrollment rate, lower secondary	5	0.4233*	0.7465*	0.3411*	0.7563*	–					
Lower secondary completion rate	6	0.1326*	0.7301*	0.3382*	0.7587*	0.8359*	–				
Adult literacy score	7	0.8680*	0.7543*	0.5664*	0.7417*	0.6776*	0.3611*	–			
Adult numeracy score	8	0.7789*	0.6972*	0.5306*	0.6814*	0.6617*	0.3688*	0.9609*	–		
Lim et al. data, secondary	9	0.8616*	0.7156*	0.5100*	0.6751*	0.5866*	0.6024*	0.8001*	0.7714*	–	
Gov. expenditure on sec. ed. as % of GDP	10	0.2820*	0.3230*	0.0628*	0.2741*	0.3674*	0.3140*	0.5260*	0.5594*	0.2398*	–

(continued)

Table 3.15 (continued)

Secondary level—science

		1	2	3	4	5	6	7	8	9	10
Learning outcomes—sec—science	1	–									
Years of schooling	2	0.5719*	–								
GDP per capita	3	0.5544*	0.3769*	–							
Secondary enrollment rate	4	0.4390*	0.8319*	0.3707*	–						
Total net enrollment rate, lower secondary	5	0.3742*	0.7465*	0.3411*	0.7563*	–					
Lower secondary completion rate	6	0.1465*	0.7301*	0.3382*	0.7587*	0.8359*	–				
Adult literacy score	7	0.7492*	0.7543*	0.5664*	0.7417*	0.6776*	0.3611*	–			
Adult numeracy score	8	0.7013*	0.6972*	0.5306*	0.6814*	0.6617*	0.3688*	0.9609*	–		
Lim et al. data, secondary	9	0.9261*	0.7156*	0.5100*	0.6751*	0.5866*	0.6024*	0.8001*	0.7714*	–	
Gov. expenditure on sec. ed. as % of GDP	10	0.1668*	0.3230*	0.0628*	0.2741*	0.3674*	0.3140*	0.5260*	0.5594*	0.2398*	–

Table 3.16 Test linking architecture

Linking number	Anchored assessment	Level	Subject	Reference assessment	List of countries used for linking
1	FIMS, SIMS, FISS, SISS, IAEP, first wave of TIMSS & PIRLS, RLS	P + S	M + S + R	NAEP	USA
2	LLECE	P	M + S	TIMSS	Colombia, Chile, Honduras, El Salvador
3	LLECE	P	R	PIRLS	Colombia, Chile, Honduras
4	SACMEQ	P	M + S	TIMSS	Botswana, South Africa
5	SACMEQ	P	R	PIRLS	South Africa
6	PISA	S	M + S	TIMSS	Australia, Bulgaria, Canada, Chile, Chinese Taipei, Colombia, Czech Republic, Finland, Georgia, Hong-Kong China, Hungary, Indonesia, Israel, Italy, Japan, Jordan, Kazakhstan, Republic of Korea, Latvia, Lebanon, Lithuania, North Macedonia, Malaysia, Malta, Netherlands, New Zealand, Norway, Qatar, Romania, Russian Federation, Serbia, Singapore, Slovakia, Slovenia, Sweden, Thailand, Tunisia, Turkey, USA, UAE
7	EGRA	P	R	PIRLS	Egypt, Honduras, Indonesia
8	PASEC Round I	P	M + R	SACMEQ	Mauritius
9	PASEC Round II	P	M + R	EGRA	Senegal

Notes For representation, we include countries used at any point in time for each test linking procedure. Since tests should be administered in adjacent years to be linked for a given round, some countries are not included in some rounds. This is especially the case with linking number 6. A more detailed architecture by year is available on request

The goal of linking is to summarize the difference in difficulty between two tests X and Y. We would like to link test X on the scale of test Y, which is a *Reference Test*, while test X is the *Anchored Test*. For instance, we would like to link a test like *PISA 2003* on another assessment like *TIMSS 2003*. Therefore, *PISA 2003* will be the *Anchored Test X* while *TIMSS 2003* will be the *Reference Test Y*.

Mean linking. In mean linking, *Anchored Test X* is considered to differ in difficulty from *Reference Test Y* by a constant amount along the score scale. Define *Anchored Test X* as the new test, let X represent the random variable score on score X, and let x

Table 3.17 Proportion of missing values, learning outcomes data

	01 MEAN	02 PRI	03 SEC	04 MATH	05 READ	06 SCIE	07 PRI + M	08 PRI + R	09 PRI + S	10 SEC + M	11 SEC + R	12 SEC + S	Total
1970	0.46	0.51	0.64	0.53	0.48	0.61	0.63	0.54	0.72	0.65	0.73	0.64	0.60
1975	0.43	0.49	0.64	0.53	0.46	0.61	0.63	0.51	0.73	0.65	0.73	0.64	0.59
1980	0.43	0.48	0.63	0.52	0.45	0.61	0.63	0.50	0.73	0.64	0.73	0.64	0.58
1985	0.43	0.48	0.63	0.52	0.45	0.60	0.63	0.50	0.73	0.65	0.73	0.63	0.58
1990	0.33	0.41	0.56	0.43	0.37	0.52	0.57	0.44	0.68	0.56	0.65	0.56	0.51
1995	0.33	0.41	0.56	0.42	0.36	0.52	0.55	0.44	0.67	0.56	0.65	0.56	0.50
2000	0.34	0.42	0.56	0.44	0.37	0.52	0.57	0.45	0.68	0.57	0.65	0.56	0.51
2005	0.35	0.43	0.56	0.44	0.39	0.52	0.57	0.47	0.68	0.57	0.65	0.56	0.51
2010	0.33	0.42	0.55	0.44	0.37	0.52	0.57	0.45	0.68	0.56	0.65	0.55	0.51
2015	0.32	0.40	0.55	0.43	0.35	0.52	0.57	0.44	0.68	0.56	0.64	0.55	0.50
2020	0.37	0.45	0.53	0.42	0.42	0.51	0.57	0.49	0.68	0.54	0.65	0.53	0.51
Total	0.37	0.45	0.58	0.46	0.41	0.55	0.59	0.48	0.70	0.59	0.68	0.58	0.54

Note "Mean" = mean of all existing levels and skills. "PRI" = primary level, "SEC" = secondary level, "MATH" or "M" = mathematics, "READ" or "R" = reading, "SCIE" or "R" = science

Table 3.18 Proportion of imputed values, learning outcomes data

	01 MEAN	02 PRI	03 SEC	04 MATH	05 READ	06 SCIE	07 PRI + M	08 PRI + R	09 PRI + S	10 SEC + M	11 SEC + R	12 SEC + S	Total
1970	0.84	0.86	0.75	0.81	0.83	0.77	0.82	0.86	0.76	0.75	0.70	0.75	0.80
1975	0.84	0.89	0.75	0.81	0.83	0.77	0.85	0.88	0.78	0.75	0.70	0.75	0.81
1980	0.80	0.89	0.70	0.77	0.80	0.72	0.85	0.88	0.78	0.70	0.63	0.70	0.78
1985	0.73	0.81	0.59	0.69	0.72	0.62	0.74	0.81	0.64	0.59	0.51	0.59	0.69
1990	0.71	0.72	0.68	0.66	0.69	0.59	0.64	0.71	0.53	0.68	0.62	0.68	0.67
1995	0.52	0.56	0.52	0.45	0.49	0.39	0.44	0.54	0.34	0.52	0.45	0.52	0.48
2000	0.42	0.51	0.37	0.34	0.38	0.29	0.37	0.49	0.32	0.36	0.27	0.37	0.38
2005	0.31	0.36	0.28	0.22	0.29	0.20	0.22	0.35	0.19	0.27	0.20	0.28	0.27
2010	0.11	0.21	0.11	0.07	0.11	0.04	0.14	0.20	0.10	0.08	0.06	0.11	0.11
2015	0.08	0.13	0.10	0.07	0.07	0.03	0.09	0.11	0.03	0.07	0.02	0.10	0.08
2020	0.27	0.32	0.16	0.21	0.24	0.13	0.21	0.29	0.09	0.14	0.05	0.16	0.20
Total	0.50	0.56	0.44	0.44	0.48	0.37	0.45	0.54	0.35	0.43	0.35	0.44	0.45

Note "Mean" = mean of all existing levels and skills. "PRI" = primary level, "SEC" = secondary level, "MATH" or "M" = mathematics, "READ" or "R" = reading, "SCIE" or "R" = science

Table 3.19 Variables related to the quantity of schooling and proxies for learning outcomes

Variable	Levels of schooling	Years available	% of missing values	% of imputation
Group 1—Proxies for learning outcomes with large missing values				
% of teachers who are female	All levels	2000–2020	20	41
% of qualified teachers	All levels	2000–2020	62	34
% of trained teachers	All levels	2000–2020	62	25
Group 2—Proxies for learning outcomes with few missing values				
Repetition rate	P—LS	1970–2020	21	45
Pupil-teacher ratio	All levels	1970–2020	21	35
Government expenditure per student (% of GDP per capita)	P—S—T	1970–2020	18	69
Government expenditure on education, total (% of government expenditure)	–	1970–2020	23	50
Government expenditure on education, total (% of GDP)	–	1970–2020	21	45
Group 3—Variables related to school enrollment				
Completion rate (%)	P—LS	1970–2020	11	50
Gross enrollment ratio (%)	P—LS	1970–2020	10	29
Survival rate to the last grade of primary education (%)	P	1970–2020	6	64
Total net enrollment rate (%)	P—LS	1970–2020	11	52
Out-of-school rate for each age group (%)	P—LS	1970–2020	11	53
Adjusted net enrollment rate (%)	P	1970–2020	11	55
Enrollment rate (%)	P—S—T	1970–2020	6	52
Average years of schooling, 15–64 age group	P—S—T	1970–2020	6	27
GDP per capita	–	1970–2020	13	10
Group 4—Alternative measure for learning outcomes				
Literacy data for developing countries	P	1970–2005	77	8
Adult literacy data	A	1950–2015	0	0

Note Levels of schooling are pre-primary (PP), primary (P), lower-secondary (LS), secondary (S), upper-secondary (US), tertiary (T), Adult (A). For average years of schooling, we also add "total schooling". Degree of imputation is lower for literacy variable, since data are not available for most developed countries and after 2005. Source of data and definitions are available in Table 3.14

Table 3.20 Regression of GDP per capita growth 1970–2020 on education variables, initial values

	(1)	(2)	(3)	(4)	(5)	(6)	(7)	(8)	(9)	(10)	(11)	(12)
	All countries				OECD countries				Non-OECD countries			
Initial GDP pc	−0.455***	−0.427***	−0.557***	−0.460***	−0.654**	−0.549***	−0.621***	−0.639**	−0.520***	−0.267***	−0.541***	−0.589***
	(0.133)	(0.074)	(0.088)	(0.120)	(0.243)	(0.180)	(0.217)	(0.232)	(0.169)	(0.089)	(0.116)	(0.125)
Years of Schooling	0.168***		0.079**		0.071		0.037		0.272***		0.165**	
	(0.051)		(0.037)		(0.043)		(0.040)		(0.081)		(0.063)	
Quality of Schooling		0.671***	0.574***			0.363*	0.271			0.866***	0.706***	
		(0.116)	(0.116)			(0.187)	(0.184)			(0.111)	(0.119)	
LAYS				0.225***				0.087*				0.492***
				(0.060)				(0.051)				(0.094)
Physical Capital	0.251	0.19	0.203	0.219	0.136	−0.041	−0.017	0.097	0.295**	0.278**	0.314***	0.287**
	(0.153)	(0.138)	(0.135)	(0.155)	(0.149)	(0.137)	(0.154)	(0.140)	(0.143)	(0.130)	(0.107)	(0.124)
R-squared	0.217	0.412	0.446	0.23	0.506	0.533	0.549	0.509	0.343	0.531	0.631	0.483
Countries	79	79	79	79	29	29	29	29	50	50	50	50

*** $p < 0.01$, ** $p < 0.05$, * $p < 0.1$

Data sources As described in the text. Note: Dependent variable: Growth of GDP per capita (1970–2020). Robust standard errors are in parentheses. Education variables are computed as the initial value in 1970 or the closest year represent a particular score on *Anchored Test X*. Define Test Y as the reference test, let Y represent the random variable score on *Reference Test Y*, and let y represent a particular score on Test Y. Define $\mu(X)$ as the mean on Test X and $\mu(Y)$ as the mean on *Reference Test Y* for a population of pupils. In mean linking, scores on the two tests that are an equal distance away from their respective means are set equal:

$$X - \mu(X) = Y - \mu(Y) \tag{3.10}$$

We then solve for y and obtain

$$linking_Y^m(x) = y = x - \mu(X) + \mu(Y) \tag{3.11}$$

In this equation, $linking_Y^m(x)$ refers to a score x on *Anchored Test X* transformed to the scale of *Reference Test Y* using mean equating. In other words, mean equating involves the addition of a constant $(-\mu(X)+\mu(Y))$ to all raw scores on *Anchored Test X* to find anchored scores on *Reference Test Y*. This linking methodology assumes that assessments have the same distribution, which is often unlikely.

Linear linking. Linear linking allows for the differences in difficulty between the two tests to vary along the score scale. In this case, scores that are an equal distance from their means in standard deviation units are set equal. Define $\sigma(X)$ and $\sigma(Y)$ as the standard deviations of *Anchored Test X* and *Reference Test Y*, respectively. The linear conversion sets standardized deviation scores (z-scores) on the two tests to be equal such that

$$\frac{x - \mu(X)}{\sigma(X)} = \frac{y - \mu(Y)}{\sigma(Y)} \tag{3.12}$$

Solving for y in Eq. (3.3),

$$linking_Y^l(X) = y = \sigma(Y)\left[\frac{x - \mu(X)}{\sigma(X)}\right] + \mu(Y) \tag{3.13}$$

where $linking_Y^l(X)$ is the linear conversion equation for converting observed scores on *Anchored Test X* to the scale of *Reference Test Y*. By rearranging terms, an alternate expression for $linking_Y^l(X)$ is

$$linking_Y^l(X) = y = \frac{\sigma(Y)}{\sigma(X)}x + \left[\mu(Y) - \frac{\sigma(Y)}{\sigma(X)}\mu(X)\right] \tag{3.14}$$

This expression is a linear equation of the form *slope (x)* + *intercept* with:

$$slope = \frac{\sigma(Y)}{\sigma(X)}, \textit{ and intercept} = \mu(Y) - \frac{\sigma(Y)}{\sigma(X)}\mu(X) \tag{3.15}$$

In linear linking, scores on *Anchored Test X* are adjusted, allowing for the tests to be differentially difficult along the score scale. Note that if the standard deviations for the two tests were equal, this assumes the distribution is the same, and Eq. (3.3) could be simplified to Eq. (3.2). In this case, we are left with an adjustment by a constant amount that is equal to the difference between the *Reference Test Y* and the *Anchored Test X* means, as in mean linking.

In summary, in mean linking we transform original to anchored scores by setting the deviation scores on the two tests equal, whereas in linear linking we set the standardized deviation scores (*z-scores*) on the two tests equal.

In our case, the difficulty between tests is different, especially between regional and international assessments. Thus, linear linking is best suited to our purposes. However, linear linking does not enable linking assessments over time, since assessments vary, rendering standard deviation comparisons misleading.

Pseudo-linear linking. Altinok et al. (2018) use a fusion of mean and linear linking to obtain anchored scores. This estimation method uses the difference in means in the *Anchored Test X* and *Reference Test Y* as a coefficient adjustment, which can be considered as an exchange rate between achievement tests:

$$linking_Y^{pl}(X) = y = \frac{\mu(Y)}{\mu(X)}x \tag{3.16}$$

where $linking_Y^{pl}(X)$ is the pseudo-linear conversion equation for converting observed scores on *Anchored Test X* to the scale of *Reference Test Y* and $\frac{\mu(Y)}{\mu(X)}$ can be considered as an exchange rate between the two tests. We prefer to use this hybrid approach instead of linear linking to preserve the over-time comparability of anchored tests. If we use the linear-linking approach, this limits comparability if standard deviations are not stable over time, as is often the case.

Hanushek and Woessmann (2012) adopt a similar approach, but adjust the coefficient with both means and standard deviations:

$$linking_Y^{pl2}(X) = y = \left[\frac{\mu(Y)}{\mu(X)} \times \frac{\sigma(Y)}{\sigma(X)}\right]x \tag{3.17}$$

where $linking_Y^{pl2}(X)$ is the pseudo-linear conversion equation for converting observed scores on *Anchored Test X* to the scale of *Reference Test Y*. The main drawback of this methodology is the potential variation in standard deviations for a given country over time. This assumption is particularly tenuous for developing countries, limiting the ability to make credible comparisons of education quality over time.

Equipercentile linking. Equipercentile linking was developed by Braun P.W. (1982). Equipercentile linking is best used when X and Y differ nonlinearly in difficulty. For instance, *Anchored Test X* could be more difficult than *Reference Test Y* for high scores but less difficult for low scores. The equipercentile linking function is developed by identifying scores on *Anchored Test X* that have the same percentile ranks as scores on *Reference Test Y*. Consider the following definitions of terms, where X and Y are continuous random variables.

F(x) is the cumulative distribution function of *X* in the population. This is defined as the proportion of examinees in each population who score at or below *x* on test X for a given population *T*. Formally: $F(x) = P\{X \leq x|T\}$ where $P\{.|T\}$ is the probability or population proportion in each population *T*.

G(y) is the cumulative distribution function of *Y* in the population. This is defined as the proportion of examinees in each population who score at or below *y* on test Y for a given population *T*. Formally: $G(y) = P\{Y \leq y|T\}$ where $P\{.|T\}$ is the probability or population proportion in each population *T*.

In equipercentile linking, we set the cumulative distributions of X and Y equal:

$$F(x) = G(y) \tag{3.18}$$

When the cumulative distribution functions are continuous and strictly increasing, we can always solve for y:

$$linking_Y^e(X) = G^{-1}[F(x) \tag{3.19}$$

where G^{-1} is the inverse of the cumulative distribution function *G(y)*.

In summary, equipercentile linking is broken down into three main steps: we first find the percentile rank of *x* in the *Anchored Test X* distribution. Then we find the score that has the same percentile rank in the *Reference Test Y* distribution. Then we find the equivalent score of *Reference Test Y* for *Reference Test* X based on their common percentile.

A limitation of simple equipercentile linking is that when score scales are discrete, which is the case for ISATs and RSATs, we are not able to find corresponding scores for test scores or percentiles not observed in the sample. For example, if in the observed sample, the closest percentile matches are a score with a 47.2 percentile on *Reference Test X* and a score on *Reference Test Y* with a 47.6 percentile, we have rough equivalence, but do not have an exact percentile match.

One approach to dealing with this limitation is to use percentile ranks. However, this might not yield adequate precision. Moreover, this approach does not enable future linking above the highest or lowest observed scores used for equating. Increasing sample sizes can alleviate these concerns to an extent, but is often insufficient. To this end, smoothing methods have been developed to deal with sampling error and produce estimates of the empirical distributions and equipercentile relationship best characterizing the underlying population. This enables interpolation at each point on the curve, enhancing the precision of the equating exercise.

Two general types of smoothing can be conducted. In *presmoothing*, the score distributions are smoothed using polynomial loglinear presmoothing (Holland & Thayer, 2000); in *postsmoothing*, the equipercentile equivalents are smoothed using cubic-spline postsmoothing (Kolen, 1984). We use the *presmoothing* loglinear method, which is the method used by the ETS, and is based on Von Davier and Yamamoto (2004) and (Holland & Thayer, 1987, 2000).[38]

Three assumptions must hold for the linking methods above to be valid. First, they must test the same underlying population. Given that we are using sample-based ISATs and RSATs and equate using overlapping countries, this assumption is satisfied if the population tested is similar and participation rates reach a certain threshold or non-participation is random. Second, tests should measure similar proficiencies. We link across precise dimensions such as subject and schooling level (primary vs. secondary) to increase the likelihood of proficiency overlap. Finally, the distribution of proficiency should be similar across tests. We address this assumption by equating using an average across countries that participate in both tests. The reliability of the equating exercise is enhanced with an increase in the number of countries that take both tests being equated. We include robustness checks to demonstrate the sensitivity of our results to this effect. We also include confidence intervals for our estimates to quantify the degree of uncertainty.

In order to obtain comparable means scores across achievement tests, we use pseudo-linear linking, also called the "exchange rate" approach. This methodology enables credible over-time comparisons, a central feature of our panel dataset, and is consistent with a growing literature in economics on globally comparable education quality data.

References

AERA NCME, A. P. A. (1999). The standards for educational and psychological testing. *American Psychological Association.*

Aghion, P., Howitt, P., Brant-Collett, M., & García-Peñalosa, C. (1998). *Endogenous growth theory.* MIT press.

Albano, A. D. (2016). Equate: An R package for observed-score linking and equating. *Journal of Statistical Software, 74*(8), 1–36.

Altinok, N. (2017). Mind the Gap: Proposal for the standardized measure for SDG4-Education 2030 Agenda. *UIS Information Paper, 46.*

Altinok, N., Angrist, N., & Patrinos, H. A. (2018). Global data set on education quality (1965–2015). *World Bank Policy Research Working Paper, 8314.*

Altinok, N., & Aydemir, A. (2017). Does one size fit all? The impact of cognitive skills on economic growth. *Journal of Macroeconomics, 53*, 176–190. https://doi.org/10.1016/j.jmacro.2017.06.007

Altinok, N., & Diebolt, C. (2024). Cliometrics of learning-adjusted years of schooling: Evidence from a new dataset. *Cliometrica, 18(3)*, 691–764. https://doi.org/10.1007/s11698-023-00276-x

Altinok, N., Diebolt, C., & Demeulemeester, J.-L. (2014). A new international database on education quality: 1965–2010. *Applied Economics, 46*(11), 1212–1247.

Altinok, N., & Murseli, H. (2007). International database on human capital quality. *Economics Letters, 96*(2), 237–244. https://doi.org/10.1016/j.econlet.2007.01.009

Angrist, N., Djankov, S., Goldberg, P. K., & Patrinos, H. A. (2021). Measuring human capital using global learning data. *Nature, 592*(7854), 403–408.

[38] We used R Statistics software for the equipercentile linking. In particular, we use the "equate" package. See Albano (2016) for more information.

Angrist, N., Patrinos, H. A., & Schlotter, M. (2013). An expansion of a global data set on educational quality: A focus on achievement in developing countries. *The World Bank: Policy Research Working Papers*. https://doi.org/10.1596/1813-9450-6536
Arellano, M., & Bover, O. (1995). Another look at the instrumental variable estimation of error-components models. *Journal of Econometrics, 68*(1), 29–51.
ASER. (2021). *Annual status of education report 2021*. ASER Centre. http://www.asercentre.org/Keywords/p/394.html
Avvisati, F. (2021). *How much do 15-year-olds learn over one year of schooling?* OECD Publishing.
Barro, R. J., & Lee, J.-W. (2013). A new data set of educational attainment in the world, 1950–2010. *Journal of Development Economics, 104*, 184–198.
Bloom, B. S., & (DHEW), O. of E. (1969). *Cross-National study of educational attainment: Stage I of the IEA investigation in six subject areas* (Vol. II). The IEA.
Blundell, R., & Bond, S. (1998). Initial conditions and moment restrictions in dynamic panel data models. *Journal of Econometrics, 87*(1), 115–143.
Bold, T., Filmer, D., Martin, G., Molina, E., Stacy, B., Rockmore, C., Svensson, J., & Wane, W. (2017). Enrollment without learning: Teacher effort, knowledge, and skill in primary schools in Africa. *Journal of Economic Perspectives, 31*(4), 185–204. https://doi.org/10.1257/jep.31.4.185
Braun P.W., H. I. H. (1982). Observed-score test equating: A mathematical analysis of some ETS equating procedures. In P. W. H. & D. B. Rubin (Ed.), *Test equating* (pp. 9–49). Academic.
Burstein, L. (1992). *The IEA study of mathematics III: Student growth and classroom processes*. Elsevier.
Campbell, K., & Mullis, M. (2001). *Framework and spesifications for PIRLS assesment*.
Casassus, J., Froemel, J. E., Palafox, J. C., & Cusato, S. (1998). *First international comparative study of language, mathematics, and associated factors in third and fourth grade*. Latin American Laboratory for Evaluation of the Quality of Education.
Chinapah, V., H'ddigui, E. M., Kanjee, A., Falayajo, W., Fomba, C. O., Hamissou, O., Rafalimanana, A., & Byomugisha, A. (2000). *With Africa for Africa. Towards quality education for All. 1999 MLA project*. ERIC. https://files.eric.ed.gov/fulltext/ED444931.pdf
Comber, L. C., & Keeves, J. P. (1973). *Science education in nineteen countries*. IEA.
Das, J., & Zajonc, T. (2010). India shining and Bharat drowning: Comparing two Indian states to the worldwide distribution in mathematics achievement. *Journal of Development Economics, 92*(2), 175–187.
De la Fuente, A., & Doménech, R. (2021). Cross-country data on skills and the quality of schooling: A selective survey. *Available at SSRN 3975955*.
Demirgüç-Kunt, A., & Torre, I. (2022). Measuring human capital in middle income countries. *Journal of Comparative Economics, 50*(4), 1036–1067.
Diebolt, C. (2016). *Cliometrica after 10 years: Definition and principles of cliometric research* (Vol. 10, pp. 1–4). Springer.
Diebolt, C., & Haupert, M. (2019a). *Handbook of Cliometrics* (C. S. Reference, Ed., 2nd ed., Vol. 2). Springer Nature.
Diebolt, C., & Haupert, M. (2019b). Measuring success: Clio and the value of database creation. *Annali Della Fondazione Luigi Einaudi, 53*(2), 59–79.
Diebolt, C., & Haupert, M. (2020). How cliometrics has infiltrated economics—And helped to improve the discipline. *Annali della Fondazione Luigi Einaudi, 54*(1), 219–230.
Diebolt, C., & Haupert, M. (2021). Cliometrics: Past, present, and future. In *Oxford Research Encyclopedia of Economics and Finance*. Oxford University Press. https://doi.org/10.1093/acrefore/9780190625979.013.552
Diebolt, C., & Haupert, M. (2022a). Cliometrics and the future of economic history. *Essays in Economic & Business History, 40*, 1–20.
Diebolt, C., & Haupert, M. (2022b). The Role of cliometrics in history and economics. In *Bloomsbury History: Theory and Method*. Bloomsbury Publishing.
Diebolt, C., Haupert, M., & Springer. (2019). Handbook of Cliometrics. In *Springer References* (2nd ed.). Springer Nature.

Dunn, L. (1959). *Series of plates for the Peabody picture vocabulary test.* American Guidance Service, Inc.
Elley, W. B. (1994). *The IEA study of reading literacy: Achievement and instruction in thirty-two school systems.* Pergamon Press.
Filmer, D., Rogers, H., Angrist, N., & Sabarwal, S. (2020). Learning-adjusted years of schooling (LAYS): Defining a new macro measure of education. *Economics of Education Review, 77*, Article 101971.
Flotts, M. P., Manzi, J., Jiménez, D., Abarzúa, A., Cayuman, C., & García, M. J. (2015). *Informe de resultados TERCE: logros de aprendizaje.* OREALC. https://unesdoc.unesco.org/notice?id=p::usmarcdef_0000243532
Foshay, A. W., Thorndike, R. L., Hotyat, F., Pidgeon, D. A., & Walker, D. A. (1962). *Educational achievements of thirteen-year olds in twelve countries: Results of an international research project, 1959–61* (Vol. 4). Unesco.
Gakidou, E., Cowling, K., Lozano, R., & Murray, C. J. L. (2010). Increased educational attainment and its effect on child mortality in 175 countries between 1970 and 2009: A systematic analysis. *The Lancet, 376*(9745), 959–974.
Garden, R. A. (1987). The second IEA mathematics study. *Comparative Education Review, 31*(1), 47–68.
Glawe, L., & Wagner, H. (2022). Is schooling the same as learning?—The impact of the learning-adjusted years of schooling on growth in a dynamic panel data framework. *World Development, 151*, Article 105773.
Gustafsson, M. A. (2014). *Education and country growth models.* Stellenbosch University.
Hanushek, E. A. (2002). Publicly provided education. *Handbook of Public Economics, 4*, 2045–2141.
Hanushek, E. A., & Kimko, D. D. (2000). Schooling, labor-force quality, and the growth of nations. *The American Economic Review, 90*(5), 1184.
Hanushek, E. A., Ruhose, J., & Woessmann, L. (2017). Economic gains from educational reform by US States. *Journal of Human Capital, 11*(4), 447–486.
Hanushek, E. A., & Woessmann, L. (2007). The Role of school improvement in economic development. *NBER Working Papers, 12832.*
Hanushek, E. A., & Woessmann, L. (2008). The role of cognitive skills in economic development. *Journal of Economic Literature, 46*(3), 607–668.
Hanushek, E. A., & Woessmann, L. (2012). Do better schools lead to more growth? Cognitive skills, economic outcomes, and causation. *Journal of Economic Growth, 17*(4), 267–321. https://doi.org/10.1007/s10887-012-9081-x
Hanushek, E. A., & Woessmann, L. (2015). *The knowledge capital of nations: Education and the economics of growth.* MIT Press.
Holland, P. W., & Dorans, N. J. (2006). Linking and equating. *Educational Measurement, 4*, 187–220.
Holland, P. W., & Hoskens, M. (2003). Classical test theory as a first-order item response theory: Application to true-score prediction from a possibly nonparallel test. *Psychometrika, 68*(1), 123–149.
Holland, P. W., & Thayer, D. T. (1987). Notes on the use of log-linear models for fitting discrete probability distributions. *ETS Research Report Series, 1987*(2), i–40.
Holland, P. W., & Thayer, D. T. (2000). Univariate and bivariate loglinear models for discrete test score distributions. *Journal of Educational and Behavioral Statistics, 25*(2), 133–183.
Honaker, J., King, G., & Blackwell, M. (2011). Amelia II: A program for missing data. *Journal of Statistical Software, 45*(1), 1–47.
International Association for the Evaluation of Educational Achievement. (1988). *Science achievement in seventeen countries. A preliminary report.* IEA.
Keeves, J. P., & A, I. E. (1992). *Learning science in a changing world. Cross-National studies of science achievement: 1970 to 1984.* IEA.

Kolen, M. J. (1984). Effectiveness of analytic smoothing in equipercentile equating. *Journal of Educational Statistics, 9*(1), 25–44.
Kolen, M. J., & Brennan, R. L. (2014). *Test equating, scaling, and linking: Methods and practices.* Springer Science & Business Media.
Kraay, A. C. (2018). Methodology for a World Bank human capital index. In *Policy Research Working Paper* (Vol. WPS8593). The World Bank.
Le Nestour, A., Moscoviz, L., & Sandefur, J. (2022). The long-run decline of education quality in the developing world. In C. for G. Development (Ed.), *CGD Working Paper 608.* https://www.cgdev.org/publication/long-rundecline-education-quality-developing-world
Lee, J., & Barro, R. J. (2001). Schooling quality in a cross–section of countries. *Economica, 68*(272), 465–488.
Lee, J.-W., & Lee, H. (2016). Human capital in the long run. *Journal of Development Economics, 122*, 147–169.
Lim, S. S., Updike, R. L., Kaldjian, A. S., Barber, R. M., Cowling, K., York, H., Friedman, J., Xu, R., Whisnant, J. L., & Taylor, H. J. (2018). Measuring human capital: A systematic analysis of 195 countries and territories, 1990–2016. *The Lancet, 392*(10154), 1217–1234.
Linn, R. L. (1993). Educational assessment: Expanded expectations and challenges. *Educational Evaluation and Policy Analysis, 15*(1), 1–16.
Livingstone, I. (1986). *Second international mathematics study: Perceptions of the intended and implemented mathematics curriculum.* Office of Educational Research and Improvement, US Department of Education.
Lucas, R. (1988). On the mechanics of economic development. *Journal of Monetary Economics, 22*(1), 3–42. https://EconPapers.repec.org/RePEc:eee:moneco:v:22:y:1988:i:1:p:3-42
Mankiw, N. G., Romer, D., & Weil, D. N. (1992). A contribution to the empirics of economic growth. *The Quarterly Journal of Economics, 107*(2), 407–437.
Martin, M. O., Mullis, I. V. S., Foy, P., & Stanco, G. M. (2012). *TIMSS 2011 International Results in Science.* TIMSS International Study Center.
Martin, M. O., Mullis, I. V. S., & Kennedy, A. M. (2007). *Progress in International Reading Literacy Study (PIRLS): PIRLS 2006 Technical Report.* ERIC.
McEwan, P. J. (2015). Improving learning in primary schools of developing countries: A meta-analysis of randomized experiments. *Review of Educational Research, 85*(3), 353–394.
Mislevy, R. J. (1992). *Linking educational assessments: Concepts, issues, methods, and prospects.*
Mourshed, M., Chijioke, C., & Barber, M. (2010). *How the world's best performing school systems keep getting better*. McKinsey.
Mullis, I., Martin, M. O., Foy, P., Kelly, D. L., & Fishbein, B. (2020). TIMSS 2019 international results in mathematics and science. In *Retrieved from Boston College, TIMSS & PIRLS International Study Center website:* https://timssandpirls.bc.edu/timss2019/international-results; https://timss2019.org/reports/wp-content/themes/timssandpirls/download-center/TIMSS-2019-International-Results-in-Mathematics-and-Science.pdf
Mullis, I. V. S., Martin, M. O., & Foy, P. (2008). TIMSS 2007 international mathematics report. Findings from IEA's Trends in International Mathematics and Science Study at the Fourth and Eighth Grades. *International Mathematics Report. TIMSS&PIRLS International Study Center, Boston College.*
Mullis, I. V. S., Martin, M. O., Foy, P., & Arora, A. (2012a). *TIMSS 2011 international results in mathematics.* ERIC.
Mullis, I. V. S., Martin, M. O., Foy, P., & Arora, A. (2012b). *TIMSS 2011 international results in mathematics.* ERIC.
Mullis, I. V. S., Martin, M. O., Foy, P., & Drucker, K. T. (2012c). *PIRLS 2011 international results in reading.* ERIC.
Mullis, I. V. S., Martin, M. O., Foy, P., & Hooper, M. (2016). *TIMSS 2015 international results in mathematics.* ERIC.
Mullis, I. V. S., Martin, M. O., Foy, P., & Hooper, M. (2017). *PIRLS 2016 International Results in Reading.* International Association for the Evaluation of Educational Achievement.

Mullis, I. V. S., Martin, M. O., Gonzalez, E. J., & Chrostowski, S. J. (2004). *TIMSS 2003 International Mathematics Report: Findings from IEA's Trends in International Mathematics and Science Study at the Fourth and Eighth Grades*. ERIC.
Mullis, I. V. S., Martin, M. O., Gonzalez, E. J., Gregory, K. D., Garden, R. A., O'Connor, K. M., Chrostowski, S. J., & Smith, T. A. (2000). *TIMSS 1999 international mathematics report*. Boston: International Study Center, Lynch School of Education, Boston College.
Mullis, I. V. S., Martin, M. O., Gonzalez, E. J., & Kennedy, A. M. (2003). *PIRLS 2001 international report*. International Association for the Evaluation of Educational Achievement.
Mullis M.O. Foy P. & Hooper M., I. V. M. (2016a). *TIMSS 2015 International Results in Mathematics*.
Mullis M.O., Foy P., & Hooper M., I. V. M. (2016b). *TIMSS 2015 International Results in Science*.
National Academies of Sciences, E., & Medicine. (2017). *Evaluation of the achievement levels for mathematics and reading on the National Assessment of Educational Progress*. National Academies Press.
OECD. (2004). *Learning for tomorrow's world: First Results from PISA 2003*. OECD Publishing.
OECD. (2007). *PISA 2006: Science Competencies for Tomorrow's World*. OECD Publishing.
OECD. (2010a). *PISA 2009 results: Learning trends: changes in student performance since 2000* (vol. v). OECD Publishing.
OECD. (2010b). *PISA 2009 results: What students know and can do: Student performance in reading*. OECD Publishing.
OECD. (2013). *PISA 2012 results: What students know and can do* (Rev. ed., Vol. 1, February 2014). OECD Publishing. https://doi.org/10.1787/9789264208780-en
OECD. (2016). *PISA 2015 Results* (Vol. I). OECD Publishing. https://doi.org/10.1787/9789264266490-en
OECD. (2019). *PISA 2018 results* (Vol. I). OECD Publishing. https://doi.org/10.1787/5f07c754-en
OECD. (2021). *Education at a Glance 2021*. OECD Publishing. https://doi.org/10.1787/b35a14e5-en
OECD. (2023). *PISA 2022 results* (Vol. I). OECD. https://doi.org/10.1787/53f23881-en
Olson, J. F., Martin, M. O., & Mullis, I. V. S. (2008). *TIMSS 2007 technical report*. TIMSS & PIRLS International Study Center.
Patrinos, H. A., & Angrist, N. (2018). Global dataset on education quality: A review and update (2000–2017). In *Policy Research Working Paper*. The World Bank.
Peaker, G. F. (1975). *An empirical study of education in twenty-one countries: A technical report. International Studies in Evaluation VIII*. Almqvist and Wiksell.
Raju, N. S. (1988). The area between two item characteristic curves. *Psychometrika, 53*(4), 495–502.
Raven, J. C. (1936). *Mental tests used in genetic, The performance of related indiviuals on tests mainly educative and mainly reproductive* (MSC Thesis). University London.
Robitaille, D. F., & Garden, R. A. (1989). *The IEA study of mathematics II: Contexts and outcomes of school mathematics* (Vol. 2). Pergamon.
Sandefur, J. (2016). *Internationally comparable mathematics scores for Fourteen African Countries*.
Schleicher, A. (2019). *PISA 2018: Insights and Interpretations*. In OECD Publishing.
Thorndike, R. L. (1973). *Reading comprehension education in Fifteen Countries: An empirical study*. (I. I. I. International Studies in Evaluation, Ed.). Almqvist and Wiksell.
Treviño, E., Fraser, P., Meyer, A., Morawietz, L., Inostroza, P., & Naranjo, E. (2015). *Informe de resultados TERCE: factores asociados*. OREALC. https://unesdoc.unesco.org/notice?id=p::usmarcdef_0000243533
Treviño, E., & OREALC. (2014). *Factors associated with student achievement. Results of the Second Comparative and Explanatory Regional Study (SERCE)*.
UNESCO Institute of Statistics. (2019a). Costs and Benefits of Different Approaches to Measuring the Learning Proficiency of Students. *UIS Information Paper, 53*. http://uis.unesco.org/sites/default/files/documents/ip53-costs-benefits-approaches-measuring-proficiency-2019-en.pdf
UNESCO Institute of Statistics. (2019b). How Fast Can Levels of Proficiency Improve ? Examining Historical Trends to Inform SDG 4.1.1 Scenarios. *UIS Information Paper, 62*.

UNESCO/Unicef, & OREALC/UNESCO. (2021). *Los aprendizajes fundamentales en América Latina y el Caribe. Evaluación de logros de los estudiantes. Estudio Regional Comparativo y Explicativo (ERCE 2019).*

Uwezo. (2014). *Are our children learning? Literacy and Numeracy Across East Africa.* Uwezo East Africa.

Von Davier, M., & Yamamoto, K. (2004). Partially observed mixtures of IRT models: An extension of the generalized partial-credit model. *Applied Psychological Measurement, 28*(6), 389–406.

Vos, T., Abajobir, A. A., Abate, K. H., Abbafati, C., Abbas, K. M., Abd-Allah, F., Abdulkader, R. S., Abdulle, A. M., Abebo, T. A., & Abera, S. F. (2017). Global, regional, and national incidence, prevalence, and years lived with disability for 328 diseases and injuries for 195 countries, 1990–2016: A systematic analysis for the Global Burden of Disease Study 2016. *The Lancet, 390*(10100), 1211–1259.

Wagner, D. A. (2011). *Smaller, quicker, cheaper: Improving learning assessments for developing countries.* UNESCO.

Wagner, D. A. (2017). Children's Reading in Low-Income Countries. *The Reading Teacher, 71*(2), 127–133.

Walker, D. A., Arnold, A. C., & Wolf, R. M. (1976). The IEA six subject survey: An emprical study of education in twenty-one countries. *International Studies in Evaluation; IX.*

Wechsler, D. (1949). *Wechsler intelligence scale for children : manual.* Psychological Corp.

Westbury, I., & Travers, K. (1990). *Second international mathematics study.* University of Illinois.

World Bank. (2018). *World development report 2018: Learning to realize education's promise.* The World Bank.

Wu, M. (2010). Comparing the Similarities and Differences of PISA 2003 and TIMSS. *OECD Education Working Papers, 32*, 0–1.

Chapter 4
Mapping Educational Inequality Worldwide

Abstract This chapter introduces the first international, long-term database of skill equity, harmonizing student achievement surveys to enable robust cross-country and temporal comparisons. By moving beyond averages, our multidimensional approach captures inequalities across socio-economic groups and performance thresholds. The findings reveal stark contrasts between regions and demonstrate that high performance and equity can indeed coexist, reshaping our understanding of both the efficiency and fairness of education systems worldwide.

4.1 Introduction

Today, perhaps more than ever, many countries are faced with a twofold challenge: how to keep up with international competition, while at the same time preserving real equity within their populations. Education is at the heart of this challenge. As a major factor in boosting productivity and hence economic growth, the expectations placed on schools are enormous. Not only must it train productive future workers, it must also meet democratic demands for equity.

Equitable access to education has been mentioned several times in international conventions. The 1948 Universal Declaration of Human Rights and the 1966 International Covenant on Economic, Social and Cultural Rights state that education must be equally accessible to all on the basis of merit and individual capacity (United Nations, 2017a, 2017b).

Beyond human rights and justice issues, there are numerous studies demonstrating the economic and social benefits of education (Hanushek & Woessmann, 2012; UNESCO, 2014). Work linked to human capital theory and the returns to education has highlighted that increased schooling is associated with better individual incomes, reduced poverty as well as more sustained growth in the wealth of Nations (Becker, 1975, 2002).

With the adoption of the Sustainable Development Goals (SDGs) as well as the 2015 Education 2030 Framework for Action, equity has received particular attention on the international agenda. In the field of education, SDG 4 calls on UN members

N. Altinok and C. Diebolt, *Edumetrics*, Population Economics,
https://doi.org/10.1007/978-3-032-13277-2_4

to "ensure inclusive and equitable quality education and promote lifelong learning opportunities for all" (United Nations, 2015).

Our work aims to provide original data on skills equity. The present work focuses more on the equity of education systems via a multidimensional measure. Following the work of Jacob and Holsinger (2008, p. 4), we define equality as "*the state of being equal in terms of quantity, rank, status, value or degree*", while equity "*considers the social justice ramifications of education in relation to the fairness, justness and impartiality of its distribution at all levels or educational sub-sectors*".

Our work is the first to propose equity indicators for skills, from both an international and a temporal perspective. Other databases exist, but only use data from homogeneous sources, which greatly reduces the number of countries, the temporal scope and the dimensions of educational inequality. One example is UNESCO's World Inequality Database on Education (WIDE), which compiles data on various aspects of education, but does not perform anchoring and adjustment analysis. Although a large amount of data is available on the WIDE website,[1] it mainly comes from household surveys such as DHS (Demographic Health Surveys) or MICS (Multiple Indicator Cluster Surveys). Furthermore, no data harmonization is proposed, which severely limits the use of such data. Other organizations collect similar data, without however having a general and comparative vision. For example, EDPC-FHI 360 (Education Policy and Data Center—Family Health International) collects a wide range of data on education in general, and gender inequality in particular. Organizations such as the OECD and UIS-UNESCO[2] carry out similar work. However, no international database on inequalities currently exists. The data presented above is mainly a compilation of results from household surveys or general education statistics.

In our study, we propose to bring together all surveys of student achievement in order to obtain a comparable international basis. Our methodology is mainly based on the original approach developed in Altinok and Diebolt (2024). The main added value of our work concerns the unequal dimension of school skills. Indeed, most previous work has focused on the average performance of education systems. However, it seems increasingly important to question the potential gaps that may exist between different strata of the population. Several lines of analysis are being explored, ranging from the analysis of the gap between deciles (similar to the approach developed by Piketty [2013]), using different performance thresholds, but also using a more conventional approach to the gaps between students' socio-economic levels.

We believe that this work contributes to the analysis of school inequalities in three ways. The first is the temporal and comparative approach of our study, which combines the advantages of longitudinal and cross-sectional studies. The database we have built enables us to compare inequalities in school skills not only between countries, but also over time (between 1970 and 2020). This dual dimension represents a significant advance for future analyses including educational inequalities. Secondly, we use several indicators and methodological approaches to inequalities,

[1] The address is https://www.education-inequalities.org/ (accessed on 13/06/2025).

[2] The OECD offers various statistics on educational inequality via its data portal.

thus improving the robustness of the results found. As a rule, data on inequalities cover only one dimension. However, the many limitations often call into question the robustness of analyses. By allowing multiple variables measuring the same concept of inequality to be crossed, we improve the robustness of our data. A three-pronged approach is used, which may or may not confirm major trends in qualitative democratization. Finally, our study uses an original historical approach in education, both quantitative and trend-finding, enabling us to bypass the problems of measurement error often inherent in international surveys.

The results shed new light on the intersection between quality and equity in education systems. The database provides a global and regional ranking of countries according to the quality and equity of their education systems. Asian countries such as Singapore and South Korea dominate, while sub-Saharan Africa lags behind. Analysis of skill thresholds slightly alters the overall ranking, with Russia and Finland coming out on top, depending on the indicators. Finally, equity adjusted by school access and completion nuances the results, revealing unexpected cases such as Cambodia and Indonesia.

Analysis of educational inequalities according to socio-economic status reveals marked discrepancies, particularly in Western countries, despite their high average performance. In sub-Saharan Africa, inequalities are less marked, but performance is very low, particularly for disadvantaged pupils. Latin America shows the greatest gaps between rich and poor pupils, especially for the advanced proficiency threshold. Only developed and Asian countries enable disadvantaged pupils to achieve high levels of performance. Countries such as Finland and the United States show that it is possible to combine performance and equity, unlike France and Turkey, where inequalities remain very marked.

Educational inequalities are multiple and cannot be summed up in a single dimension. Some countries, such as France and Belgium, have high levels of inequality in several indicators. Others, like Iceland or Japan, manage to maintain a low level of inequality whatever the measure used. Finally, countries such as Finland, Ireland and Canada combine high performance with strong equity, showing that efficiency and justice are not incompatible.

The hypothesis of equity convergence is generally confirmed, particularly in OECD countries, where initially highly unequal countries are progressing less rapidly than others. Adjustment of the equity index by school completion rates shows a more marked convergence in the long term, especially in developing countries. Sub-Saharan Africa is a good example of this trend, thanks to the increasing democratization of education. However, some countries, such as Thailand and Malaysia, are seeing a decline in equity, revealing contrasting trajectories depending on the region.

In order to carry out this project, we first present the original data produced on inequalities in educational attainment. The methodology used to construct the data is described, followed by a general analysis of inequalities. Finally, we explore some questions that can be addressed with the data constructed.

4.2 Data and Methodology

4.2.1 Data: Youth and Adult Skills Surveys

The assessment of the extent of inequalities is based on the dimension of learning achievement, measured through an exercise in standardization of international surveys. The international database on student learning mobilizes results from various international (TIMSS, PIRLS and PISA[3]), regional (PASEC, LLECE, SACMEQ and EGRA[4]) or hybrid (EGRA[5]) surveys. Other assessments focus on adult skills (IALS, PIAAC[6]). We present these surveys very briefly. Further information can be found in works on the quality of education (Altinok & Diebolt, 2024).

The international assessments are by far the ones that cover the most countries, and the ones that have been the driving force behind the other assessments. We will briefly present these assessments below. The first internationally comparable measures of individual achievement were initiated in the early 1960s by the International Association for the Evaluation of Educational Achievement (IEA). Less well known to the general public, these assessments began with the participation of OECD countries in a variety of fields, although mathematics, science and reading were among the most widely tested. From the 1990s onwards, IEA assessments adopted the *item* response theory method. This transformation enabled the assessments to be comparable over time, but also to have more skill areas tested (by means of "cahiers tournants", which consist in testing only part of all the items with the students, and thus having a higher total number of items submitted to the students than in tests based on the so-called classic theory, see in particular Bertrand and Blais, 2004). The TIMSS assessment began in 1995, focusing on mathematics and science. Since then, several waves of tests have been carried out every 4 years.[7] The IEA has also been assessing students' literacy skills since the 1970s. However, it was the PIRLS survey that brought young people's literacy skills to the fore. The assessment evaluates the skills of grade 4 students every 5 years, starting in 2001.[8] Alongside the IEA surveys, it is the PISA assessment that has received the most media coverage, particularly in Europe. PISA is an assessment developed by the OECD and launched in 2000. Testing 15-year-old

[3] Respectively *Trends on International Mathematics and Science Study*, *Progress on International Reading Literacy Study* and *Programme for International Student Assessment*.

[4] Respectively Programme d'Analyse des Systèmes Educatifs de la Confemen, Laboratorio Latinoamericano de Evaluación de la Calidad de la Educación, Southern and Eastern Africa Consortium for Monitoring Educational Quality…

[5] Early Grade Reading Assessment.

[6] Respectively *International Adult Literacy Survey* and *Programme for the International Assessment of Adult Competencies*.

[7] The second wave can be found in 1999, then 2003, 2007… The latest wave with available data is 2019.

[8] The different test waves are 2001, 2006, 2011, 2016 and 2021. As the data for PIRLS 2021 have not been fully published at the time of writing, we include only temporary results, based on average country scores.

students in three skill areas (mathematics, science and literacy), PISA has become the survey covering the most countries in the world. Organized every 3 years, seven different waves have been carried out up to 2018, with over 70 countries participating in the latest wave.

Aware that international assessments were not adapted to their audiences, some countries joined forces in the 90s to organize regional surveys. Two surveys concern the African continent. While PASEC focuses mainly on French-speaking countries, SACMEQ[9] brings together English-speaking countries. Several waves of PASEC tests have been carried out, but it is above all the last two waves in 2014 and 2019 that have adopted the standards of international assessments. The SACMEQ survey was more prolific when it began in 1995, but seems to have slowed down, following methodological problems.[10] On the Latin American continent, the LLECE organization has also carried out 4 different waves of tests on primary school pupils in some fifteen countries, including Mexico and Honduras.

In addition to international and regional assessments, there is also a hybrid assessment that focuses on developing countries, irrespective of the continent to which they belong. The EGRA test is a rapid assessment of pupils' reading ability in the early grades. With dozens of countries having participated in this assessment, it was important to include it in our measurement of literacy skills. Adult skills surveys (IALS and PIAAC) can also be useful in better assessing students' skills. Using a specific methodology, some authors have in fact obtained panel data of young adults' skill levels (Schwerdt & Wiederhold, 2019). Most developing countries organize household surveys, most often financed by the World Bank or UNICEF. These surveys include tests in reading and mathematics. A recent study pooled most of the results from participating countries to obtain comparable literacy scores across several countries (Le Nestour et al., 2022).

All the surveys used to obtain the database can be found in Table 4.8 (Appendix A). Below, we discuss the methodology used to produce the database.

4.2.2 General Methodology

Before preparing data on specific sub-samples or thresholds, our work required the construction of an international database on the quality of education systems. The detailed methodology of our approach can be found in Altinok and Diebolt (2024). Below, we present the general approach very briefly, before moving on to the dimension of educational inequalities proper.

---

[9] SACMEQ changed its name a few years ago to SEACMEQ (The Southern and Eastern Africa Consortium for Monitoring Educational Quality).

[10] There is no critical study of the fourth wave of SACMEQ, but the lack of publication of the results indicates unease about methodological difficulties. A critical publication by Nic Spaull sheds some light on these limitations. See https://nicspaull.com/2016/09/14/serious-technical-concerns-about-sacmeq-iv-results-presented-to-parliament/ (accessed June 19, 2025).

One of the main challenges we face in analyzing assessments of student learning is the lack of comparability between these different surveys. It is often difficult, if not impossible, to make reliable comparisons, not only between the surveys themselves, but also between different waves of the same survey. This heterogeneity compromises the interpretation of results and limits the scope of the conclusions that can be drawn from them.

Our study aims to overcome this difficulty by mapping the international surveys presented in the previous section, through the development of common scales. Given the methodological and conceptual diversity of student achievement surveys, it is imperative that a rigorous adjustment strategy be put in place to enable their alignment. In the absence of such an adjustment, any attempt to compare countries that have participated in different assessments would introduce substantial biases. For example, a country could obtain a higher score in one survey than in another, not because of any real improvement in performance, but simply because of a lower level of difficulty in the survey in question. A direct comparison, without adjustment, between the results of two surveys carried out at different times could thus lead to erroneous interpretations, such as an artificial drop in student levels.

To ensure comparability both between countries and over time, our approach is based on harmonizing the various international and regional surveys, using common measurement scales. This harmonization requires a specific methodology, based on the exploitation of data from countries that participated simultaneously in several surveys conducted over the same period (cf. Angrist et al., 2021). These overlaps constitute an essential anchor point for establishing robust statistical equivalences between the different assessments.

By combining data from countries that have participated in several international assessments, it is possible to estimate conversion rates between the different surveys, analogous to exchange rates between currencies. This methodological approach, used to harmonize the scores of assessments conducted since the 1990s, has been mobilized in several previous works (Angrist et al., 2013; Filmer et al., 2018; Gust et al., 2022). Complementing this method, a temporal anchoring strategy was implemented to link older surveys—particularly those conducted before the 1990s—with more recent ones. Inspired by the pioneering work of Hanushek and Kimko (2000), this strategy is based on the use of US results from the National Assessment of Educational Progress (NAEP) as a reference point. This anchorage enables the first international surveys to be integrated into a consistent measurement scale over time.[11]

In the case of PISA and TIMSS, the use of a global conversion rate is generally sufficient to guarantee comparability of data between these two programs.[12] However, a major innovation in our work lies in the application of multiple imputation methods, which make it possible to exploit variables that are highly correlated

[11] Details of the methodology used to obtain a database covering over 130 countries are presented in Altinok and Diebolt (2024).

[12] Assuming that the average scores of countries participating in TIMSS 1999 and PISA 2000 in mathematics are equal to 520 in TIMSS and 495 in PISA, then the conversion rate between PISA and TIMSS will be $525/495 = 1.06$. PISA scores will thus be re-evaluated upwards by around 6.06%.

with educational attainment to extend the temporal and geographical coverage of the data. This approach makes it possible to estimate the educational performance of countries that did not participate in all the surveys.

The imputation procedure is based on the use of the Amelia II statistical package (Honaker et al., 2011), which is particularly well suited to the construction of panel databases. It enables the generation of consistent time series over almost half a century (1970–2020),[13] whereas existing databases, such as that of Angrist et al. (2021), only cover a more recent period (2010–2020). By combining the techniques of anchoring by conversion rate and by reference to NAEP, with multiple imputation, it is thus possible to produce comparable learning achievement scores for over a hundred countries over a long period.

These methods make it possible to build a panel database on the quality of education, structured by school level (primary, secondary) and skill area (mathematics, reading, science). This database covers the majority of OECD countries, as well as a large number of developing countries, for the period from 1970 to 2020.[14]

The extension proposed in this analysis concerns the unequal dimension of learning achievement. While almost all OECD countries have achieved universal schooling in quantitative terms, this is not yet the case in many developing countries. It therefore seems crucial to broaden the analysis of learning achievement to include the measurement of inequalities in access to and completion of basic levels of education, in particular primary and secondary. To this end, we propose adjustments to achievement indicators based on standardized measures of access to and completion of education.

Cameron et al. (2018) propose a typology of different approaches to measuring equity in school skills. Some of these approaches are based on a unidimensional logic—for example, the attainment of minimum standards or equality of conditions—while others mobilize a multidimensional perspective, including concepts such as impartiality, meritocracy or even redistribution. The degree of meritocracy in an education system can be assessed by the link between a performance measure (e.g., progression to a higher level of education) and a measure of individual merit (such as a score on a standardized test), while checking for the absence of correlation with exogenous factors, such as socio-economic status. In theory, a truly meritocratic education system should thus lead to equivalent results between students, regardless of their social background.

---

[13] Details of the multiple imputation procedure can be found in Altinok and Diebolt (2024). In contrast to Lim et al. (2018), we employ this multiple imputation method using different steps to minimize measurement error. Specifically, eight steps are implemented, ranging from predicting scores for countries with the most observations over a short period (between 1995 and 2020, step number 1) to countries with very little data on education quality and over a longer period (between 1970 and 2020, step number 8). This imputation procedure uses explanatory factors previously selected via multiple regression and includes several explanatory variables.

[14] It should be noted that we use the term "panel" in the sense that cross-sectional data are pooled without longitudinal follow-up. However, as the data are statistically representative of the different countries included in the surveys, we can consider them as a panel for monitoring the performance of education systems.

Cameron et al. (2018) also discuss the notion of impartiality, which they link to the concepts of equality of opportunity (Berne & Stiefel, 1984) and horizontal equity (Stewart, 2005). In normative terms, impartiality assumes that educational resources are distributed without discrimination, irrespective of factors such as gender, economic situation or geographical location. In practice, it is measured by the absence of a statistical relationship between an educational variable and individual circumstances. Perfect impartiality is achieved when this relationship is non-existent.

There are five main methods for measuring impartiality (Cameron et al., 2018). The most accessible involves disaggregating data according to different sub-groups (urban/rural, rich/poor, girl/boy) and comparing indicators in tables or graphical representations. This method facilitates international and temporal comparisons. More elaborate approaches involve the use of ratios, such as parity indices, often mobilized to measure gender inequalities. These indicators are particularly well suited to binary variables. For ordinal variables such as wealth, interquartile or inter-decile comparisons are preferable. The interquartile ratio, for example, is calculated by dividing the score of the top quartile by that of the bottom quartile. This method limits the influence of extreme values (outliers) and better represents the central distribution of performance.

Parity indices are recommended in particular for monitoring the Sustainable Development Goals (SDGs), in order to account for disparities between socio-demographic groups (gender, residence, economic status). Other, more advanced methods rely on covariation analysis (correlation coefficient, elasticity, R^2 coefficient of determination) or on concentration indicators, such as the Lorenz curve or the Gini index. A final category of measures concerns group-level cumulative information, enabling us to assess the equality of conditions using indicators such as the standard deviation.

Given the multidimensional nature of educational inequalities, our analysis is based on three main axes of measurement. The first is to reproduce the data-anchoring methodology, shifting the focus from average scores to performance thresholds and decile scores. Unlike the method based on conversion rates, here we use the so-called equipercentile approach (Kolen & Brennan, 2014), which enables fine-grained anchoring by taking into account the full distribution of scores in each survey. In concrete terms, this method involves associating the percentiles of a reference survey with those of another survey, via the calculation of conversion coefficients specific to each percentile. On average, around one hundred coefficients are generated for each pair of surveys. This approach enables us to better reflect the differences in distribution between evaluations, thus avoiding the bias that could be introduced by a comparison based solely on averages. Indeed, two surveys may present different score amplitudes, reflecting varying skill ranges. The aim of this method is to estimate, in a robust way, the proportion of students reaching certain performance thresholds. By taking account of the internal distribution of scores, it guarantees greater comparability of results over time and between countries, particularly when we wish to study learning inequalities.

In our analysis, we pay particular attention to the proportion of students reaching different proficiency thresholds, mobilizing the levels defined by the IEA, close to those adopted by the OECD as part of the PISA program. Two thresholds are at the heart of our approach: a Minimum Competence Threshold (MCT) and an Advanced Competence Threshold (ACT).

The Minimum Proficiency Level (MPL) is designed to quantify the proportion of students achieving a basic level of proficiency deemed necessary to cope with the demands of everyday life. This threshold is explicitly recommended as part of the Sustainable Development Goals (SDGs) (UNESCO Institute for Statistics, 2019). In IEA surveys, it corresponds to the Low International Benchmark, set at 400 points. Students reaching this level are able to mobilize fundamental skills in areas such as mathematics, reading or science. For example, at primary level, they are able to perform simple arithmetic operations, solve problems with few parameters, manipulate fractions or common geometric shapes, and read and interpret simple graphs or tables (see Table 4.9, Appendix A).

In contrast, the Advanced Proficiency Level (APL)—Seuil Avancé de Compétence (SAC)—identifies the proportion of students achieving levels of academic excellence. This threshold, corresponding to the IEA's Advanced International Benchmark, is set at 625 points. Students who reach this threshold demonstrate not only a thorough command of basic knowledge, but also the ability to mobilize it rigorously in complex contexts. They can, for example, solve problems requiring the use of advanced mathematical concepts such as fractions, decimals or abstract forms of reasoning. These students are able to explain their reasoning in a structured way and adapt their knowledge to new situations.

Evaluating these two thresholds enables us to make a balanced diagnosis of education systems: a country in which a very large majority of pupils achieve the SMC can be considered as equitable. If this country also manages to develop a significant proportion of pupils reaching the SAC, it can then be described as both equitable and high-performing.

Above these thresholds, we carry out a distributive analysis of performance by calculating average scores per decile. This approach draws on Piketty's (2013) work on income inequality, transposing the logic to school results. More specifically, we look at deciles 1 and 9, i.e. respectively the average score of the lowest-performing 10% of pupils and that of the highest-performing 10%. The interdecile ratio (D9/D1) is thus an indicator of the extent of educational inequality. A country where this ratio tends toward 1 reflects a relative homogeneity of educational performance. Conversely, a high ratio suggests that only the most advantaged or high-achieving pupils are progressing, to the detriment of the lowest performers, reflecting an unequal education system. Measuring the interdecile ratio thus enables us to assess a country's level of internal equity, by comparing the gap between extreme performances, both over time and internationally.

A second strand of our analysis of educational inequality focuses on performance gaps between distinct social groups, particularly as a function of socio-economic level. This approach is in line with classic work in the sociology of education (Ballantine et al., 2021), which highlights the way in which social affiliations influence access to learning.

From this perspective, Stewart (2005) introduces the concept of horizontal inequalities, i.e. inequalities that occur between culturally defined groups (ethnicity, religion, social class, region, etc.), as opposed to "vertical" inequalities, often measured by unidimensional variables such as income. Horizontal inequalities tend to be maintained, or even amplified over time, due to their cumulative nature, whether economic, social or political (Stewart & Langer, 2008). They can thus have deleterious long-term effects on a country's social cohesion and political stability (Stewart, 2005). Systemic discrimination against certain groups is also economically inefficient, as it leads to under-utilization of the potential of talented individuals from marginalized groups (Stewart, 2008). Studies such as Cederman et al. (2011) have shown that the persistence of such inequalities increases the risk of conflict and instability.

In this context, the analysis of educational inequalities cannot ignore differences between population sub-groups. Although our anchoring method is initially based on overall scores, it is adapted to take account of the specificities of these sub-populations through ratios calculated during the multiple imputation procedure. More specifically, we replicate the anchoring method for each subgroup, then use ratios of absolute differences between groups to estimate missing data. Multiple dimensions of differentiation are taken into account: gender (girls/boys), location (urban/rural), school type (public/private) and socio-economic level (segmented into quartiles). For each of these categories, average scores are calculated, offering a multidimensional reading of school inequalities. To our knowledge, our database represents a first in terms of the wealth of indicators available for the study of group inequalities.

However, for the purposes of this study, and in line with the literature in the sociology of education, we are focusing our attention on the variability of scores linked to socio-economic level. Although other dimensions are available in the general database, our analysis is based exclusively on this dimension. To this end, we have constructed an index of socio-economic level from the data available in each survey. Given the heterogeneity of indicators between surveys, it is impossible to develop a strictly standardized scale. Nevertheless, as our method is based on the differences between quartiles for each survey—by dividing the population into four equal parts—this lack of standardization does not hinder the temporal comparability of the results.

All the variables used to construct this index are presented in Table 4.10 in Appendix A. The analysis is therefore based on the difference in score between the top quartile (Q_4)—representing the 25% of students from the most advantaged families—and the bottom quartile (Q_1)—corresponding to the 25% least advantaged. The greater this differential, the greater the educational inequalities are considered to be.[15] This differential is one of the main indicators used to assess the equity of education systems in our database.

[15] It remains possible that if the structure of the population changes over time, as, for example, with the arrival of large numbers of poor immigrants in a country, the interquartile range may be modified exogenously. However, it should be noted here that France is not the only country to have experienced a large influx of immigrants, and international comparisons can help to highlight any gaps between France and other countries.

For all existing data, we calculate a gap between one category and another. For example, if a country has a score of 550 for its students included in the 4th quartile of the socio-economic index, against 520 points for those included in the first quartile, the indicator used is obtained by subtracting the first number by the second, i.e. $550 - 520 = 30$. We replicate this calculation in a similar way to the existing data set, and proceed with multiple imputation based on this ratio and not on the scores of each category. When we have more than two categories, as is the case for socio-economic level quartiles, we calculate several ratios: the ratios between quartile 4 and quartile 1 (Q_4/Q_1), but also other quartile pairs (e.g., Q_4/Q_2).

Estimating gaps rather than scores for each sub-group by multiple imputation has several advantages:

- It is possible to anchor and adjust for inequality dimensions without being directly influenced by the level of educational quality, and by allowing for temporal smoothing of deviations. Instead of predicting scores for each sub-sample, we prefer to analyze and predict deviations calculated on the differences in performance between sub-samples. In this way, the variance can evolve with a smoothing and global consistency constraint, independently of the average score (via the method proposed by Honaker et al. (2011)).
- Statistical analysis of imputation is facilitated because the use of deviations prevents the natural existence of structural effects in the data: it is highly likely that some low-performing systems are also the most unequal, but this should not be translated into a statistical constraint. By using ratios instead of scores, we avoid creating structural biases.
- Calculating scores for each sub-sample is facilitated by using the scores already anchored in the general database (Altinok & Diebolt, 2024) and provides overall consistency to the scores. Indeed, the use of prediction for each sub-sample could lead to discrepancies and contradictions in performance between sub-groups and the general population.

The last point is crucial, as it could lead to major deviations in performance within sub-samples. Indeed, every anchoring and imputation method has its own limitations and can lead to estimation bias. Performance for a sub-sample is calculated directly on real data, and then recalculated only in the final step, taking into account its initial weighting. So, if in our data, the geographical location in a rural area of the school tested accounts for around 30% of the proportion of students, we reuse this ratio to obtain the rural score after carrying out the anchoring procedure. To do this, we simply combine the score for the general population with the estimated gap between urban and rural areas, while taking into account the weighting of rural within the overall system.[16]

The indicators presented above each measure a particular dimension, and can relate to measures of effectiveness, efficiency or equity. First, we propose to construct

[16] When data on the proportion of each sub-sample in the general population are not available, we use the most likely data, i.e. those for the nearest year, or failing that, the average proportion of the sub-sample for the country concerned.

an indicator of educational effectiveness. This is based on the assumption that a system can be considered efficient if it succeeds in getting all its students to reach the minimum performance threshold (*MPL*), without sacrificing those who could also reach the excellence threshold (*APL*). However, it is virtually impossible to have the entire population reach the threshold of excellence. For this reason, we weight the value relative to this threshold to obtain our efficiency index:

$$efficacy_{country,t} = \frac{(MPL + 2 \times APL)}{2} \times 10 \tag{4.1}$$

with $MPL = Minimum\ Proficiency\ Level\ \&\ APL = Advanced\ Proficiency\ Level$

So, let's assume a country A where 80% of the population reaches the minimum threshold and only 5% manages to reach the excellence threshold. Conversely, in country B, almost the entire population reaches the minimum threshold (95%), with almost a fifth reaching the excellence threshold (20%). The efficiency index will be equal to 450 in country A versus 675 for country B, i.e. a difference of 50% in favor of the latter country.

Beyond efficiency, a system can also be measured by its degree of equity, i.e. the extent to which it enables everyone to succeed, regardless of their initial resources. The notion of equity is fairly subjective, but often refers to the notion of equality of opportunity to succeed, irrespective of individual characteristics. Equity does not imply perfect equality between all students, but equal access and success justified by factors independent of socio-economic characteristics or based on various dimensions (such as gender, immigrant status or religion). It is impossible to combine all possible dimensions. The one that is often used, given the ease of obtaining comparable data, refers to the socio-economic status of parents. However, the measure of socio-economic level is quite heterogeneous and could be interpreted differently depending on the economic level of the country. A more neutral measure refers to the analysis of deciles. More specifically, the gap between deciles 1 and 9 can measure a degree of inequality, in much the same way as the Gini index. We therefore propose to measure the equity of education systems by combining the extreme deciles in terms of student scores. The *Bottom* 10% decile is calculated as the average score of students in the bottom 10%. In contrast, the Top 10% score refers to the average score obtained by the top 10% of students. The greater the deviation from the median score, the more inequitable an education system is considered to be. More generally, the formula we use is as follows:

$$equity_{absolute,t} = \left(1 - \frac{Top_{10\%} - Bottom_{10\%}}{Median\_score}\right) \times 1{,}000 \tag{4.2}$$

where $Bottom_{10\%}$ is the average score obtained by the bottom 10% of students, $Top_{10\%}$ is the average score obtained by the top 10% and $Median\_score$ is the median score.

This equity index then represents the standardized score of the gap between the best and worst performers, relative to the median score. If an education system is selective and does not include the entire school-age population, the equity index may be overestimated. Let's assume a country where only half the population aged 15 actually attends school. In this case, the equity index will tend to overestimate the level of equity in the country, if we assume that the population excluded from the education system would have performed less well if they had attended school. To take account of this exclusion bias, we calculate an adjusted equity index where we include the school completion rate:

$$equity_{adjusted,t} = \left(1 - \frac{Top_{10\%} - Bottom_{10\%}}{Median\_score}\right) \times completionrate \times 1{,}000, \quad (4.3)$$

where *completionrate* represents the completion rate for the school level under consideration.

4.3 Results

4.3.1 The Database

We have obtained a multidimensional database on inequalities based on school skills. As the database is based on several indicators, it enables inequalities to be viewed from different angles (Fig. 4.1). Beyond the average scores generally used in almost all previous work, we propose a measure of inequalities based on differences in performance between different groups of pupils. Four divisions are used, namely the gender of the student (girls or boys), the type of school locality (urban or rural), the language spoken by the student at home (main test language or other language), socio-economic status (measured in quartiles) and finally the status of the school (private or public). In addition, inequality is also measured by the proportion of students reaching the various performance thresholds (i.e. the minimum and advanced proficiency thresholds). It's important to note that data disaggregation for each dimension is also possible for proficiency thresholds. Thus, it is also possible to compare the proportion of students by gender for each proficiency threshold. A final dimension covers the gaps between deciles within each country. The interdecile gap (between deciles 1 and 9) measures the difference in performance between the top 10% and the bottom 10%.

This database includes data on educational inequalities for around 140 countries (see Table 4.1). Data on average scores concern more countries than those on inequalities (165 versus around 140, respectively). The main reason for this is the impossibility of making subdivisions on certain surveys, such as those relating to the skills of the very young (*EGRA*), where only average scores can be extracted. As these surveys are by nature targeted at rural populations, we preferred not to calculate scores for sub-samples and performance thresholds based on these assessments. The data available vary according to year and indicator (Table 4.2). While the total

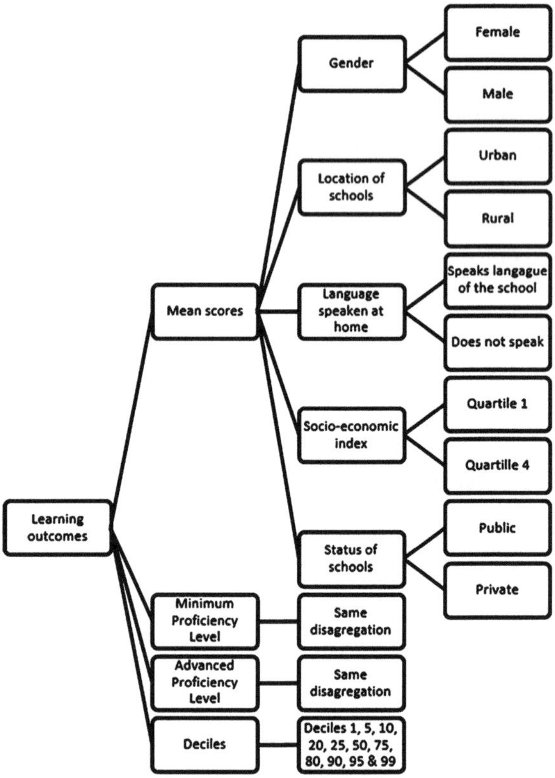

Fig. 4.1 Disaggregation of the dataset on equity for learning outcomes (*Notes* For definitions of different indicators, please refer to Sect. 2.2. *Source* Authors based on international and regional student achievements tests)

number of observations is close to 1,500 for the average score, over 1,100 observations are available for the socio-economic index (noted "dif_0ses4") and around half that number for the distinction according to school type (public or private). As the number of surveys has increased since the late 1990s, data availability is higher for the period 1995–2020, while it is lower for the 1970s. The rate of missing values is therefore higher for this decade, while it remains below 40% for the recent period (see Table 4.9). The multiple imputation procedure has made it possible to obtain more information on the equity of education systems. More specifically, it is the 70s and 90s that are concerned by this procedure (Table 4.10), while the last two decades have little imputation (around 20%). Since we have used quantitative indicators such as completion rates, the imputation procedure has also concerned these measures, even if data availability is more present for this type of indicator.

A wide range of indicators are used to measure inequalities in learning achievement. In addition to the proportion of pupils reaching the competency thresholds, we also calculate performance gaps between sub-populations divided according to certain criteria such as gender, type of tenancy, language spoken at home, socio-economic status or type of school (public or private). Analysis of correlations highlights the consistency of the different dimensions of equity. However, some indicators

Table 4.1 Descriptive statistics

Variable	Number	Countries	Mean	SD	Minimum	Maximum	Decile 10	Decile 90
Mean score	1547	165	420.3	75.9	249.5	599.2	324.8	524.5
Minimum Prof. Level	1385	139	66.1	23.4	20.3	100.0	31.1	94.1
Advanced Prof. Level	1365	138	5.7	5.6	0.0	37.8	0.5	13.3
Efficacy score	1365	138	389.1	162.5	104.0	866.0	160.9	594.9
Gender Gap	1415	154	6.8	8.3	–12.6	49.3	–2.7	17.4
Male score	1444	157	420.8	76.9	243.0	590.9	320.3	523.4
Female score	1444	157	427.8	77.1	256.5	610.4	326.5	528.2
Location Gap	1090	140	26.3	17.5	–42.0	84.7	5.3	48.7
Urban score	1095	142	450.9	65.9	271.0	608.8	360.8	533.5
Rural score	1095	142	424.7	72.3	239.1	576.4	329.5	517.7
Language spoken Gap	1066	148	26.9	23.5	–42.9	87.6	–2.7	56.3
Not speakers score	1069	150	424.1	61.9	237.3	582.3	342.2	500.5
Speakers score	1069	150	451.0	69.6	275.4	602.2	359.0	537.1
SES Gap	1101	147	62.7	18.2	6.5	116.6	39.7	84.7
SES Quarter 1 score	1107	150	411.4	67.3	232.8	552.1	320.5	495.4
SES Quarter 4 score	1107	150	473.9	73.6	281.6	646.2	372.7	566.1
Status of School Gap	605	126	36.2	24.9	–39.6	126.9	3.5	67.8
Public School score	608	127	475.6	71.4	281.5	629.9	374.4	560.0
Private School score	608	127	439.5	72.4	281.3	589.5	345.1	525.5
Interdecile Gap	1358	137	202.8	47.8	–114.9	317.8	141.0	252.8
Decile 10 Mean score	1376	139	341.8	69.4	136.3	537.9	246.0	432.0
Decile 90 Mean score	1376	139	544.8	76.7	312.3	728.7	426.4	633.0

(continued)

Table 4.1 (continued)

Variable	Number	Countries	Mean	SD	Minimum	Maximum	Decile 10	Decile 90
Completion Rate	1995	205	59.0	31.1	0.6	100.0	12.7	97.0
Equity score	1285	129	497.1	73.1	24.2	647.2	411.6	579.4
Adjusted Equity score	1211	126	369.0	147.9	19.5	630.3	146.6	546.2

Notes For definitions of different indicators, please refer to Sect. 2.2
Source Authors based on international and regional student achievements tests

measure specific dimensions of inequality (Table 4.11): for example, the correlation between gender and socio-economic status is rather weak (0.14), as is that between gender and type of locality (–0.08). These weak correlations thus underline the multi-dimensional nature of inequalities in educational attainment, and reinforce the idea of analyzing educational inequalities from several angles rather than via a single indicator.

The international average score over the half-century is 420 points, compared with the 500-point average generally obtained by *OECD* countries in assessments such as *PISA*. The standard deviation is 75 points, which may seem lower than that of *PISA* surveys. It should be noted that this standard deviation is based on data per country and not per pupil, as it is calculated on aggregate data (*macro* versus *micro*). Logically, the variability of scores between countries taken as a whole is lower than that between students in all countries.

The main contribution of our database relates to the different dimensions of inequality. Thus, we find that around 66.1% of the population tested over the last half-century meets the minimum performance threshold, with fairly wide variations between countries and years, since this threshold varies between 20.3% and 100%. Very few students worldwide reach the advanced proficiency threshold (less than 6%), although some countries manage to get more than one in three students to reach this threshold. The efficiency index is calculated by combining the two performance thresholds (see Eq. 4.1, Sect. 2.2). It can be an interesting indicator of the effectiveness of an education system, based on its propensity to simultaneously achieve universalization of basic skills, but also to target a certain proportion of students with a view to reaching a threshold of excellence (see Sect. 2.2 for more information). The average efficiency score is 390 points.

Our database also focuses on differences between sub-populations. While girls outperform boys by an average of 6.8 points, urban students score 25 points higher than rural students. As expected, discrimination based on students' origin is strong and exceeds that found via the other dimensions: there is a 27-point gap between students who do not speak the test language at home. The gap between students' socio-economic levels reinforces this hypothesis of discrimination, with almost 60 points separating the extreme quartiles of this composite index. A form of spatial segregation can be seen in the difference between public and private schools, since

Table 4.2 Observations by country-year

year	qual0t	qual1t	qual3t	diff_0gend	diff_0loca	diff_0lang	diff_0ses4	diff_0priv	diff_decile	comp_lsec	eq_qual0t	eq_qual1t	eff_qual
1970	122	11[illegible]	109	113	74	74	77	30	109	135	103	90	109
1975	127	113	110	114	74	74	77	30	110	168	104	99	110
1980	128	113	111	114	76	74	77	30	111	171	105	102	111
1985	128	113	111	114	76	74	78	30	111	179	105	102	111
1990	150	135	132	135	95	93	97	32	131	186	125	114	132
1995	151	136	133	136	106	100	101	34	132	191	126	120	133
2000	149	133	131	134	111	107	107	64	130	193	124	118	131
2005	147	132	131	134	119	110	114	73	130	195	124	119	131
2010	150	132	131	142	121	119	127	91	130	197	124	119	131
2015	153	133	132	141	121	122	125	94	131	198	123	118	132
2020	142	134	134	138	117	119	121	97	133	182	122	110	134
Total	1547	1385	1365	1415	1090	1066	1101	605	1358	1995	1285	1211	1365

Notes "qual0t" = mean score; "qual1t" = MPL; "qual3t" = APL; "dif_0gend" = gender ratio; "dif_0loca" = location ratio; "dif0_lang" = language ratio; "dif0_ses4" = socic-economic status ratio; "dif0_priv" = public/private school status ratio; "dif_decile" = interdecile gap; "complsec" = completion rate, lower secondary level; "eq_qual0t" = equity index; "eq-qual1t" = adjusted equit index; "eff_qual" = efficacy index
Source Authors based on international and regional student achievements tests

private schools perform better than public schools. A final approach to inequality refers to the gap between extreme deciles. In theory, egalitarian education systems should have few performance gaps within the population. Any gap between the extreme deciles can then characterize a form of inequality. We find an average gap of 200 points between deciles 10 and 90: while the lowest-performing 10% have an average score of 341 points, the highest-performing 10% manage to achieve a score of 541 points. From these differences between the deciles, it is possible to obtain an equity score (see Eq. 4.2). On average, equity in education systems is equal to around 500 points, varying from 24.2 points to over 647 points depending on the country and the year. It is important to note that equity can be influenced by access to schooling for the most disadvantaged. The use of the adjusted equity indicator goes some way to resolving this bias (see Eq. 4.3). The adjusted equity score then drops by around 130 to an average of 369 points.

4.3.2 A Multidimensional Analysis of Educational Inequalities

As the database presents multiple inequality indicators for a large proportion of the world's countries, a benchmarking analysis may prove interesting. We therefore rank countries within regions using the main quality and equity indicators (see Tables 4.3 and 4.4). The maps in Figs. 4.2–4.4 show the differences in performance between regions, with Latin America and sub-Saharan Africa in particular lagging far behind. The proportions of students reaching the advanced competency threshold are highest in East Asia, North America and some European countries (Fig. 4.3). Equity—adjusted by school access and completion—seems to be more of a concern in Asian countries, but also in a few European countries such as Finland.

We continue our analysis with the ranking of countries within each region. The global ranking is also shown to the right of the countries (Tables 4.3 and 4.4). In line with the results found in the PISA tests, the best performing countries in terms of average scores are Singapore, South Korea and Japan in Asia, while Estonia and Ireland are among the top performers in the West. The best-performing countries are Chile, Trinidad & Tobago and Cuba in Latin America, while Malta, Israel and Bahrain are the best performers in the Middle East-North Africa (*MENA*) region.

As our database allows us to capture not only average performance, but also performance thresholds, we find that the ranking of countries is slightly altered when we analyze the distribution of scores. For example, Russia is among the top performers in terms of the minimum skills threshold, while Finland is among the top performers in terms of the advanced skills threshold. African countries appear to be largely under-performing, whatever the indicator selected, the best country being Ghana, but ranked 60th for the advanced skills threshold.

The efficiency score aggregates the two performance thresholds, providing a more global picture (see Eq. 4.1 in Sect. 2.2). In this respect, countries such as the United

Table 4.3 Country rankings by education quality and skills thresholds (2020)

Ranking	EAP	W	West	W	LAC	W	MENA	W	SSA	W
Learning outcomes (mean scores)										
1	Singapore	1	Estonia	6	Chile	58	Malta	43	Rwanda	88
2	Korea R	2	Liechtenstein	8	Trinidad & T	62	Israel	44	Gabon	94
3	Japan	3	Ireland	9	Cuba	63	Bahrain	48	Mauritius	100
Minimum Proficiency Level										
1	Japan	1	Estonia	1	Chile	60	Malta	49	Mauritius	84
2	Singapore	3	Russian Fed	8	Costa Rica	62	Israel	51	Seychelles	93
3	Korea Rep	4	Ireland	9	Uruguay	64	Bahrain	57	Tanzania U.R	100
Advanced Proficiency Level										
1	Singapore	1	Estonia	6	Cuba	58	Israel	25	Ghana	60
2	Korea Rep	2	United Kingdom	7	Trinidad & T	59	United Arab Em	46	Botswana	61
3	Hong Kong	3	Finland	9	Jamaica	74	Malta	47	Mauritius	69
Efficacy Score										
1	Singapore	1	Estonia	6	Chile	61	Israel	37	Mauritius	83
2	Korea Rep	2	United Kingdom	8	Trinidad & T	64	Malta	47	Seychelles	90
3	Japan	3	Finland	9	Cuba	67	Bahrain	55	Botswana	95

Notes Rankings are presented within regions in columns and for the world as a whole in "W" columns. For example, Singapore ranks first in the world for learning outcomes and in the East Asia and Pacific region. Korea ranks second for learning tests, 3rd for Minimum Proficiency Level (MPL) and 2nd for Advanced Proficiency Level (APL). South Asian countries are not represented, as there are only five countries in this zone. Western countries include North America, Europe and Central Asia. The complete results are presented in Table 4.14
Source Authors based on international and regional student achievements tests

Kingdom and Finland rank among the top 10 countries in the world, while countries such as Mauritius and the Seychelles lag far behind (in 83rd and 90th place respectively).

The most efficient and effective countries can also be the most equitable (Table 4.4). For example, Japan is the fourth most equitable country according to our equity indicator, while it ranks third in terms of education quality. Among Western countries, Ireland, Denmark and Russia are among the best performers when it comes to adjusted equity in access to education. The gross equity index seems to favor countries where access to schooling is underdeveloped, such as Benin, which ranks 8th. However, once school access and completion are taken into account, the best African country is Kenya, in 70th place. Taking school access and completion into

Table 4.4 Ranking of countries for equity scores and socio-economic gaps (2020)

Ranking	EAP	W	West	W	LAC	W	MENA	W	SSA	W
Equity Scores										
1	Macao, China	1	Russia	2	Costa Rica	30	Jordan	69	Benin	8
2	Japan	4	Latvia	3	Mexico	44	Algeria	75	Gabon	11
3	Vietnam	6	Ireland	5	Chile	53	Bahrain	81	Senegal	12
Equity Scores (adjusted)										
1	Japan	2	Ireland	1	Mexico	33	Malta	53	Kenya	70
2	Vietnam	5	Denmark	3	Ecuador	36	Iran	62	Mauritius	78
3	Korea R	8	Russia	4	Chile	47	Israel	63	Botswana	79
Socioeconomic Gap (relative)										
1	Macao	5	Uzbekistan	4	Honduras	3	Kuwait	1	Gabon	23
2	Cambodia	6	Russian Fed	10	Cuba	8	Algeria	2	Burundi	29
3	Indonesia	7	Kazakhstan	13	Nicaragua	14	Bahrain	11	Congo, D.R	30

Notes Rankings are presented within regions in columns and for the world as a whole in "W" columns. For example, Singapore ranks first in the world for learning outcomes and in the East Asia and Pacific region. Japan ranks second for equity score and 1st for adjusted equity score. South Asian countries are not represented, as there are only five countries in this zone. Western countries include North America, Europe and Central Asia. Full results are presented in Table 4.15
Source Authors based on international and regional student achievements tests

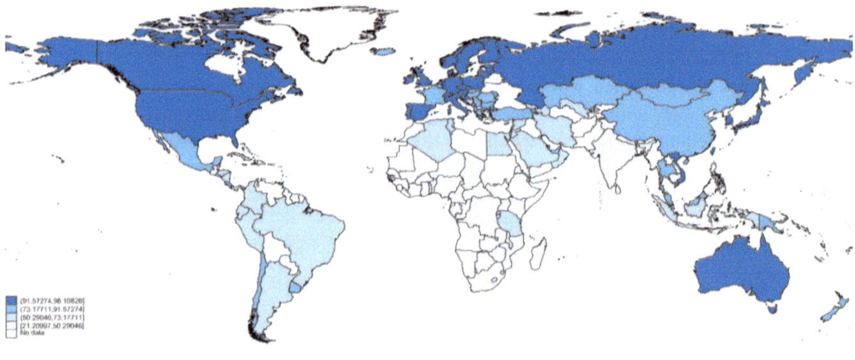

Fig. 4.2 Proportion of students reaching the minimum competency threshold (MPL) (*Source* Authors based on international and regional student achievements tests)

account therefore appears to be of prime importance if we wish to compare countries with different economic levels. Results concerning the gap between families' socio-economic status can also provide information on the equity of education systems. Here too, the ranking of countries is modified. Instead of measuring a raw performance gap, we put it into perspective with the average score. Medium-performing

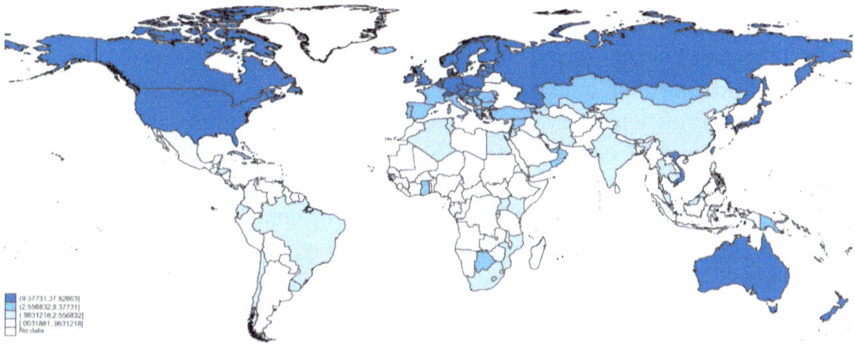

Source: authors based on international and regional student achievements tests.

Fig. 4.3 Proportion of students reaching the Advanced Proficiency Level (APL) (*Source* authors based on international and regional student achievements tests)

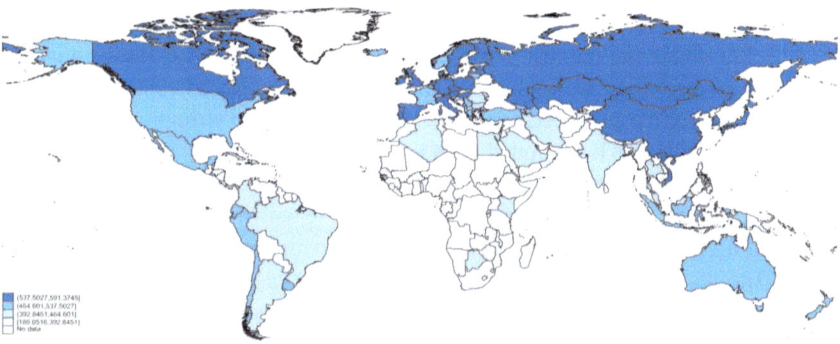

Source: authors based on international and regional student achievements tests.

Fig. 4.4 Equity scores (adjusted by interdecile gap and completion rates) (*Source* authors based on international and regional student achievements tests)

countries such as Cambodia and Indonesia appear to have a lower than expected level of inequality, as they rank 6th and 7th, respectively, in the international rankings.

4.3.3 An Overview of Educational Inequalities Worldwide

The most common measure of inequality often refers to the performance gap between families' socio-economic status. We explore these gaps within world regions (Fig. 4.5) and for a sample of countries (Fig. 4.6) for three indicators in 2020: the average score, the minimum competency threshold (MPL) and the advanced competency threshold (APL). This shows that gaps are widest in Western countries, which are also those with the highest average performance. Sub-Saharan African countries, on the other hand, seem to stand out for their lower inequality, but also for their much lower performance than other regions (Part A of Fig. 4.5). The results concerning the Minimum Proficiency Level (*MPL*) confirm and even reinforce this observation: on average, only 40% of pupils in sub-Saharan Africa reach the minimum performance threshold, while only 22% of children from families with low socio-economic capital achieve it. Latin America appears here as the continent with the widest gap between extreme socio-economic statuses (Part B, Fig. 4.5). In regions such as Latin America, sub-Saharan Africa and the Middle East (*MENA*), only students from families rich in socio-economic capital manage to reach the advanced threshold. It's only in Asia and the developed countries that students with low socio-economic capital are able to reach this threshold. Thus, we deduce that even if inequalities remain high within developed countries, pupils from poor families seem to perform better than the average of pupils living in developing regions such as Latin America or the Middle East. Beyond regional averages, it may be interesting to analyze the situation in certain countries (Fig. 4.6). South Africa is an atypical case in point: its performance is rather weak, with an average score below 400 points (Part A, Fig. 4.6), but where the poorest perform around 100 points lower. The inequalities seem even greater when we look at the minimum proficiency threshold (25% gap, Part B, Fig. 4.6) or the advanced proficiency threshold, where virtually no pupil from the poorest quartile can be included (Part C, Fig. 4.6).

The position of a developed country like France is quite similar to that of a developing country like Turkey: performance is in line with the international average, but inequalities are very high: pupils from families with low socio-economic capital score 100 points lower than those with high capital. The case of a country like Finland seems to offer a rather original situation where performance is high, while avoiding excessive disparities between families' socio-economic levels. When we turn to the advanced skills threshold, inequalities seem to emerge more clearly: almost no high achievers from families with low socio-economic capital in France or Turkey reach this threshold, whereas they represent almost a fifth of the population to do so in Finland, suggesting greater equity in this country (Part C, Fig. 4.6). The situation in the USA is quite similar to that in Finland, calling into question the idea that inequality is higher in Anglo-Saxon countries than in continental Europe.

Inequalities are multidimensional, and it would be simplistic to reduce them to a single dimension. We can see this quite clearly in Fig. 4.7, where we cross-reference the two main inequality indicators, namely the relative gap between socio-economic statuses and our equity indicator based on the gaps between deciles. There is certainly a negative correlation, as expected, between the indicators, with some countries such as France, Belgium and Israel showing high inequality across both indicators. However, some countries (on the bottom left) appear to have less inequality on a socio-economic level, while equity based on the interdecile gap is stronger. This is the case of Iceland and Slovenia. Some countries manage to achieve a lower level of inequality, whatever the indicator used (countries at top left). This is the case, for example, of Japan and Ireland.

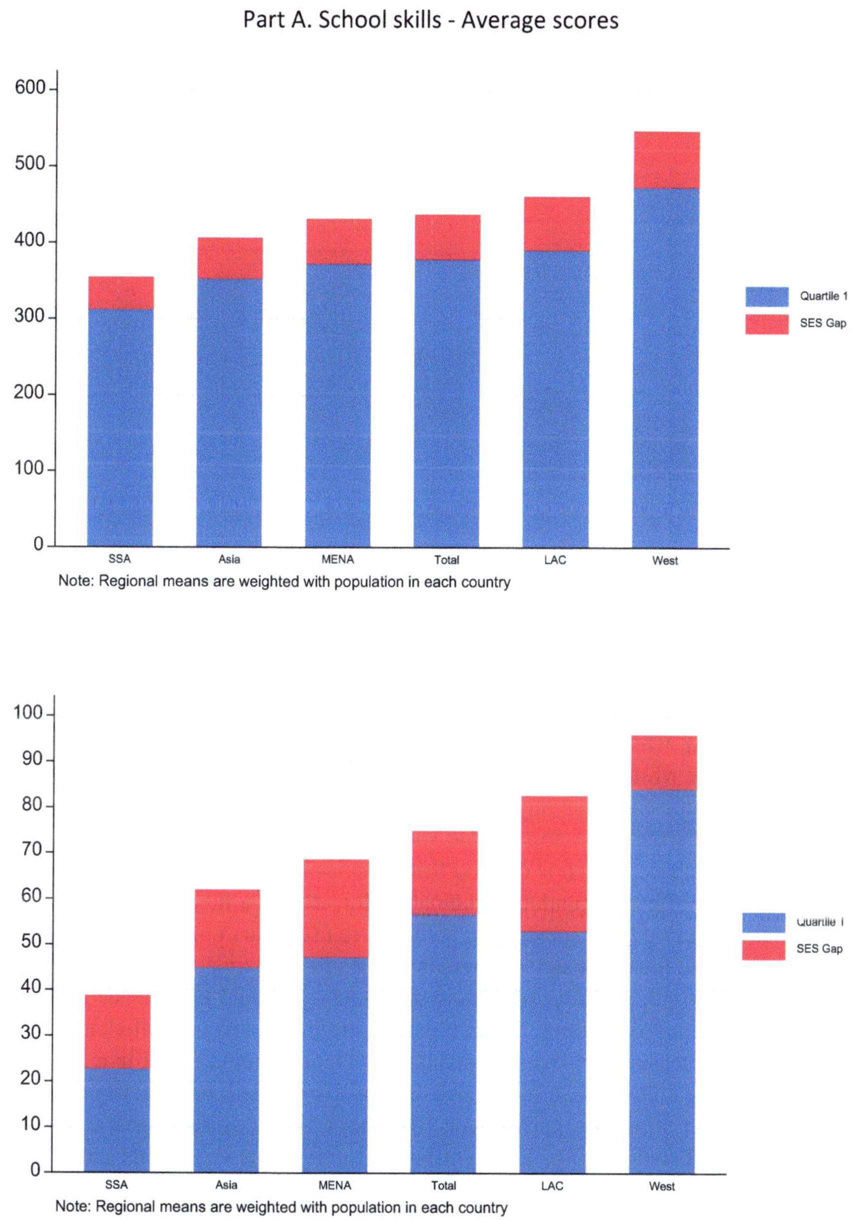

Fig. 4.5 Regional inequality by socio-economic status (2020) (*Notes* LAC = Latin America and Caribbean countries, SSA = Sub-Saharan Africa; MENA = Middle-East and North Africa, Asia = all Asian countries, West = mainly high-income countries. *Source* Authors based on international and regional student achievements tests)

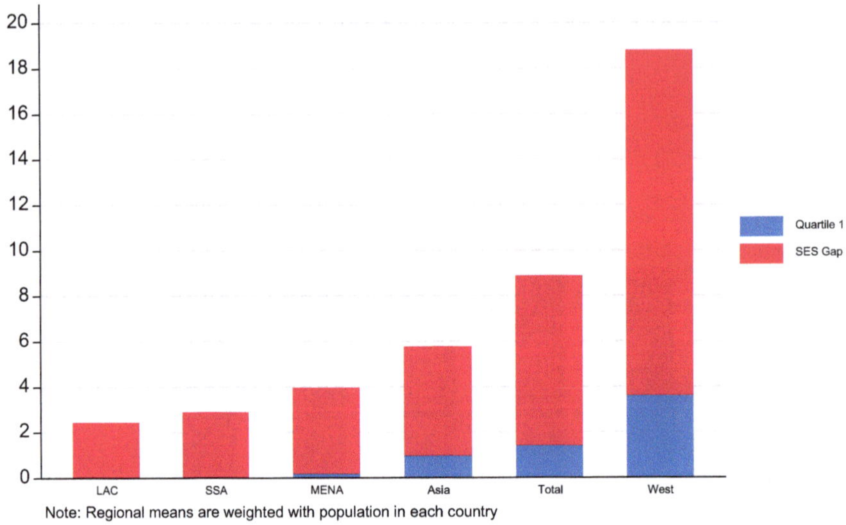

Fig. 4.5 (continued)

The best-performing countries are not necessarily the most unequal (Fig. 4.8). Several scenarios are possible. While some countries are indeed in this situation (e.g., France and Germany), others have lower quality and high inequality (e.g., Switzerland and Austria), while countries such as Ireland, Finland and Canada manage to reduce inequality while still achieving high performance. Of course, the choice of inequality indicator can alter the positioning of countries, but we believe that the equity indicator is the most appropriate for international comparisons, due to the nature of our database, which is derived from various heterogeneous surveys.

Our database offers comparative indicators for around a hundred countries, as well as data spanning half a century. It is therefore useful to compare the evolution of inequalities and the efficiency of education systems over time. Assuming convergence, countries with initially low levels of efficiency should experience stronger growth in efficiency over time. Thus, crossing the initial level of efficiency with the growth rate measured in terms of standard deviation should result in a negative relationship. This convergence hypothesis is partially verified, particularly over the long term for the minimum performance threshold, and to a lesser extent for the advanced skills threshold (Fig. 4.9, right-hand graphs). This shows that initial efficiency scores (i.e. in 1970) are well correlated negatively with changes in efficiency over time. Data by region are presented in Table 4.5. The efficiency of education systems increases everywhere in the short and long term, except in Asian countries where it is already very high initially. Efficiency seems to increase the most in Latin America, whatever the period analyzed. On the contrary, the region that has seen the least change in efficiency is the Middle East and North Africa, particularly over the last two decades. It is also possible to analyze the situation of individual countries. For example, while the efficiency of France's education system was lagging behind

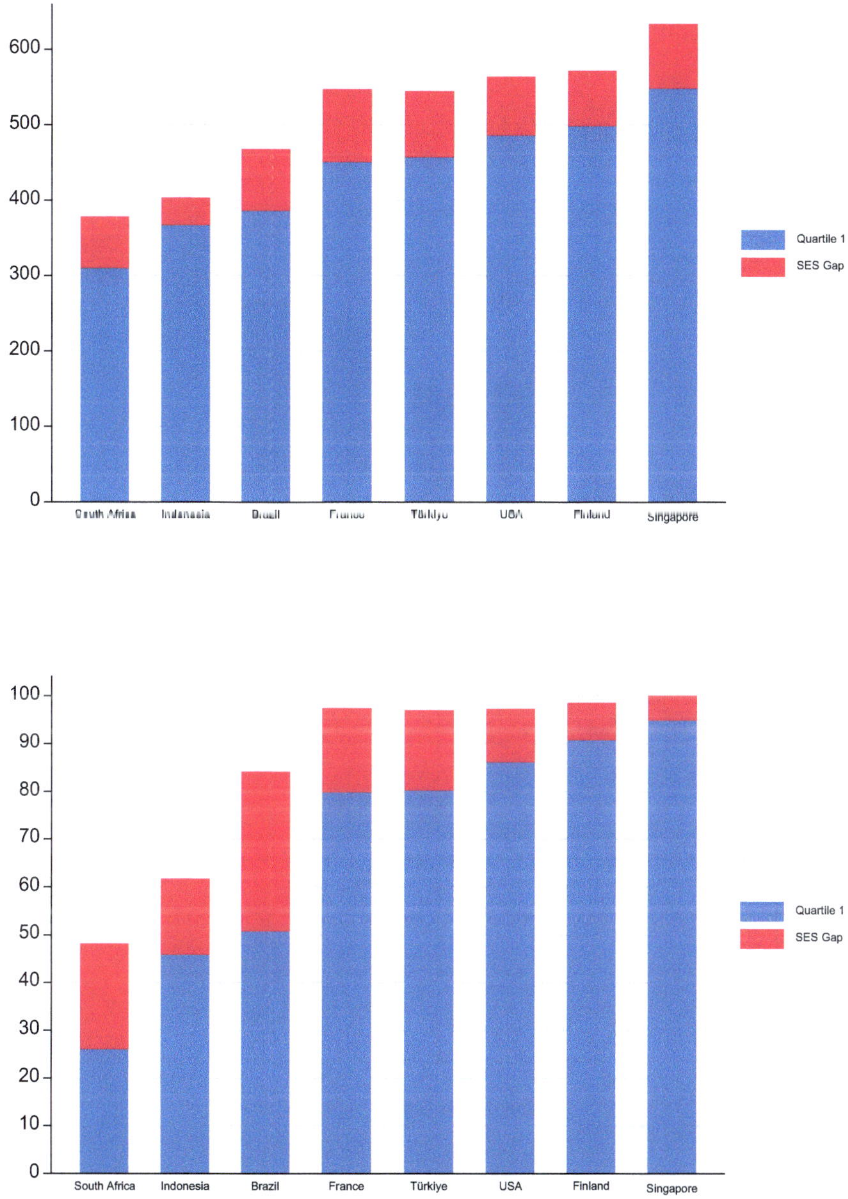

Fig. 4.6 Inequalities by socio-economic status for selected countries (2020) (*Source* authors based on international and regional student achievements tests)

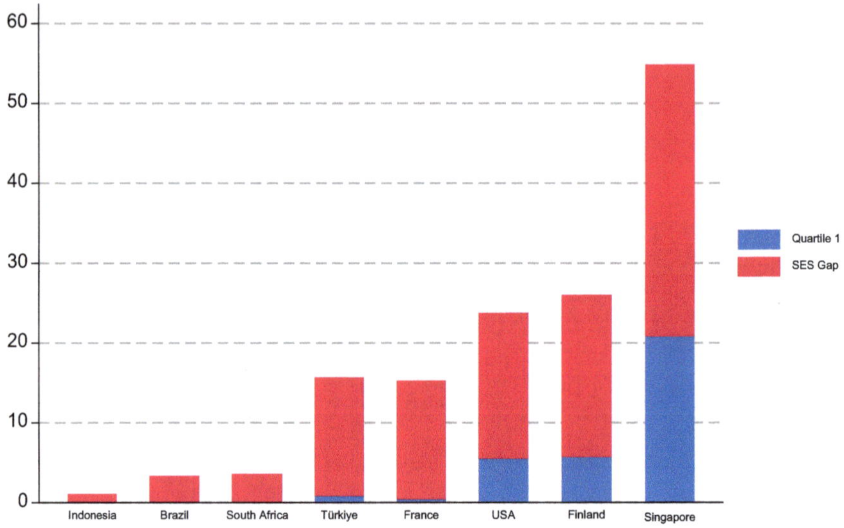

Fig. 4.6 (continued)

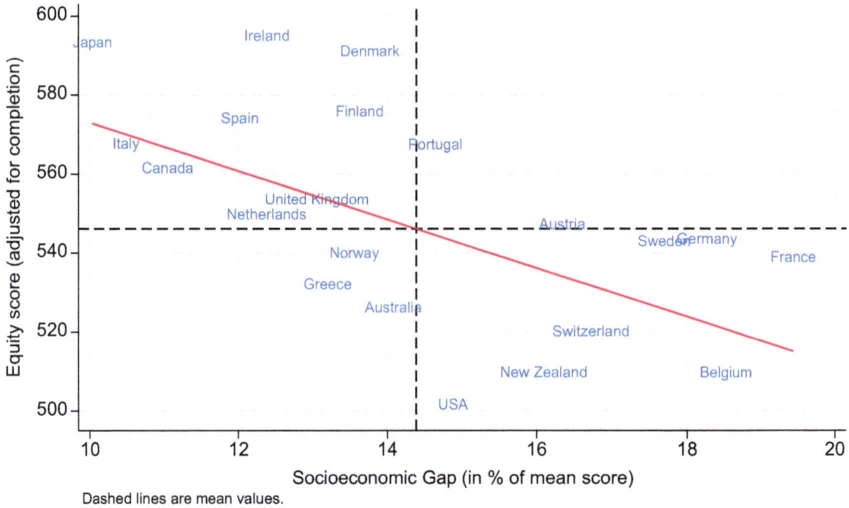

Fig. 4.7 Socio-economic inequalities and equity scores in 2020, OECD countries (*Source* authors based on international and regional student achievements tests)

in the 1970s, its growth has been more sustained than that of other countries. On the contrary, Japan's lead has been partly made up, although the latter is still managing to improve its efficiency over time. In the short term, convergence is clearly not taking place. Japan's lead seems to be strengthening, while France's lag seems to be widening. Details of the evolution of efficiency for each country are available in

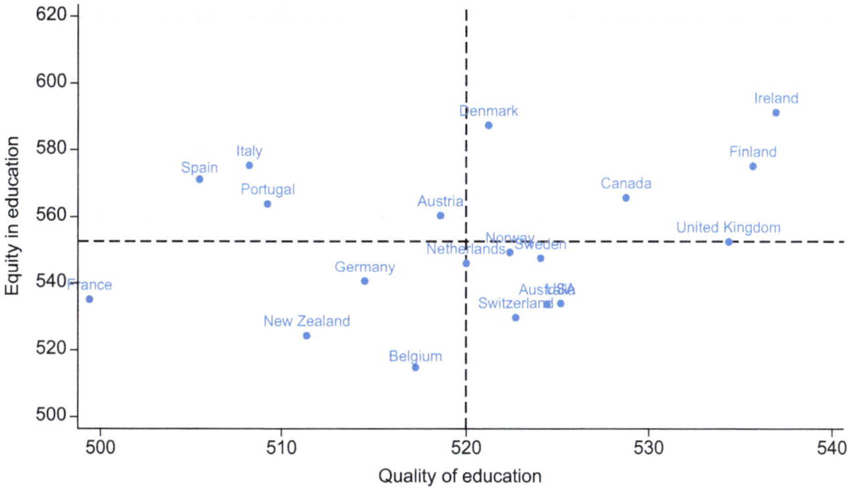

Fig. 4.8 Quality and equity of education in 2020, OECD countries (*Source* Authors based on international and regional student achievements tests)

Table 4.12. The convergence hypothesis is called into question when all countries are grouped together, whether in the short or long term (Fig. 4.15). Similarly, a wide variety of situations seems to emerge in the case of developing countries (Fig. 4.16). While some countries appear to be experiencing a slowdown in efficiency over the short and long term, as a result of convergence (such as Cuba and Indonesia), others are not following the convergence trajectory, such as Armenia and Turkey. These countries, which initially had a certain lead over other developing countries, are experiencing fairly sustained growth in efficiency (Fig. 4.16).

The hypothesis of convergence of the equity index is tested in Fig. 4.10 for OECD countries. Convergence appears to be more effective in the case of equity than efficiency, particularly in the short term. Under the hypothesis of generalized school enrollment in all countries, the quantitative indicator—the secondary school completion rate—perfectly meets the convergence hypothesis. Although convergence seems less pronounced in the short term, it remains effective.[17] Our equity index also seems to meet the convergence hypothesis: countries where inequalities were initially high are also those where they are progressing least. This is the case, for example, in Ireland and Canada. On the contrary, some countries with low initial inequality tend to converge toward the more equitable countries (such as Denmark and the UK).

[17] A lower level of convergence in the short term can be explained by the fact that many countries have already achieved universal enrolment, making the rate of growth in completion rates close to zero for developed countries.

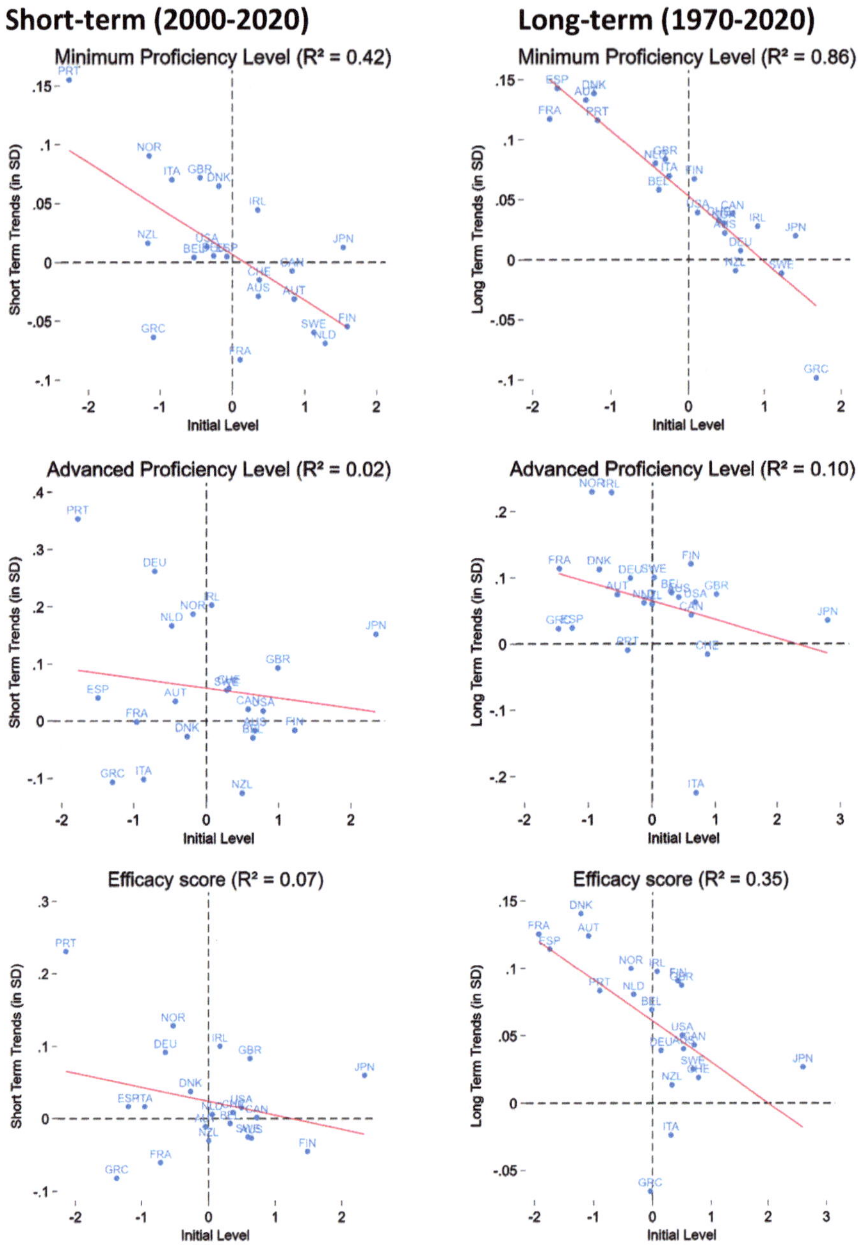

Fig. 4.9 Efficacy trends based on competency thresholds—OECD countries (*Source* Authors based on international and regional student achievements tests)

Table 4.5 Trends in the efficiency of education systems (1970–2020 and 2000–2020)

	Short-term trends								
	Initial level (2000)			Final Level (2020)			20-Year Trends		
Regions	MPL	APL	Efficacy	MPL	APL	Efficacy	MPL	APL	Efficacy
Asia	78.4	9.9	501.5	76.8	10.7	501.08	–1.62	0.77	–1.80
West	86.2	7.7	508.5	87.8	8.6	525.07	1.61	0.86	3.86
LAC	58.1	2.2	312.1	62.3	1.3	325.10	4.24	–0.81	6.54
MENA	60.2	3.4	335.5	61.8	3.0	339.00	1.62	–0.46	1.36
SSA	34.7	0.8	178.1	36.7	1.0	191.49	2.05	0.27	8.77
Total	67.0	5.3	389.3	68.6	5.6	400.54	1.61	0.31	4.11
	Long-term trends								
	Initial level (1970)			Final Level (2020)			50-Year Trends		
Regions	MPL	APL	Efficacy	MPL	APL	Efficacy	MPL	APL	Efficacy
Asia	75.4	10.7	489.4	76.8	10.7	501.08	1.36	0.01	–0.40
West	83.4	7.9	496.3	87.8	8.6	525.07	4.38	0.69	6.55
LAC	51.5	2.7	284.3	60.9	1.3	317.46	9.37	–1.37	12.61
MENA	52.8	4.4	308.0	61.8	3.0	339.00	9.04	–1.42	11.34
SSA	33.1	1.6	182.9	36.7	1.3	196.19	3.59	–0.35	9.75
Total	63.1	5.7	373.4	68.3	5.5	397.67	5.18	–0.22	7.30

Notes "MPL" = Minimum Proficiency Level; "APL" = Advanced Proficiency Level; "Efficacy" = efficacy index. *Source* Authors based on international and regional student achievements tests

Correcting the equity index by the completion rate is particularly useful for developing countries over the long term. However, some countries such as Spain and Portugal, which were lagging behind in quantitative terms, are seeing their equity levels improve more than other countries, once equity has been corrected by the quantitative dimension (Fig. 4.11). Of the 20 OECD countries in our sample, New Zealand, Sweden and Australia show the least progress in the equity index over the long term, while Portugal, Germany and Spain show the most. Over the last two decades, the variations seem to diverge for certain countries such as France and Sweden, which are experiencing a decline in equity, while a clear improvement can be seen in countries such as Denmark and Italy (Fig. 4.12). Fairness managed to increase slightly in Finland and Spain, countries which already had fairness levels above the average for other OECD countries. Equity is improving on average in all regions, but it is especially in sub-Saharan Africa (*SSA*) where it is progressing rapidly, when corrected by education access and completion rates (Table 4.6). This is reassuring, given that most *SSA* countries began democratizing their education systems at the dawn of the twentieth century. As access to schooling has increased, our adjusted equity index mechanically increases, reinforcing the hypothesis of convergence between the world's regions. The convergence test for all countries is partly confirmed (Fig. 4.17), particularly in the short term and when equity is adjusted by school completion. However, the situation seems more heterogeneous when it comes to developing countries (Fig. 4.18), where we see countries significantly improving their equity (e.g., South Africa), while others seem to be reducing it quite sharply (e.g., Thailand and Malaysia).[18]

4.3.4 Some Possible Analyses Based on Inequality Data

Data on educational inequalities can be useful in several fields of application. As the data offered by our database is multidimensional, it can be used, for example, in an analysis of gender inequalities. By analyzing gender inequalities in mathematics and reading performance within OECD countries, we find that girls outperform boys in reading, while the reverse is true in mathematics, whether at primary (Fig. 4.13) or secondary (Fig. 4.14) level. However, the gender gap in mathematics is most pronounced in countries such as Canada and Portugal (a gap of around 20 points), while it is smallest in Finland (around 5 points). In reading, girls outperform boys in all OECD countries, but these inequalities are most pronounced in Finland and Norway, whatever the school level studied.

Another possible application relates to monitoring the Sustainable Development Goals set for 2030. In Goal 4.1.1, it is expected that pupils at primary and secondary levels will have access to quality universal schooling (UNESCO Institute for Statistics, 2017). Thus, reaching the minimum competency threshold can be a target to be achieved (Altinok, 2017). We use the combination between the proportion of students reaching the minimum competency threshold adjusted by the school completion rate in each school level (Table 4.7). We then use the growth rates observed during the period 2000–2020 to predict the proportions of students who could reach the SDG target in 2030 and 2050. At global level, we find that fewer than six out of ten students reach the *SDG* target at primary and secondary level. Forecasts for 2030 underline the impossibility of reaching the *MDG* target for some regions, such as sub-Saharan Africa, where only one child in four is expected to eventually meet the *MDG* requirements. Even in developed countries, the *SDG* target is still relevant, with around 7% of primary school pupils expected to miss the target at primary level, compared with almost 15% at secondary level. Even by 2050, this target seems unattainable for many countries, particularly in the Middle East and North Africa (*MENA*). In the countries of this region, only two-thirds of secondary school pupils are likely to reach this target by 2050, if the trend observed in the past continues to 2050. Finally, even if these forecasts are based on questionable assumptions, they provide useful information for future decisions regarding sustainable development targets in education.

---

[18] Data for each country are available for the year 2020 in Table 4.13.

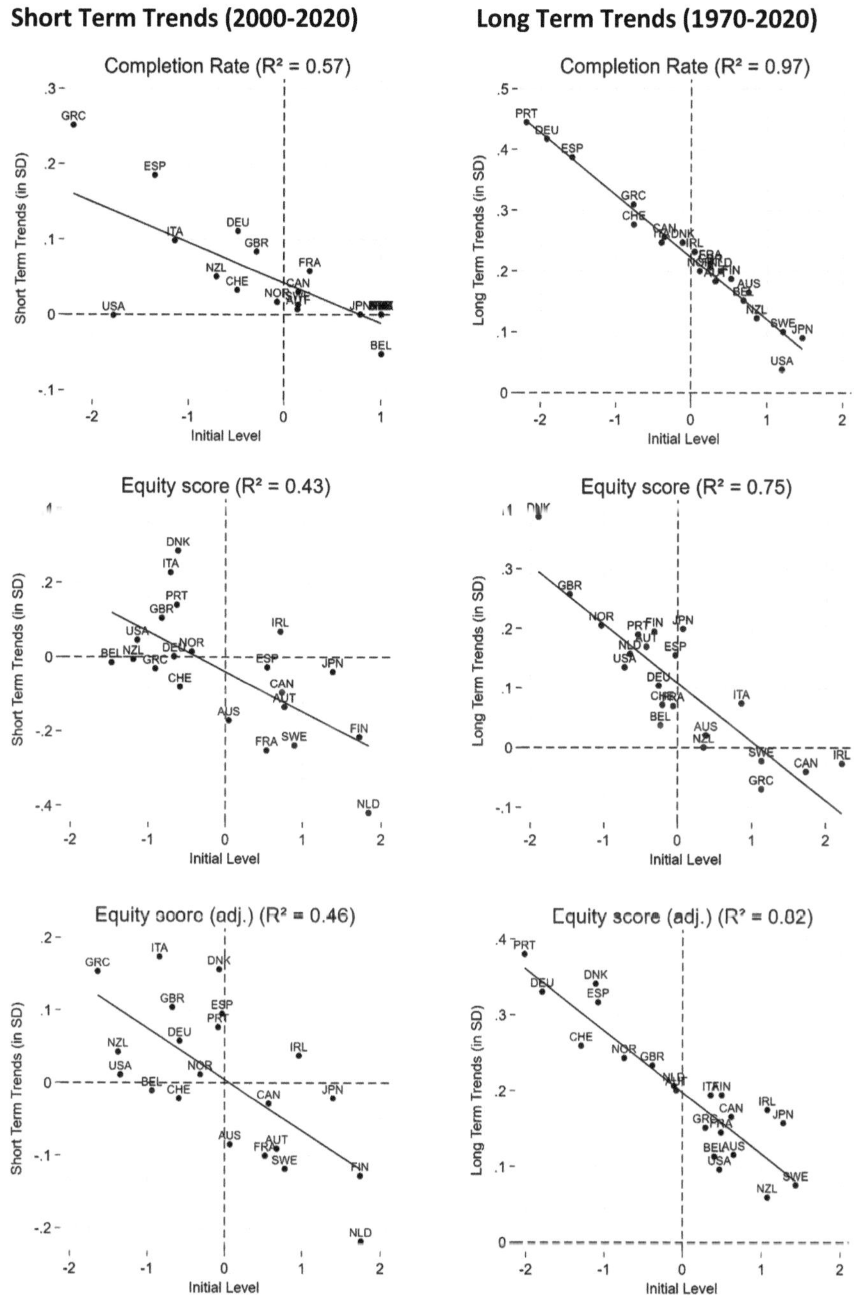

Fig. 4.10 Equity trends based on deciles, OECD countries (*Source* Authors based on international and regional student achievements tests)

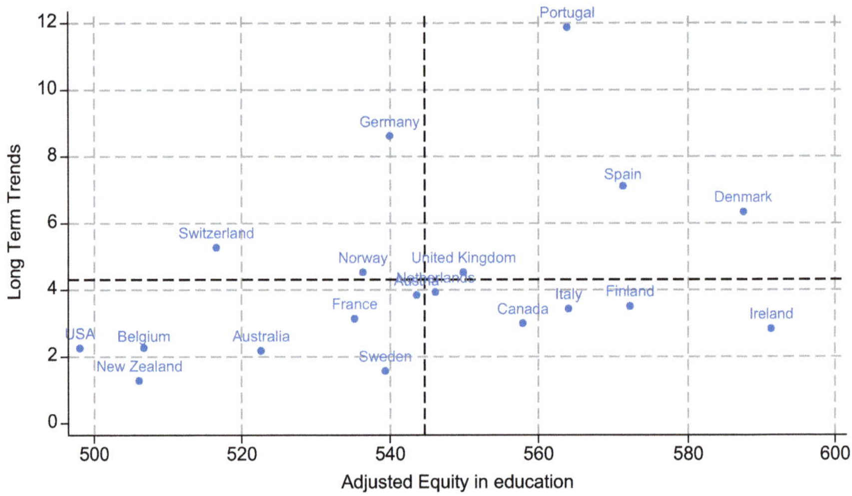

Fig. 4.11 Adjusted equity and long-term trends, OECD countries (*Source* Authors based on international and regional student achievements tests)

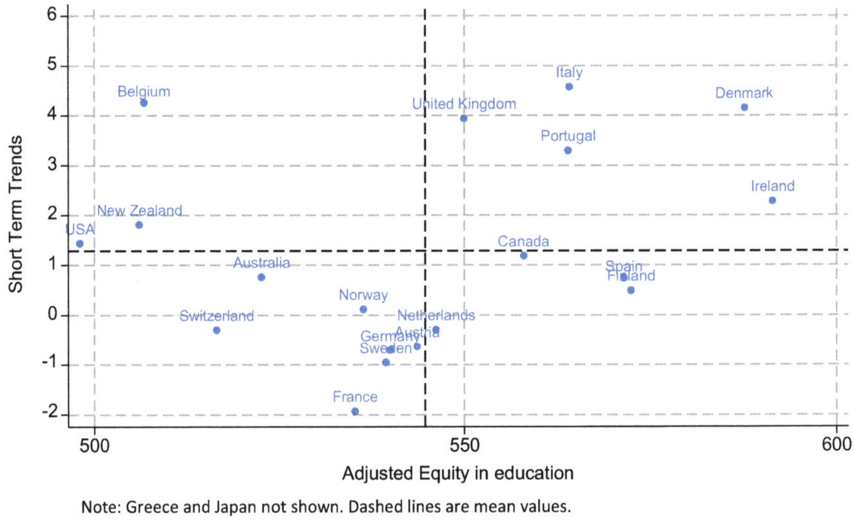

Fig. 4.12 Adjusted equity and short-term trends, OECD countries (*Source* Authors based on international and regional student achievements tests)

Table 4.6 Regional trends in equity indicators (1970–2020 and 2000–2020)

	Short-term trends								
	Initial level (2000)			Final Level (2020)			20-Year Trends		
Regions	Completion	Equity	Equity (adj.)	Completion	Equity	Equity (adj.)	Completion	Equity	Equity (adj.)
Asia	66.2	550	480	83.1	539	502	16.9	–1.2	7.7
West	87.5	542	509	92.8	545	524	5.3	0.9	3.8
LAC	70.3	471	364	80.5	499	431	10.2	6.6	21.0
MENA	65.3	443	369	78.3	455	414	13.0	3.1	14.2
SSA	27.4	452	186	45.7	494	296	18.2	55.5	122.5
Total	63.4	500	394	75.9	515	443	12.5	13.4	34.5
	Long-term trends								
	Initial level (1970)			Final Level (2020)			50-Year Trends		
Regions	Completion	Equity	Equity (adj.)	Completion	Equity	Equity (adj.)	Completion	Equity	Equity (adj.)
Asia	42.9	533	324	82.6	539	502	39.7	2.4	87.4
West	68.4	521	418	91.8	545	524	23.4	5.4	29.1
LAC	45.3	438	212	81.0	494	416	35.7	13.4	134.6
MENA	29.4	408	230	77.4	455	406	48.0	13.0	134.9
SSA	12.5	440	114	45.7	495	296	33.1	21.0	320.0
Total	41.7	477	280	75.7	514	438	34.0	10.6	132.2

Notes LAC = Latin America and Caribbean countries, SSA = Sub-Saharan Africa; MENA = Middle East and North Africa, Asia = all Asian countries, West = mainly high-income countries
Source Authors based on international and regional student achievements tests

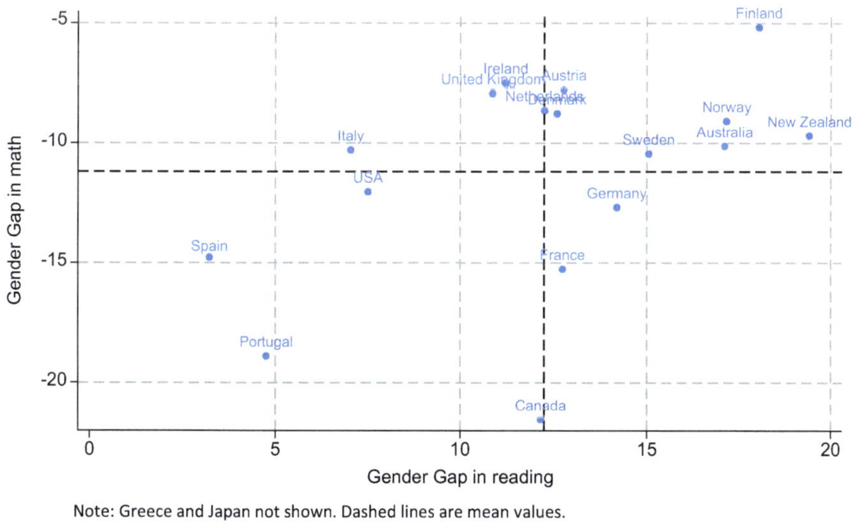

Fig. 4.13 Gender inequalities at primary level (*Source* Authors based on international and regional student achievements tests)

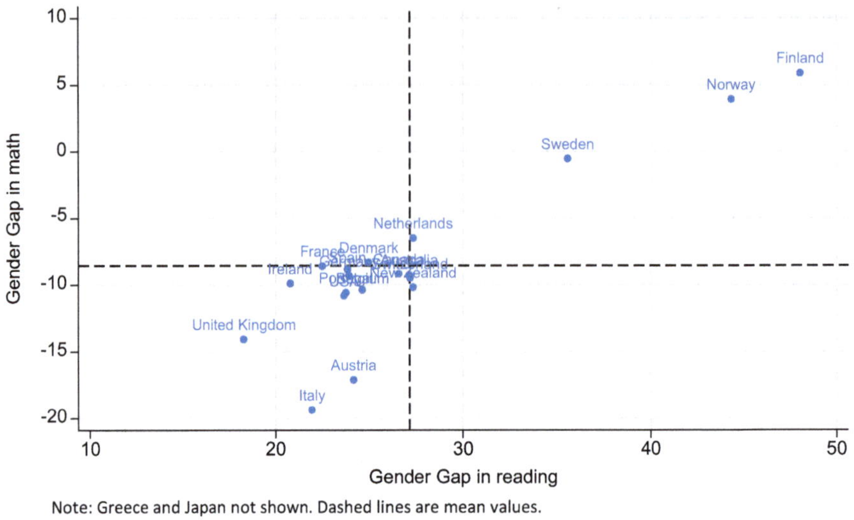

Fig. 4.14 Gender inequalities at secondary level (*Source* Authors based on international and regional student achievements tests)

Table 4.7 Projections for the education indicator in the SDGs (Objective 4.1.1)

	2020				2030				2050			
	Primary		Secondary		Primary		Secondary		Primary		Secondary	
Regions	MPL	Adj. MPL	MPL	Adj. MPL	MPL	Adj. MPL	MPL	Adj. MPL	MPL	Adj. MPL	MPL	Adj. MPL
	(1)	(2)	(3)	(4)	(5)	(6)	(7)	(8)	(9)	(10)	(11)	(12)
Asia	62	56	77	68	84	75	83	77	84	75	83	79
West	89	88	85	81	94	93	87	85	95	94	87	86
LAC	68	65	71	61	64	62	69	63	67	66	71	67
MENA	53	51	67	56	63	60	69	62	64	61	70	66
SSA	24	19	n.a	n.a	26	23	n.a	n.a	28	26	n.a	n.a
World	62	58	72	64	68	64	80	76	70	66	81	78

Notes "MPL" = "Minimum Proficiency Level"; "Adj. MPL" = "MPL adjusted for completion"; "n.a." = not available

Source Authors based on international and regional student achievements tests

4.4 Limitations of the Database

All data production inevitably generates limitations and biases. We discuss these and try to see to what extent it is important to take them into account when using these data in subsequent analyses. The limitations of our study can be divided into three parts: those that relate directly to assessments of achievement, and those that concern the use of specific inequality indicators such as ratios. Furthermore, the methodology used may lead to estimation bias. The use of supplied data also calls for a parsimonious approach when comparing countries over time.

4.4.1 Inherent Limitations of Student Achievement Surveys

The main advantage of using surveys of pupil achievement is that data are available for many countries in different parts of the world. However, these surveys are heterogeneous, both in the content of the items used to measure skills, and in the definitions given to social groups. The limitations are detailed in Altinok and Diebolt (2024). Here, we recall some of their concepts.

It should first be stressed that, although performance tests are intended to provide a representative measure of skills within the population, there is no guarantee that score distributions from different assessments will be similar. It is not uncommon, for example, for a country that has participated in several assessments to display distinct score distributions depending on the tests considered—notably between an international survey such as PISA and a regional test such as LLECE. The "conversion rate" approach we use is based on the implicit assumption that score distributions between assessments are comparable. However, this assumption can be called into question, as each assessment is based on its own psychometric methodology and offers different items, whose level of difficulty may vary. As a result, the score distributions observed can take divergent forms. For example, the items proposed in the LLECE study may be more accessible overall than those used in the TIMSS program. This difference in difficulty may result in a right-skewed (positive) distribution for TIMSS—suggesting a greater concentration of low scores—and an inverse skew for LLECE. Such disparities can influence the definition of proficiency thresholds, leading to divergent results for countries that have been assessed in several schemes simultaneously. Altinok and Diebolt (2024) have shown that such discrepancies exist between, on the one hand, certain regional assessments such as PASEC and SACMEQ and international assessments such as PISA or TIMSS, without these being such as to call into question the anchoring methodology. Furthermore, since we use the percentile-based anchoring method (known as equipercentile linking), differences in score distributions between surveys for the same countries are partly reduced. The use of direct conversion rates between average scores would have led to estimation bias.

Another factor likely to generate estimation bias lies in the differences between the populations tested, depending on the assessments used for the anchoring process. A particularly significant distinction concerns the case of the PISA program, which differs from other international assessments in the way it selects participants: PISA assesses students on the basis of their age, whereas the other systems are based on the level of schooling attended. This methodological divergence can have significant implications in national contexts marked by high repetition or dropout rates. Indeed, assessments targeting a given grade level may exclude some students who have repeated a year, whereas assessments based on age will include these students, whether or not they are behind in their school career. In a framework that assumes comparability of the populations assessed between different surveys, this structural difference may introduce a bias into the estimates produced. However, the work of Wu (2010) suggests that the differences observed between TIMSS and PISA are not statistically significant, which allows certain comparisons to be made. It is also worth pointing out that repetition and dropout rates tend to reduce over time, bringing the populations tested in PISA and TIMSS closer together.

Similarly, the representativeness of sub-populations can be biased. Achievement surveys are stratified so that the target population is representative. Generally, the representativeness of target populations is based on multiple criteria such as geographical location, gender and school size. However, such surveys cannot guarantee that population sub-groups (such as pupils living in rural areas) are representative of the rural population. This is even truer of students who do not speak the test language at home. However, this limitation needs to be put into perspective, because by having a fairly large sample of students taking the test, representativeness can be achieved indirectly: by randomly selecting students from different geographical locations, there is no legitimate reason to think that certain categories of students would be more likely to be chosen to take a test than others. Thus, we can reasonably assume that the sub-categories prepared in our database may be comparable between surveys and at least partially representative of the population.

Measuring inequalities in skills frees us from the need to use indicators as proxies for the qualitative dimension of education. Alternative measures, such as the completion rate in a given grade, are imperfect. These measures are biased because there are wide differences in the quality of education between countries and over time. For example, it is rather counter-intuitive to assume that the same completion rate produces the same stock of skills between countries with different socio-economic characteristics. However, surveys of student achievement also have their own limitations when the dimension analyzed concerns educational inequalities. For example, surveys use different definitions for different urban and rural groups. They have different sample sizes, and this may call into question the possibility of calculating scores for sub-groups with few observations. They may also present "floor" and "ceiling" threshold effects. Some tests, such as PISA, are rather difficult. Some countries whose quality is too low run the risk of seeing their students among the lowest scores, calling into question the very notion of performance gaps between sub-groups. Assessments of student achievement are generally limited to a single grade or a given age. This is not necessarily the best way of analyzing inequalities in skills, as the whole part relating to the added value of skills is neglected. The ideal situation would be to have several skill measurement periods, and to assess the progress made by different population groups. Our database allows for such comparability over time and between countries.

Another limitation relates to the variability of the content assessed and its effects on the comparability of results. The nature of the content assessed is another factor that can compromise the comparability of results between different international surveys. While assessments such as PISA or PASEC III place greater emphasis on the evaluation of cross-curricular or cognitive skills, other tests—such as TIMSS or SACMEQ—rely more heavily on national curricula. This distinction can lead to significant gaps in performance, particularly in education systems that are strongly focused on academic knowledge to the detriment of generic skills. This situation mainly concerns developing countries, but can also be observed in certain contexts in developed countries. To empirically assess the impact of this difference, Altinok and Diebolt (2024) conducted an analysis of countries that participated simultaneously in the TIMSS and PISA surveys, targeting those where the average school level tested in PISA corresponded approximately to grade 9. Although this selection restricts the number of countries studied in relation to all "duplicate" countries, it does limit certain sources of variability. The authors find small differences between the PISA and TIMSS tests, pointing out that an estimate combining heterogeneous surveys does not call into question the robustness of the results.

4.4.2 Limitations on Inequality Indicators

Beyond the data used, a database requires the use of specific indicators. The indicator we will be using the most is the ratio, calculated by dividing the performance of one group by that of another. For example, the locality ratio is calculated by dividing the performance of students living in urban areas by that of students living in rural areas. This type of measurement has clear advantages, such as being easy to understand and independent of absolute values. Thus, even if there are differences in score levels between surveys, the use of a ratio reduces the bias related to the construction of score scales within assessments. On the contrary, the more heterogeneous the score scales, the more biased a performance gap would be. A ratio calculated on the basis of performance ratios between sub-groups avoids this type of bias. The interdecile ratio is also an approach free from this type of bias. However, although the biases inherent in measurement scales are partly reduced, there remains the possibility of deviations in ratios when extreme values are included within sub-populations or when they are not distributed according to a linear, Gaussian curve. In particular, if a large part of the population falls outside the measurement range of a survey, the low representativeness of this sample may lead to the calculation of ratios that are not valid. This may be the case for very poor countries that have taken part in assessments such as PISA. As the distribution of scores does not follow a normal distribution and is mainly present in low scores, the calculation of a ratio between two population groups may not represent the real difference that would have existed between these groups if the test had taken into account a greater variability of scores within the given country. We are unable to quantify this type of bias. However, given that our database includes regional surveys focused on developing countries, we can assume that this type of bias is reduced in our database.

The use of indicators such as the interquartile range may also present limitations. Analysis in terms of the interquartile range focuses exclusively on the 50% of the distribution that lies between the 25% and 75% quartiles. This can be seen as a weakness for this indicator, as the whole inequality analysis is based on just two points of a distribution. It is possible to have the same interquartile range with very different distributions between countries (Omoeva et al., 2018). This dimension of inequality should then be complemented by additional indicators such as ratios between subgroups. The main strength of our database is that it offers a variety of measures relating to inequality, enabling us to supplement the usual indicators with others and thus improve the robustness of any comparative analysis.

4.4.3 Limitations of the Anchoring Methodology

The anchoring strategy adopted is based on a strong assumption: the conversion rate anchoring method based on "duplicate" countries (having participated in several evaluations) only reflects differences between evaluations, independently of national specificities. In other words, linking coefficients are interpreted as "exchange rates" between international assessments. This hypothesis assumes, for example, that the differences observed in the results obtained by Argentina between the LLECE and PISA surveys are exclusively due to the methodological characteristics specific to each assessment, and not to structural elements of the Argentine education system.

However, when matching is based on a limited number of duplicate countries, this hypothesis becomes particularly fragile. Country-specific effects (institutional factors, educational policies, socio-economic context) can then explain a significant proportion of the discrepancies observed, introducing a significant estimation bias. However, this bias tends to diminish as the number of duplicate countries used in the linking equations increases.

In this context, the present study has adapted the initial methodology to include all available valuations in the calculation of "exchange rates", with the aim of reducing the influence of potentially unobserved country fixed effects. In addition, the work of Altinok (2017) has empirically tested this validity hypothesis, by comparing the linking equations between different waves of surveys. Two main findings emerge: on the one hand, country-specific factors do indeed influence the linkage results, beyond test characteristics alone. This means that the estimation method is exposed to a bias linked to these country fixed effects. On the other hand, increasing the number of duplicate countries is essential to mitigate the impact. This requirement has guided the methodological adaptation proposed in this research, which aims to reinforce the robustness of the results by broadening the base of countries taken into account in the matching equations.

The database used to measure equity in education is based on a specific multiple imputation protocol (Honaker et al., 2011), which aims to compensate for missing data in school performance indicators from regional and international tests. This process, while rigorous, nevertheless introduces a certain margin of error into the final estimates of equity scores. In order to limit this potential bias, a rigorous selection of explanatory variables was made, focusing on those likely to provide a substantial explanation of quality and disparities within school systems. These variables, detailed in Altinok and Diebolt (2024), mainly include proxy indicators of schooling quality such as the proportion of qualified teachers, repetition rates at different levels and school completion rates.

These variables were integrated into the multiple imputation process, significantly enriching the data set on learning equity. This methodological framework also made it possible to extend the analysis of schooling quality and equity ratios between subgroups of pupils. Although this method minimizes estimation error, it can lead to outliers. These can be exacerbated when comparing groups of students by gender, locality or socio-economic level, as samples become smaller. However, we have tried to minimize these estimation errors as much as possible by dividing the imputation method into 10 different steps. As indicated in Altinok and Diebolt (2024), this imputation procedure first focuses on developed countries with the highest survey participation and for recent years (1995–2020). In subsequent stages, the imputation procedure is extended to other less frequently surveyed countries, including the predictions from the previous imputation. This approach is extended to other years and countries, until a large database is obtained, including around 100 countries and data from 1970 to 2020. It goes without saying that any form of imputation can lead to measurement errors, and these exist in our database.

4.5 Conclusion

The main contribution of our present work is the availability of a database on educational inequalities. To the best of our knowledge, this is the first database to bring together information on educational inequalities worldwide over a period spanning half a century (1970–2020).

Not only is this database a novelty, it will also help to inform future work in a number of disciplines (notably economics, sociology and education science), as the data provided enables us to grasp the multidimensionality of educational inequalities. Indeed, measuring inequalities with a single indicator would appear to be both reductive and erroneous, since inequalities can take many forms. We therefore propose to distinguish several population groups to see to what extent their performance may differ, without any legitimate reason (distinction according to gender, type of tenancy, language spoken at home, status of the school or socio-economic status of the families). In addition to this approach to inequalities by sub populations, we measure these through competency scales and deduce an efficiency score for education systems. This measure of efficiency is available for over 100 countries and over 50 years, providing a global view of the efficiency of education systems. In addition to these approaches, we also produce an inequality dimension based on deciles. More specifically, by comparing the gap between extreme deciles and relating it to the median score, we can obtain a measure of inequality based on the differences between extreme performances within each country. We can then deduce an equity indicator, which is adjusted by indicators of educational access and completion.

The database provided uses a standardized methodology, enabling it to be updated with the output of future surveys. As such, the next time the results of the *PISA 2025* survey are published, it will be possible to update this database. In this way, the approach used enables us to increase both the temporal interval of the data, and the anchoring of the data. In fact, with the availability of new data, the anchoring methodology is improved, as new countries provide new information on the measurement of inequalities. This in turn strengthens the quality of the adjustments made, and hence the measurement of inequalities.

Appendix A

See Tables 4.8, 4.9, 4.10 and 4.11.

Appendix B: Equity and Efficacy Dimensions

See Tables 4.12, 4.13, 4.14, 4.15, 4.16 and 4.17.

See Figs. 4.15–4.18

Table 4.8 International surveys of student achievement

No	Years	Organization	Abbrev	Subject	Number of countries or regions	Grade	Included
1	1959–60	IEA	–	M,S,L	12	7/8	
2	1964	IEA	FIMS	M	12	7/FS	■
3	1970–71	IEA	SSS-RC	L	15	4/8/FS	
4	1970–72	IEA	FISS	S	19	4/8/FS	■
5	1980–82	IEA	SIMS	M	19	8/FS	■
6	1983–84	IEA	SISS	S	23	4/8/FS	■
7	1988/ 1990–91	NCES	IAEP	M,S	6-19	4/7-8	
8	1990–91	IEA	RLS	L	32	3-4/ 7-8	■
9	1995/ 1999/ 2003/ 2007/ 2011/ 2015/2019	IEA	TIMSS	M,S	45-38-26-48-66-65-64	3-4/ 7-8/ FS	■
10	1992–97	UNESCO	MLA	M,S,L	72	6-8	
11	1997/ 2006/ 2013/2019	UNESCO	LLECE	M,S,L	13-16-15-16	3-6	■
12	1999/ 2002/2007	UNESCO	SACMEQ	M,L	7-15-16	6 6	■
13	2000/ 2010/ 2014/2019	CONFEMEN	PASEC	M,L	22-22-10-14	2/5 then 3-6	■
14	2001/ 2006/ 2011/2016	IEA	PIRLS	L	35-41-55-50	4	■
15	2000/ 2003/ 2006/ 2009/ 2012/ 2015/2018	OECD	PISA	M,S,L	43-41-57-74-65-71-79	Age 15	■
16	2010/ 2015/2019	USAID/RTI	EGRA	L	29-40-5	1 to 6	■
17	2008–2019	ASER	ASER	L	2	1 to 6	■

(continued)

Table 4.8 (continued)

No	Years	Organization	Abbrev	Subject	Number of countries or regions	Grade	Included
18	1994–1998	OECD	IALS	L	22	Adults	
19	2011–2017	OECD	PIAAC	L	39	Adults	■

Note IEA = "International Association for the Evaluation of Educational Achievement", NCES = "National Center for Education Statistics", CONFEMEN = "Conférence des Ministres de l'Education des Etats et Gouvernements de la Francophonie", OECD = "Organisation for Economic Co-operation and Development", USAID = "United States Agency for International Development", RTI = "Research Triangle Institute", ASER = "Australian Council for Educational Research", FIMSS = "First International Mathematics Study", SSS-RC = "Six Subject Survey: Reading Comprehension", FISS = "First International Science Study", SIMS = "Second International Mathematics Study", IAEP = "International Assessment of Educational Progress", RLS = "Reading Literacy Study", TIMSS = "Trends on International Mathematics and Science Study", MLA = "Monitoring Learning Achievement", LLECE = "Latin American Laboratory for Evaluation of the Quality of Education", SACMEQ = "The Southern and Eastern Africa Consortium for Monitoring Educational Quality", PASEC = "Programme d'Analyse des Systèmes Educatifs de la Confemen", PIRLS = "Progress in International Reading Literacy Study", PISA = "Programme of International Student Assessment", EGRA = "Early-Grade Reading Assessment", IALS = "International Adult Literacy Survey", PIAAC = "Programme for International Assessment of Adult Competencies". Subjects: M = mathematics; S = science; L = reading. FS = "fin du secondaire, équivalent au lycée"

Table 4.9 Proportion of missing values

Year	[01]	[02]	[03]	[04]	[05]	[06]	[07]	[08]	[09]	[10]	[11]	[12]	[13]	Total
1970	0.46	0.51	0.52	0.50	0.67	0.67	0.66	0.87	0.52	0.41	0.55	0.60	0.52	0.57
1975	0.44	0.50	0.52	0.50	0.67	0.67	0.66	0.87	0.52	0.26	0.54	0.56	0.52	0.56
1980	0.44	0.50	0.51	0.50	0.67	0.67	0.66	0.87	0.51	0.25	0.54	0.55	0.51	0.55
1985	0.44	0.50	0.51	0.50	0.67	0.67	0.66	0.87	0.51	0.21	0.54	0.55	0.51	0.55
1990	0.34	0.41	0.42	0.41	0.58	0.59	0.57	0.86	0.43	0.18	0.45	0.50	0.42	0.47
1995	0.34	0.40	0.42	0.40	0.54	0.56	0.56	0.85	0.42	0.16	0.45	0.47	0.42	0.46
2000	0.35	0.42	0.43	0.41	0.51	0.53	0.53	0.72	0.43	0.15	0.46	0.48	0.43	0.44
2005	0.36	0.42	0.43	0.41	0.48	0.52	0.50	0.68	0.43	0.14	0.46	0.48	0.43	0.44
2010	0.34	0.42	0.43	0.38	0.47	0.48	0.44	0.60	0.43	0.14	0.46	0.48	0.43	0.42
2015	0.33	0.42	0.42	0.38	0.47	0.46	0.45	0.59	0.43	0.13	0.46	0.48	0.42	0.42
2020	0.37	0.41	0.41	0.39	0.48	0.47	0.46	0.57	0.41	0.19	0.46	0.51	0.41	0.43
Total	0.38	0.45	0.45	0.43	0.56	0.57	0.56	0.76	0.46	0.20	0.49	0.52	0.45	0.48

Notes [01] = MEAN; [02] = PRI; [03] = SEC; [04] = MATH; [05] = READ; [06] = SCIE; [07] = PRI + M; [08] = PRI + R; [09] = PRI + S; [10] = SEC + M; [11] = SEC + R; [12] = SEC + S; where PRI = Primary; SEC = Secondary; MATH = M = Mathematics; READ = R = Reading; SCIE = S = Science

Table 4.10 Proportion of imputed values

Year	[01]	[02]	[03]	[04]	[05]	[06]	[07]	[08]	[09]	[10]	[11]	Total
1970	0.84	0.82	0.82	0.83	0.73	0.76	0.74	0.80	0.10	0.82	0.82	0.66
1975	0.84	0.82	0.82	0.83	0.73	0.76	0.74	0.80	0.10	0.82	0.82	0.67
1980	0.80	0.78	0.77	0.78	0.67	0.72	0.69	0.77	0.10	0.78	0.78	0.63
1985	0.73	0.70	0.69	0.71	0.61	0.62	0.58	0.73	0.10	0.70	0.70	0.57
1990	0.71	0.67	0.67	0.68	0.57	0.57	0.56	0.4[illegible]	0.10	0.67	0.67	0.55
1995	0.52	0.46	0.45	0.47	0.34	0.35	0.36	0.15	0.10	0.45	0.46	0.38
2000	0.42	0.35	0.34	0.36	0.25	0.25	0.25	0.08	0.10	0.33	0.35	0.28
2005	0.31	0.23	0.23	0.26	0.18	0.18	0.17	0.05	0.10	0.23	0.23	0.20
2010	0.11	0.15	0.15	0.09	0.03	0.04	0.04	0.02	0.10	0.15	0.15	0.10
2015	0.08	0.16	0.15	0.09	0.02	0.02	0.02	0.01	0.10	0.16	0.16	0.09
2020	0.27	0.23	0.23	0.27	0.14	0.14	0.16	0.09	0.09	0.24	0.23	0.19
Total	0.50	0.47	0.46	0.47	0.34	0.35	0.34	0.22	0.10	0.47	0.47	0.37

Notes [01] = MEAN; [02] = PRI; [03] = SEC; [04] = MATH; [05] = READ; [06] = SCIE; [07] = PRI + M; [08] = PRI + R; [09] = PRI + S; [10] = SEC + M; [11] = SEC + R; [12] = SEC + S; where PRI = Primary; SEC = Secondary; MATH = M = Mathematics; READ = R = Reading; SCIE = S = Science

Table 4.11 Correlation table

		[01]	[02]	[03]	[04]	[05]	[06]	[07]	[08]	[09]	[10]	[11]	[12]	[13]	[14]
qual0t	[01]	1													
qual1t	[02]	0.96**	1												
		0.00													
qual3t	[03]	0.79**	0.73**	1											
		0.00	0.00												
dif_0gend	[04]	0.05	0.05	0.04	1										
		0.08	0.07	0.19											
dif_0loca	[05]	–0.34**	–0.34**	–0.26**	–0.08**	1									
		0.00	0.00	0.00	0.01										
dif_0lang	[06]	0.40**	0.36**	0.34**	–0.31**	–0.10**	1								
		0.00	0.00	0.00	0.00	0.00									
dif_0ses4	[07]	0.34**	0.33**	0.23**	–0.14**	0.01	0.43**	1							
		0.00	0.00	0.00	0.00	0.67	0.00								
dif_0rses4	[08]	–0.22**	–0.21**	–0.18**	–0.13**	0.27**	0.24**	0.83**	1						
		0.00	0.00	0.00	0.00	0.00	0.00	0.00							
dif_0priv	[09]	–0.17**	–0.19**	–0.28**	–0.05	0.16**	0.01	0.28**	0.39**	1					
		0.00	0.00	0.00	0.09	0.00	0.79	0.00	0.00						
comp_pri	[10]	0.65**	0.68**	0.42**	0.19**	–0.17**	0.14**	0.41**	0.09**	0	1				
		0.00	0.00	0.00	0.00	0.00	0.00	0.00	0.00	0.92					
comp_lsec	[11]	0.72**	0.72**	0.47**	0.17**	–0.25**	0.12**	0.41**	0.06	–0.05	0.82**	1			
		0.00	0.00	0.00	0.00	0.00	0.00	0.00	0.06	0.27	0.00				
eq_qual0t	[12]	0.61**	0.55**	0.44**	–0.18**	–0.27**	0.23**	–0.03	–0.46**	–0.23**	0.16**	0.28**	1		

(continued)

Table 4.11 (continued)

		[01]	[02]	[03]	[04]	[05]	[06]	[07]	[08]	[09]	[10]	[11]	[12]	[13]	[14]
		0.00	0.00	0.00	0.00	0.00	0.00	0.28	0.00	0.00	0.00	0.00			
eq_qual1t	[13]	0.85**	0.85**	0.60**	0.06*	–0.32**	0.20**	0.29**	–0.18**	–0.13**	0.85**	0.92**	0.56**	1	
		0.00	0.00	0.00	0.04	0.00	0.00	0.00	0.00	0.00	0.00	0.00	0.00		
eff_qual	[14]	0.97**	0.97**	0.87**	0.05	–0.34**	0.38**	0.32**	–0.21**	–0.24**	0.63**	0.68**	0.55**	0.81**	1
		0.00	0.00	0.00	0.08	0.00	0.00	0.00	0.00	0.00	0.00	0.00	0.00	0.00	

Notes "qual0t" = mean score; "qual1t" = MPL; "qual3t" = APL; "dif_0gend" = gender ratio; "dif_0loca" = location ratio; "dif0_lang" = language ratio; "dif0_ses4" = socio-economic status ratio; "dif0_priv" = public/private school status ratio; "dif_decile" = interdecile gap; "complsec" = completion rate, lower secondary level; "eq_qual0t" = equity index; "eq-qual1t" = adjusted equity index; "eff_qual" = efficacy index

$*p < 0.05$; $**p < 0.01$; p-value appears below correlation coefficient

Table 4.12 Ranking of countries according to efficiency, short-term trends

		Minimum proficiency level (%)			Advanced proficiency level (%)			Efficacy index (score points)		
Region	Country	R. Rank	W. Rank	Value	R. Rank	W. Rank	Value	R. Rank	W. Rank	Value
Asia	Australia	8	31	92.1	7	16	13.8	7	16	599
Asia	Brunei	13	63	75.8	11	62	3.3	13	63	412
Asia	Cambodia	18	111	40.5	17	88	1.6	18	111	219
Asia	Chin. Taipei	5	6	96.4	5	5	21.3	5	5	694
Asia	China	10	47	86.1	15	80	2	11	56	451
Asia	Hong Kong	4	5	96.6	3	3	21.9	4	4	702
Asia	India	17	110	43.9	14	78	2.1	17	108	241
Asia	Indonesia	16	95	53.9	19	119	0.6	16	99	275
Asia	Japan	1	2	97.8	4	4	21.9	3	3	708
Asia	Korea Rep	3	4	96.7	2	2	25.3	2	2	737
Asia	Macao	7	10	95.5	6	8	16.1	6	7	639
Asia	Malaysia	14	68	73.7	13	70	2.5	14	66	394
Asia	Mongolia	12	61	76.5	12	67	3	12	62	412
Asia	New Zealand	9	38	89.4	8	21	12	9	30	566
Asia	Papua New Guinea	11	54	84	10	54	4.9	10	54	469
Asia	Philippines	19	120	31.9	18	113	0.7	19	121	166
Asia	Singapore	2	3	97.5	1	1	37.8	1	1	866
Asia	Thailand	15	69	73.4	16	81	2	15	70	386
Asia	Vietnam	6	7	95.7	9	27	10.6	8	22	584
West	Albania	45	59	79.9	43	57	3.8	44	58	438

(continued)

Table 4.12 (continued)

Region	Country	Minimum proficiency level (%)			Advanced proficiency level (%)			Efficacy index (score points)		
		R. Rank	W. Rank	Value	R. Rank	W. Rank	Value	R. Rank	W. Rank	Value
West	Armenia	33	42	88.5	41	55	4.6	37	48	488
West	Austria	15	22	93.5	19	29	10.3	21	29	570
West	Azerbaijan	48	76	69.6	47	77	2.2	48	76	369
West	Belgium	27	35	90.8	10	17	13.6	13	20	590
West	Belgium Flemish	14	21	93.7	30	40	7.2	25	34	541
West	Belgium French	39	50	85.1	40	53	4.9	42	53	475
West	Bosnia	47	72	72.5	44	63	3.2	46	65	395
West	Bulgaria	43	56	81.8	24	34	8.9	35	45	498
West	Canada	7	14	94.6	9	15	13.9	8	14	612
West	Croatia	16	23	93.5	29	39	7.3	26	35	540
West	Cyprus	28	36	90.6	33	43	6.6	32	42	519
West	Czech Rep	11	18	94.2	16	24	11.5	14	21	586
West	Denmark	5	12	94.8	21	31	10.2	17	25	576
West	Estonia	1	1	98.1	1	6	16.7	1	6	658
West	Finland	6	13	94.8	3	9	15.9	3	9	632
West	France	31	40	88.7	28	38	7.9	31	41	522
West	Georgia	46	70	73	50	91	1.5	47	73	380
West	Germany	25	33	91.7	14	22	11.7	18	26	576
West	Greece	38	48	85.8	39	52	5.5	38	49	484
West	Hungary	26	34	91.6	20	30	10.3	22	31	560

(continued)

Table 4.12 (continued)

		Minimum proficiency level (%)			Advanced proficiency level (%)			Efficacy index (score points)		
Region	Country	R. Rank	W. Rank	Value	R. Rank	W. Rank	Value	R. Rank	W. Rank	Value
West	Iceland	37	46	86.6	32	42	7.1	34	44	504
West	Ireland	3	9	95.5	8	14	14	6	12	617
West	Italy	19	26	93	31	41	7.1	27	36	536
West	Kazakhstan	35	44	86.7	42	56	4.4	40	51	478
West	Kosovo	51	91	56.4	51	117	0.6	51	93	289
West	Latvia	4	11	95.4	22	32	9.6	20	28	573
West	Liechenstein	9	16	94.3	4	10	14.7	5	11	618
West	Lithuania	13	20	93.8	18	28	10.5	19	27	574
West	Luxembourg	29	37	89.7	23	33	9.4	24	33	542
West	Moldova	42	55	83.7	45	66	3	43	57	448
West	Montenegro	44	58	79.9	46	73	2.2	45	60	422
West	Netherlands	17	24	93.1	15	23	11.5	16	24	581
West	North Macedonia	49	80	66.9	48	89	1.6	49	81	351
West	Norway	20	27	93	13	20	12.8	12	19	593
West	Poland	12	19	94.2	6	12	14.2	7	13	613
West	Portugal	22	29	92.5	25	35	8.7	23	32	549
West	Romania	41	53	84	36	48	5.8	39	50	479
West	Russian Fed	2	8	95.6	7	13	14.1	4	10	620
West	Scotland	34	43	87.9	34	44	6.6	33	43	505
West	Serbia	36	45	86.7	37	50	5.5	36	46	489

(continued)

Table 4.12 (continued)

		Minimum proficiency level (%)			Advanced proficiency level (%)			Efficacy index (score points)		
Region	Country	R. Rank	W. Rank	Value	R. Rank	W. Rank	Value	R. Rank	W. Rank	Value
West	Slovak Republic	30	39	89.1	27	37	8.1	29	39	526
West	Slovenia	8	15	94.5	17	26	11	15	23	583
West	Spain	23	30	92.3	35	45	6.3	30	40	524
West	Sweden	18	25	93	12	19	13.1	11	18	596
West	Switzerland	21	28	92.8	11	18	13.3	10	17	597
West	Turkey	32	41	88.7	26	36	8.3	28	38	526
West	USA	24	32	91.8	5	11	14.6	9	15	605
West	Ukraine	40	52	84.1	38	51	5.5	41	52	475
West	United Kingdom	10	17	94.3	2	7	16.2	2	8	633
West	Uzbekistan	50	83	61.4	49	90	1.5	50	85	322
LAKE	Argentina	11	86	60.5	16	120	0.6	12	87	308
LAC	Brazil	8	77	67.6	8	92	1.4	9	79	352
LAKE	Chile	1	60	79.2	4	76	2.2	1	61	417
LAKE	Colombia	10	79	67.1	13	107	0.8	10	82	344
LAKE	Costa Rica	2	62	76.3	15	112	0.7	5	69	389
LAKE	Cuba	7	73	71.3	1	58	3.7	3	67	394
LAC	Dominican Rep	19	117	37	18	133	0.1	19	118	186
LAC	Ecuador	9	78	67.3	5	82	1.9	8	78	355
LAC	El Salvador	14	96	53.4	9	99	1	14	97	277
LAKE	Guatemala	17	106	46.8	12	105	0.9	16	105	243
LAKE	Honduras	13	92	55.5	6	83	1.8	13	91	295

(continued)

Table 4.12 (continued)

		Minimum proficiency level (%)			Advanced proficiency level (%)			Efficacy index (score points)		
Region	Country	R. Rank	W. Rank	Value	R. Rank	W. Rank	Value	R. Rank	W. Rank	Value
LAKE	Jamaica	12	87	60.3	3	74	2.2	11	84	323
LAKE	Mexico	4	65	74.9	14	111	0.7	6	72	382
LAKE	Nicaragua	15	99	51.4	19	134	0	15	103	257
LAKE	Panama	16	103	47.9	17	132	0.2	18	107	241
LAKE	Paraguay	18	107	46.6	11	104	0.9	17	106	242
LAC	Peru	6	71	72.5	10	103	1	7	75	372
LAKE	Trinidad & T	5	67	74.3	2	59	3.7	2	64	408
LAKE	Uruguay	3	64	75	7	85	1.7	4	68	392
MENA	Algeria	13	94	54.1	10	84	1.8	13	94	288
MENA	Bahrain	3	57	81.6	4	49	5.6	3	55	464
MENA	Egypt	15	98	52.4	13	93	1.4	15	98	276
MENA	Iran I.R	6	75	70.6	8	75	2.2	6	74	375
MENA	Israel	2	51	84.1	1	25	11.1	1	37	532
MENA	Jordan	11	89	56.5	15	95	1.3	12	92	295
MENA	Kuwait	10	88	57.3	12	87	1.6	10	88	303
MENA	Lebanon	12	90	56.5	9	79	2	11	89	303
MENA	Malta	1	49	85.5	3	47	6.1	2	47	488
MENA	Morocco	17	105	47.1	18	122	0.4	17	109	240
MENA	Oman	8	82	64.5	7	68	2.8	8	80	351
MENA	Palestine	14	97	52.5	11	86	1.7	14	96	279
MENA	Qatar	5	74	70.7	6	65	3.2	5	71	385

(continued)

Table 4.12 (continued)

		Minimum proficiency level (%)			Advanced proficiency level (%)			Efficacy index (score points)		
Region	Country	R. Rank	W. Rank	Value	R. Rank	W. Rank	Value	R. Rank	W. Rank	Value
MENA	Saudi Arabia	9	85	61.2	17	114	0.7	9	86	313
MENA	Syrian A.R	7	81	65.2	5	64	3.2	7	77	358
MENA	Tunisia	16	101	51.1	16	97	1.2	16	101	268
MENA	United Arab Em	4	66	74.7	2	46	6.1	4	59	435
MENA	Yemen	18	128	27.5	14	94	1.3	18	126	151
SSA	Benin	9	113	39	23	127	0.3	12	116	198
SSA	Botswana	4	102	50.3	2	61	3.4	3	95	286
SSA	Burkina Faso	11	115	37.3	23	127	0.3	13	117	189
SSA	Burundi	20	126	29.4	23	127	0.3	20	127	150
SSA	Cameroon	17	123	31	23	127	0.3	18	124	158
SSA	Chad	27	134	21.2	23	127	0.3	27	134	109
SSA	Congo	16	122	31.4	23	127	0.3	17	123	160
SSA	Congo, D.R	26	133	22.6	16	116	0.7	26	133	119
SSA	Eswatini	10	114	38.2	9	101	1	10	114	201
SSA	Gabon	7	109	45.3	18	121	0.5	7	110	231
SSA	Ghana	6	108	46.4	1	60	3.6	4	100	268
SSA	Kenya	5	104	47.7	8	100	1	6	104	249
SSA	Lesotho	19	125	29.5	13	109	0.8	19	125	155
SSA	Madagascar	25	132	24.1	15	115	0.7	24	131	127

(continued)

Table 4.12 (continued)

Region	Country	Minimum proficiency level (%)			Advanced proficiency level (%)			Efficacy index (score points)		
		R. Rank	W. Rank	Value	R. Rank	W. Rank	Value	R. Rank	W. Rank	Value
SSA	Malawi	22	129	26.8	12	108	0.8	22	129	142
SSA	Mauritius	1	84	61.4	3	69	2.6	1	83	333
SSA	Mozambique	13	118	36	4	71	2.3	9	113	203
SSA	Namibia	15	121	31.6	10	102	1	15	120	168
SSA	Niger	24	131	24.8	23	127	0.3	25	132	127
SSA	Senegal	8	112	40.2	23	127	0.3	8	112	204
SSA	Seychelles	2	93	54.9	5	72	2.3	2	90	298
SSA	South Africa	12	116	37.2	6	96	1.3	11	115	199
SSA	Tanzania U.R	3	100	51.2	11	106	0.9	5	102	265
SSA	Togo	21	127	29.3	23	127	0.3	21	128	149
SSA	Uganda	18	124	30.7	7	98	1.1	16	122	164
SSA	Zambia	23	130	25.9	14	110	0.7	23	130	137
SSA	Zimbabwe	14	119	35.1	17	118	0.6	14	119	182

Notes R. Rank = Regional Rank; W. Rank = World Rank

Table 4.13 Country equity rankings based on deciles

		Equity (score points)			Adjusted equity (score points)			Socio-economic status (relative)		
Region	Country	R. Rank	W. Rank	Value	R. Rank	W. Rank	Value	R. Rank	W. Rank	Value
Asia	Australia	10	50	534	7	35	523	9	58	14.1
Asia	Brunei	14	84	499	9	55	467	17	95	18.0
Asia	China	7	16	581	4	9	564			
Asia	Hong Kong	5	9	589	6	25	540	4	9	9.7
Asia	India	15	86	495	12	69	433	12	66	15.3
Asia	Indonesia	16	89	487	10	56	466	3	7	9.4
Asia	Japan	2	4	593	1	2	590	5	12	10.0
Asia	Korea Rep	8	19	572	3	8	564	8	45	13.3
Asia	Malaysia	13	74	509	11	57	463	16	88	17.0
Asia	Mongolia	9	41	542	5	21	542	15	87	17.0
Asia	New Zealand	11	65	524	8	41	506	13	76	16.1
Asia	Philippines	17	122	334	14	104	280	11	60	14.4
Asia	Thailand	12	66	524	13	77	403	14	81	16.4
Asia	Vietnam	3	6	591	2	5	573	6	19	11.1
West	Albania	35	59	528	34	44	503	10	24	11.9
West	Armenia	28	46	537	30	39	514	15	31	12.2
West	Austria	18	31	560	14	18	544	35	79	16.3
West	Azerbaijan	44	82	500	39	52	475	14	28	12.1
West	Belgium	42	71	515	31	40	507	44	102	18.5
West	Bulgaria	46	93	476	43	82	393	49	116	22.5

(continued)

Table 4.13 (continued)

		Equity (score points)			Adjusted equity (score points)			Socio-economic status (relative)		
Region	Country	R. Rank	W. Rank	Value	R. Rank	W. Rank	Value	R. Rank	W. Rank	Value
West	Canada	13	25	566	10	14	558	6	18	11.0
West	Cyprus	17	29	561	17	22	542	20	38	13.0
West	Czech Rep	11	23	568	18	23	541	34	77	16.3
West	Denmark	4	10	587	2	3	587	26	52	13.8
West	Estonia	10	22	571	21	27	539	7	20	11.3
West	Finland	8	18	575	4	6	572	24	50	13.6
West	France	29	47	535	24	30	535	46	106	19.4
West	Georgia	43	76	506	32	42	505	8	21	11.4
West	Germany	26	43	541	19	24	540	43	98	18.3
West	Greece	34	58	529	26	32	529	22	44	13.2
West	Hungary	21	36	550	16	20	542	47	112	20.1
West	Iceland	36	60	527	38	49	492	27	55	13.9
West	Ireland	3	5	591	1	1	591	17	33	12.4
West	Italy	7	17	575	6	10	564	4	16	10.5
West	Kazakhstan	19	32	560	9	13	560	3	13	10.1
West	Latvia	2	3	602	8	12	563	5	17	10.6
West	Liechenstein	14	26	566	11	15	550			
West	Lithuania	12	24	567	25	31	529	28	57	14.1
West	Luxembourg	31	49	534	37	48	493	39	89	17.1

(continued)

Table 4.13 (continued)

		Equity (score points)			Adjusted equity (score points)			Socio-economic status (relative)		
Region	Country	R. Rank	W. Rank	Value	R. Rank	W. Rank	Value	R. Rank	W. Rank	Value
West	Moldova	41	70	519	41	60	450	38	86	16.9
West	Montenegro	37	62	526	33	43	504	9	22	11.7
West	Netherlands	24	39	546	13	17	546	16	32	12.4
West	North Macedonia	47	105	454	42	76	405	45	104	19.0
West	Norway	22	37	549	23	29	536	23	48	13.5
West	Poland	15	27	565	15	19	542	32	71	15.4
West	Portugal	16	28	564	7	11	564	29	61	14.6
West	Romania	45	90	486	40	59	452	50	118	22.7
West	Russian Fed	1	2	604	3	4	582	2	10	9.9
West	Serbia	38	63	526	35	45	503	36	80	16.3
West	Slovenia	6	15	581	27	34	525	19	36	12.6
West	Spain	9	21	571	5	7	571	12	26	12.0
West	Sweden	23	38	548	20	26	539	41	91	17.7
West	Switzerland	33	57	530	28	37	517	37	84	16.7
West	Turkey	27	45	540	22	28	538	40	90	17.5
West	USA	30	48	534	36	46	498	31	65	14.9
West	Ukraine	39	64	525	29	38	515	30	63	14.8
West	United Kingdom	20	34	553	12	16	550	21	41	13.0
LAKE	Argentina	14	96	473	8	61	450	18	107	19.5
LAC	Brazil	13	95	473	13	75	409	17	105	19.1

(continued)

Table 4.13 (continued)

		Equity (score points)			Adjusted equity (score points)			Socio-economic status (relative)		
Region	Country	R. Rank	W. Rank	Value	R. Rank	W. Rank	Value	R. Rank	W. Rank	Value
LAKE	Chile	3	53	533	3	47	494	7	70	15.4
LAKE	Colombia	7	73	509	9	64	447	15	101	18.4
LAKE	Costa Rica	1	30	560	7	58	459	9	75	15.9
LAKE	Cuba	18	104	457	11	71	425	2	8	9.7
LAKE	Dominican Rep	12	92	479	12	72	422	8	72	15.7
LAKE	Ecuador	5	61	526	2	36	523	6	64	14.9
LAKE	El Salvador	6	68	522	6	54	469	11	83	16.7
LAKE	Guatemala	9	83	499	16	93	338	13	96	18.1
LAKE	Honduras	11	88	493	18	96	306	1	3	8.1
LAC	Mexico	2	44	540	1	33	525	5	56	13.9
LAKE	Nicaragua	4	55	531	15	85	377	3	14	10.1
LAKE	Panama	15	98	470	14	80	399	19	115	21.7
LAKE	Paraguay	17	103	462	17	95	318	10	78	16.3
LAKE	Peru	8	78	504	4	50	489	14	100	18.4
LAKE	Trinidad & T	16	102	467	10	66	442	12	85	16.9
LAKE	Uruguay	10	87	494	5	51	487	16	103	18.7
MENA	Algeria	2	75	507	4	65	444	2	2	7.5
MENA	Egypt	10	109	435	9	81	395	10	67	15.3
MENA	Iran I.R	6	94	476	2	62	450	16	111	20.0
MENA	Israel	8	99	469	3	63	448	14	97	18.2
MENA	Jordan	1	69	521	10	83	393	12	69	15.3
MENA	Kuwait	13	117	418	7	73	418	1	1	5.1

(continued)

Table 4.13 (continued)

		Equity (score points)			Adjusted equity (score points)			Socio-economic status (relative)		
Region	Country	R. Rank	W. Rank	Value	R. Rank	W. Rank	Value	R. Rank	W. Rank	Value
MENA	Malta	4	85	496	1	53	472	7	49	13.6
MENA	Morocco	11	113	431	13	94	325	5	39	13.0
MENA	Oman	12	116	419	11	84	386	9	54	13.8
MENA	Palestine	5	91	484	6	68	434	8	53	13.8
MENA	Qatar	9	108	438	8	74	415	11	68	15.3
MENA	Saudi Arabia	7	97	472	5	67	435	4	15	10.2
MENA	Tunisia	14	118	417	12	88	353	13	94	18.0
SSA	Benin	1	8	590	7	90	351	11	93	17.9
SSA	Botswana	21	112	431	3	79	401	8	62	14.8
SSA	Burkina Faso	4	20	572	14	101	289	7	47	13.4
SSA	Burundi	6	35	550	17	105	279	2	29	12.1
SSA	Cameroon	9	52	533	11	98	300	15	113	20.4
SSA	Congo	5	33	560	10	97	305	12	99	18.4
SSA	Eswatini	10	54	531	4	86	372	4	34	12.5
SSA	Ghana	23	115	421	8	91	351	5	40	13.0
SSA	Kenya	14	80	503	1	70	427			
SSA	Lesotho	16	101	467	12	99	294			
SSA	Madagascar	11	72	513	19	107	259	14	110	20.0
SSA	Malawi	13	79	503	20	108	223			
SSA	Mauritius	20	111	432	2	78	401			
SSA	Mozambique	8	51	533	21	109	197			

(continued)

Table 4.13 (continued)

		Equity (score points)			Adjusted equity (score points)			Socio-economic status (relative)		
Region	Country	R. Rank	W. Rank	Value	R. Rank	W. Rank	Value	R. Rank	W. Rank	Value
SSA	Namibia	19	110	435	9	92	346			
SSA	Senegal	3	12	584	13	100	293	9	74	15.9
SSA	South Africa	24	121	339	16	103	281	13	108	19.7
SSA	Tanzania U.R	12	77	506	18	106	271			
SSA	Togo	7	40	543	6	89	352	17	119	27.2
SSA	Uganda	17	106	450	22	110	185			
SSA	Zambia	15	100	468	5	87	369			

Notes R. Rank = Regional Rank; W. Rank = World Rank. For details, please consult Sect. 2.2

Table 4.14 Efficacy of schooling systems around the World, 2000–2020

Short-term trends									
	Initial level (2000)			Final level (2020)			20-year trends		
Countries	MPL	APL	Efficacy	MPL	APL	Efficacy	MPL	APL	Efficacy
Albania	59.6	1.8	317	79.9	3.8	438	20.3	2.0	38.3
Algeria	50.1	2.6	276	54.1	1.8	288	4.0	–0.8	4.4
Argentina	64.8	2.2	346	60.5	0.6	308	–4.4	–1.6	–11.0
Armenia	78.1	3.4	424	88.5	4.6	488	10.5	1.2	15.1
Australia	93.4	14.0	607	92.1	13.8	599	–1.4	–0.2	–1.4
Austria	95.0	9.9	574	93.5	10.3	570	–1.5	0.4	–0.6
Azerbaijan	71.9	2.0	380	69.6	2.2	369	–2.3	0.1	–2.7
Bahrain	69.5	3.9	386	81.6	5.6	464	12.1	1.7	20.0
Belgium	90.6	13.9	592	90.8	13.6	590	0.2	–0.3	–0.4
Belgium Flemish	96.6	7.9	562	93.7	7.2	541	–2.9	–0.6	–3.7
Belgium French	85.5	5.1	478	85.1	4.9	475	–0.3	–0.2	–0.7
Benin	30.5	0.5	158	39.0	0.3	198	8.5	–0.3	25.1
Bosnia	73.9	3.2	401	72.5	3.2	395	–1.4	0.0	–1.7
Botswana	40.3	2.3	224	50.3	3.4	286	10.0	1.2	27.4
Brazil	61.0	1.3	318	67.6	1.4	352	6.6	0.1	10.5
Brunei	70.6	3.2	385	75.8	3.3	412	5.2	0.0	6.8
Bulgaria	88.6	9.1	534	81.8	8.9	498	–6.7	–0.2	–6.7
Burkina Faso	32.1	0.3	163	37.3	0.3	189	5.2	0.0	15.9
Burundi	28.3	0.3	145	29.4	0.3	150	1.2	–0.1	3.6

(continued)

Table 4.14 (continued)

Short-term trends									
	Initial level (2000)			Final level (2020)			20-year trends		
Countries	MPL	APL	Efficacy	MPL	APL	Efficacy	MPL	APL	Efficacy
Cambodia	40.5	1.6	219	40.5	1.6	219	0.0	0.0	0.0
Cameroon	42.0	0.3	213	31.0	0.3	158	–10.9	0.0	–25.7
Canada	94.9	13.6	611	94.6	13.9	612	–0.3	0.2	0.1
Chad	25.8	0.7	136	21.2	0.3	109	–4.6	–0.4	–19.8
Chile	68.0	1.9	359	79.2	2.2	417	11.2	0.2	16.3
Chin. Taipei	97.4	19.3	681	96.4	21.3	694	–1.1	1.9	2.0
China	84.3	3.6	457	86.1	2.0	451	1.9	–1.5	–1.3
Colombia	59.1	0.8	304	67.1	0.8	344	8.0	0.0	13.2
Congo	27.3	0.8	144	31.4	0.3	160	4.1	–0.5	10.7
Congo, D.R	25.2	0.3	129	22.6	0.7	119	–2.6	0.3	–7.8
Costa Rica	76.0	0.9	389	76.3	0.7	389	0.4	–0.2	–0.1
Croatia	92.6	6.7	530	93.5	7.3	540	0.8	0.6	1.9
Cuba	85.6	11.1	539	71.3	3.7	394	–14.3	–7.4	–27.0
Cyprus	84.0	4.9	469	90.6	6.6	519	6.7	1.7	10.8
Czech Rep	94.0	10.9	579	94.2	11.5	586	0.2	0.6	1.2
Denmark	91.7	10.5	563	94.8	10.2	576	3.1	–0.3	2.2
Dominican Rep	29.6	0.4	152	37.0	0.1	186	7.3	–0.3	22.2
Ecuador	58.2	2.5	316	67.3	1.9	355	9.1	–0.6	12.3
Egypt	64.5	3.5	358	52.4	1.4	276	–12.1	–2.2	–23.0

(continued)

Table 4.14 (continued)

Short-term trends									
	Initial level (2000)			Final level (2020)			20-year trends		
Countries	MPL	APL	Efficacy	MPL	APL	Efficacy	MPL	APL	Efficacy
El Salvador	47.2	2.3	259	53.4	1.0	277	6.2	–1.3	7.1
Estonia	95.7	14.5	623	98.1	16.7	658	2.4	2.2	5.5
Eswatini	34.6	0.3	175	38.2	1.0	201	3.6	0.7	14.3
Finland	97.3	16.0	647	94.8	15.9	632	–2.6	–0.2	–2.3
France	92.6	7.9	542	88.7	7.9	522	–3.9	0.0	–3.6
Gabon	38.1	0.4	195	45.3	0.5	231	7.2	0.0	18.6
Georgia	69.7	1.5	363	73.0	1.5	380	3.3	0.0	4.6
Germany	91.5	8.8	546	91.7	11.7	576	0.3	2.9	5.5
Ghana	53.1	3.7	303	46.4	3.6	263	–6.7	–0.1	–11.3
Greece	88.9	6.6	510	85.8	5.5	484	–3.0	–1.2	–5.2
Guatemala	47.1	2.5	251	46.8	0.9	243	–0.3	–1.6	–6.8
Honduras	49.6	2.4	272	55.5	1.8	295	5.9	–0.6	8.7
Hong Kong	98.0	20.4	695	96.6	21.9	702	–1.4	1.5	1.1
Hungary	93.9	11.3	583	91.6	10.3	560	–2.4	–1.0	–3.8
Iceland	92.1	7.2	532	86.6	7.1	504	–5.4	–0.1	–5.4
India	42.3	3.7	249	43.9	2.1	241	1.6	–1.6	–3.3
Indonesia	57.9	0.8	298	53.9	0.6	275	–4.1	–0.2	–7.5
Iran I.R	66.3	3.6	367	70.6	2.2	375	4.3	–1.4	2.0
Ireland	93.4	11.7	585	95.5	14.0	617	2.1	2.2	5.6
Israel	81.6	9.1	498	84.1	11.1	532	2.6	2.0	6.7

(continued)

Table 4.14 (continued)

Short-term trends

	Initial level (2000)			Final level (2020)			20-year trends		
Countries	MPL	APL	Efficacy	MPL	APL	Efficacy	MPL	APL	Efficacy
Italy	89.7	8.2	531	93.0	7.1	536	3.3	–1.1	1.0
Jamaica	60.3	2.2	323	60.3	2.2	323	0.0	0.0	0.0
Japan	97.2	20.3	688	97.8	21.9	708	0.6	1.7	2.9
Jordan	65.6	1.2	340	56.5	1.3	295	–9.1	0.1	–13.2
Kazakhstan	83.3	5.3	469	86.7	4.4	478	3.3	–0.8	1.7
Kenya	44.0	0.5	225	47.7	1.0	249	3.7	0.5	10.4
Korea Rep	98.5	21.3	706	96.7	25.3	737	–1.8	4.0	4.4
Kosovo	46.9	0.3	238	56.4	0.6	289	9.5	0.3	21.2
Kuwait	49.8	2.7	276	57.3	1.6	303	7.5	–1.1	9.8
Latvia	92.2	8.2	543	95.4	9.6	573	3.2	1.4	5.6
Lebanon	58.5	1.3	306	56.5	2.0	303	–2.0	0.7	–1.0
Lesotho	23.8	0.3	122	29.5	0.8	155	5.7	0.5	27.7
Liechenstein	92.3	8.5	546	94.3	14.7	618	2.1	6.2	13.2
Lithuania	92.0	8.5	544	93.8	10.5	574	1.8	2.1	5.5
Luxembourg	84.8	4.1	465	89.7	9.4	542	4.9	5.3	16.6
Macao	90.7	10.6	559	95.5	16.1	639	4.8	5.5	14.2
Madagascar	39.4	0.3	200	24.1	0.7	127	–15.3	0.4	–36.3
Malawi	20.8	0.3	107	26.8	0.8	142	6.0	0.5	33.0
Malaysia	98.9	1.6	511	73.7	2.5	394	–25.2	0.9	–22.9
Malta	82.3	6.0	471	85.5	6.1	488	3.2	0.1	3.6

(continued)

Table 4.14 (continued)

Short-term trends									
	Initial level (2000)			Final level (2020)			20-year trends		
Countries	MPL	APL	Efficacy	MPL	APL	Efficacy	MPL	APL	Efficacy
Mauritius	51.5	1.4	271	61.4	2.6	333	9.8	1.2	22.6
Mexico	66.2	1.5	346	74.9	0.7	382	8.7	–0.8	10.3
Moldova	83.3	3.4	450	83.7	3.0	448	0.4	–0.4	–0.3
Mongolia	72.6	4.1	403	76.5	3.0	412	4.0	–1.1	2.2
Montenegro	72.9	1.6	381	79.9	2.2	422	7.1	0.6	10.8
Morocco	45.9	1.2	241	47.1	0.4	240	1.2	–0.8	–0.7
Mozambique	28.0	0.3	143	36.0	2.3	203	8.0	2.1	42.6
Namibia	27.9	0.4	143	31.6	1.0	168	3.7	0.6	17.3
Netherlands	96.4	9.7	579	93.1	11.5	581	–3.3	1.8	0.3
New Zealand	88.6	13.3	576	89.4	12.0	566	0.8	–1.4	–1.7
Nicaragua	48.5	0.5	248	51.4	0.0	257	2.9	–0.5	3.8
Niger	23.6	0.7	125	24.8	0.3	127	1.2	–0.4	1.4
North Macedonia	70.1	3.1	381	66.9	1.6	351	–3.2	–1.5	–8.0
Norway	88.7	10.8	551	93.0	12.8	593	4.3	2.0	7.6
Oman	58.5	2.3	315	64.5	2.8	351	6.0	0.5	11.2
Palestine	61.2	4.2	348	52.5	1.7	279	–8.7	–2.5	–19.7
Panama	46.1	0.6	236	47.9	0.2	241	1.8	–0.4	2.0
Papua New Guinea	81.4	4.6	453	84.0	4.9	469	2.6	0.3	3.6
Paraguay	47.2	2.1	257	46.6	0.9	242	–0.6	–1.2	–5.8
Peru	42.8	0.9	223	72.5	1.0	372	29.8	0.0	66.7

(continued)

Table 4.14 (continued)

Short-term trends

	Initial level (2000)			Final level (2020)			20-year trends		
Countries	MPL	APL	Efficacy	MPL	APL	Efficacy	MPL	APL	Efficacy
Philippines	47.5	3.1	269	31.9	0.7	166	–15.6	–2.5	–38.1
Poland	87.7	7.8	516	94.2	14.2	613	6.4	6.5	18.8
Portugal	85.1	4.8	474	92.5	8.7	549	7.4	3.9	15.9
Puerto Rico	62.2	1.3	324	62.2	1.3	324	0.0	0.0	0.0
Qatar	60.8	3.1	335	70.7	3.2	385	9.9	0.1	15.0
Romania	82.5	5.5	467	84.0	5.8	479	1.6	0.4	2.4
Russian Fed	93.1	12.7	593	95.6	14.1	620	2.5	1.4	4.5
Saudi Arabia	61.6	2.4	332	61.2	0.7	313	–0.4	–1.7	–5.8
Scotland	87.9	6.9	509	87.9	6.6	505	0.0	–0.3	–0.7
Senegal	29.5	0.3	150	40.2	0.3	204	10.7	0.0	35.7
Serbia	83.3	6.2	478	86.7	5.5	489	3.3	–0.6	2.2
Seychelles	53.3	1.3	280	54.9	2.3	298	1.7	1.0	6.4
Singapore	94.6	31.7	791	97.5	37.8	866	2.9	6.1	9.5
Slovak Republic	94.8	8.4	557	89.1	8.1	526	–5.7	–0.3	–5.6
Slovenia	89.3	10.4	550	94.5	11.0	583	5.2	0.6	5.8
South Africa	37.5	2.6	213	37.2	1.3	199	–0.3	–1.3	–6.7
Spain	92.1	5.9	519	92.3	6.3	524	0.2	0.4	1.1
Sweden	95.9	12.5	605	93.0	13.1	596	–2.8	0.6	–1.4
Switzerland	93.5	12.7	594	92.8	13.3	597	–0.7	0.6	0.5
Syrian A.R	63.9	5.4	374	65.2	3.2	358	1.3	–2.3	–4.3

(continued)

Table 4.14 (continued)

Short-term trends									
	Initial level (2000)			Final level (2020)			20-year trends		
Countries	MPL	APL	Efficacy	MPL	APL	Efficacy	MPL	APL	Efficacy
Tanzania U.R	45.7	0.5	233	51.2	0.9	265	5.5	0.5	13.8
Thailand	82.5	1.9	431	73.4	2.0	386	–9.1	0.1	–10.4
Togo	33.4	0.6	173	29.3	0.3	149	–4.1	–0.4	–13.9
Trinidad & T	69.4	3.6	383	74.3	3.7	408	4.9	0.1	6.6
Tunisia	47.6	0.7	245	51.1	1.2	263	3.5	0.5	9.1
Turkey	80.0	4.5	445	88.7	8.3	525	8.7	3.8	18.3
USA	91.2	14.4	600	91.8	14.6	605	0.6	0.2	0.8
Uganda	29.5	0.3	150	30.7	1.1	164	1.2	0.8	9.3
Ukraine	82.9	5.8	472	84.1	5.5	475	1.3	–0.3	0.6
United Arab Em	72.2	6.9	430	74.7	6.1	435	2.5	–0.8	1.1
United Kingdom	90.9	15.2	606	94.3	16.2	633	3.4	1.0	4.5
Uruguay	73.2	1.9	385	75.0	1.7	392	1.8	–0.2	1.8
Uzbekistan	61.4	1.5	322	61.4	1.5	322	0.0	0.0	0.0
Vietnam	91.5	9.5	552	95.7	10.6	584	4.2	1.1	5.8
Yemen	24.0	1.8	138	27.5	1.3	151	3.5	–0.5	9.3
Zambia	23.0	0.3	118	25.9	0.7	137	2.9	0.5	16.3
Zimbabwe	33.2	0.5	171	35.1	0.6	182	1.9	0.1	6.2
Total	67.3	5.3	389	69.0	5.6	401	1.6	0.3	4.1

Notes Short-term trends: between 2000 and 2020. For details, please consult Sect. 2.2

Table 4.15 Efficacy of schooling systems around the World, 1970–2020

Long-term trends									
	Initial level (1970)			Final level (2020)			50-year trends		
Countries	MPL	APL	Efficacy	MPL	APL	Efficacy	MPL	APL	Efficacy
Albania	63.7	2.3	342	79.9	3.8	438	16.2	1.5	28.1
Algeria	49.6	4.4	292	54.1	1.8	288	4.5	–2.6	–1.2
Argentina	56.6	2.5	308	60.5	0.6	308	3.8	–1.9	0.0
Armenia	75.1	3.2	407	88.5	4.6	488	13.4	1.4	19.8
Australia	89.5	12.0	567	92.1	13.8	599	2.6	1.9	5.5
Austria	78.1	8.3	474	93.5	10.3	570	15.4	2.0	20.4
Azerbaijan	72.8	1.5	379	69.6	2.2	369	–3.2	0.7	–2.5
Bahrain	64.9	4.9	373	81.6	5.6	464	16.7	0.7	24.2
Belgium	84.1	11.5	536	90.8	13.6	590	6.7	2.0	10.1
Belgium Flemish	95.7	14.5	624	93.7	7.2	541	–2.1	–7.3	–13.3
Belgium French	84.9	6.9	494	85.1	4.9	475	0.2	–2.0	–3.7
Benin	30.3	0.4	155	39.0	0.3	198	8.6	–0.1	27.1
Bolivia	46.4	2.0	252	46.4	2.0	252	0.0	0.0	0.0
Bosnia	74.2	2.8	399	72.5	3.2	395	–1.7	0.4	–1.1
Botswana	36.7	4.2	225	50.3	3.4	286	13.6	–0.7	27.0
Brazil	54.1	3.3	303	67.6	1.4	352	13.5	–1.9	16.0
Brunei	69.2	6.2	408	75.8	3.3	412	6.6	–3.0	0.8
Bulgaria	82.4	9.0	502	81.8	8.9	498	–0.5	–0.1	–0.7
Burkina Faso	30.0	0.3	153	37.3	0.3	189	7.3	0.0	23.9

(continued)

Table 4.15 (continued)

Long-term trends

	Initial level (1970)			Final level (2020)			50-year trends		
Countries	MPL	APL	Efficacy	MPL	APL	Efficacy	MPL	APL	Efficacy
Burundi	30.6	0.8	160	29.4	0.3	15[illegible]	−1.1	−0.5	−6.5
Cambodia	60.3	1.6	219	40.5	1.6	21[illegible]	−19.8	0.0	0.0
Cameroon	32.5	0.3	165	31.0	0.3	158	−1.5	0.0	−4.5
Canada	90.2	12.7	578	94.6	13.9	61[illegible]	4.4	1.1	5.8
Chad	29.0	1.9	164	21.2	0.3	109	−7.8	−1.6	−33.7
Chile	44.1	6.8	289	79.2	2.2	41[illegible]	35.0	−4.7	44.5
Chin. Taipei	89.0	18.6	631	96.4	21.3	694	7.4	2.6	10.0
China	80.6	3.6	439	86.1	2.0	451	5.5	−1.6	2.7
Colombia	54.1	3.4	304	67.1	0.8	344	13.0	−2.6	12.9
Congo	24.7	0.3	126	31.4	0.3	160	6.7	0.0	26.7
Congo, D.R	23.4	0.7	124	22.6	0.7	119	−0.8	0.0	−3.4
Costa Rica	68.4	1.0	352	76.3	0.7	389	8.0	−0.4	10.3
Croatia	94.1	7.1	542	93.5	7.3	540	−0.7	0.1	−0.4
Cuba	68.0	9.0	430	71.3	3.7	394	3.3	−5.3	−8.5
Cyprus	97.6	3.8	526	90.6	6.6	519	−7.0	2.8	−1.4
Czech Rep	94.4	13.9	611	94.2	11.5	586	−0.2	−2.4	−4.1
Denmark	78.8	7.2	466	94.8	10.2	576	16.0	2.9	23.5
Dominican Rep	24.5	1.7	140	37.0	0.1	186	12.5	−1.6	32.9
Ecuador	48.9	2.8	273	67.3	1.9	355	18.3	−1.0	30.0

(continued)

Table 4.15 (continued)

Long-term trends									
	Initial level (1970)			Final level (2020)			50-year trends		
Countries	MPL	APL	Efficacy	MPL	APL	Efficacy	MPL	APL	Efficacy
Egypt	60.5	5.6	358	52.4	1.4	276	–8.1	–4.2	–22.9
El Salvador	42.3	4.0	251	53.4	1.0	277	11.0	–2.9	10.3
Estonia	97.8	14.0	628	98.1	16.7	658	0.3	2.8	4.7
Eswatini	32.5	0.3	165	38.2	1.0	201	5.6	0.7	21.4
Finland	87.0	12.7	562	94.8	15.9	632	7.8	3.2	12.5
France	75.2	4.9	425	88.7	7.9	522	13.6	3.0	23.0
Gabon	33.5	0.3	170	45.3	0.5	231	11.8	0.2	36.0
Georgia	70.8	0.8	362	73.0	1.5	380	2.1	0.7	4.9
Germany	90.8	9.1	545	91.7	11.7	576	0.9	2.6	5.6
Ghana	53.6	6.0	328	46.4	3.6	268	–7.2	–2.4	–18.3
Greece	97.2	4.8	534	85.8	5.5	484	–11.4	0.6	–9.5
Guatemala	44.4	2.4	246	46.8	0.9	243	2.4	–1.5	–1.3
Honduras	47.0	2.9	264	55.5	1.8	295	8.4	–1.1	12.0
Hong Kong	86.9	18.4	619	96.6	21.9	702	9.6	3.5	13.5
Hungary	92.8	12.2	586	91.6	10.3	560	–1.2	–2.0	–4.4
Iceland	85.0	5.3	478	86.6	7.1	504	1.7	1.8	5.5
India	51.4	8.2	339	43.9	2.1	241	–7.5	–6.1	–29.1
Indonesia	75.5	1.6	393	53.9	0.6	275	–21.6	–1.0	–30.0
Iran I.R	37.4	5.7	244	70.6	2.2	375	33.2	–3.5	53.6
Ireland	92.3	8.0	541	95.5	14.0	617	3.2	6.0	14.1

(continued)

Table 4.15 (continued)

Long-term trends									
	Initial level (1970)			Final level (2020)			50-year trends		
Countries	MPL	APL	Efficacy	MPL	APL	Efficacy	MPL	APL	Efficacy
Israel	45.0	9.7	322	84.1	11.1	532	39.1	1.4	65.1
Italy	84.9	13.0	555	93.0	7.1	535	8.1	–5.9	–3.3
Jamaica	60.3	2.2	323	60.3	2.2	323	0.0	0.0	0.0
Japan	95.5	21.0	687	97.8	21.9	703	2.3	0.9	3.0
Jordan	63.0	2.8	343	56.5	1.3	295	–6.5	–1.5	–14.0
Kazakhstan	83.5	5.5	472	86.7	4.4	473	3.2	–1.1	1.1
Kenya	40.8	0.6	210	47.7	1.0	249	6.9	0.4	18.2
Korea Rep	93.2	23.2	698	96.7	25.3	737	3.5	2.1	5.5
Kosovo	44.6	0.8	231	56.4	0.6	289	11.8	–0.1	25.1
Kuwait	46.4	3.7	269	57.3	1.6	303	10.9	–2.0	12.8
Latvia	85.9	7.4	504	95.4	9.6	573	9.6	2.1	13.7
Lebanon	59.2	1.9	316	56.5	2.0	303	–2.8	0.1	–4.1
Lesotho	21.0	0.8	113	29.5	0.8	155	8.5	0.0	38.1
Liechenstein	97.7	15.2	640	94.3	14.7	618	–3.4	–0.5	–3.4
Lithuania	84.5	9.1	513	93.8	10.5	574	9.3	1.5	11.9
Luxembourg	77.6	5.5	443	89.7	9.4	542	12.1	3.9	22.4
Macao	84.7	11.2	535	95.5	16.1	639	10.7	5.0	19.3
Madagascar	31.1	0.3	158	24.1	0.7	127	–7.0	0.4	–19.7
Malawi	22.3	0.7	119	26.8	0.8	142	4.5	0.0	19.1
Malaysia	82.6	2.7	440	73.7	2.5	394	–8.9	–0.2	–10.6
Malta	72.3	4.7	409	85.5	6.1	488	13.2	1.3	19.4

(continued)

Table 4.15 (continued)

Long-term trends									
	Initial level (1970)			Final level (2020)			50-year trends		
Countries	MPL	APL	Efficacy	MPL	APL	Efficacy	MPL	APL	Efficacy
Mauritius	48.6	1.7	260	61.4	2.6	333	12.8	0.9	28.0
Mexico	60.8	1.9	323	74.9	0.7	382	14.1	–1.2	18.1
Moldova	79.3	2.2	418	83.7	3.0	448	4.3	0.8	7.2
Mongolia	70.4	4.9	401	76.5	3.0	412	6.1	–2.0	2.8
Montenegro	74.3	1.1	383	79.9	2.2	422	5.6	1.1	10.2
Morocco	39.7	1.8	217	47.1	0.4	240	7.4	–1.4	10.6
Mozambique	29.0	3.1	175	36.0	2.3	203	7.1	–0.7	15.9
Namibia	26.1	0.5	136	31.6	1.0	168	5.5	0.4	23.5
Netherlands	83.8	9.9	518	93.1	11.5	581	9.3	1.6	12.1
New Zealand	90.4	10.4	556	89.4	12.0	566	–1.0	1.6	1.9
Nicaragua	44.2	0.7	228	51.4	0.0	257	7.2	–0.7	12.6
Niger	24.5	0.3	125	24.8	0.3	127	0.3	0.0	1.1
Nigeria	52.9	9.5	383	49.8	8.4	323	–3.0	–1.1	–15.6
North Macedonia	68.7	2.9	373	66.9	1.6	351	–1.8	–1.3	–5.9
Norway	89.5	6.8	515	93.0	12.8	593	3.5	6.0	15.1
Oman	55.8	2.7	307	64.5	2.8	351	8.7	0.1	14.4
Palestine	60.3	3.8	340	52.5	1.7	279	–7.8	–2.1	–17.8
Panama	43.1	0.7	223	47.9	0.2	241	4.7	–0.5	8.3
Papua New Guinea	81.4	8.6	493	84.0	4.9	469	2.6	–3.7	–4.9
Paraguay	41.6	2.3	230	46.6	0.9	242	5.0	–1.3	5.0

(continued)

Table 4.15 (continued)

Long-term trends									
	Initial level (1970)			Final level (2020)			50-year trends		
Countries	MPL	APL	Efficacy	MPL	APL	Efficacy	MPL	APL	Efficacy
Peru	47.5	1.8	255	72.5	1.0	372	25.1	–0.8	45.9
Philippines	37.8	3.8	227	31.9	0.7	166	–5.9	–3.1	–26.7
Poland	89.2	12.2	568	94.2	14.2	613	4.9	2.1	8.0
Portugal	79.1	8.9	485	92.5	8.7	549	13.4	–0.2	13.4
Puerto Rico	62.2	1.3	324	62.2	1.3	324	0.0	0.0	0.0
Qatar	54.1	3.5	306	70.7	3.2	385	16.5	–0.3	26.0
Romania	75.7	5.8	436	84.0	5.8	479	8.4	0.1	9.8
Russian Fed	99.7	12.0	618	95.6	14.1	620	–4.1	2.1	0.2
Saudi Arabia	55.7	3.9	318	61.2	0.7	313	5.5	–3.3	–1.6
Scotland	83.8	11.8	536	87.9	6.6	505	4.1	–5.2	–5.8
Senegal	33.3	1.5	181	40.2	0.3	204	6.9	–1.2	12.4
Serbia	85.3	6.4	490	86.7	5.5	489	1.3	–0.8	–0.3
Seychelles	50.8	0.7	261	54.9	2.3	298	4.2	1.6	14.1
Singapore	60.7	29.5	598	97.5	37.8	866	36.8	8.4	44.8
Slovak Republic	95.5	8.2	560	89.1	8.1	526	–6.4	–0.2	–6.0
Slovenia	88.8	11.7	561	94.5	11.0	583	5.7	–0.7	3.9
South Africa	36.8	5.4	238	37.2	1.3	199	0.4	–4.1	–16.5
Spain	75.8	5.7	436	92.3	6.3	524	16.5	0.6	20.4
Sweden	94.3	10.5	577	93.0	13.1	596	–1.3	2.6	3.4
Switzerland	89.0	13.7	582	92.8	13.3	597	3.8	–0.4	2.5

(continued)

Table 4.15 (continued)

Long-term trends

	Initial level (1970)			Final level (2020)			50-year trends		
Countries	MPL	APL	Efficacy	MPL	APL	Efficacy	MPL	APL	Efficacy
Syrian A.R	60.6	6.2	365	65.2	3.2	358	4.6	–3.0	–2.1
Tanzania U.R	47.7	1.6	255	51.2	0.9	265	3.5	–0.7	4.1
Thailand	81.9	7.1	481	73.4	2.0	386	–8.5	–5.2	–19.6
Togo	25.0	0.4	129	29.3	0.3	149	4.3	–0.2	15.5
Trinidad & T	58.9	3.8	333	74.3	3.7	408	15.4	–0.2	22.6
Tunisia	41.0	2.5	230	51.1	1.2	268	10.1	–1.3	16.2
Turkey	72.4	6.9	431	88.7	8.3	526	16.3	1.4	22.0
USA	87.3	13.0	566	91.8	14.6	605	4.5	1.6	6.9
Uganda	33.1	2.2	187	30.7	1.1	164	–2.4	–1.1	–12.2
Ukraine	83.3	5.6	472	84.1	5.5	475	0.8	–0.1	0.6
United Arab Em	62.7	9.8	411	74.7	6.1	435	12.0	–3.7	5.7
United Kingdom	84.6	14.2	565	94.3	16.2	633	9.7	2.0	12.0
Uruguay	69.4	2.2	370	75.0	1.7	392	5.6	–0.5	6.1
Uzbekistan	61.4	1.5	322	61.4	1.5	322	0.0	0.0	0.0
Venezuela	45.6	0.3	231	45.4	0.3	230	–0.2	0.0	–0.4
Vietnam	92.1	10.5	565	95.7	10.6	584	3.6	0.1	3.4
Yemen	22.1	1.5	126	27.5	1.3	151	5.3	–0.2	19.5
Zambia	23.7	0.9	128	25.9	0.7	137	2.2	–0.2	7.5
Zimbabwe	24.6	0.3	126	35.1	0.6	182	10.5	0.3	44.0
Total	63.3	5.7	373	68.5	5.5	398	5.2	–0.2	7.8

Notes Long-term trends: between 1970 and 2020. For details, please consult Sect. 2.2

Table 4.16 Equity of schooling systems around the World, 2000–2020

Short-term trends									
	Initial level (2000)			Final level (2020)			20-year trends		
Countries	Completion	Equity	Equity (adj)	Completion	Equity	Equity (adj)	Completion	Equity	Equity (adj)
Albania	81.6	425.8	382	94.4	528.5	503	12.8	24.1	31.6
Algeria	51.8	483.4	313	80.9	507.1	444	29.1	4.9	42.1
Argentina	85.2	431.5	396	89.7	473.0	450	4.5	9.6	13.8
Armenia	87.5	520.4	472	96.9	537.2	514	9.4	3.2	8.9
Australia	100.0	561.1	547	100.0	533.8	523	0.0	–4.9	–4.5
Austria	96.0	581.9	570	96.4	560.4	544	0.4	–3.7	–4.6
Azerbaijan	38.2	507.1	319	89.2	499.8	475	50.9	–1.4	48.9
Bahrain	85.0	448.2	412	89.0	500.0	450	4.0	11.6	9.2
Belgium	100.0	517.3	510	96.9	514.9	507	–3.1	–0.5	–0.6
Benin	15.2	520.3	139	45.5	590.1	351	30.3	13.4	152.2
Botswana	92.3	319.7	302	92.6	431.5	401	0.4	34.9	32.8
Brazil	72.1	465.2	398	71.0	473.0	409	–1.1	1.7	2.8
Brunei	73.7	479.9	422	86.4	498.6	467	12.7	3.9	10.6
Bulgaria	76.4	536.7	467	60.8	475.9	393	–15.5	–11.3	–15.7
Burkina Faso	6.5	524.0	83	35.7	571.7	289	29.2	9.1	247.6
Burundi	6.9	544.8	88	35.3	550.3	279	28.4	1.0	216.1
Cameroon	19.7	550.3	187	46.8	533.0	300	27.1	–3.1	60.3
Canada	96.0	581.0	566	97.8	565.8	558	1.8	–2.6	–1.5
Chad	8.8	499.4	79	14.8	488.3	111	6.0	–2.2	41.1
Chile	79.8	485.4	431	87.2	532.7	494	7.4	9.7	14.5

(continued)

Table 4.16 (continued)

Short-term trends

	Initial level (2000)			Final level (2020)			20-year trends		
Countries	Completion	Equity	Equity (adj)	Completion	Equity	Equity (adj)	Completion	Equity	Equity (adj)
Chin. Taipei	92.0	610.8	584	95.6	582.7	573	3.6	–4.6	–1.8
China	63.6	571.9	446	99.1	581.1	564	35.5	1.6	26.5
Colombia	67.0	443.4	368	74.5	509.4	447	7.5	14.9	21.5
Congo	27.2	515.7	188	46.3	559.9	305	19.1	8.6	62.8
Congo, D.R	13.1	470.7	142	58.7	514.6	189	45.7	9.3	33.3
Costa Rica	43.7	548.5	360	64.0	560.5	459	20.3	2.2	27.6
Croatia	74.5	598.3	492	87.0	582.9	527	12.5	–2.6	7.1
Cuba	94.9	503.9	480	90.9	456.6	425	–4.0	–9.4	–11.4
Cyprus	91.3	539.2	508	93.0	560.9	542	1.7	4.0	6.7
Czech Rep	88.0	556.6	524	90.1	568.1	541	2.1	2.1	3.2
Denmark	100.0	542.0	542	100.0	587.5	587	0.0	8.4	8.4
Dominican Rep	60.8	402.2	282	84.3	479.3	422	23.5	19.2	50.0
Ecuador	57.1	483.0	369	98.6	526.2	523	41.5	8.9	41.6
Egypt	80.1	480.1	413	83.9	435.1	395	3.7	–9.4	–4.2
El Salvador	66.3	462.9	366	79.5	522.4	469	13.2	12.9	28.2
Estonia	81.7	565.0	502	91.7	570.9	539	10.0	1.0	7.4
Eswatini	33.8	497.9	256	59.3	530.7	372	25.6	6.6	44.9
Finland	100.0	609.5	610	100.0	575.2	572	0.0	–5.6	–6.1

(continued)

Table 4.16 (continued)

Short-term trends									
	Initial level (2000)			Final level (2020)			20-year trends		
Countries	Completion	Equity	Equity (adj)	Completion	Equity	Equity (adj)	Completion	Equity	Equity (adj)
France	96.6	575.4	565	100.0	535.2	535	3.4	–7.0	–5.2
Gabon	48.2	532.0	322	48.2	586.8	322	0.0	10.3	0.0
Georgia	91.3	478.3	459	99.6	505.8	505	8.4	5.7	9.9
Germany	93.1	540.6	523	99.7	540.8	540	6.6	0.0	3.2
Ghana	53.4	345.9	226	75.5	420.6	351	22.1	21.6	55.1
Greece	85.0	533.6	484	100.0	528.6	529	15.0	–0.9	9.2
Guatemala	29.6	507.2	209	58.8	498.6	338	29.2	–1.7	61.8
Honduras	37.1	458.2	257	45.0	493.4	306	7.9	7.7	18.9
Hong Kong	71.9	647.2	542	85.6	589.4	540	13.7	–8.9	–0.5
Hungary	94.5	573.7	555	97.0	549.5	542	2.5	–4.2	–2.3
Iceland	83.0	579.4	529	87.4	526.6	492	4.4	–9.1	–6.9
India	53.6	464.9	292	84.7	495.0	433	31.1	6.5	48.2
Indonesia	63.2	484.4	379	92.2	487.0	466	29.0	0.5	22.9
Iran I.R	77.0	500.4	417	89.8	475.6	450	12.8	–5.0	8.1
Ireland	100.0	580.5	580	100.0	591.4	591	0.0	1.9	1.9
Israel	90.7	468.5	449	89.9	469.2	448	–0.8	0.2	–0.3
Italy	90.0	539.3	513	95.8	575.4	564	5.9	6.7	9.9
Japan	99.0	599.8	597	99.0	593.4	590	0.0	–1.1	–1.0

(continued)

Table 4.16 (continued)

Short-term trends									
	Initial level (2000)			Final level (2020)			20-year trends		
Countries	Completion	Equity	Equity (adj)	Completion	Equity	Equity (adj)	Completion	Equity	Equity (adj)
Jordan	78.1	498.5	433	61.9	520.6	393	–16.3	4.4	–9.2
Kazakhstan	94.9	528.9	497	100.0	560.2	560	5.1	5.9	12.7
Kenya	78.2	447.0	357	78.8	502.7	427	0.7	12.5	19.7
Korea Rep	99.0	633.6	630	97.0	572.4	564	–2.0	–9.7	–10.5
Kuwait	100.0	396.8	397	100.0	418.0	418	0.0	5.3	5.3
Latvia	78.5	568.5	498	89.6	601.6	563	11.1	5.8	13.0
Lesotho	23.9	464.0	183	47.6	467.4	294	23.7	0.7	60.8
Liechenstein	93.9	545.4	561	94.9	565.7	550	0.9	3.7	–2.0
Lithuania	84.4	569.4	519	91.5	567.3	529	7.1	–0.4	2.0
Luxembourg	87.9	515.3	471	96.6	533.8	493	8.7	3.6	4.6
Macao	72.4	576.2	485	82.4	613.0	542	10.0	6.4	11.6
Madagascar	13.3	560.6	139	36.5	513.0	259	23.2	–8.5	87.0
Malawi	22.2	465.5	192	23.5	503.0	223	1.3	8.1	15.8
Malaysia	88.4	639.8	598	83.9	508.6	463	–4.5	–20.5	–22.5
Malta	79.4	474.4	415	96.5	495.9	472	17.1	4.5	13.8
Mauritius	75.4	364.7	318	86.6	432.2	401	11.2	18.5	26.1
Mexico	70.2	502.4	413	94.4	540.4	525	24.2	7.6	27.3
Moldova	86.9	523.6	484	83.7	518.9	450	–3.2	–0.9	–7.0

(continued)

Table 4.16 (continued)

Short-term trends

	Initial level (2000)			Final level (2020)			20-year trends		
Countries	Completion	Equity	Equity (adj)	Completion	Equity	Equity (adj)	Completion	Equity	Equity (adj)
Mongolia	62.7	530.0	395	100.0	541.6	542	37.3	2.2	37.1
Montenegro	86.9	507.0	464	94.8	526.2	504	7.9	3.8	8.7
Morocco	33.4	430.6	325	66.6	430.6	325	33.2	0.0	0.0
Mozambique	3.9	508.4	51	23.3	533.5	197	19.4	4.9	288.5
Namibia	52.1	390.7	262	73.1	434.5	346	21.0	11.2	32.4
Netherlands	100.0	613.0	610	100.0	546.2	546	0.0	–10.9	–10.4
New Zealand	92.0	525.4	494	95.0	524.4	506	3.0	–0.2	2.5
Nicaragua	44.5	514.1	281	66.4	530.6	377	21.9	3.2	34.4
Niger	4.8	509.1	63	17.2	398.1	156	12.5	–21.8	147.1
North Macedonia	91.4	458.9	430	86.5	454.3	405	–4.8	–1.0	–5.8
Norway	95.0	547.2	533	96.0	549.4	536	1.0	0.4	0.6
Oman	68.2	347.2	271	86.8	418.5	386	18.7	20.5	42.5
Palestine	65.2	473.5	381	84.5	484.1	434	19.3	2.2	14.0
Panama	61.6	456.3	356	76.3	470.2	399	14.7	3.0	12.3
Paraguay	69.3	464.4	367	71.7	462.1	318	2.4	–0.5	–13.6
Peru	75.3	385.8	335	93.8	504.2	489	18.5	30.7	46.3
Philippines	71.4	306.9	257	79.5	334.3	280	8.1	8.9	9.0
Poland	98.8	535.2	527	94.6	565.0	542	–4.2	5.6	2.8

(continued)

Table 4.16 (continued)

Short-term trends

	Initial level (2000)			Final level (2020)			20-year trends		
Countries	Completion	Equity	Equity (adj)	Completion	Equity	Equity (adj)	Completion	Equity	Equity (adj)
Portugal	100.0	541.6	542	100.0	563.9	564	0.0	4.1	4.1
Puerto Rico	74.8	493.7	411	82.3	493.7	411	7.5	0.0	0.0
Qatar	79.6	372.0	337	91.9	438.5	415	12.3	17.9	23.3
Romania	84.1	503.9	447	88.6	486.4	452	4.5	–3.5	1.1
Russian Fed	93.6	558.4	514	97.3	604.3	582	3.7	8.2	13.4
Saudi Arabia	66.1	462.1	343	85.7	472.3	435	19.6	2.2	26.9
Senegal	13.4	494.4	131	38.5	583.6	293	25.1	18.0	124.3
Serbia	96.1	490.9	482	94.6	526.0	503	–1.5	7.1	4.3
Seychelles	63.5	419.5	332	70.9	448.8	380	7.4	7.0	14.5
Slovak Republic	74.6	591.1	503	79.3	530.3	456	4.7	–10.3	–9.4
Slovenia	87.9	552.7	498	86.2	581.4	525	–1.7	5.2	5.5
South Africa	71.7	24.2	21	80.6	339.3	281	8.9	1302.0	1234.8
Spain	89.0	575.7	544	100.0	571.3	571	11.0	–0.8	5.1
Sweden	96.0	585.6	574	96.8	547.7	539	0.8	–6.5	–6.0
Switzerland	93.0	542.8	523	95.0	529.8	517	1.9	–2.4	–1.2
Tanzania U.R	12.6	462.8	137	30.7	505.8	271	18.1	9.3	98.0
Thailand	100.0	576.4	535	80.6	523.7	403	–19.4	–9.2	–24.7
Togo	22.4	531.1	242	45.6	543.2	352	23.1	2.3	45.4

(continued)

Table 4.16 (continued)

Short-term trends									
	Initial level (2000)			Final level (2020)			20-year trends		
Countries	Completion	Equity	Equity (adj)	Completion	Equity	Equity (adj)	Completion	Equity	Equity (adj)
Trinidad & T	72.7	442.8	380	88.5	466.7	442	15.8	5.4	16.1
Tunisia	58.4	392.5	278	73.4	416.9	353	15.0	6.2	26.9
Turkey	79.4	527.9	459	100.0	540.2	538	20.6	2.3	17.0
USA	87.0	526.8	495	86.9	534.1	498	–0.1	1.4	0.6
Uganda	14.9	412.5	131	28.2	450.1	185	13.3	9.1	41.1
Ukraine	97.9	535.1	519	100.0	524.9	515	2.1	–1.9	–0.8
United Arab Em	70.5	436.6	346	82.3	413.7	395	11.7	–5.2	14.2
United Kingdom	94.0	535.9	520	99.0	552.6	550	5.0	3.1	5.8
Uruguay	85.3	490.3	454	96.8	494.5	487	11.5	0.8	7.2
Vietnam	68.9	577.0	479	99.3	590.9	573	30.4	2.4	19.7
Zambia	24.0	419.8	165	63.2	468.2	369	39.1	11.5	123.4
Zimbabwe	45.0	411.6	280	47.3	424.5	285	2.3	3.1	1.9
Total	69.5	500.5	394	80.4	515.1	443	10.9	13.8	34.5

Notes Short-term trends: between 2000 and 2020. For details, please consult Sect. 2.2

Table 4.17 Equity of schooling systems around the World, 1970–2020

Long-term trends									
	Initial level (1970)			Final level (2020)			50-year trends		
Countries	Completion	Equity	Equity (adj)	Completion	Equity	Equity (adj)	Completion	Equity	Equity (adj)
Albania	85.4	429.4	385	94.4	528.5	503	9.0	23.1	30.6
Algeria	10.6	502.6	101	80.9	507.1	444	70.3	0.9	340.7
Argentina	16.8	409.0	193	89.7	473.0	450	72.9	15.6	132.7
Armenia	90.0	500.5	480	96.9	537.2	514	6.9	7.3	7.1
Australia	74.5	525.4	437	100.0	533.8	523	25.5	1.6	19.5
Austria	68.0	491.7	395	96.4	560.4	544	28.4	14.0	37.5
Azerbaijan	89.7	508.1	469	89.2	499.8	475	–0.6	–1.6	1.3
Bahrain	51.1	420.9	312	89.0	500.0	450	37.9	18.8	44.3
Belgium	73.4	499.7	423	96.9	514.9	507	23.5	3.0	19.8
Benin	3.3	500.4	38	45.5	590.1	351	42.1	17.9	816.8
Bolivia	47.4	430.6	300	85.1	430.6	300	37.8	0.0	0.0
Botswana	9.3	299.8	63	92.6	431.5	401	83.3	43.9	535.6
Brazil	100.0	410.6	411	71.0	473.0	409	–29.0	15.2	–0.3
Brunei	47.0	443.6	338	86.4	498.6	467	39.4	12.4	38.0
Bulgaria	87.7	478.9	446	60.8	475.9	393	–26.9	–0.6	–11.8
Burkina Faso	1.2	504.8	20	35.7	571.7	289	34.5	13.3	1344.9
Burundi	0.9	540.0	26	35.3	550.3	279	34.4	1.9	965.7
Cameroon	4.0	514.2	131	46.8	533.0	300	42.8	3.6	129.2
Canada	58.1	582.0	436	97.8	565.8	558	39.7	–2.8	28.1
Chad	1.6	481.7	45	14.8	488.3	111	13.2	1.4	148.0

(continued)

Table 4.17 (continued)

Long-term trends									
	Initial level (1970)			Final level (2020)			50-year trends		
Countries	Completion	Equity	Equity (adj)	Completion	Equity	Equity (adj)	Completion	Equity	Equity (adj)
Chile	29.0	503.4	281	87.2	532.7	494	58.2	5.8	75.9
Chin. Taipei	71.6	564.5	475	95.6	582.7	573	24.0	3.2	20.8
China	8.1	561.0	280	99.1	581.1	564	91.0	3.6	101.3
Colombia	24.5	399.9	150	74.5	509.4	447	50.0	27.4	197.7
Congo	15.4	484.8	199	46.3	559.9	305	30.9	15.5	53.3
Congo, D.R	12.9	458.4	169	58.7	514.6	189	45.8	12.3	11.7
Costa Rica	19.4	500.9	233	64.0	560.5	459	44.5	11.9	97.0
Croatia	71.4	591.8	450	87.0	582.9	527	15.7	–1.5	17.1
Cuba	8.5	442.3	213	90.9	456.6	425	82.4	3.2	100.0
Cyprus	43.0	603.4	364	93.0	560.9	542	50.0	–7.0	48.8
Czech Rep	38.0	542.0	473	90.1	568.1	541	52.1	4.8	14.5
Denmark	61.7	430.4	336	100.0	587.5	587	38.3	36.5	75.1
Dominican Rep	22.1	387.9	113	84.3	479.3	422	62.2	23.6	274.6
Ecuador	25.3	447.7	201	98.6	526.2	523	73.3	17.5	159.6
Egypt	33.7	427.3	171	83.9	435.1	395	50.1	1.8	131.5
El Salvador	15.5	439.8	152	79.5	522.4	469	64.0	18.8	209.2
Estonia	91.2	566.2	509	91.7	570.9	539	0.5	0.8	5.8
Eswatini	16.2	508.9	148	59.3	530.7	372	43.1	4.3	150.3

(continued)

Table 4.17 (continued)

Long-term trends

Countries	Initial level (1970)			Final level (2020)			50-year trends		
	Completion	Equity	Equity (adj)	Completion	Equity	Equity (adj)	Completion	Equity	Equity (adj)
Finland	71.0	496.2	429	100.0	575.2	572	29.0	15.9	33.5
France	67.0	507.0	428	100.0	535.2	535	33.0	5.6	25.0
Gabon	11.7	482.3	194	48.2	586.8	322	36.4	21.7	66.3
Georgia	100.0	507.4	481	99.6	505.8	505	−0.4	−0.3	5.0
Germany	35.0	498.7	296	99.7	540.8	540	64.7	8.4	82.5
Ghana	44.7	377.1	182	75.5	420.6	351	30.8	11.5	92.4
Greece	52.0	556.6	417	100.0	528.6	529	48.0	−5.0	26.8
Guatemala	10.9	492.5	78	58.8	498.6	338	47.9	1.2	335.9
Honduras	17.2	434.9	114	45.0	493.4	306	27.8	13.4	169.3
Hong Kong	33.0	576.1	340	85.6	589.4	540	52.6	2.3	58.8
Hungary	31.0	538.4	337	97.0	549.5	542	66.0	2.1	60.8
Iceland	69.5	539.6	446	87.4	526.6	492	17.9	−2.4	10.4
India	33.4	490.2	170	84.7	495.0	433	51.4	1.0	155.3
Indonesia	15.0	644.9	170	92.2	487.0	466	77.2	−24.5	174.0
Iran I.R	25.1	514.0	211	89.8	475.6	450	64.7	−7.5	112.8
Ireland	64.0	602.2	462	100.0	591.4	591	36.0	−1.8	27.9
Israel	67.6	340.4	362	89.9	469.2	448	22.3	37.8	23.9
Italy	57.5	545.2	421	95.8	575.4	564	38.3	5.5	34.1

(continued)

Table 4.17 (continued)

Long-term trends									
	Initial level (1970)			Final level (2020)			50-year trends		
Countries	Completion	Equity	Equity (adj)	Completion	Equity	Equity (adj)	Completion	Equity	Equity (adj)
Japan	85.0	512.6	474	99.0	593.4	590	14.0	15.8	24.5
Jordan	16.1	458.1	246	61.9	520.6	393	45.8	13.6	59.5
Kazakhstan	94.0	533.1	520	100.0	560.2	560	6.0	5.1	7.7
Kenya	11.5	437.7	131	78.8	502.7	427	67.3	14.9	227.1
Korea Rep	38.0	587.7	374	97.0	572.4	564	59.0	–2.6	50.9
Kuwait	54.0	345.3	196	100.0	418.0	418	46.0	21.0	112.8
Latvia	91.5	538.3	463	89.6	601.6	563	–2.0	11.8	21.5
Lebanon	36.9	412.2	321	58.4	376.4	278	21.5	–8.7	–13.2
Lesotho	7.4	429.2	119	47.6	467.4	294	40.2	8.9	147.8
Liechenstein	93.9	584.6	561	94.9	565.7	550	0.9	–3.2	–2.0
Lithuania	82.8	537.6	451	91.5	567.3	529	8.8	5.5	17.4
Luxembourg	47.0	482.5	336	96.6	533.8	493	49.6	10.6	46.8
Macao	18.7	549.1	209	82.4	613.0	542	63.7	11.6	158.8
Madagascar	10.4	540.5	105	36.5	513.0	259	26.1	–5.1	146.4
Malawi	28.4	460.6	113	23.5	503.0	223	–4.9	9.2	97.3
Malaysia	100.0	586.7	545	83.9	508.6	463	–16.1	–13.3	–15.1
Malta	49.0	426.3	299	96.5	495.9	472	47.5	16.3	58.0
Mauritius	39.9	324.8	187	86.6	432.2	401	46.7	33.1	114.7

(continued)

Table 4.17 (continued)

Long-term trends

	Initial level (1970)			Final level (2020)			50-year trends		
Countries	Completion	Equity	Equity (adj)	Completion	Equity	Equity (adj)	Completion	Equity	Equity (adj)
Mexico	33.8	478.1	201	94.4	540.4	525	60.7	13.0	160.9
Moldova	88.4	506.0	450	83.7	518.9	450	–4.7	2.5	0.2
Mongolia	62.5	489.1	398	100.0	541.6	542	37.5	10.7	36.2
Montenegro	86.9	545.3	464	94.8	526.2	504	7.9	–3.5	8.7
Morocco	6.2	430.6	325	66.6	430.6	325	60.4	0.0	0.0
Mozambique	6.6	468.9	67	23.3	533.5	197	16.6	13.8	192.3
Namibia	36.0	398.9	241	73.1	434.5	346	37.1	8.9	43.8
Netherlands	69.0	482.4	394	100.0	546.2	546	31.0	13.2	38.8
New Zealand	76.0	524.2	462	95.0	524.4	506	19.0	0.0	9.5
Nicaragua	8.1	477.2	80	66.4	530.6	377	58.3	11.2	370.4
Niger	0.7	491.5	19	17.2	398.1	156	16.5	–19.0	699.6
Nigeria	6.4	516.4	245	51.1	531.1	311	44.7	2.8	27.0
North Macedonia	88.3	447.6	403	86.5	454.3	405	–1.8	1.5	0.6
Norway	65.0	466.2	357	96.0	549.4	536	31.0	17.8	50.4
Oman	0.6	355.1	48	86.8	418.5	386	86.3	17.8	704.6
Palestine	57.3	481.8	360	84.5	484.1	434	27.2	0.5	20.5
Panama	33.9	395.8	199	76.3	470.2	399	42.4	18.8	100.8
Paraguay	23.7	431.4	142	71.7	462.1	318	47.9	7.1	123.9

(continued)

Table 4.17 (continued)

Long-term trends

	Initial level (1970)			Final level (2020)			50-year trends		
Countries	Completion	Equity	Equity (adj)	Completion	Equity	Equity (adj)	Completion	Equity	Equity (adj)
Peru	28.3	367.6	170	93.8	504.2	489	65.6	37.2	187.7
Philippines	54.5	270.8	189	79.5	334.3	280	25.0	23.5	48.3
Poland	38.0	486.8	320	94.6	565.0	542	56.6	16.1	69.1
Portugal	31.0	487.0	283	100.0	563.9	564	69.0	15.8	99.4
Puerto Rico	74.8	493.7	411	82.3	493.7	411	7.5	0.0	0.0
Qatar	39.8	327.2	240	91.9	438.5	415	52.1	34.0	72.8
Romania	53.0	453.6	334	88.6	486.4	452	35.6	7.2	35.3
Russian Fed	38.8	624.6	416	97.3	604.3	582	58.5	–3.2	40.1
Saudi Arabia	25.9	399.8	185	85.7	472.3	435	59.8	18.2	135.5
Senegal	8.4	523.4	95	38.5	583.6	293	30.1	11.5	207.5
Serbia	96.9	505.6	464	94.6	526.0	503	–2.3	4.0	8.4
Seychelles	23.4	391.2	232	70.9	448.8	380	47.5	14.7	64.1
Slovak Republic	77.5	585.5	516	79.3	530.3	456	1.7	–9.4	–11.8
Slovenia	73.1	541.9	453	86.2	581.4	525	13.1	7.3	15.9
South Africa	29.9	91.8	42	80.6	339.3	281	50.7	269.5	571.9
Spain	40.0	508.3	337	100.0	571.3	571	60.0	12.4	69.3
Sweden	81.2	556.7	484	96.8	547.7	539	15.5	–1.6	11.6
Switzerland	52.1	500.8	325	95.0	529.8	517	42.9	5.8	59.0

(continued)

Table 4.17 (continued)

Long-term trends									
	Initial level (1970)			Final level (2020)			50-year trends		
Countries	Completion	Equity	Equity (adj)	Completion	Equity	Equity (adj)	Completion	Equity	Equity (adj)
Tanzania U.R	4.8	458.4	71	30.7	505.8	271	25.9	10.3	282.9
Thailand	2.6	577.8	84	80.6	523.7	403	77.9	–9.4	382.0
Togo	4.8	511.9	41	45.6	543.2	352	40.8	6.1	762.4
Trinidad & T	33.0	369.0	241	88.5	466.7	442	55.5	26.5	83.5
Tunisia	13.2	323.0	97	73.4	416.9	353	60.2	29.1	264.2
Turkey	13.8	589.5	294	100.0	540.2	538	86.2	–8.4	82.7
USA	81.0	479.4	427	86.9	534.1	498	5.9	11.4	16.6
Uganda	3.8	377.3	70	28.2	450.1	185	24.5	19.3	164.5
Ukraine	96.1	527.9	516	100.0	524.9	515	3.9	–0.6	–0.2
United Arab Em	17.6	364.3	208	82.3	413.7	395	64.6	13.6	90.2
United Kingdom	67.0	448.3	377	99.0	552.6	550	32.0	23.3	45.7
Uruguay	46.3	425.5	303	96.8	494.5	487	50.6	16.2	60.9
Venezuela	30.3	462.0	276	76.1	455.1	238	45.8	–1.5	–13.5
Vietnam	14.2	545.5	244	99.3	590.9	573	85.1	8.3	135.0
Zambia	20.5	379.3	160	63.2	468.2	369	42.6	23.4	130.4
Zimbabwe	14.8	355.3	33	47.3	424.5	285	32.5	19.5	765.1
Total	42.2	475.6	280	80.0	513.0	438	37.8	10.9	132.2

Notes Long-term trends: between 1970 and 2020. For details, please consult Sect. 2.2

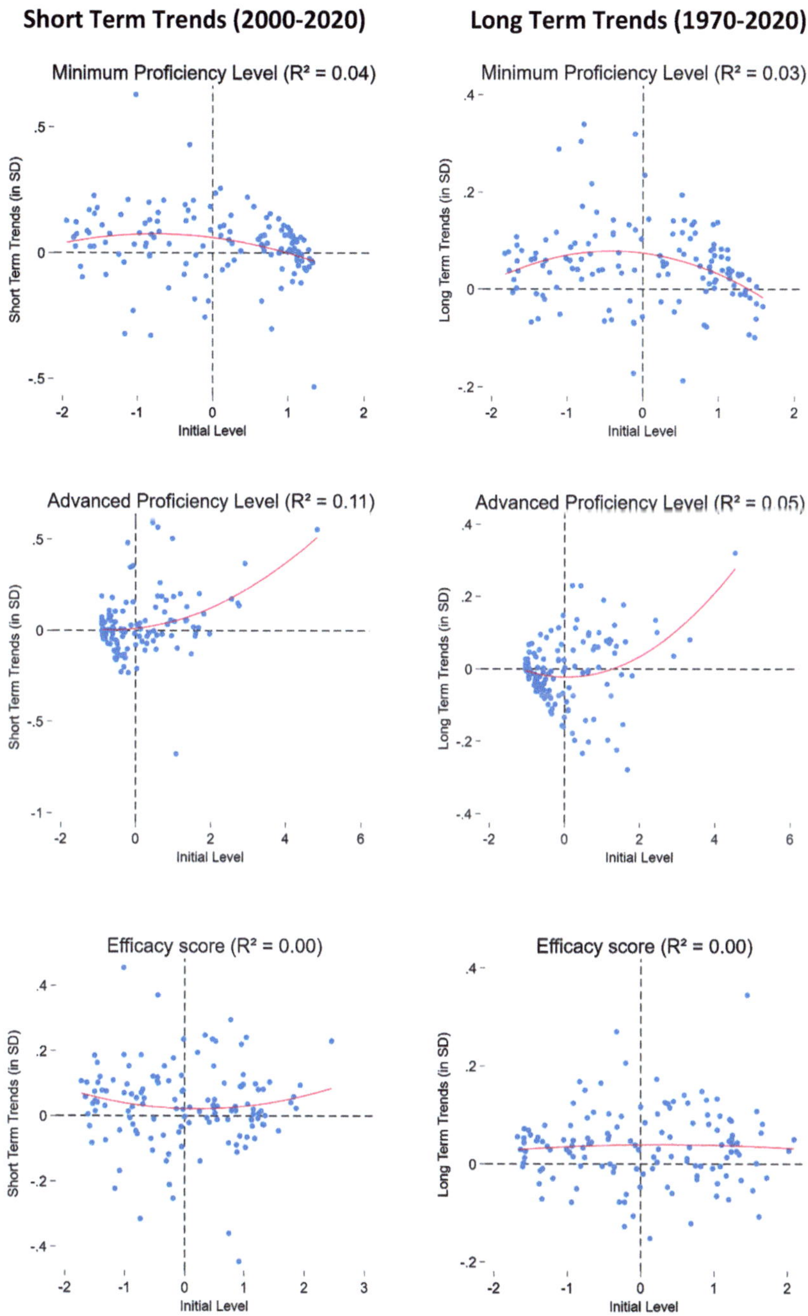

Fig. 4.15 Efficiency trends by skill level—World

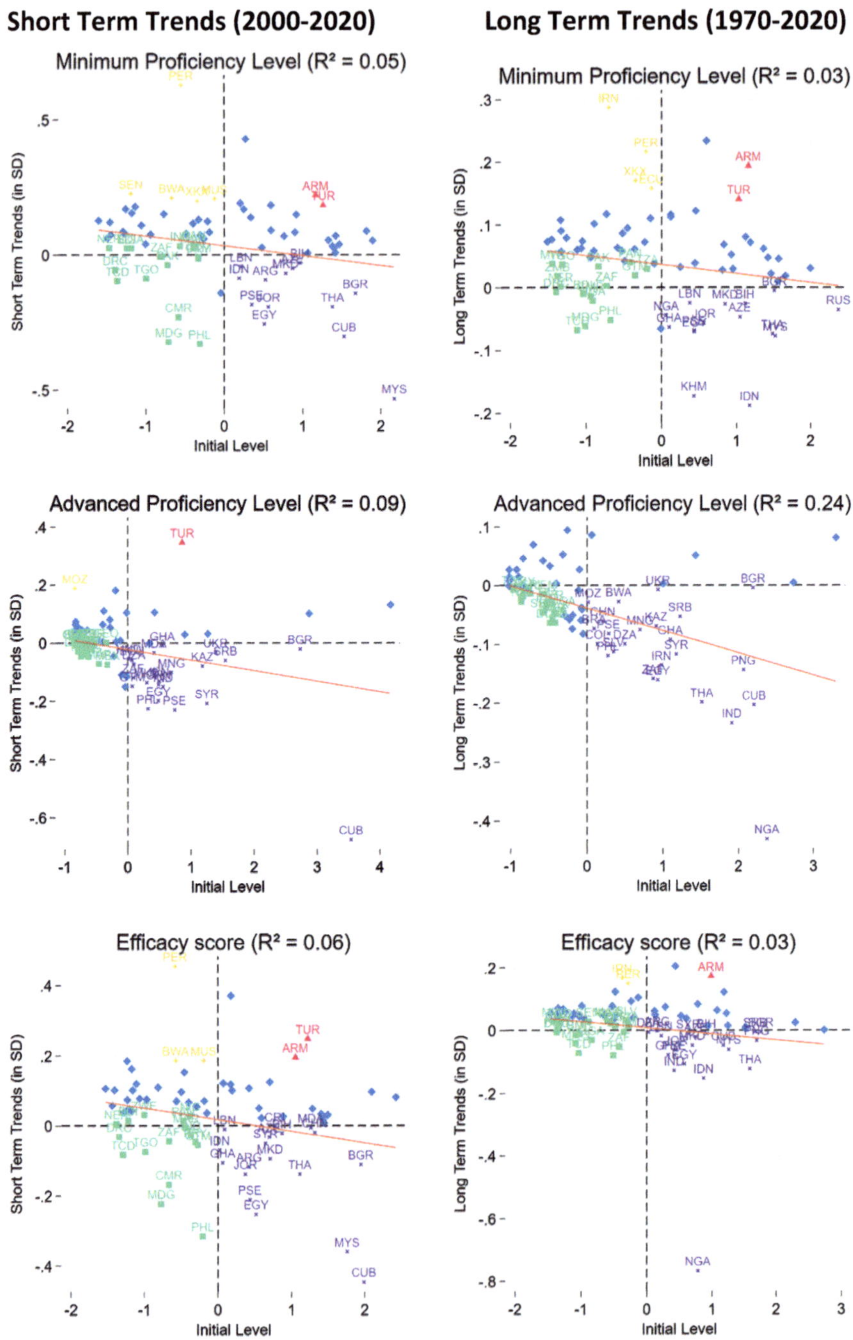

Fig. 4.16 Efficiency trends by skill level—Developing countries

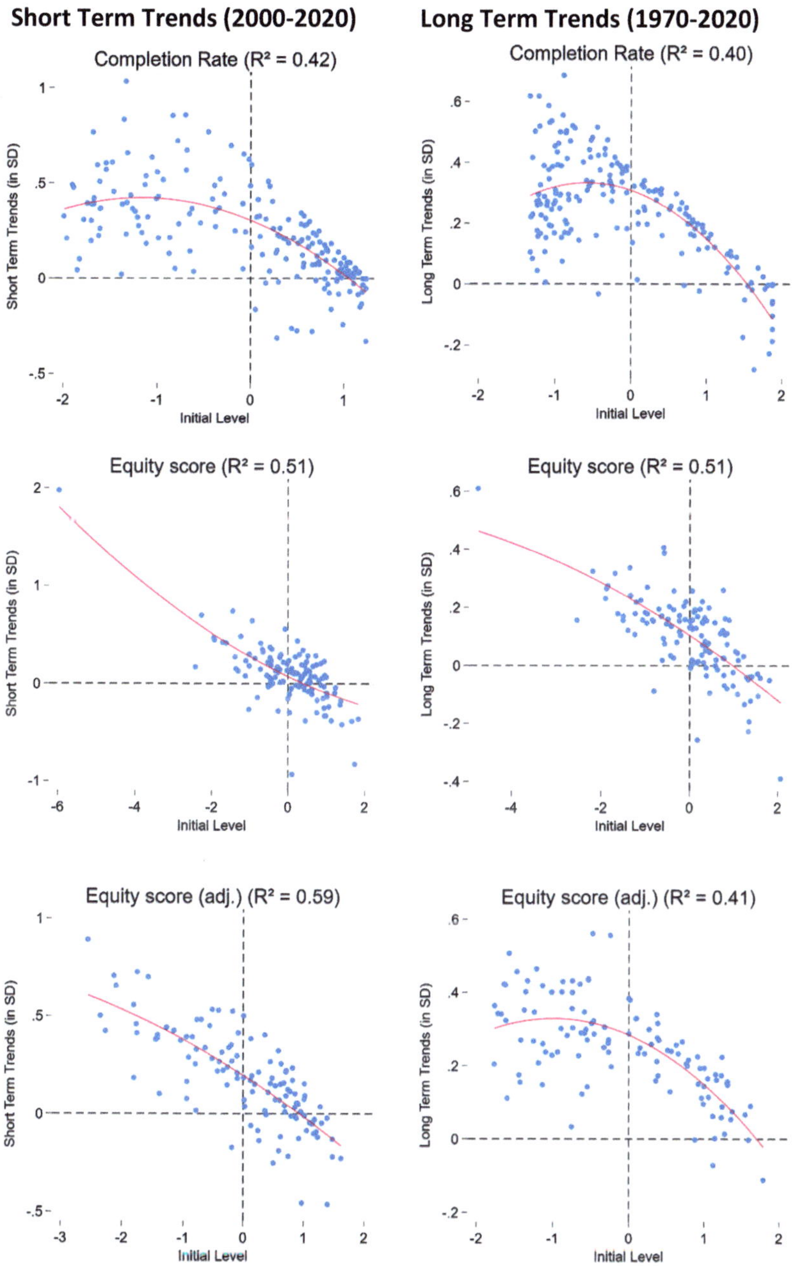

Fig. 4.17 Equity trends based on deciles—World

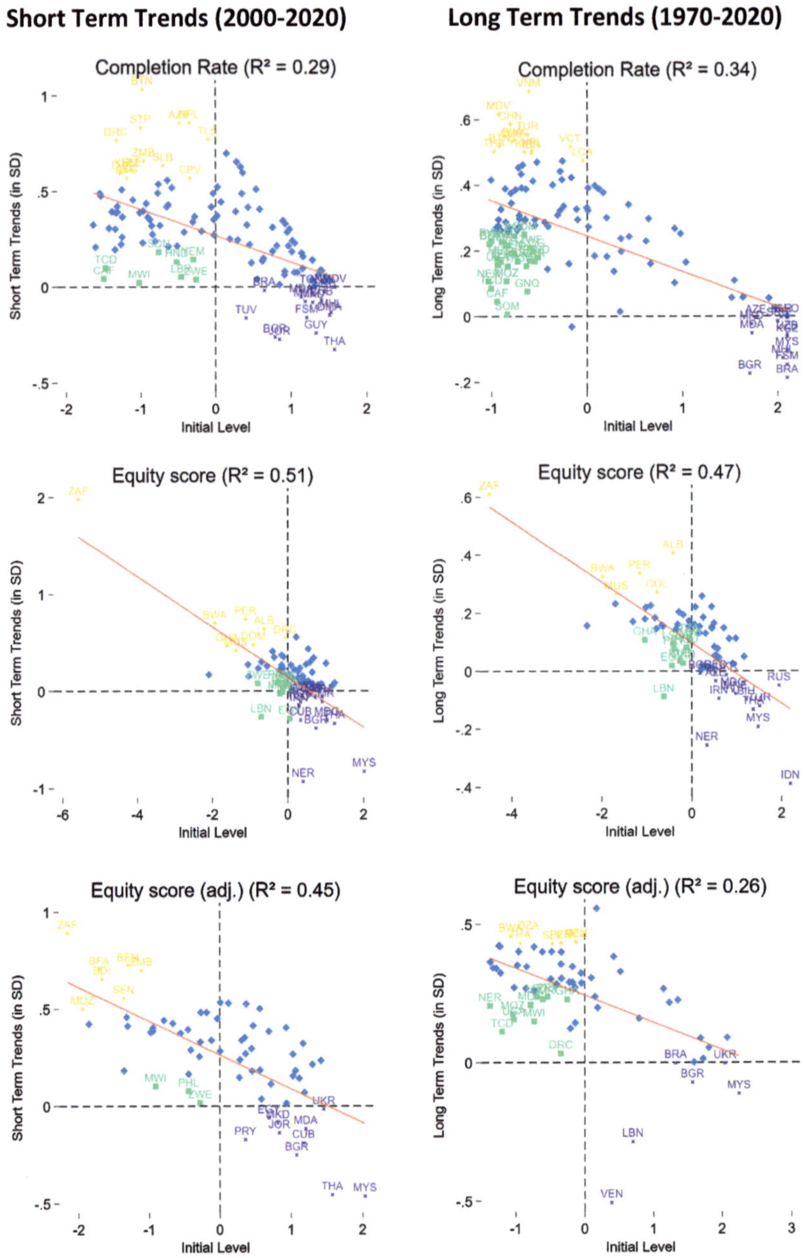

Fig. 4.18 Equity trends based on deciles—Developing countries

References

Altinok, N. (2017). Mind the gap: Proposal for the standardized measure for SDG4-Education 2030 Agenda. *UIS Information Paper, 46.*

Altinok, N., & Diebolt, C. (2024). Cliometrics of learning-adjusted years of schooling: Evidence from a new dataset. *Cliometrica, 18*(3), 691–764. https://doi.org/10.1007/s11698-023-00276-x

Angrist, N., Djankov, S., Goldberg, P. K., & Patrinos, H. A. (2021). Measuring human capital using global learning data. *Nature, 592*(7854), 403–408.

Angrist, N., Patrinos, H. A., & Schlotter, M. (2013). An expansion of a global data set on educational quality: A focus on achievement in developing countries. *The World Bank: Policy Research Working Papers.* https://doi.org/10.1596/1813-9450-6536

Ballantine, J. H., Stuber, J., & Everitt, J. G. (2021). *The sociology of education.* Routledge. https://doi.org/10.4324/9781003023715

Becker, G. S. (1975). *Human capital: A theoretical and empirical analysis, with special reference to education.* http://www.nber.org/chapters/c3730.pdf

Becker, G. S. (2002). The age of human capital. In E. P. Lazear (Ed.), *Education in the twenty-first century.* Hoover Institution Press. http://media.hoover.org/sites/default/files/documents/0817928928_3.pdf

Berne, R., & Stiefel, L. (1984). *The measurement of equity in school finance: conceptual, methodological, and empirical dimensions.* Johns Hopkins University Press. https://books.google.fr/books?id=TiydAAAAMAAJ

Bertrand, R., & Blais, J.-G. (2004). *Modèles de mesure: l'apport de la théorie des réponses aux items.* PUQ.

Cederman, L.-E., Weidmann, N. B., & Gleditsch, K. S. (2011). Horizontal Inequalities and Ethnonationalist Civil War: A Global Comparison. *American political science review, 105*(3), 478–495. https://doi.org/10.1017/S0003055411000207

Cameron, S., Daga, R., & Outhred, R. (2018). Setting out a conceptual framework for measuring equity in learning. In UIS-UNESO (Ed.), Handbook on Measuring Equity in Education (UIS-UNESCO, pp. 16–45). UNIS-UNESCO

Filmer, D., Rogers, F. H., Angrist, N., & Sabarwal, S. (2018). *Learning-Adjusted Years of Schooling (LAYS): Defining a new macro measure of education.* The World Bank.

Gust, S., Hanushek, E. A., & Woessmann, L. (2022). Global universal basic skills: current deficits and implications for world development. *National Bureau of Economic Research Working Paper Series, 30566.* https://doi.org/10.3386/w30566

Hanushek, E. A., & Kimko, D. D. (2000). Schooling, labor-force quality, and the growth of nations. *The American Economic Review, 90*(5), 1184.

Hanushek, E. A., & Woessmann, L. (2012). Do better schools lead to more growth? Cognitive skills, economic outcomes, and causation. *Journal of Economic Growth, 17*(4), 267–321. https://doi.org/10.1007/s10887-012-9081-x

Honaker, J., King, G., & Blackwell, M. (2011). Amelia II: A program for missing data. *Journal of Statistical Software, 45*(1), 1–47.

Jacob, W. J., & Holsinger, D. B. (2008). *Inequality in education: A critical analysis. In Inequality in education: Comparative and international perspectives* (pp. 1–33). Springer.

Kolen, M. J., & Brennan, R. L. (2014). *Test equating, scaling, and linking: Methods and practices.* Springer Science & Business Media.

Le Nestour, A., Moscoviz, L., & Sandefur, J. (2022). *The long-run decline of education quality in the developing world.* In C. for G. Development (Ed.), CGD Working Paper 608. https://www.cgdev.org/publication/long-rundecline-education-quality-developing-world

Lim, S. S., Updike, R. L., Kaldjian, A. S., Barber, R. M., Cowling, K., York, H., Friedman, J., Xu, R., Whisnant, J. L., & Taylor, H. J. (2018). Measuring human capital: A systematic analysis of 195 countries and territories, 1990–2016. *The Lancet, 392*(10154), 1217–1234.

OECD. (2023). *PISA 2022 results* (Vol. I). OECD. https://doi.org/10.1787/53f23881-en

Omoeva, C., Moussa, W., & Hatch, R. (2018). Proposed operationalisation of equity measurement. In UIS-UNESCO (Ed.), *Handbook on measuring equity in education* (UIS-UNESCO, pp. 46–79). UIS-UNESCO.

Piketty, T. (2013). Capital in the twenty-first century. In *Les Livres du nouveau monde*. Seuil.

Schwerdt, G., & Wiederhold, S. (2019). A Macroeconomic Analysis of Literacy and Economic Performance. Mimeo. https://doi.org/http://www.dataangel.ca/docs/A%20Macroeconomic%20Analysis%20of%20Literacy_February2019.pdf

Stewart, F. (2005). Horizontal Inequalities: A Neglected Dimension of Development. In *Wider perspectives on global development* (pp. 101–135). Palgrave Macmillan UK. https://doi.org/10.1057/9780230501850_5

Stewart, F. (2008). Horizontal Inequalities and Conflict: An Introduction and some Hypotheses. In *Horizontal inequalities and conflict* (pp. 3–24). Palgrave Macmillan UK. https://doi.org/10.1057/9780230582729_1

Stewart, F., & Langer, A. (2008). Horizontal Inequalities: Explaining Persistence and Change. In *Horizontal inequalities and conflict* (pp. 54–82). Palgrave Macmillan UK. https://doi.org/10.1057/9780230582729_4

UNESCO. (2014). *Sustainable development begins with education: How education can contribute to the proposed post-2015 goals*. http://unesdoc.unesco.org/images/0023/002305/230508e.pdf

UNESCO Institute for Statistics. (2017). *Metadata for the global and thematic indicators for the follow-up and review of SDG 4 and Education 2030*. UNESCO Institute for Statistics. http://uis.unesco.org/sites/default/files/documents/sdg4-metadata-global-thematic-indicators.pdf

UNESCO Institute of Statistics. (2019). Costs and benefits of different approaches to measuring the learning proficiency of students. *UIS Information Paper, 53*. http://uis.unesco.org/sites/default/files/documents/ip53-costs-benefits-approaches-measuring-proficiency-2019-en.pdf

United Nations. (2015). *Transforming our world: The 2030 agenda for sustainable development*. http://www.un.org/ga/search/view_doc.asp?symbol=A/RES/70/1

United Nations. (2017a). *International covenant on economic, social and cultural rights*. http://www.ohchr.org/EN/ProfessionalInterest/Pages/CESCR.aspx

United Nations. (2017b). *Universal declaration of human rights*. http://www.un.org/en/universaldeclaration-human-rights/index.html

Chapter 5
The Price of Educational Inequality: Fifty Years of Education and Growth in France

Abstract This chapter examines the structural dynamics of educational inequality, situating France within a half-century of international comparisons. We combine longitudinal and cross-sectional data for nearly 130 countries (1970–2020), enabling robust counterfactual analyses. Our findings reveal France's persistent struggles: too many students fail to master basic skills, while socio-economic gaps remain among the widest in the OECD. By contrasting extremes—top versus bottom performers, privileged versus disadvantaged—we highlight the dual failure of low equity and limited performance. Ultimately, the chapter quantifies both the social and economic costs of inequality, underscoring the urgent need for more effective and fair education systems.

> Unless a society completely eliminates the ties between parent and child, inequality between parents guarantees a certain level of inequality in the opportunities available to children. The only real question is about the severity of the inequality.
>
> Christopher Jencks (1979), p. 18.

5.1 Introduction

Today, perhaps more than ever, many countries are faced with a twofold challenge: how to keep up with international competition while preserving real equity within their populations. Education is at the heart of this challenge. As a major factor in productivity and, by extension, economic growth, the expectations placed on schools are enormous (Wasmer et al., 2007), and regularly give rise to cries for the reduction or even elimination of inequalities, so that tomorrow everyone can still find their place in society (Duru-Bellat, 2009, 2017).

The Coleman Report in the USA and the work of Bourdieu and Passeron (1964) have, historically, highlighted questions about the nature, sources and causes of educational inequality. Today, while education systems in developed countries have succeeded in enrolling almost all their populations between the ages of 6 and 16, the

N. Altinok and C. Diebolt, *Edumetrics*, Population Economics,
https://doi.org/10.1007/978-3-032-13277-2_5

major question no longer concerns the quantity of education. In fact, the question now refers more to analyzing a "*qualitative* democratization" (Merle, 2020; Prost, 1986), since questions of access seem to have been partly resolved (Thélot & Vallet, 2000). As a result, questions about educational inequalities are prompting us to question the way we measure and understand how educational achievements are statistically linked to individuals' characteristics, such as their social origin or socio-economic level (Felouzis, 2020; Felouzis & Charmillot, 2012; Lafontaine et al., 2013; Ly & Riegert, 2015).

This article is part of this dynamic. It combines the advantages of longitudinal and cross-sectional studies. We use several indicators and different inequality methodologies to question the state of knowledge and to improve the robustness of the results found. In so doing, we also seek to address the problems of measurement error inherent in international surveys.

While longitudinal analyses are able to capture fixed effects and retrace school career paths, cross-sectional approaches have the advantage of enabling a more comparative reading and, in so doing, including many countries. With this in mind, we propose a hybrid, counterfactual approach. Using cross-sectional data spread over time, we analyze educational inequalities based on a database of learning outcomes for almost 130 countries between 1970 and 2020. In doing so, we combine the advantages of cross-sectional data (comparability with other education systems) with those of longitudinal analyses (the ability to trace the evolution of inequalities over time). We also use the double-difference method, with a view to "purging" exogenous effects similar to all developed countries (exogenous fixed effects), but also in order to detect structural changes in the French education system.[1] In very concrete terms, and in order to make a robust assessment of the evolution of educational inequalities in France, we compare French data with those from similar countries over a 50-year period, studying several dimensions of inequality. To the best of our knowledge, this is the first cliometric research study, mobilizing an original database and counterfactual modalities, devoted to the structural and spatial dynamics of the unequal dimension of educational attainment in France and worldwide.

Our first indicator concerns threshold inequalities between individuals. Measured by the proportion of pupils reaching the minimum competency threshold, it highlights France's backwardness, particularly at primary level and in mathematics. While most OECD countries succeed in getting almost all their populations to reach a minimum level of competence, this is far from being the case in France. Nearly 15% of French CM1 pupils are unable to perform simple calculations, while significantly fewer pupils in neighboring countries suffer from this shortcoming.

With this in mind, we believe that analyzing the difference between top and bottom performers can be an original way of measuring inequalities. In line with Piketty's (2013) analysis, we measure inequalities by comparing extreme deciles. Admittedly, the gap between the best and worst performers has tended to narrow over the past

[1] In a way, our approach can be seen as a natural, quasi-experimental experiment, with France as the control group and the other OECD countries as the control group.

half-century, but in the case of France, we observe at best a stabilization over the past two decades.

Another dimension of our analysis refers to the performance gap between students from families richly endowed with socio-economic capital and less-favored students.[2] We note that the gap is particularly significant in France, while other countries, notably those with an Anglo-Saxon culture, observe smaller gaps. We find, for example, that the gap is almost 100 points in France, equivalent to almost 3 years of lost learning for pupils from the poorest families (Avvisati & Givord, 2023).

In any case, like Jencks (1979), we believe that the main problem with inequalities is not to eliminate them entirely, but to reduce their severity. In this sense, we are testing the extent to which France's position appears to be singular. By calculating the trajectory gaps between France on the one hand and other developed countries on the other, we seek to measure a potential divergence in France's trajectory. Indeed, unlike Canada, the UK or Finland, France is simultaneously failing to ensure that its pupils acquire the minimum skills, while also failing to have an equitable system with small gaps between different population groups. In so doing, our results confirm the initial intuitions of Meuret (2012) which suggested that equity and performance inevitably go hand in hand.

In the remainder of this article, we first present the original data produced on inequalities in educational achievement. The methodology used to construct the data is explained, and the analysis of inequalities is presented. The latter focuses on several dimensions that confirm or refute the trends observed. As an extension, we measure the price of educational inequalities, i.e. their economic cost, using a historical macro-simulation model based on a counterfactual approach. We conclude our analysis by elaborating typical ideals for education systems, comparing their average performance with the level of educational inequalities.

5.2 Data and Methodology

5.2.1 Assessments of Student Achievement

Our assessment of the extent of inequalities is based on the dimension of learning achievement, measured through a standardization exercise of international surveys. The international database on student learning mobilizes results from various surveys (TIMSS, PIRLS and PISA[3]). Other assessments focus on adult skills (IALS,

[2] This measure is based primarily on the "escs" indicator developed by the OECD. We reproduce it using similar indicators for the other surveys. See Sect. 2.2.2 for a detailed presentation.

[3] *Trends on International Mathematics and Science Study*, *Progress on International Reading Literacy Study* and *Programme for International Student Assessment*, respectively.

PIAAC[4]). We present these surveys very briefly. More information can be found in previous works (Altinok & Diebolt, 2024a, 2024b).

The International Association for the Evaluation of Educational Achievement (IEA) was the first organization to conduct international surveys of student achievement. Following a pilot survey in the 1960s (Foshay et al., 1962), several assessments have tested primary and secondary school pupils in mathematics and science, but it is above all the TIMSS assessment that has left its mark on the international community. This survey began in 1995 and focuses on mathematics and science. Since then, several waves of tests have been carried out every 4 years.[5] The IEA has also assessed students' reading skills since the 1970s, but it is undeniably the PIRLS survey that has highlighted young people's reading skills. Parallel to the IEA surveys, the PISA assessment has attracted a great deal of media attention, particularly in Europe; PISA being an assessment developed by the OECD. It was launched in 2000. Testing 15-year-old students in three skill areas (mathematics, science and reading), PISA has become the most widely distributed survey in the world. Organized every 3 years, eight different waves have been carried out up to 2022, with over 70 countries participating in the latest wave. Alongside assessments of student achievement, adult skills surveys (IALS and PIAAC) can also be very useful in better assessing student skills. Using a specific methodology, some authors have, in fact, obtained panel data relating to the skill levels of young adults (Schwerdt & Wiederhold, 2019). All the surveys used to obtain the database can be found in Table A1 (Appendix A).

5.2.2 *General Methodology*

5.2.2.1 Quality of Education Database

Before preparing data on specific sub-samples or thresholds, our work required the construction of an international database on the quality of education systems. The detailed methodology of our approach can be found in Altinok and Diebolt (2024b). Below, we present the general approach very briefly, before moving on to the dimension of educational inequalities proper.

Our research is based on a grouping of different international surveys (presented in the previous section) on comparable scales. Since these surveys are diverse in nature, we had to devise a methodology that would enable us to adjust them to each other, in order to avoid any potential bias. We therefore proceeded to anchor the surveys, in order to envisage comparisons in time and space. The general idea behind our approach is to use the results from countries that participated simultaneously in several surveys over the same period (Angrist et al., 2021).

---

[4] Respectively *International Adult Literacy Survey* and *Programme for the International Assessment of Adult Competencies*.

[5] The second wave dates from 1999, then 2003, 2007… The latest wave with available data dates from 2019. The 2023 assessment has not yet been published at the time of writing.

In fact, by combining all the countries that have participated in several assessments, it is possible to calculate *conversion rates*, as one would do for an exchange rate between currencies, for example. This method is used to adjust the scores of surveys carried out from the 1990s onwards and has already been implemented by previous research (Angrist et al., 2013, 2021; Gust et al., 2024). An additional approach was also implemented to anchor the surveys to each other over time, and especially before 1990. Following the pioneering approach of Hanushek and Kimko (2000), it is thus possible to anchor data from international surveys by referring to the results of the United States in the *National Assessment of Educational Progress* (NAEP).[6]

As for PISA and TIMSS, the calculation of a general *conversion rate* is sufficient to obtain a comparable database in terms of learning achievement.[7] What is new, however, is the implementation of the multiple imputation method used in Lim et al. (2018). By using data that are highly correlated with learning achievement, our research not only extends the period covered by learning achievement assessments, but also enables us to predict scores for countries that have not participated in all these assessments.

This imputation procedure uses the "Amelia II" package (Honaker et al., 2011) and proves useful for obtaining panel data covering almost half a century (1970–2020).[8] Indeed, the database prepared by Angrist et al. (2021) only covers the period 2010–2020. The use of multiple imputation and the oldest surveys, using anchoring by the conversion rate and through NAEP evaluation, therefore enables us to obtain comparable scores for the main OECD countries between 1970 and 2020.

5.2.2.2 Extending the Base to Educational Inequalities

The use of anchoring methods enables us to obtain a panel database on the quality of education. In very concrete terms, data on the quality of education are spread over

[6] Details of the methodology used to obtain a database covering more than 130 countries can be found in Altinok and Diebolt (2024b). In this article, we focus on the results for France, comparing the hexagon with a sample of 20 OECD countries. As a reminder, it should be noted here that the database we have created naturally contains a wider and more detailed sample of data.

[7] Assuming that the average mathematics scores of countries participating in TIMSS 1999 and PISA 2000 are equal to 520 in TIMSS and 495 in PISA, then the conversion rate between PISA and TIMSS will be $525/495 = 1,06$. PISA scores will thus be re-evaluated upwards by around 6.06%.

[8] Details of the multiple imputation procedure can be found in Altinok and Diebolt (2024b). Unlike Lim et al. (2018), we employ this multiple imputation method using different steps to minimize measurement error. Specifically, eight steps are implemented, ranging from the prediction of scores for countries with the most observations over a short period (between 1995 and 2020, step number 1) to those for countries with very little data on education quality and over a longer period (between 1970 and 2020, step number 8). This imputation procedure uses explanatory factors previously selected via multiple regression and includes several explanatory variables.

several school levels (primary, secondary) and skills domains (mathematics, reading, science) and are available between 1970 and 2020 for most OECD countries.[9]

The extension proposed here concerns the unequal dimension of educational attainment. We consider universal schooling in the core OECD countries, leaving aside inequalities in access to and completion of the basic school levels of primary and secondary education. In other words, we focus our analysis exclusively on the dimension of learning achievement.

To this end, we have adopted three main approaches.

Firstly, we reproduce the data anchoring methodology almost identically, focusing on performance thresholds and scores in the various deciles. The approach used is very similar to that for average scores, with the difference that we prefer to use the "*equipercentile*" anchoring method instead of the "*conversion rate*" method, in order to calibrate each performance threshold between countries and over time (Kolen & Brennan, 2014). The main advantage of this method is that it takes into account the distribution of scores within each database. In concrete terms, instead of anchoring average scores with *conversion rates*, we anchor each percentile of a reference survey with the same percentile of another survey by calculating conversion coefficients. Around a hundred of these coefficients are calculated for a pair of surveys (each referring to a particular percentile). This allows us to take into account any differences in score distribution within each survey. Since we wish to calculate the proportions of students exceeding performance thresholds, it is indeed important to take into account the distribution of scores within each assessment before anchoring the surveys to each other.

We also calculate the proportions of students reaching different competency thresholds. These are the two levels we are most interested in. Our performance thresholds are based on those developed by the IEA, and are quite similar to those defined by the OECD in the PISA test. The first level refers to a "Minimum Competence Threshold" (MCT). Its main aim is to highlight the proportion of a population that achieves a certain level of competence, in order to obtain minimum skills for everyday activities. The Sustainable Development Goals explicitly refer to this minimum threshold (UIS, 2019). The minimum competence threshold refers to the IEA's minimum benchmark, the "*Low International Benchmark*", which corresponds to a threshold of 400 points. Students who reach this threshold have basic skills in mathematics, reading and science.[10] At primary level, they can perform basic arithmetic operations on one- and two-digit numbers, and solve problems involving a small number of parameters. Students can handle fractions and common geometric shapes. Statistically, they can read and complete bar graphs and tables (see Table A2. in Appendix A).

---

[9] It should be noted here that we use the term "panel" in the sense that the cross-sectional data are pooled without longitudinal follow-up. However, as the data are statistically representative of the different countries included in the surveys, we can consider them as a panel for monitoring the performance of education systems.

[10] This threshold is very close to the level 2 defined in the PISA assessment (OECD, 2023).

Alongside this minimum threshold, it is interesting to look at the proportion of students reaching the Advanced Competence Threshold (ACT). The main purpose of the latter is to measure the proportion of the population achieving a high level on tests of student achievement, and thus to see the proportion of elites within each country. For the purposes of this article, we use the IEA's "*Advanced International Benchmark*", which is set at a level of 625 points.[11] At this level, primary school pupils can apply their knowledge and understanding in a variety of complex situations and explain their reasoning rigorously. It's no longer a question of having basic knowledge, but rather of being able to use it in complex situations and knowing exactly which ones to mobilize, while mobilizing more sophisticated tools (such as the use of fractions or decimals). The use of multidimensional tools is essential to reach this advanced level. Table A2 shows in greater detail the skills acquired for each skill area and threshold. In particular, we analyze the proportion of students reaching the minimum competency threshold (MCS), compared with the proportion reaching the advanced competency threshold (ACS). A country that manages to get almost its entire population to reach the minimum threshold can be considered egalitarian. If the same country also manages to get a proportion of students above the advanced skills threshold, it will be both egalitarian and successful.

In addition to average scores, we also calculate scores for each decile. The gap between deciles may prove to be a means of measuring educational inequality, in the light of the approach developed by Piketty (2013) with regard to income inequality. In doing so, we calculate scores at deciles 1 and 9, i.e. respectively the average score of the lowest and highest performing 10%.[12] An egalitarian country should logically obtain an inter-decile ratio close to 1, indicating a very small gap in performance between the two extreme deciles. Conversely, an unequal country, which succeeds in making the best performers do better while neglecting the worst performers, will have a high inter-decile ratio. Measuring the inter-decile ratio therefore enables us to assess the level of inequality in France, compared with other countries.

An additional focus of our research on educational inequalities concerns the potential differences in performance that may exist between populations with specific characteristics, such as coming from a family with or without high socio-economic capital. This refers to the classic analysis of inequalities in the sociology of education (Felouzis, 2020). It's important to note that the initial anchoring is done on the scores of each sub-population, but ratios are only used in the multiple imputation procedure. The approach adopted here is to replicate the initial anchoring methods on sub-populations, then use ratios marking the absolute differences between sub-populations to perform data imputation. More specifically, we calculate ratios

[11] It is important to note that this threshold is very close in secondary education to level 5 of the PISA study. The thresholds are close to 625 points for the 3 skill areas, bearing in mind that we use approximately the same threshold in reading. More precisely, the threshold is 607 points in mathematics, 633 points in science and 626 points in reading. See OECD (2023), pages 92, 99–100 and 103 for the definition of thresholds according to the PISA assessment.

[12] Contrary to the analysis of Piketty (2013), it is not appropriate to refer to percentiles in international tests, due to the small number of students taking part in the survey compared to a country's total workforce or population.

between different population groups. The dimensions of this differentiation can be multiple: differences between genders (girls and boys), between the type of locality (urban and rural), between the type of school (public and private) or between the socio-economic level of families (calculated as quartiles).

In this research, we use only the variability of scores relating to differences in socio-economic level. To this end, we have calculated socio-economic level scales within all surveys, using available data. It is impossible to have a standardized, similar scale for all surveys, since data on socio-economic characteristics differ between the different assessments. However, as we use the quartile spread for each index (i.e. by splitting the distribution of scores into four equal parts), comparison between different periods should not suffer from the lack of standardization of the scales of this index between surveys. The choice of variables used to calculate this index is presented in Table A3 in Appendix A. If students with the highest socio-economic levels have significantly higher scores than those from families without social and economic capital, the country can be considered unequal in terms of educational achievement.

We use an index of socio-economic level, obtained from virtually all the assessments included in our database. As the measurement of this index is quite heterogeneous between surveys, it is more the absolute gap between quartiles that will weigh in our analysis. The bottom quartile (Q_1) will measure the average score of students from the 25% of families with the lowest socio-economic status. We then measure the level of inequality by calculating the difference in performance between the top quartile (Q_4) and the bottom quartile (Q_1). The greater the difference, the greater the inequality.[13]

For all existing data, we calculate a difference between one category and another. For example, if a country has a score of 550 for its students included in the 4thquartile of the socio-economic index against 520 points for those included in the first quartile, the indicator used is obtained by subtracting the first number by the second, i.e.: $550 - 520 = 30$.. We replicate this calculation in a similar way to the existing data set, and proceed with multiple imputation based on this ratio and not on the scores of each category. When we have only two categories left, as is the case for socio-economic level quartiles, we calculate several ratios: the ratios between quartile 4 and quartile 1 (Q_4/Q_1), but also other quartile pairs (). Q_4/Q_2.

Estimating gaps rather than scores for each sub-group by multiple imputation has several advantages.

- It is possible to anchor and adjust for inequality dimensions without being directly influenced by the level of educational quality, and by allowing temporal smoothing of deviations. Instead of predicting scores for each sub-sample, we

[13] However, it remains possible that if the population structure changes over time, with the arrival of large numbers of poor immigrants in a country for example, the interquartile range may be modified exogenously. The imputation method we use allows us, at least partially, to take into account structural differences specific to certain countries, since we mobilize a specific procedure to take into account country fixed effects.

prefer to analyze and predict deviations calculated on the differences in performance between sub-samples. This variance can then evolve with a smoothing and global consistency constraint, independently of the average score (via the method proposed by Honaker et al., 2011).
- Statistical analysis of imputation is facilitated because the use of deviations prevents the natural existence of structural effects in the data: it is highly probable that some poorly performing systems are also the most unequal, but this should not be translated into a statistical constraint. Using ratios instead of scores avoids generating structural biases.
- Calculating scores for each sub-sample is facilitated by using the scores already anchored in the general database (the one provided in Altinok & Diebolt, 2024b) and allows overall consistency to the scores. Indeed, the use of prediction for each sub-sample could lead to divergences and contradictions in performance between sub-groups and the general population.

This last point is crucial, as it could lead to major deviations in performance within sub-samples. Indeed, every anchoring and imputation method has its own limitations and can lead to estimation bias. Performance for a sub-sample is calculated directly on real data, and then recalculated only in the final step, taking into account its initial weighting. So, if in our data, the private education sector accounts for around 10% of the proportion of students, we reuse this ratio to obtain the private score after carrying out the anchoring procedure. To do this, we simply combine the score for the general population with the estimated gap between the public and private sectors, while taking into account the weighting of the private sector within the overall system.[14]

5.2.3 Analysis Method

5.2.3.1 Double-Difference Analysis

Since the recent decline in France's performance could, theoretically, be the result of other countries catching up, we decided to undertake an analysis with a counterfactual dimension. In doing so, we decided to calculate France's performance gap in relation to countries with *ceteris paribus* the same characteristics in the 1970s, namely the historical members of the OECD. We then calculated the performance gap between France and these countries in subsequent years, for the previously selected inequality indicators. If the gap proved significant, then we could deduce that the trajectory followed by France is, indeed, the result of actions or, as the case may be, non-actions, specific to the country and not the consequence of any catch-up phenomenon.

[14] When data on the proportion of each sub-sample in the general population are not available, we use the most probable data, i.e. those for the nearest year, or failing that, the average proportion of the sub-sample for the country concerned.

In more formal terms, we assume an inequality indicator (denoted *ineq*) for France and a panel of countries similar to France:

$$ineq_{FRA,1970} = X \; et \; ineq_{OECD,1970} = Y \tag{5.1}$$

We calculate the change in inequality for France between two periods:

$$\Delta ineq_{FRA,t \rightarrow t+10} = ineq_{FRA,t+10} - ineq_{FRA,t} \tag{5.2}$$

In a similar way, we calculate the variation in inequality for the control group (here the 21 main OECD countries):

$$\Delta ineq_{OECD,t \rightarrow t+10} = ineq_{OECD,t+10} - ineq_{OECD,t} \tag{5.3}$$

We assume that a significant effect of inequality in France will be observed by calculating the difference between the variation in France's performance and that of the panel of countries previously selected (double-difference method).

Thus:

$$\Delta ineq_{FRA-net,t \rightarrow t+10} = \left(ineq_{FRA,t+10} - ineq_{FRA,t}\right) - \left(ineq_{OECD,t+10} - ineq_{OECD,t}\right) \tag{5.4}$$

We are, of course, aware that the main drawback of this double-difference approach lies in the potential presence of measurement errors that bias the net effect of the variation in France's inequalities. Indeed, if there is a measurement error that would overestimate inequalities in a given year, then the variation calculated between two periods would be mainly due to this measurement error. To circumvent this estimation bias, we propose two alternatives. First, we calculated the absolute inequality gap between France and the panel considered for each period:

$$ineq_{FRA-relative,t} = ineq_{FRA-abs,t} - ineq_{OECD-abs,t} \tag{5.5}$$

Then, by calculating the average of these inequalities, we were able to see whether the inequalities observed in France are really different from those of other so-called similar countries:

$$ineq_{mean,FRA-relative,t} = \frac{\sum_{t=1}^{n} ineq_{FRA-relative,t}}{n} \tag{5.6}$$

Another method was to widen the interval of years used to calculate variation, in order to temper possible estimation biases. Instead of taking an interval of 10 years, we could take intervals of 5, 15 or 20 years:

$$\Delta ineq_{FRA-dif,t \rightarrow t+10} = \left(ineq_{FRA,t+10} - ineq_{FRA,t}\right) - \left(ineq_{OECD,t+10} - ineq_{OECD,t}\right) \tag{5.7}$$

5.2.3.2 Modeling the Economic Cost of Educational Inequality

In order to assess the price, i.e. the economic cost, of educational inequalities in France, we have used and re-adapted a forecasting model developed by Hanushek and his co-authors (cf. in particular Hanushek & Woessmann, 2012; Hanushek et al., 2017a; Hanushek et al., 2017b; Hanushek et al., 2020; Gust et al., 2024). In these forecasting models (whose general features are presented in Appendix B), a macro-simulation of the impact on economic growth of an educational reform is estimated. As an extension of these precursor models, our approach here has a counterfactual dimension, since we measure the trajectory that France might have experienced if it had implemented a more effective policy to reduce inequalities over the past half-century.[15]

With this in mind, our first scenario aims to measure the economic gains of an educational policy explicitly seeking to improve the performance in tests of educational achievement of the school population belonging to the poorest quartile.[16] Indeed, assuming that their performance is improved and brought down to the level of those belonging to the richest quartile, we can estimate the potential gain in economic growth that France would have experienced in the event of the implementation of a policy of equity, which we refer to here as "positive discrimination".

In such a model, the skill levels of each cohort are not identical to those of the workforce in the country under consideration. We are simply estimating a situation in which an educational policy would be implemented and would progressively concern the entire population over the period 1970–2050. In short, the initial workforce takes on the skill level existing before a potential reform. This workforce will then be partially, then totally, replaced by a population that has experienced the reform. This period will last several years, given that the working life cycle is 40 years ($W = 40$) *ceteris paribus*. So, for each new cohort, students who have experienced the educational reform represent only a fraction of the total French workforce, i.e. 2.5% each year.

In very concrete terms, we calculate the skill level of the workforce for each year between 1970 and 2050 by replacing the oldest workers with those from the new cohorts (i.e. $\overline{A}_t$) weighted as $1/W$, where W is life expectancy at work. In calculating the gain in cognitive skills from such a reform, we consider 4 phases:

---

[15] Our approach seems more coherent than that followed by Hanushek and his co-authors, insofar as the growth surplus measured by an educational policy is measured on the basis of economic and educational figures for the past and present periods, without assuming, as these authors do, a similarity of these effects in the decades to come.

[16] It should be noted here that neither our approach, nor those of Hanushek and his co-authors, includes the cost of a reform and the exact means of achieving the educational policy concerned. It goes without saying that including the costs of reforms would inevitably reduce their beneficial effects. In our view, the costs would be far less than the economic benefits. As for the policies to be implemented to achieve the set objectives, we believe that they should be discussed upstream and represent a global project for society, rather than being, all too often, the result of successive patchwork reforms, with no real support, as we have been observing for decades in the case of France.

1. School reform ($t = 1, \ldots, R$): during the reform of duration R, workers with an initial skill level are gradually replaced by more skilled workers.
2. Main replacement ($t = R + 1, \ldots, W$): workers with the initial skill level (i.e. before the reform) are replaced by new workers for the next ($W - R$) years.
3. Quality reinforcement ($t = W + 1, \ldots, W + R$): for the following R years, some workers who have partially experienced the reform are replaced by workers who have fully experienced the reform.
4. Population with complete reform ($t = W + R + 1, \ldots$): the entire workforce concerned has a skill level at the level of the desired reform.

Our reform scenario therefore assumes a progression of 15 years before the reform is fully operational (parameter R). This means that the educational levels of each of the first cohorts following the educational reform will have different (and better) levels of educational attainment. For each year of the simulation, we calculate the GDP growth rate resulting from the educational reform as follows:

$$g_t^{reform} = p + \gamma \overline{A}_t \quad (5.8)$$

GDP with or without the reform evolves as follows:

$$GDP_t^{\Delta} = \left(1 + g_t^{\Delta}\right) \times GDP_t^{\Delta}, \quad (5.9)$$

where $\Delta \in (reform, withoutreform)$

The total value V of the reform is given by the sum of the present values of the annual differences between GDP with and without the reform:

$$V = \sum_{t=1}^{S} \left(GDP_t^{reform} - GDP_t^{without\ reform}\right) \times (1 + d)^{-t}, \quad (5.10)$$

where S is the end of the simulation period and d is the discount rate.

5.3 Multidimensional Measurement of Educational Inequality

5.3.1 *General Results*

Before analyzing the various dimensions of inequality, it may be interesting to situate France in relation to other countries in terms of average performance (Fig. 5.1).

Lagging some 30 points behind Germany at primary level, France's performance at secondary level is in the middle of the pack. Nevertheless, it is clear that some education systems, such as Canada, Finland and Ireland, manage to achieve respectable

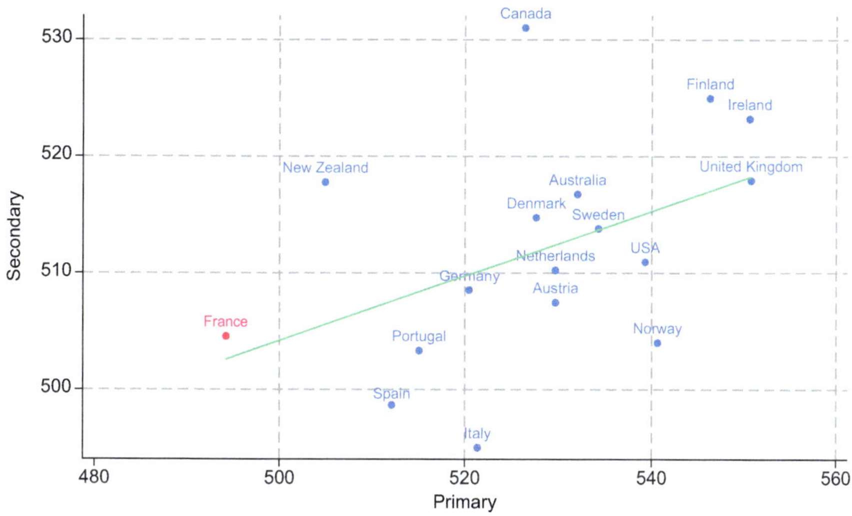

Fig. 5.1 France's performance based on average scores (*Source* Altinok and Diebolt [2024a])

performance at both levels. It is also important to note that there is a strong correlation in the performance of the two school levels presented in this graph (correlation close to 45%).[17]

As already mentioned in the introduction to this article, the main innovation of our work lies in the availability of comparable data for inequalities in educational attainment over almost half a century (1970–2020). While almost the entire population manages to achieve a minimum level of schooling up to the end of secondary school ("quantitative democratization"), the question of inequalities must be analyzed not in terms of the quantity of education, but rather in terms of its quality ("qualitative democratization", Prost, 1986).

Table 5.1 shows the main features of our database on educational inequalities. Our method is comparative and focuses here on countries similar to France, the OECD countries and more precisely the 20 countries which, *ceteris paribus*, make up the heart of the OECD[18] and which we call OECD-20. Restricting ourselves to these countries offers a double advantage: the availability of long-term data, and the fact of placing France around countries that have almost all achieved universal primary and secondary schooling by the early 2000s. France's average scores are systematically lower than the OECD-20 average, but a more pronounced catch-up is

[17] A more detailed analysis of French performance can be found in Altinok and Diebolt (2024a).

[18] We refer to these countries as "historic OECD members", and select mainly countries with strong similarities to France: Australia, Austria, Belgium, Canada, Denmark, Finland, France, Germany, Greece, Ireland, Italy, Netherlands, New Zealand, Norway, Portugal, Spain, Sweden, Switzerland, United Kingdom and United States. Asian countries perform better than Western countries in achievement surveys. However, certain cultural specificities may explain these differences (see Boman, 2022). For the purposes of this article, therefore, we prefer to focus on non-Asian OECD countries.

observed for France over the past half-century. Inequalities can be examined from the angle of the proportion of pupils reaching the minimum competency threshold. This underlines the fact that France is lagging far behind, with a tendency to fall further behind by 2020.

It is also interesting to note that the cumulative proportions for the two thresholds studied show that France lags behind by around 8% (i.e. 105% vs. 97% for the OECD and France, respectively): this would mean that France is unable to obtain an overall stock of competent students capable of meeting both the demand for basic skills and the demand for advanced skills. An alternative approach to inequality is to compare the scores of different deciles. We thus calculate the inter-decile ratio between the extreme deciles (i.e. the average score of the top 10%, compared with that of the bottom 10%). The variation in these inequalities has been rising over half a century at primary level, with the top decile having a score around 50% higher than the bottom decile: the inter-decile ratio at primary level has risen from 1.44 to 1.52. At secondary level, this ratio has tended to increase, with the top decile having a score around 50% higher than the bottom decile. At secondary level, this ratio tends to decline by around 9%, from 1.66 to 1.57. Compared with the OECD-20, this trend appears to have been less marked at primary level over the half-century studied. However, over the last two decades, the inter-decile ratio in secondary education has fallen slightly in France, following the same trend as in OECD-20 countries.

These variations are all relative, and can sometimes be explained by a slowing down of the elites, while the least successful have stagnating scores. An alternative approach is to use the absolute difference in performance between quartiles based on the socio-economic level of the families of the students tested. We can see that absolute differences between quartiles are widening at both school levels in France, whereas they are tending to narrow at primary level in OECD countries. Over the recent period, the increase in inequality seems to have been more pronounced in France, particularly at secondary level (+24% versus + 4%).[19]

5.3.2 *Lagging Performance in Terms of Proficiency Thresholds and the Inter-Decile Gap*

Most empirical studies of educational achievement focus on average scores, and often highlight France's weaker performance (cf. for example Colmant & Le Cam, 202; Salles & Le Cam, 2020). However, trends can vary according to different skill levels. It is quite possible to observe a simultaneous increase in the quality of learning at the highest levels, while at the same time seeing a decline in the performance of students at the lowest levels.

[19] Results obtained using rates of change of interquartile ranges for each sub-sample:+24% $= (116, 07 - 93, 73)/93, 73$ and.+4% $= (92, 70 - 89, 43)/89, 43$

Table 5.1 Database on educational inequalities (1970–2020)

	Level			Variation	
	1970	2000	2020	1970–2020	2000–2020
France					
Average score	450.41	513.20	499.38	48.97	–13.82
Minimum Proficiency Level (MPL)	75.18	92.64	88.73	13.55	–3.91
Advanced Proficiency Level (APL)	4.89	7.89	7.87	2.98	–0.02
Cumulative thresholds (MPL + APL)	80.07	100.53	96.61	16.53	–3.93
Inequality by decile, primary	1.44	1.44	1.52	0.08	0.08
Inequality by decile, secondary	1.66	1.50	1.57	–0.09	0.07
Deviation from mean score, SES, primary	57.12	60.97	73.59	16.47	12.62
Deviation from average score, SES, secondary	77.77	93.73	116.07	38.30	22.34
Deviation from minimum threshold, SES, primary	18.60	9.37	17.31	–1.29	7.94
Deviation from minimum threshold, SES, secondary	13.33	8.61	16.47	3.14	7.86
OECD 20					
Average score	493.33	521.24	520.28	26.95	–0.97
Minimum Proficiency Level (MPL)	86.54	92.30	92.63	6.09	0.33
Advanced Proficiency Level (APL)	10.40	11.47	12.10	1.71	0.63
Cumulative thresholds (MPL + APL)	96.94	103.77	104.73	7.79	0.96
Inequality by decile, primary	1.60	1.49	1.44	–0.16	–0.05
Inequality by decile, secondary	1.57	1.51	1.55	–0.02	0.04
Deviation from mean score, SES, primary	58.49	57.30	53.65	–4.84	–3.65
Deviation from mean score, SES, secondary	72.93	89.43	92.70	19.78	3.28
Deviation from minimum threshold, SES, primary	13.85	10.39	7.58	–6.27	–2.81
Deviation from minimum threshold, SES, secondary	7.81	10.00	11.73	3.92	1.73

Source Authors

To analyze these possibilities in more detail, we calculate the proportions of students reaching different competency thresholds. More specifically, we are interested in two levels (see Sect. 2.2.2). The first level refers to a Minimum Proficiency Level (MPL). Its main purpose is to highlight the proportion of a population that achieves a standard level of competence in order to obtain useful skills for everyday activities. Alongside this minimum threshold, it may also be interesting to look at the proportion of students reaching the Advanced Proficiency Level (APL). The main purpose of the latter is to measure the proportion of the population achieving high levels on tests of student achievement, and thus to see the proportion of elites within each country.

France's performance for the minimum proficiency level is presented in Table 5.2. An equitable country can be defined as one in which virtually all its children achieve a common core of skills. For a country like France, we would expect to see rates approaching 100% in all skill areas, and for both primary and secondary school levels. Yet the results are far from perfect equity in terms of learning achievement.

While France is in a rather good position in most areas, a fairly significant drop-off is observed in mathematics at primary level: only 84% of French pupils reach the minimum competency threshold, compared with an average of 93% for OECD-20 countries (columns 11 and 15). An analysis of trends in the proportion of pupils achieving the minimum competency threshold shows a sharp drop in mathematics results at primary level since the 1990s, when France's performance was well above the OECD-20 average. Although there has been a similarly sharp drop in mathematical performance at secondary level, France's performance remains around average in terms of the proportion of students reaching the minimum threshold. Columns 17 and 18 of Table 5.2 show the differences in performance for this threshold between France and the OECD (see Eq. 5.5): whereas in 1970 France was lagging behind in all areas, it would appear that this gap has narrowed, even if it remains systematic and widespread (i.e. the values in these columns are all negative). The following columns highlight a regression in equity at secondary level over half a century: while the share of students with a minimum level of competency stagnated in OECD countries between 2000 and 2020, in the case of France it fell by almost 4%. At primary level and over the long term, France is progressing faster than the OECD (respectively + 16% versus + 9.7% per decade), suggesting a convergence in performance between the countries. However, a more detailed analysis shows that this convergence is taking place above all in reading, while the proportion of students reaching the minimum threshold is tending to stagnate in mathematics.

Our research also makes it possible to compare long periods with more recent series, in order to assess any contradictory trends. This is what we observe when we compare the long term with the short term (50 years and 20 years, respectively, see columns 19–22).

In fact, over the last two decades, France's performance has fallen behind, and the proportion of the population with minimum skills even seems to be declining in all skill areas (the figures in column 21 are all negative). A comparison of the respective short-term variations underlines France's underperformance in terms of inequality: while OECD countries manage to increase the proportion of pupils reaching the minimum performance threshold in primary mathematics by around 5%, this same proportion falls by more than 5% in France. The double-difference method confirms the previous results (see columns 23–24 and Eq. 5.4): in the short term, France's trajectory lags behind that of the OECD. On the contrary, a certain catching-up is observed over the long term, meaning that France's recent underperformance is not the direct consequence of pre-2000 policies (except perhaps for primary math).

A system can be considered effective if it succeeds in getting all its pupils to progress, with almost all of its population above a minimum threshold, but also if

Table 5.2 Comparative trends in the proportion of pupils exceeding the minimum threshold

	1970		1980		1990		2000		2010		2020	
	Value	S.E.	Value	S.E.	Value	S.E.	Value	S.E.	Value	S.E.	Value	S.E.
	(1)	(2)	(3)	(4)	(5)	(6)	(7)	(8)	(9)	(10)	(11)	(12)
Mean	75	(6.1)	81	(2.6)	92	(2.8)	93	(3.2)	90	(3.0)	89	(2.5)
Primary	71	(3.4)	77	(3.3)	92	(3.3)	91	(3.3)	90	(3.3)	87	(3.3)
Reading	58	(2.9)	73	(2.7)	96	(2.7)	95	(2.4)	95	(2.7)	94	(2.4)
Mathematics	82	(3.4)	81	(3.3)	91	(3.3)	89	(3.3)	86	(3.3)	84	(3.3)
Sciences	75	(3.2)	79	(3.1)	89	(3.1)	89	(3.1)	87	(3.1)	85	(3.3)
Secondary	79	(6.1)	84	(2.6)	91	(2.8)	94	(3.2)	91	(3.0)	90	(2.5)
Reading	75	(2.8)	83	(2.7)	94	(2.7)	97	(2.7)	94	(3.2)	93	(2.7)
Mathematics	81	(6.1)	85	(2.6)	91	(2.8)	94	(3.2)	88	(3.0)	88	(2.5)
Sciences	80	(3.6)	84	(3.5)	89	(3.5)	91	(3.8)	90	(3.4)	89	(2.6)

	OECD Level				Difference with OECD		Long Term (LT) Variation		Short Term (ST) Variation		Double differences	
	1970	S.E.	2020	S.E.	1970	2020	France	OECD	France	OECD	ST	LT
	(13)	(14)	(15)	(16)	(17)	(18)	(19)	(20)	(21)	(22)	(23)	(24)
Mean	86	(3.9)	92	(2.5)	–10.9	–3.6	13.6	6.3	–3.9	0.3	–4.2	7.3
Primary	84	(4.8)	94	(2.6)	–12.8	–6.6	15.9	9.7	–3.9	2.8	–6.7	6.2
Reading	81	(3.0)	95	(2.4)	–23.4	–1.5	36.3	14.4	–1.6	1.4	–3.0	21.9
Mathematics	85	(4.9)	93	(2.5)	–3.3	–9.9	1.5	8.1	–5.9	4.7	–10.6	–6.7
Sciences	85	(3.8)	94	(2.7)	–10.7	–9.1	10.0	8.4	–4.3	2.9	–7.2	1.6
Secondary	88	(3.8)	91	(2.5)	–8.9	–0.9	11.2	3.2	–3.9	–1.8	–2.1	8.0
Reading	88	(3.2)	94	(2.6)	–13.1	–0.9	18.1	5.9	–3.7	–1.7	–2.0	12.2

(continued)

Table 5.2 (continued)

	OECD Level				Difference with OECD		Long Term (LT) Variation		Short Term (ST) Variation		Double differences	
	1970	S.E.	2020	S.E.	1970	2020	France	OECD	France	OECD	ST	LT
	(13)	(14)	(15)	(16)	(17)	(18)	(19)	(20)	(21)	(22)	(23)	(24)
Mathematics	86	(3.9)	89	(2.5)	–4.2	–1.0	6.3	3.0	–6.6	–2.5	–4.1	3.3
Sciences	89	(3.7)	90	(2.7)	–9.2	–0.8	9.2	0.8	–1.4	–1.3	–0.1	8.4

Notes The first twelve columns show the proportion of French pupils reaching the minimum proficiency threshold, with standard errors in brackets (calculated by adding the errors in assessment measurement and those in imputation). Comparative data for the OECD-20 and the percentage point gap are then presented (columns 13–22). Short- and long-term trends show whether or not France's trajectory follows that of the OECD. It can be seen, for example, that France has increased the proportion of pupils reaching the minimum threshold in reading at primary level by almost 36.3% over the long term, compared with 14.4% for the OECD average. On the other hand, progress in primary mathematics has been slower (1.5% versus 8.1% respectively), whereas France had a shortfall of 3.3% in 1970. The double-difference approach is presented in columns 23 and 24 for the short and long term (CT and LT respectively). Values in bold indicate a significant difference at the 5% threshold. *Source* authors some of its pupils reach an advanced threshold. In this case, performance and the level of inequality can be measured by comparing the proportion of pupils reaching these two extreme thresholds.

In Fig. 5.2 crosses these two parameters for each school level and the two main domains of reading and mathematics for the year 2020. The first result to highlight is the correlation between the two thresholds: empirically, there seems to be no dilemma between having a population with basic skills or focusing on an elite in terms of school skills. Countries such as Ireland, Norway, the Netherlands and the UK show that it is possible to have almost the entire population achieve the minimum competency threshold, while at the same time having a significant proportion of pupils exceed the advanced proficiency level. At primary level, France's position is rather unusual in this respect: fewer than one pupil in twenty achieves the advanced proficiency level at primary level, whether in reading or mathematics, whereas the average is 12% and 10%, respectively. The French education system is thus struggling to get its primary school pupils to achieve excellence, while also showing a relative deficit in the proportion of the population with basic skills. This is clearly visible in mathematics, where France lags behind in both thresholds (Quadrant A). At secondary level (Quadrants C and D), France's position is in the low middle, suggesting that inequalities are most concentrated in mathematics at primary level, even if they exist in the other dimensions.

The increase in inequality could, however, benefit the elites. We would then see a simultaneous reduction in the proportion of students reaching the minimum threshold and an increase in those reaching the advanced threshold. We might therefore ask whether recent years have seen an improvement in the proportions of students reaching the various competency thresholds. This would represent an improvement in equity, particularly if the proportion of students reaching the minimum proficiency level were to increase in such a way as to close the French gap.

Since we observe a form of convergence in scores and a continuous rise since the 1970s in most OECD countries (see our previous study, Altinok & Diebolt, 2024a), we prefer to compare the *relative* evolution of the proportion of students reaching the two proficiency thresholds. In line with an absolute difference analysis, we compare France's relative position to OECD countries at both proficiency thresholds (Fig. 5.3). When the values are negative, this means that France is lagging behind other OECD countries, even if an absolute increase in performance can be observed via the simple difference method.

In Quadrant A, we can see that in 2010, France was lagging behind both in terms of the minimum threshold and the proportion of students reaching the advanced proficiency level (a gap of around 4% for both thresholds). The trend since 2010 seems to be toward a *relative* reinforcement of inequalities, as the gap in the proportion of students reaching the minimum proficiency level rises from 4 to 10% in 2020. On the contrary, the years 1985, 1990 and 1995 seem to indicate a *relative* improvement in the proportion of students exceeding the minimum proficiency level. The 80 s and 90 s could thus be seen as decades of reduced inequalities in mathematical achievement,

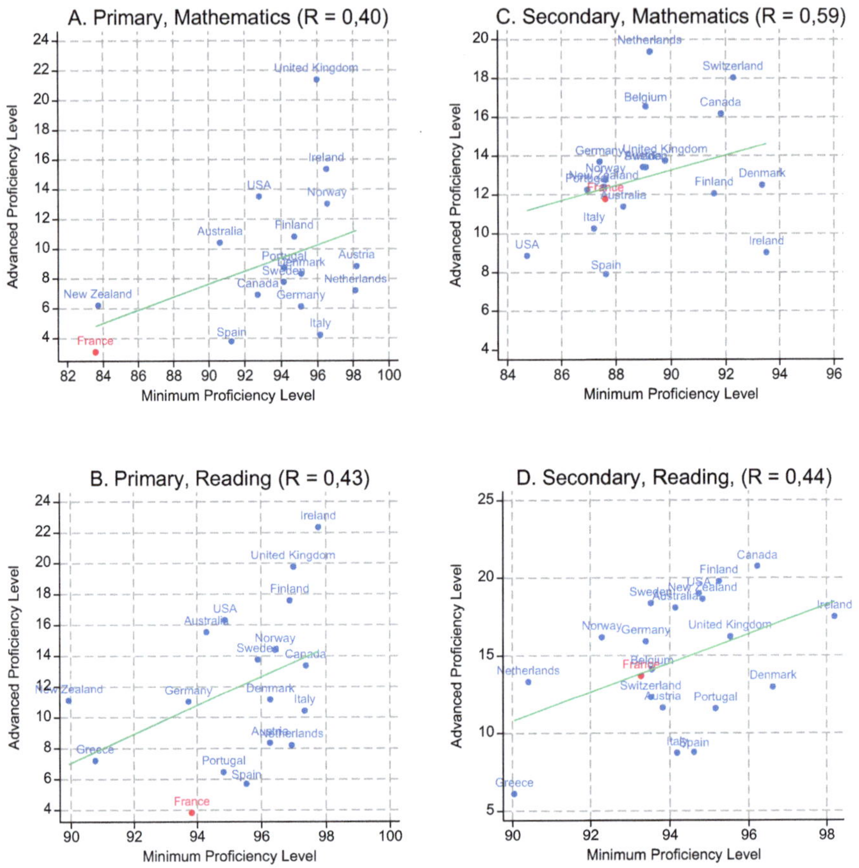

Fig. 5.2 France's relative position in performance thresholds, year 2020 (*Notes* The minimum proficiency level refers to a threshold at which students can perform basic tasks in everyday life, while the advanced threshold refers more to complex tasks that can help them to be more innovative. See text and Appendix A3 for more precise definitions. *Source* Authors)

while the last two decades seem to argue in favor of an accentuation of these.[20] The trend over the last two decades has been toward an overall decline in performance, in both minimum and elite skills.

An alternative to performance thresholds in the analysis of school inequalities is to analyze the inter-decile ratio. To do this, we calculate scores for the two extreme deciles. The last decile represents the score obtained by students ranked in the top 10% of a country, while the first decile covers the score of the bottom 10%. The

[20] It is important to remember that the analyses carried out in Fig. 5.3 are in relative terms: it is not so much the increase in proportions for each threshold that interests us, but rather the difference in variation between France and the OECD countries. This is a simple difference approach between French performance and that of the OECD.

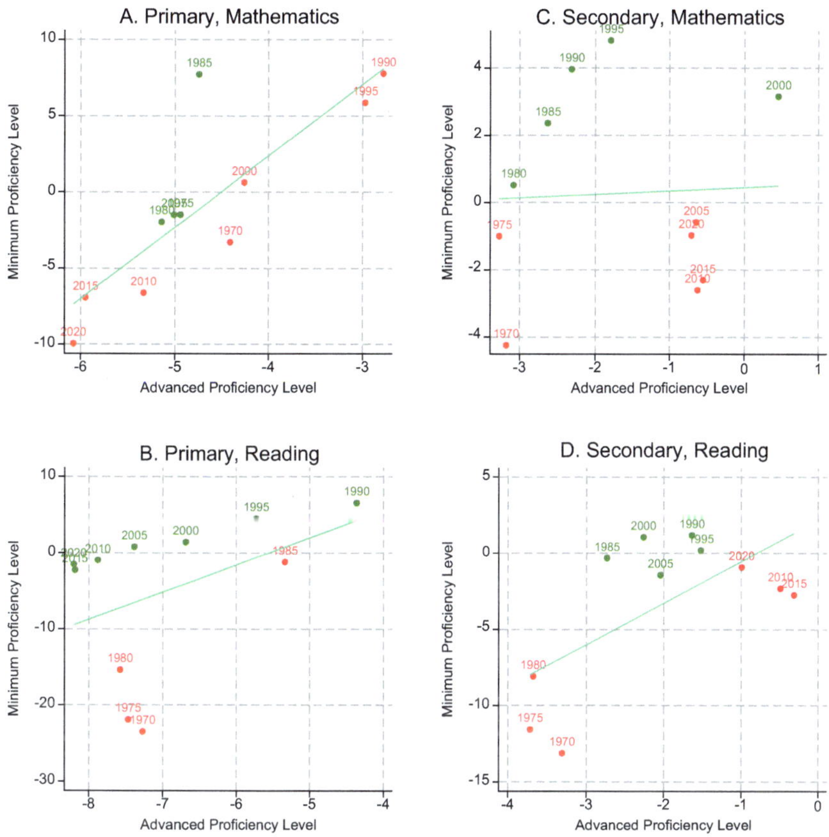

Fig. 5.3 Variations relative to the OECD for skill thresholds (*Notes* For each period, we compare the value of the thresholds for France with the average observed for the OECD-20. A negative value means that the proportion of French students reaching a threshold is below the OECD-20 average. For example, in 2015, French pupils had a deficit of around 6% in reaching the advanced proficiency level in mathematics at primary level. At the same time, the deficit was close to 5% for the minimum proficiency level. *Source* authors)

inter-decile ratio is calculated by dividing the score of the best performers by that of the worst performers. The results are presented in Table 5.3.

Generally speaking, we can see that, on average, the top 10% have a score around 50% higher than the bottom 10%, and that this difference is similar to that observed within OECD countries (i.e. the ratio is close to 1.50). The relative gap with the OECD average even shows less inequality in France: whereas in 1970, the inter-decile gap was 1.60 for the OECD, it was only 1.55 in France. In the short term, however, inequality seems to be increasing in France, whereas it is stagnating in the

OECD: in France, it has risen by around 7.7% over the last two decades, compared with a 0.5% fall in the OECD as a whole.[21]

These trends conceal disparities between school levels and in terms of skill areas (Table 5.3). Since our database provides separate trends for three skill areas, we can compare trends and highlight the weak points of the French education system. Once again, France's "weakest link" is in mathematics at primary level: while OECD countries have managed to reduce the inter-decile gap by around 9.3% over the last two decades, this same gap is increasing by 11.8% per decade in France. At secondary school level, inequalities appear to be rising much faster in France than in the OECD, particularly in mathematics (+7.4% vs. + 4.0%, respectively). The evolution of inequalities over the short term highlights a fairly homogeneous picture for France: gaps are increasing everywhere between deciles (i.e. see the positive sign of the figures in column 13). The double-difference method confirms that the French trajectory cannot be explained exclusively by exogenous factors (columns 15 and 16), since the coefficients are all positive, suggesting a worsening of inequality in France, independently of that observed in other similar countries.

5.3.3 The Socio-Economic Dimension of Inequality

The sociology of education looks at inequalities in educational achievement by measuring any gaps in performance between different socio-economic strata. The most appropriate indicator is a synthetic socio-economic index, measured on the whole population and standardized using the quartile method (see Sect. 2.2 for more information). It is interesting to compare the average performance of a population with the possible performance gap between the two extreme quartiles of this socio-economic index, i.e. between the 25% of students belonging to families with the highest socio-economic capital and the 25% with the lowest capital. The results presented in Fig. 5.4 suggest that there is no systematic relationship between mean score and socio-economic inequality (the correlation coefficient is less than –0.04). There is therefore no inevitability in having an unequal system as long as performance is set at a threshold. The results largely confirm those found with inter-decile analysis. For example, countries such as Canada and Ireland have rather low levels of inequality compared to other countries, while at the same time having high performance.

Table 5.4 presents inequality data, broken down by skill area and grade level. In 2020, the level of inequality in France appears to be around 21 points higher than the OECD average. In our previous work, we found an overall rise in school performance over the past half-century for OECD countries. At the same time, inequalities have been rising over the long term in France, with an increase of around 30 points for the country as a whole, or the equivalent of one school year's lost competence for

[21] The variations shown in columns 11–14 correspond to variations per decade. This makes it possible to compare short- and long-term trends.

Table 5.3 Double differences in the inter-decile ratio in education

	1970	1980	1990	2000	2010	2020	OECD Level 2020	
							1970	2020
	(1)	(2)	(3)	(4)	(5)	(6)	(7)	(8)
Mean	1.55	1.52	1.46	1.47	1.53	1.55	1.59	1.50
Primary	1.44	1.44	1.42	1.44	1.48	1.52	1.61	1.44
Reading	1.43	1.41	1.39	1.41	1.41	1.45	1.66	1.41
Mathematics	1.37	1.43	1.47	1.51	1.59	1.63	1.49	1.49
Sciences	1.43	1.41	1.39	1.41	1.41	1.45	1.66	1.41
Secondary	1.66	1.59	1.50	1.50	1.58	1.57	1.57	1.55
Reading	1.65	1.57	1.46	1.41	1.50	1.51	1.55	1.49
Mathematics	1.61	1.58	1.47	1.49	1.65	1.63	1.56	1.62
Sciences	1.65	1.57	1.46	1.41	1.50	1.51	1.55	1.49
	Difference with OECD		Long Term (LT) Variation		Short Term (ST) Variation		Double differences	
	1970	2020	France	OECD	France	OECD	Short Term	Long Term
	(9)	(10)	(11)	(12)	(13)	(14)	(15)	(16)
Mean	–3.9	4.5	–0.3	–8.7	7.7	–0.5	8.2	8.4
Primary	–17.5	7.8	8.1	–17.3	8.0	–5.4	13.4	25.4
Reading	–23.0	4.4	2.4	–25.0	3.7	–4.6	8.3	27.5
Mathematics	–11.3	14.5	26.0	0.2	11.8	–9.3	21.1	25.8
Sciences	–23.0	4.4	2.4	–25.0	3.7	–4.6	8.3	27.5
Secondary	8.6	1.7	–8.7	–1.7	7.4	4.0	3.5	–6.9
Reading	9.4	2.1	–13.6	–6.4	10.1	4.7	5.4	–7.3
Mathematics	5.3	1.3	1.6	5.6	14.0	5.4	8.6	–4.0
Sciences	9.4	2.1	–13.6	–6.4	10.1	4.7	5.4	–7.3

Notes Evolution is expressed in terms of the inter-decile ratio, i.e. by dividing the scores of the top 10% by those of the bottom 10%. Thus, a ratio equal to 1.60 means that the top 10% have scores 60% higher than those in the bottom 10%. *Source* authors

the poorest.[22] Inequalities are systematically more pronounced at secondary level than at primary. While the gap is 74 points in 2020 at primary level (equivalent to 2 years of schooling), it reaches 116 points at secondary level (equivalent to almost 4 years of schooling). These trends all point to widening inequalities. Inequalities are increasing in reading at primary level and in mathematics at secondary level. While over the last two decades, inequalities have risen only slightly in reading at secondary level (i.e. + 13.8 points), they have risen by 35 points in mathematics

[22] We assume that one year of learning achievement is similar to around 30 points (Avvisati, 2021; Avvisati and Givord, 2023).

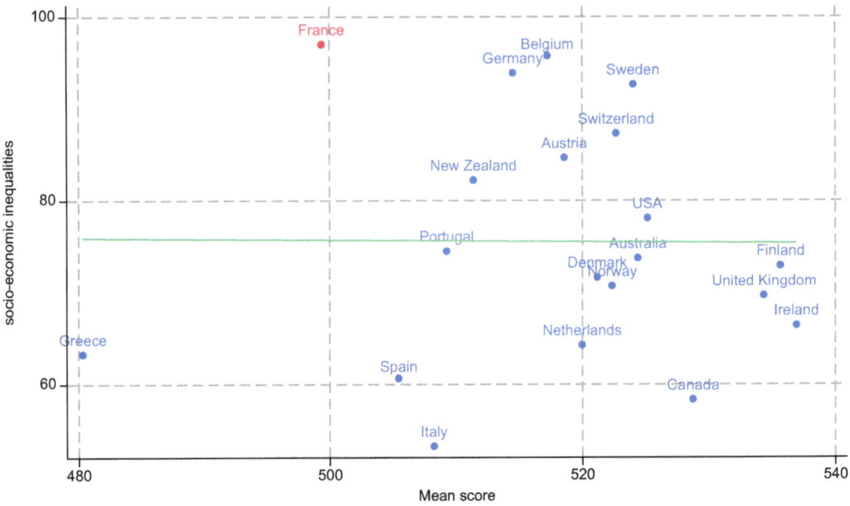

Fig. 5.4 Socio-economic level and school performance (2020, R = –0.04) (*Source* Authors)

in France, compared with only 10 points in the OECD. We therefore deduce that, although socio-economic inequalities are increasing in almost all countries, France's trajectory is on a steeper slope in terms of inequalities. Indeed, the double-difference method shows that inequality is on the rise in France, to a greater extent than in other OECD countries (see the positivity of the coefficients in columns 23 and 24).

Our database makes it possible to analyze and detect contradictory trends over different periods. Figure 5.5 underlines the importance of having sufficiently long data to better appreciate the evolution of inequalities. We can see that in 1970, there was a positive relationship between average performance and the level of inequality, which was more pronounced at primary level (Quadrants A and B).

High-performing countries such as the United States, the United Kingdom and Switzerland were also those where inequalities were significant. Recent years, however, have seen a general reversal of this trend. In 2020, the relationship is absent at both school levels. A variety of situations can be observed at primary level, while at secondary level, average performance seems to have fallen, with levels of inequality varying from country to country. Some countries, such as Finland and the Netherlands, have strong performance with low inequality, while others, such as Germany and France, have higher levels of inequality, without being able to achieve higher scores. Of course, these analyses are purely descriptive, but once again they demonstrate the value of taking a long-term look at data on education systems.

But how can we characterize the level of socio-economic inequalities in educational attainment in France? As Jencks (1979) points out, every system has some form of inequality, whether in terms of access, completion or learning achievement. The question is more to do with the amplitude of these inequalities, whether they are tolerable or not.

Table 5.4 Comparative trends in socio-economic inequalities in education

	1970		1980		1990		2000		2010		2020	
	Value	S.E.	Value	S.E.	Value	S.E.	Value	S.E.	Value	S.E.	Value	S.E.
	(1)	(2)	(3)	(4)	(5)	(6)	(7)	(8)	(9)	(10)	(11)	(12)
Mean	67	(7.0)	62	(5.8)	55	(5.9)	81	(5.9)	98	(5.8)	97	(5.2)
Primary	57	(6.2)	58	(5.6)	49	(5.5)	61	(5.3)	69	(5.1)	74	(5.5)
Reading	38	(5.9)	47	(5.5)	36	(5.3)	55	(4.9)	77	(4.3)	84	(4.3)
Mathematics	64	(6.1)	60	(5.5)	53	(5.4)	67	(5.4)	73	(5.4)	70	(6.1)
Sciences	69	(6.7)	68	(5.9)	58	(5.7)	75	(5.8)	74	(5.7)	75	(6.1)
Secondary	78	(7.8)	65	(6.0)	62	(6.3)	94	(6.4)	119	(6.6)	116	(4.9)
Reading	91	(6.2)	82	(5.8)	74	(5.7)	98	(5.7)	116	(6.6)	112	(5.1)
Mathematics	61	(9.9)	46	(5.0)	51	(6.1)	83	(6.2)	123	(6.5)	118	(4.7)
Sciences	81	(7.4)	68	(7.3)	60	(7.3)	111	(7.5)	123	(6.8)	124	(4.8)

	OECD Level				Difference with OECD		Long Term Variation		Short Term Variation		Doubles differences	
	1970	S.E.	2020	S.E.	1970	2020	Franc	OECD	Franc	OECD	Franc	OECD
	(13)	(14)	(15)	(16)	(17)	(18)	(19)	(20)	(21)	(22)	(23)	(24)
Mean	64	(7.5)	76	(5.1)	3.5	21.5	29.6	11.6	15.7	0.8	14.9	18.0
Primary	57	(7.8)	54	(5.1)	0.1	19.3	19.3	–2.7	12.6	–3.6	16.2	19.2
Reading	38	(6.6)	69	(4.5)	–0.1	14.2	45.5	31.1	28.9	13.3	15.6	14.4
Mathematics	62	(9.8)	45	(5.3)	2.4	25.4	6.5	–16.5	3.2	–12.4	15.7	23.0
Sciences	75	(7.8)	49	(5.5)	–5.8	26.3	5.5	–26.5	–0.3	–14.2	13.9	32.1
Secondary	71	(7.2)	94	(5.1)	6.4	22.4	38.3	22.3	22.3	2.7	19.7	16.0
Reading	82	(6.3)	92	(5.1)	9.5	19.9	20.3	9.9	13.8	0.9	12.9	10.4

(continued)

Table 5.4 (continued)

	OECD Level				Difference with OECD		Long Term Variation		Short Term Variation		Doubles differences	
	1970	S.E.	2020	S.E.	1970	2020	Franc	OECD	Franc	OECD	Franc	OECD
	(13)	(14)	(15)	(16)	(17)	(18)	(19)	(20)	(21)	(22)	(23)	(24)
Mathematics	62	(7.7)	96	(4.9)	–0.7	21.6	21.6	34.1	35.1	10.4	24.7	22.2
Sciences	72	(7.7)	100	(5.3)	8.1	24.3	43.5	27.3	13.2	3.7	9.6	16.2

Notes The first six columns show the interquartile range by socio-economic index, with standard errors in brackets (calculated by weighting the errors for each quartile according to the following formula: *standard error of the difference* $= \sqrt{standard\ error_{Q1}^2 + standard\ error_{Q5}^2}$). Socio-economic inequalities are measured here by the difference in performance between students from the 25% of families with the highest socio-economic index (upper quartile) and students from the most disadvantaged families (lower quartile). OECD comparative data are presented in the following columns. *Source* authors

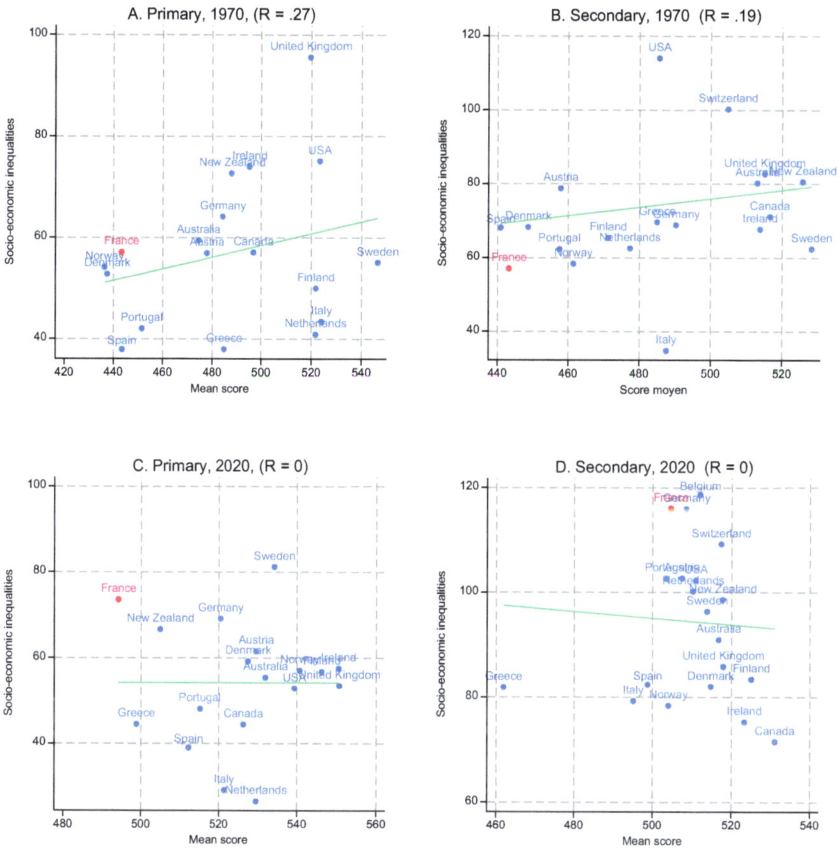

Fig. 5.5 School performance and inequalities: Is the trend reversing? (*Note* Socio-economic inequalities are measured by the difference in performance between pupils from the 20% of families with the highest socio-economic index (upper quartile) and pupils from the most disadvantaged families (lower quartile). Thus, in 2020, secondary school pupils from advantaged families score on average almost 120 points higher on tests than their colleagues from families with less socio-economic capital. *Source* Authors)

The level of inequality is shown in Fig. 5.6. The equivalent of 3 or 4 years of educational attainment separates pupils from wealthy families from those with low socio-economic capital (73 and 117 points, respectively, for primary and secondary education). France's position is in the northeast quarter of Fig. 5.6, indicating a relatively low level of inequality. In the end, inequality is only higher in Sweden at primary level. Even in the USA, where inequality is often singled out for criticism, the performance gap is only 53 points at primary level, compared with over 70 points in France.

A further observation concerns the evolution of inequality over time. The results in Table 5.4 show that inequalities have increased in most OECD countries. In the case of France, we observe an almost continuous rise in primary inequality since

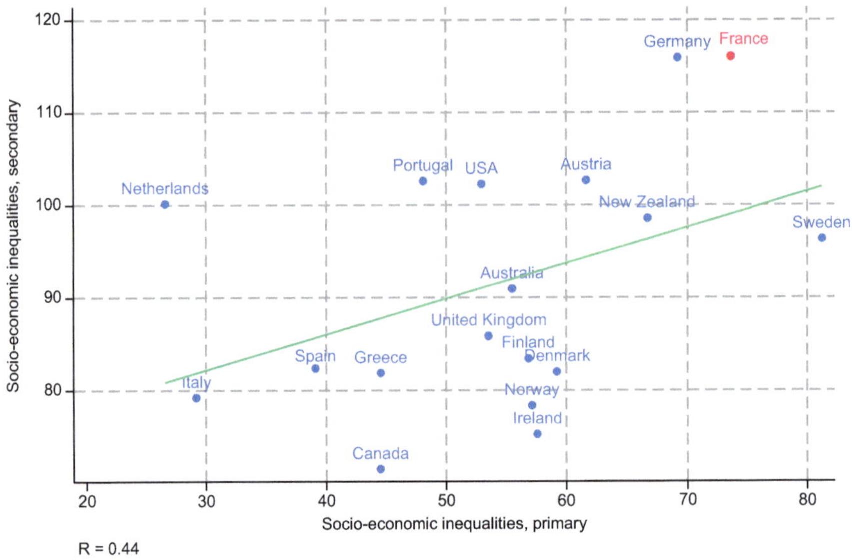

Fig. 5.6 Socio-economic inequalities at both school levels (2020) (*Notes* Socio-economic inequalities are measured by the difference in performance between students from the 25% of families with the highest socio-economic index (upper quartile) and students from the most disadvantaged families (lower quartile). *Source* Authors)

1970 (Fig. 5.7). In concrete terms, the gap between rich and poor has risen from 57 to 74 points in the space of half a century. At secondary level, the situation is clearly more critical, as inequalities were already higher in the 1970s: the level of inequality has risen by around 40 points, equivalent to a loss of 1.2 years of schooling for pupils from the poorest families. Whereas in 1970, poor pupils lagged behind pupils from families with high socio-economic capital by around 2.6 years ($78/30 = 2, 6$), by 2020 this gap had risen to almost 4 years ($116/30 = 3, 9$). It is worth noting, however, that inequalities have fallen somewhat since 2010, although they remain high.

5.3.4 *The Price of Educational Inequality: A Historical Macro-Simulation*

In the previous sections, we highlighted the extent of inequalities in education, and in particular the differences between the socio-economic levels of students' families. Tackling educational inequalities can be seen as an ultimate goal for reasons of equity: a child from a family with a low socio-economic level should have the same opportunities as one from a wealthy family. What's more, high levels of educational inequality can lead to a sub-optimal allocation of human resources within the

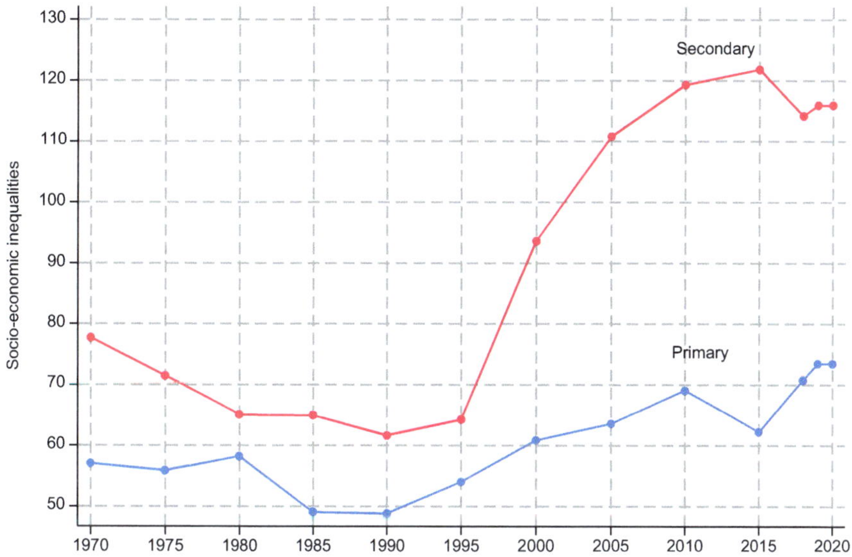

Fig. 5.7 Evolution of socio-economic inequalities (1970–2020) (*Note* Socio-economic inequalities are measured by calculating the difference between the scores of the extreme groups according to the socio-economic level of the families of the pupils tested. Differences are based on the difference between quartiles 1 and 4. A value of 80 indicates that students from the wealthiest families (i.e. the richest 25%) score 80 points higher than students from the poorest families (i.e. the poorest 25%). *Source* Authors)

workforce, and ultimately to lower productivity and hence economic growth. Recent debates concerning the slowdown or even decline in productivity have increasingly focused on the lack of highly qualified manpower, and sometimes even on the mathematical skills of young people (Martin et al., 2022). This raises the question of the economic cost of such a high level of educational inequality (Hallak, 1974). Indeed, assuming that young people from families with low levels of socio-economic capital have the same cognitive abilities as other young people, there is no legitimate reason to observe a gap of almost 97 points between the extreme quartiles (see Table 5.4). As a result, this gap may constitute a kind of resource misallocation and disrupt France's potential growth pattern.

We use here the simulation model presented in Sect. 2.3.2 (and in greater detail in Appendix B). Several scenarios are considered. The first concerns a policy of positive discrimination, whereby educational actions would be targeted primarily at pupils from the least affluent families (i.e. quartile 1). Bringing the performance of this population up to the same level as that of the richest quartile will raise the average level of performance of the whole population. As we saw earlier (see Table 5.4), this gap is around 97 points in 2020. Since the standard deviation in our databases is 100 points, and according to Hanushek and Woessmann (2012), a one-standard-deviation rise in scores increases average annual growth by around 1.98%, catching up the poorest students thus consists in raising their performance by around 1 standard deviation. As this quartile by definition represents a quarter of the population, we can assume that the overall effect to be estimated on the whole population would be an increase of 0.25 standard deviations.

According to our estimates and adopting the parameters presented in Table 5.5, we find that such a policy to combat educational inequality could have increased France's annual GDP growth rate by 0.5% in 2020 (see Table 5.6 as a summary document). The gain from educational reform would thus be €295 billion in 2020 alone, compared with over €789 billion in 2050. As inequality generates economic losses, it is possible to translate this price tag as an impediment to economic activity. Put another way, we find that the French economy would have stopped working for around 1.5 years between 1970 and 2020. Indeed, if a pro-equity policy had been implemented, GDP would have reached the value of 2,748 billion euros in 2020, compared with 2,454 billion calculated in our simulation. Taking all these differences together, the cumulative effect would be 3,570 billion euros, or around 1.5 years of economic activity equivalent to 2020.

Other scenarios are also possible. Targeting a specific population may not be enough. Another policy could aim to converge the performance of the entire population toward that of students belonging to the group of wealthy families. This equity-seeking policy would thus aim to raise the performance of students in quartiles 1, 2 and 3, so as to converge toward that of students in quartile 4. The overall effect on performance of such a reduction in inequality would be all the greater. The economic loss of not implementing such a policy is even greater: France's GDP growth rate would be 1% higher than at present. In 2020 alone, the economic loss would be $294 billion. More concretely, GDP in 2020 would have been close to $3,337 billion, versus the $2,675 billion observed. This $662 billion difference is explained by the misallocation of educational resources, and therefore the price of educational inequality. As the loss of this misallocation is realized every year, we find a cumulative loss of 1,568% of 2020 GDP. Put another way, we would lose around 17 years of economic activity up to 2050 as a result of these inequalities.

A final scenario aims not only to reduce inequalities by tackling differences in performance according to the socio-economic level of students' families, but also to raise the general level of performance by around 25 points. Combining these two factors, we find that the overall effect on the French economy would have been higher, amounting to a loss of around 1.4% of the growth rate in 2020. The economic cost of this absence of a policy focused on quality and equity would have cost France almost $1,000 billion. Put another way, while other countries would have continued to produce, this misallocation of educational resources would have prevented France from producing for almost 4 full years up to 2020. If nothing were done, the loss would amount to more than 28 equivalent years by 2050.[23]

[23] The advantage of a counterfactual analysis is that it does not quantify the cost of any policies to be implemented on the educational front. However, it goes without saying that reducing inequalities, or even improving the quality of education systems, requires specific actions. As stressed above, we believe that this must be orchestrated via a national consensus (see footnote 19).

Table 5.5 Simulation model parameters

Parameter	Definition	Base value
R	Duration of reform (years)	15
W	Working life expectancy	40
S	Simulation period (years)	80
d	Discount rate	2%
p	Growth rate without reform	2,3%
γ	Growth rate due to reform	1,98%
A*	Skills test scores	500

Notes Growth due to the reform is the result of a one-standard-deviation increase in the overall population, i.e. a 100-point rise in the average score. In the simulations carried out in our study, we use various projections which weight this coefficient according to the case

Table 5.6 The price of educational inequality: Results of counterfactual analysis

		(1)	(2)	(3)	(4)	(5)	(6)
	Year	GDP without reform (€ billions)	GDP with reform (Billions €)	Lost annual growth (%)	Annual value lost (€ billion)	Cumulative value lost(Billions €)	Years of activity lost
Scenario 1	2020	2 454	2 749	0,49	295	3 570	1,45
	2050	2 680	3 470	0,5	790	19 722	8,04
Scenario 2	2020	2 454	3 061	0,95	607	7 214	2,94
	2050	2 680	4 430	0,97	1 750	41 936	17,09
Scenario 3	2020	2 454	3 427	1,44	973	11 337	4,62
	2050	2 680	5 725	1,46	3 045	69 742	28,42

Notes Calculations were made in dollars, then converted to euros using the conversion rate €1 = $1.8. GDP without reform is calculated from 1970, the start date of the reform, and would be that obtained without educational reform. GDP with reform corresponds to the changes forecast in each scenario (see text). GDPs are updated to correspond to 2020 values. The annual growth lost corresponds to the growth points that could have been gained if the educational reform in question had been carried out. The lost value (column 4) shows the amount lost for the year in question alone (2020 or 2050). The cumulative value lost is shown in column 5. Column 6 calculates the number of years of activity lost, equivalent to that observed in 2020 without reform, i.e. 2,454 billion euros (calculated as follows: *valeur cumulée perdue/PIB*$_{2020}$)

5.4 Conclusion

The results of our research point to highly heterogeneous situations. It is undoubtedly premature to attempt to classify countries on the basis of data based solely on grade level and reduced to two or three areas of competence. The performance of an education system cannot be reduced solely to the math and reading results of pupils enrolled in grade 4 or 6 (i.e. grades often assessed in learning achievement tests). This obviously makes the measurement of inequalities more open to criticism. That said, the major interest of our research lies in the importance of a comparative vision, over a sufficiently long period of time, in order to apprehend trends and ruptures. That's why, to conclude this article, we propose a ranking of OECD countries according to several criteria.

The first criterion refers to the level of performance observed for the most recent year, while also measuring the level of inequality, based on the gaps between groups separated by their socio-economic level.

The results in Fig. 5.8 highlight the great heterogeneity of possible situations within a fairly homogeneous group of countries, which the OECD has reduced to 21 countries.[24] Some countries manage to achieve average or high performance, while at the same time having a low level of inequality (Group C, examples: Canada, Japan and Canada). In contrast, France's singular position reflects a double deficit (Group A), in terms of both average performance and inequality. In the French context, success at school appears to be strongly linked to the socio-economic characteristics of individuals, and does not depend solely on the will of the individual, thus calling into question the notion of educational justice (Bourdieu & Passeron, 1964; Duru-Bellat, 2009).

More generally, Group A countries can be seen as failing both in terms of school performance and school justice. The amplitude of inequalities is very high: on average, a pupil from a family with low socio-economic capital (i.e. among the lowest 25%) has a score more than 95 points lower than a pupil from a richly endowed family (i.e. among the highest 25%). Transformed into the equivalent of years of study, this would amount to a difference of almost 3 years, meaning that quantitative democratization is not fully complete in practice, if we take into account the stock of knowledge accumulated during compulsory schooling. In so doing, our research sheds new light and provides new evidence on the delicate issue of educational inequality. In light of the literature in the field, a plausible explanation for high inequalities could thus refer to the decline in social mix in the education system (Barthon & Monfroy, 2006; Boutchenik et al., 2021; Guillerm & Monso, 2023) or, more generally, to the strategy of school selection by parents (van Zanten, 2009, 2012).

Since we have historical data at our disposal, we have also indicated (in brackets) the evolution of inequalities within countries (these are measured by taking the difference in the gap between socio-economic level quartiles for the years 1970 and 2020). Although inequality is already high in France, it seems to have increased significantly since 1970, as in Germany and Austria.

[24] We have included Japan in this last figure because its position appears to be original in relation to other countries.

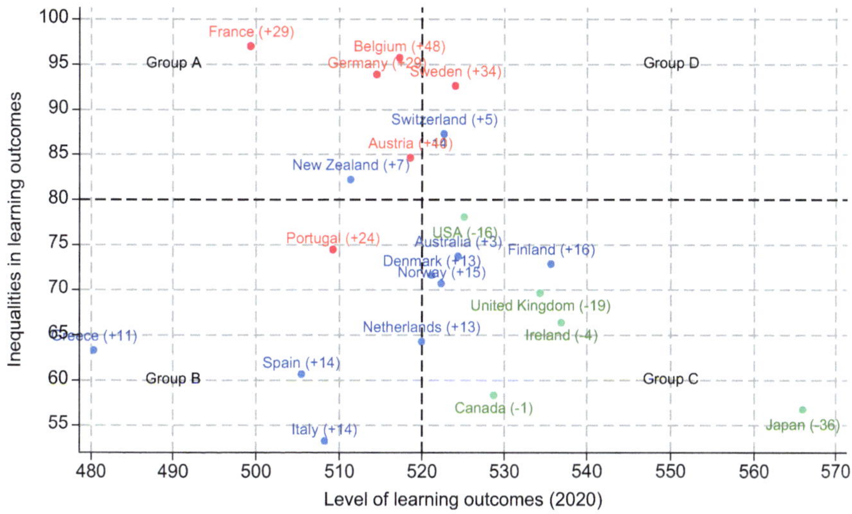

Fig. 5.8 Quality and equity of education systems (*Note* The level of educational attainment is represented by the average of scores obtained at the two school levels (primary and secondary) and three skill areas (mathematics, science and reading). The level of inequality in educational attainment represents the average difference in performance between the quartiles of socio-economic levels (i.e. the 25% most endowed with socio-economic capital and the 25% least endowed with socio-economic capital). The numbers in brackets show the variation in this gap between 1970 and 2020 for each country. In red, we indicate countries with a sharp increase in inequality, while in green, inequality appears to be decreasing. *Source* Authors)

Lahire (2019) has shown that there are close links between family socialization patterns and academic achievement at primary level, particularly through "written culture". These results are confirmed here for France. They even tend to strengthen over time. They apply not only to reading at primary level, but can also be generalized to both levels (primary and secondary), and to all three skill areas (math, reading and science) studied.

As for the price of educational inequality, we have come to the conclusion that, since 1970, everything has happened as if, measured in terms of GDP, the French economy had stopped working for about a year and a half.

Appendix A

See Table A1,A2 and A3.

Table A1 International surveys of student achievement

No	*Years*	*Organization*	*Abbrev*	*Subject*	*Number of countries or regions*	*Grade*	*Included*
1	1959–60	IEA	Pilot survey	M,S,L	12	7/8	
2	1964	IEA	FIMS	M	12	7/FS	■
3	1970–71	IEA	SSS-RC	L	15	4/8/FS	
4	1970–72	IEA	FISS	S	19	4/8/FS	■
5	1980–82	IEA	SIMS	M	19	8/FS	■
6	1983–84	IEA	SISS	S	23	4/8/FS	■
7	1988/1990–91	NCES	IAEP	M,S	6–19	4/7–8	
8	1990–91	IEA	RLS	L	32	3–4/7–8	■
9	1995/1999/2003/2007/2011/2015/2019	IEA	TIMSS	M,S	45–38-26–48-66–65-64	3–4/7–8/FS	■
10	1992–97	UNESCO	MLA	M,S,L	72	6–8	
11	1997/2006/2013/2019	UNESCO	LLECE	M,S,L	13–16-15–16	3–6	■
12	1999/2002/2007	UNESCO	SACMEQ	M,L	7–15-16	6 6	■
13	2000/2010/2014/2019	CONFEMEN	PASEC	M,L	22–22-10–14	2/5 then 3–6	■
14	2001/2006/2011/2016/2021	IEA	PIRLS	L	35–41-55–50	4	■
15	2000/2003/2006/2009/2012/2015/2018/2022	OECD	PISA	M,S,L	43–41-57–74-65–71-79	Age 15	■
16	2010/2015/2019	USAID/RTI	EGRA	L	29–40-5	1 to 6	■
17	2008–2019	ASER	ASER	L	2	1 to 6	■

(continued)

Table A1 (continued)

No	*Years*	*Organization*	*Abbrev*	*Subject*	*Number of countries or regions*	*Grade*	*Included*
18	1994–1998	OECD	IALS	L	22	Adults	
19	2011–2017	OECD	PIAAC	L	39	Adults	■

Note IEA = "International Association for the Evaluation of Educational Achievement", NCES = "National Center for Education Statistics", CONFEMEN = "Conférence des Ministres de l'Education des Etats et Gouvernements de la Francophonie", OECD = "Organisation for Economic Co-operation and Development", USAID = "United States Agency for International Development", RTI = "Research Triangle Institute", ASER = "Australian Council for Educational Research", FIMSS = "First International Mathematics Study", SSS-RC = "Six Subject Survey: Reading Comprehension", FISS = "First International Science Study", SIMS = "Second International Mathematics Study", IAEP = "International Assessment of Educational Progress", RLS = "Reading Literacy Study", TIMSS = "Trends on International Mathematics and Science Study", MLA = "Monitoring Learning Achievement", LLECE = "Latin American Laboratory for Evaluation of the Quality of Education", SACMEQ = "The Southern and Eastern Africa Consortium for Monitoring Educational Quality", PASEC = "Programme d'Analyse des Systèmes Educatifs de la Confemen", PIRLS = "Progress in International Reading Literacy Study", PISA = "Programme of International Student Assessment", EGRA = "Early-Grade Reading Assessment", IALS = "International Adult Literacy Survey", PIAAC = "Programme for International Assessment of Adult Competencies". Subjects: M = mathematics; S = science; L = reading. FS = "fin du secondaire, équivalent"

Table A2 Meaning of competency thresholds

Threshold	Score limit	Competence achieved
Minimum Proficiency Level (MPL)		
MPL—Primary, Mathematics	400	Students have a basic knowledge of mathematics. They can add, subtract, multiply and divide one- and two-digit whole numbers. They can solve problems using simple words. They have some knowledge of simple fractions and geometric shapes. Students can read and complete bar graphs and simple tables
MPL—Primary, Reading	400	When reading mainly simpler literary texts, students can: – Locate and retrieve explicitly stated information, actions or ideas – Make direct inferences about events and reasons for actions – Begin to interpret story events and central ideas When reading mainly simpler informational texts, students can: – Locate and reproduce explicitly stated information from text and other formats (e.g., graphs, diagrams) – Begin to make direct inferences about explanations, actions and descriptions
MPL—Primary, Science	400	Students show limited understanding of scientific concepts and limited knowledge of basic scientific facts
MPL—Secondary, Mathematics	400	Students have some knowledge of whole numbers and basic graphs
MPL—Secondary, Reading	400	Readers can identify the main idea in a text of average length. They can understand the relationships or interpret the meaning in a limited part of the text when the information is not prominent by producing basic inferences, and/or when the text(s) contain(s) superfluous information They can select and access a page in a set based on explicit but sometimes complex requests, and locate one or more pieces of information on the basis of multiple, partly implicit criteria Readers can, when explicitly warned, reflect on the overall purpose of medium-length texts. They can reflect on simple visual or typographical features. They can compare claims and evaluate the reasons behind them on the basis of short, explicit statements Tasks may involve comparisons or contrasts based on a single feature of the text. Typically, reflective tasks at this level ask readers to make one comparison or several connections between the text and external knowledge, drawing on personal experience and attitudes
MPL—Secondary, Science	400	Students show limited understanding of scientific principles and concepts and limited knowledge of scientific facts
Advanced Proficiency Level (APL)		

(continued)

Table A2 (continued)

Threshold	Score limit	Competence achieved
APL—Primary, Mathematics	625	Students can apply their understanding and knowledge in a variety of relatively complex situations and explain their reasoning. Students can solve a variety of multi-step written problems involving whole numbers and show an understanding of fractions and decimal numbers. They can apply their knowledge of two- and three-dimensional shapes in a variety of situations. Students can interpret and represent data to solve multi-step problems
APL—Primary, Reading	625	When reading relatively complex literary texts, students can: – Interpret story events and character actions to describe reasons, motivations, feelings and character descriptions with full ownership of the text – Begin to evaluate the effect on the reader of the author's choices of language and style When reading relatively complex informational texts, students can: – Distinguish and interpret complex information from different parts of the text, and provide complete information based on the text – Integrate information in a text to explain relationships and sequence activities – Begin to evaluate visual and textual elements to take into account the author's point of view
APL—Primary, Science	625	Students communicate their understanding of life, physical and earth sciences and demonstrate some knowledge of scientific inquiry processes. Students demonstrate knowledge of the characteristics and life processes of a variety of organisms. They can communicate understanding of relationships in ecosystems and interactions between organisms and their environment. They communicate understanding of the properties and states of matter and the properties of physical and chemical change. Students communicate understanding of the Earth's physical characteristics, processes and history, and demonstrate knowledge of the Earth's revolution and rotation
APL—Secondary, Mathematics	625	Students can apply and reason through a variety of problem situations, solve linear equations and make generalizations. They can solve a variety of fraction, proportion and percentage problems and justify their conclusions. They can understand linear functions and algebraic expressions. Students can use their knowledge of geometric figures to solve a wide range of problems involving angles, area and surface. They can calculate averages and medians and understand how changing data points can impact the average. Students can interpret a wide variety of data displays to draw and justify conclusions and solve multi-step problems. They can solve problems involving expected values

(continued)

Table A2 (continued)

Threshold	Score limit	Competence achieved
APL—Secondary, Reading	625	Readers can understand long texts, deducing what information in the text is relevant even though interesting information can easily be ignored. They can perform causal or other forms of reasoning based on a thorough understanding of long pieces of text. They can also answer questions indirectly, by inferring the relationship between the question and one or more pieces of information distributed in or between several texts and sources Reflective tasks require the generation or critical evaluation of hypotheses, based on information. Readers can make distinctions between content and purpose, and between fact and opinion as applied to complex or abstract statements. They can assess neutrality and bias based on explicit or implicit cues about both the content and/or source of information. They can also draw conclusions about the reliability of claims or conclusions presented in a text For all aspects of reading, tasks usually involve dealing with abstract or counter-intuitive concepts, going through several stages until the goal is reached. In addition, tasks at this level may require the reader to process several long texts, moving from one text to another in order to compare and contrast information
APL—Secondary, Science	625	Students communicate their understanding of concepts related to biology, chemistry, physics and earth science in a variety of contexts. Students can classify animals into taxonomic groups. They can apply their knowledge of cellular structures and their functions. Students demonstrate an understanding of diversity, adaptation and natural selection. They also recognize the interdependence of populations of organisms in an ecosystem. Students demonstrate knowledge of the composition of matter and the periodic table of elements. Students use the physical properties of matter to sort, classify and compare substances and materials. They also recognize evidence that a chemical reaction has occurred. Students communicate understanding of the spacing and motion of particles in different physical states. Students apply their knowledge of energy transfer and electrical circuits, can relate the properties of light and sound to common phenomena, and demonstrate understanding of forces in everyday contexts. Students communicate their understanding of the Earth's structure, features and processes. They demonstrate knowledge of the Earth's resources and their conservation

Sources Mullis et al. (2017), OECD (2019), Mullis et al. (2020). Our translation

Table A3 Parameters used to calculate the socio-economic index

Survey	Years	Variables	
PISA	2000–2018	escs	PISA index of economic, cultural and social status, calculated by the OECD
FIMS	1964	m1pqi14; m1pqi15	Years of education of student's mother and father
SIMS	1980	yfeduc; ymeduc	Years of education of student's mother and father
FISS Grade 4	1970	focc; q12g18; q12g16	Father's activity, number of books at home, number of magazines or newspapers read daily
FISS Grade 8	1970	fed; med; q62g55	Mother's and father's years of education, number of books at home
SISS	1980	fposted; mposted; homebook	Mother's and father's years of education after high school, number of books at home
TIMSS Grade 4	1995; 2003; 2007	asbgbook; asbgps01-asbgps04	Possession of various objects at home (4 or 5 depending on the year), number of books at home
TIMSS Grade 8	1995; 1999; 2003; 2007	bsbgbook; bsbgps01—bsbgps04; bsbgeduf; bsbgedum	Possession of miscellaneous objects at home, number of books at home; father's and mother's level of education
TIMSS Grade 4	2011; 2015; 2019	asbghrl; asbg05a-asbg05e; asbg04	Socio-economic index calculated by the IEA; possession of miscellaneous items at home (5); number of books at home
TIMSS Grade 8	2011; 2015; 2019	bsbghrl; bsbg05a-bsbg05e; bsbg04	Socio-economic index calculated by the IEA, possession of miscellaneous items at home (5), number of books at home, mother's and father's education
RLS Grade 4	1990	ashomd; asbooks; asborbo; asprhtl; asbookf	Socio-economic index calculated by IEA, books at home, study of country language, frequency of book reading
PIRLS	2001	asdgps; asbgps1-asbgps4; asbgbook	Possession of various objects at home (5), number of books at home
PIRLS	2006	asbgta1- asbgta6; asbgbook	Possession of various objects at home (5), number of books at home
PIRLS	2011; 2016	asbghrl; asbg05a-asbg05e; asbg04; asbh17b; asbh17a	Socio-economic index calculated by the IEA, possession of miscellaneous objects at home, number of books at home; father's and mother's level of education

Note variable names may vary significantly within the TIMSS and PIRLS surveys, but the meaning and definition remain identical across the different test waves. FIMS = First International Mathematics Study; SIMS = Second International Mathematics Study; FISS = First International Science Study; SISS = Second International Science Study; TIMSS = Trends on International Mathematics and Science Study; PISA = Programme for International Student Assessment; RLS = Reading Literacy Study; PIRLS = Progress in International Reading Literacy Study

Appendix B

This appendix is adapted from Hanushek and Woessmann (2011), Hanushek et al. (2017a) and Gust et al. (2024). Unlike a prediction model, we use the same assumptions but draw up a counterfactual educational policy hypothesis by asking what trajectory the French economy would have experienced if an educational policy action had been carried out as early as 1970.

The projection model is based on four different phases. First, we introduce the reform (Phase A), where the effect of the quality of education is passed on over a 15-year period. The next phase B sees older workers replaced by reform workers (i.e. young people affected by the reform and having graduated enter the labor market). This means that the reform only becomes fully effective over a period of 30 years. Thirdly, workers who were only partially affected by the reform are replaced (Phase C). Finally, all workers affected by the reform are replaced, and the effect of the reform comes to an end (Phase D).

Phase A (1970–1985): Introduction of the Reform

During the first 15 years of the educational reform, the additional growth in GDP per capita due to the reform for year t is given by

$$\Delta^{t}_{growth} = growth\,coef. \times \Delta Scores \times \frac{1}{Active\ life\ expenctancy} \times \frac{t-1970}{15} + \Delta^{t-1}_{growth} \tag{B1}$$

where the *growth coefficient* represents the effect of the one standard deviation increase in test scores obtained in the growth models of Hanushek and Woessmann (2012) and $\Delta Scores\ aux\ tests$ is the change in educational performance due to the reform analyzed. Each year, only part of the labor force is replaced by new workers who have received better education (i.e. that relating to the reform). We take this lag into account with $1/active\ life\ expectancy$, with a working life of 40 years. The $\frac{t-1970}{15}$ term shows that it takes 15 years for the reform to be fully effective.[25]

[25] In the first version of their projection model, Hanushek and Woessmann (2011) assumed that the reform would only be fully effective after 20 years; we have used the latest version of their model, in which this period is reduced to 15 years (see Gust et al., 2024). However, the results change little if this period is reduced to 20 years.

Phase B (1986–2020): Replacement of Older Workers by New Ones Who Have Benefited from the Reform

The educational reform is now fully effective, and the academic quality of all pupils remains stable at this new level. However, given that the working life span is assumed to be 40 years, there are still workers with old schooling levels who will be replaced by new workers with a higher level of quality. Thus, over the next 25 years, additional growth should follow the following path:

$$\Delta_{growth}^{t} = growth\,coeff. \times \Delta Scores \times \frac{1}{Active\ life\ expenctancy} + \Delta_{growth}^{t-1} \quad \text{(B2)}$$

Phase C (2021–2036): Replacement of Workers Who Have Received Part of the Reform with Better Quality

After 40 years, all workers who have not experienced educational reform are replaced by new workers. At the same time, the cohorts of the first 15 years have received only part of the educational reform. During this phase, these workers are replaced by cohorts who have received all the educational reform. The additional growth for the following 15 years is thus:

$$\Delta_{growth}^{t} = growth\,coeff. \times \Delta Scores \times \frac{1}{Active\ life\ expenctancy} - \left(\Delta_{cgrowth}^{t-40} - \Delta_{growth}^{t-41}\right) + \Delta_{growth}^{t-1} \quad \text{(B3)}$$

Phase D (After 2036): Educational Reform Concerns All Workers

The entire workforce has experienced the reform via the renovated education system. Additional economic growth now reaches a constant long-term level:

$$\Delta_{growth}^{t} = growth\,coeff. \times \Delta Scores \quad \text{(B4)}$$

The cumulative effect of the reform can be assessed by calculating various indicators. The total value of the reform can be obtained by calculating the current difference between GDP with and without the reform. We thus calculate the gain from improving the education system over a period of 80 years:

$$Total\ Value\ of\ the\ reform = \sum_{t=1970}^{t=2050} \left(GDP^{t}_{reform} - GDP^{t}_{without\ reform} \right). \tag{B5}$$

Expressed as a percentage of current GDP, the total value of the reform is obtained using the following equation:

$$Total\ Value\ of\ the\ reform_{in\%ofconstantGDP} = \frac{Value\ of\ the\ reform}{GDP^{2020}_{without\ reform}} \times 100. \tag{B6}$$

Other indicators can also be obtained, such as the ratio between the total value of the reform and the discounted GDP obtained over the entire duration of the reform (equation B7):

$$\begin{aligned} &Total\ Value\ of\ the\ reform_{in\ \%\ of\ GDP\ of\ 2020} \\ &= \left(\frac{Value\ of\ the\ reform_{1970-2020}}{\sum_{t=1970}^{t=2050} GDP^{t}_{without\ ref.} \times (1+d)^{(t-2020)}} \right. \\ &\left. + \frac{Value\ of\ the\ reform_{2020-2050}}{\sum_{t=1970}^{t=2050} GDP^{t}_{without\ ref.} \times (1+d)^{-(t-2020)}} \right) \times 100 \end{aligned} \tag{B7}$$

In our counterfactual analysis exercise, it is above all the potential loss of economic wealth that is appropriate to calculate up to 2020:

$$\begin{aligned} &Value\ of\ the\ reform_{1970-2020,\ \ in\ \%\ 2020\ GDP} \\ &= \left(\frac{Value\ of\ reform_{1970-2020}}{\sum_{t=1970}^{t=2050} GDP^{t}_{without\ ref.} \times (1+d)^{(t-2020)}} \right) \times 100 \end{aligned} \tag{B8}$$

On the other hand, we can also calculate how much additional GDP growth could have been achieved thanks to the reform for any year, such as 2020, using equation (B8):

$$GDP_{increase\ in\ 2020(\%)} = \frac{GDP^{2020}_{reform} - GDP^{2020}_{without\ reform}}{GDP^{2020}_{without\ reform}} \times 100. \tag{B9}$$

References

Altinok, N., & Diebolt, C. (2024a). Bref retour cliométrique sur 50 ans de performances scolaires en lecture et en mathématique en France: 1970–2020. *Revue D'economie Politique, 134*(2024/01), 81–104.

Altinok, N., & Diebolt, C. (2024b). Cliometrics of Learning-adjusted years of schooling: Evidence from a new dataset. *Cliometrica, 18*(3), 691–764.
Angrist, N., Djankov, S., Goldberg, P. K., & Patrinos, H. A. (2021). Measuring human capital using global learning data. *Nature, 592*(7854), 403–408.
Angrist, N., Patrinos, H. A., & Schlotter, M. (2013). An Expansion of a global data set on educational quality: A focus on achievement in developing countries. *The World Bank: Policy Research Working Papers.*
Avvisati, F. (2021). *How much do 15-year-olds learn over one year of schooling.* OECD Publishing.
Avvisati, F., & Givord, P. (2023). The learning gain over one school year among 15-year-olds: An international comparison based on PISA. *Labour Economics, 84*, Article 102365.
Barthon, C., & Monfroy, B. (2006). Une analyse systémique de la ségrégation entre collèges: l'exemple de la ville de Lille. *Revue française de pédagogie. Recherches en éducation, 156*, 29–38.
Boman, B. (2022). Vietnam's exceptional educational achievement: A thematic review of the emerging literature. *Discover Education, 1*(1), 14.
Bourdieu, P., & Passeron, J. -C. (1964). *Les héritiers.* Paris, Ed. de Minuit.
Boutchenik, B., Givord, P., & Monso, O. (2021). Urban segregation and college choice: What contributions to school segregation? *Revue Économique, 72*(5), 717–747.
Coleman, J. S. (1966). Equality of Educational Opportunity. *US Department of Health, Education, and Welfare, Office of Education.*
Colmant, M., & Le Cam, M. (2020). TIMSS 2019—Évaluation internationale des élèves de CM1 en mathématiques et en sciences: les résultats de la France toujours en retrait. *DEPP-MENJS Note d'information, 20*, 46.
Duru-Bellat, M. (2009). *Le mérite contre la justice.* Les Presses de Sciences Po.
Duru-Bellat, M. (2017). Eradicating all tolerance of inequality. *Revue Projet, 356*(1), 29–37.
Felouzis, G. (2020). *Les inégalités scolaires.* Presses Universitaires de France.
Felouzis, G., & Charmillot, S. (2012). *Les enquêtes PISA.* PUF.
Foshay, A. W., Thorndike, R. L., Hotyat, F., Pidgeon, D. A., & Walker, D. A. (1962). Educational achievements of thirteen-year olds in twelve countries: Results of an International research project, 1959–61, *UNESCO.*
Guillerm, M., & Monso, O. (2023). Évolution de la mixité sociale des collèges. *Note D'information, DEPP., 23*, 37.
Gust, S., Hanushek, E. A., & Woessmann, L. (2024). Global universal basic skills: Current deficits and implications for world development. *Journal of Development Economics, 166*, 103–205.
Hallak, J. (1974). *A qui profite l'école.* Presses universitaires de France.
Hanushek, E. A., & Kimko, D. D. (2000). Schooling, labor-force quality, and the growth of nations. *The American Economic Review, 90*(5), 1184–1184.
Hanushek, E. A., & Woessmann, L. (2011). How much do educational outcomes matter in OECD countries? *Economic Policy, 26*(67), 427–491.
Hanushek, E. A., Peterson, P. E., Talpey, L. M., & Woessmann, L. (2020). Long-run trends in the US SES-achievement gap. *National Bureau of Economic Research.*
Hanushek, E. A., Ruhose, J., & Woessmann, L. (2017a). Economic gains from educational reform by US states. *Journal of Human Capital, 11*(4), 447–486.
Hanushek, E. A., Ruhose, J., & Woessmann, L. (2017b). Knowledge capital and aggregate income differences: Development accounting for US states. *American Economic Journal: Macroeconomics, 9*(4), 184–224.
Hanushek, E. A., & Woessmann, L. (2012). Do better schools lead to more growth? Cognitive skills, economic outcomes, and causation. *Journal of Economic Growth, 17*(4), 267–321.
Honaker, J., King, G., & Blackwell, M. (2011). Amelia II: A program for missing data. *Journal of Statistical Software, 45*(1), 1–47.
Jencks, C. (1979). *Inequality. Influence de la famille et de l'école.* Paris, Puf.
Kolen, M. J., & Brennan, R. L. (2014). *Test equating, scaling, and linking: Methods and practices.* Springer Science & Business Media.

Lafontaine, D., Felouzis, G., Crahay, M., & Monseur, C. (2013). Des parcours scolaires émaillés de discriminations négatives. In D. Boeck (ed.), *Can school be fair and effective*? De Boeck.

Lahire, B. (2019). *La Raison scolaire. Ecole et pratiques d'écriture, entre savoir et pouvoir*. Presses Universitaires de Rennes.

Lim, S. S., Updike, R. L., Kaldjian, A. S., Barber, R. M., Cowling, K., York, H.,... & Taylor, H. J. (2018). Measuring human capital: A systematic analysis of 195 countries and territories, 1990–2016. *The Lancet*, *392*(10154), 1217–1234.

Ly, S. T., & Riegert, A. (2015). Mixité sociale et scolaire et ségrégation inter-et intra-établissement dans les collèges et lycées français. *Report by the Conseil national d'évaluation du système scolaire (CNESCO)*. https://www.cnesco.fr/wp-content/uploads/2015/05/Etat-des-lieux-Mixit%C3%A9-%C3%A0-l%C3%A9coleFrance1.pdf.

Martin, R., Renault, T., & Roux, B. (2022). Baisse de la productivite en France: échec en "maths"? Focus. *091–2022.*

Merle, P. (2020). Les inégalités scolaires (1995–2020). *Effects of social origin and gender*, *86*(3), 25–41.

Meuret, D. (2012). Plus équitable, l'école retrouirait la voie de la réussite. *Esprit*, *12*, 65–81.

Mullis, I. V., Martin, M. O., Foy, P., & Hooper, M. (2017). *PIRLS 2016 international results in reading*. International Association for the Evaluation of Educational Achievement.

Mullis, I. V. S., Martin, M. O., Foy, P., Kelly, D. L., & Fishbein, B. (2020). TIMSS 2019 international results in mathematics and science. *Retrieved from Boston College, TIMSS & PIRLS International Study Center website:* https://timssandpirls.bc.edu/timss2019/international-results

OECD. (2019). *PISA 2018 results (Volume I)*. OECD Publishing.

OECD. (2023). *PISA 2022 results (Volume I)*. OECD.

Piketty, T. (2013). *Capital in the 21st century*. Seuil.

Prost, A. (1986). *L'Enseignement s'est-il démocratisé?* Presses Universitaires de France.

Salles, F., & Le Cam, M. (2020). TIMSS 2019 Mathématiques au niveau de la classe de quatrième: des résultats inquiétants en France. *DEPP-MENJS Note d'information*, *20*, 47.

Schwerdt, G., & Wiederhold, S. (2019). *A macroeconomic analysis of literacy and economic performance*. Mimeo.

Thélot, C., & Vallet, L.-A. (2000). La réduction des inégalités sociales devant l'école depuis le début du siècle. *Economie Et Statistique/economics and Statistics*, *334*, 3–32.

UIS. (2019). How fast can levels of proficiency improve? Examining Historical Trends to Inform SDG 4.1.1 Scenarios. *UIS Information Paper*, *62.*

van Zanten, A. (2009). *Choosing your school. Stratégies familiales et médiations locales*. Paris cedex 14 Presses Universitaires de France.

van Zanten, A. (2012). School choice policies and their effects. Politique de la ville. Perspectives françaises et ouvertures internationales. L. D. f. C. d. A. Stratégique. Paris, La Documentation française, 111–130.

Wasmer, E., Fredriksson, P., Lamo, A., Messina, J., & Peri, G. (2007). *The macroeconomics of education*. Education and Training in Europe, Oxford University Press.

Chapter 6
The Price of Progress: Access, Quality and Equity in the Turkish Education System

Abstract This chapter investigates Türkiye's educational performance and inequalities through the lens of international assessments such as TIMSS, PISA, PIRLS and ABIDE. While Türkiye's strong showing in TIMSS 2023 highlights remarkable progress, questions of sample representativeness and persistent disparities temper this success. Contradictory results across assessments reveal structural weaknesses, notably regional and socio-economic inequalities that heavily shape student outcomes. By combining longitudinal and cross-sectional data for 130 countries (1970–2020), we develop a counterfactual approach to place Türkiye's trajectory in comparative perspective. Ultimately, the analysis links educational performance and equity to broader economic resilience, addressing the risk of the "middle-income trap".

6.1 Introduction

In 2023, Türkiye achieved a remarkable performance in the international TIMSS (Trends in International Mathematics and Science Study) assessment, ranking 8th out of 58 participants with an average score of 553, well above the international average (Koca et al., 2024). This progression is part of a trend of improving results for Turkish students in mathematics and science, which has been evident throughout successive cycles of TIMSS, particularly since the 2000s. Compared with previous assessments, Türkiye has consolidated its position among OECD countries, showing notable progress at both the 4th and 8th grade levels. However, while these results illustrate a significant improvement in Türkiye's education system, questions remain as to the representativeness of the 2023 sample and the structural challenges still facing the country.

According to Polat et al. (2024), the TIMSS 2023 survey in Türkiye was not carried out in some provinces due to the earthquake of February 6, 2023. Thus, students from nine provinces, including Adıyaman, Gaziantep, Hatay and Malatya, were not included in the final sample. This exclusion raises questions about the representativeness of the results obtained, given that these regions, heavily affected by

N. Altinok and C. Diebolt, *Edumetrics*, Population Economics,
https://doi.org/10.1007/978-3-032-13277-2_6

the disaster, generally experience difficulties in terms of access to quality education. Furthermore, previous studies, such as those by Spaull (2018), have already shown that sample composition can influence international rankings. In this respect, the performance observed in 2023 may not reflect the reality of the Turkish education system as a whole.

At the same time, Türkiye's results in the latest OECD PISA assessment survey do not confirm its advantageous position found in TIMSS 2023. Its mathematics score is below the OECD average (453 points compared to an average of 472). Results in reading and science confirm this central position. The question is whether these contradictions will persist over the long term and to what extent Türkiye's performance has actually improved since the advent of international surveys of student achievement.

Improving the quality of education is therefore a central issue if Türkiye is to avoid falling into the "middle-income trap". As various researchers have pointed out (Suna & Özer, 2021), the level of qualification of the working population is a decisive factor for sustained, inclusive economic growth. Despite progress in access to education, imbalances persist, particularly in terms of the quality of teaching and performance gaps between schools and regions.

According to Sarıer (2020), performance in mathematics and science is strongly influenced by students' socio-economic status, reflecting persistent inequalities in access to quality education. To avoid this pitfall and foster sustainable development, it is essential to reduce these disparities and improve the quality of education overall. Indeed, studies have shown that countries that have successfully overcome this trap have implemented education policies that promote research, innovation and the development of advanced skills (Yediyıldız & Ustun, 2024).

Overall, the trend in Türkiye's school enrollment rate is positive, with increasing participation in secondary and tertiary education. According to the OECD, between 2003 and 2018, Türkiye doubled the number of students eligible for the PISA test, and the country significantly reduced the number of young people not in education or training (OECD, 2021). The 4 + 4 + 4 reform has played a crucial role in this progress, extending the duration of compulsory education and promoting greater access to education for girls. In addition, the "2023 Vision" project has also helped to improve the quality of the Turkish education system by focusing on pedagogical innovation, teacher training and the reduction of educational inequalities (MEB, 2018).

Türkiye's school enrollment rate has undergone significant change over the decades, but the country remains marked by significant regional disparities. Despite this expansion in access to education, significant gaps remain between provinces. According to Çelik and Gür (2013), in 2012, provinces such as Bilecik, Rize, Artvin and Bolu had secondary school enrollment rates above 90%, while regions such as Bitlis, Şanlıurfa, Şırnak and Siirt remained around 40%. This situation highlights the persistent challenges of educational equity and the need for targeted policies to improve access to education in disadvantaged areas. In addition, the study by

Uysal and Gelbal (2018) indicates that regional economic development directly influences access to education, with wealthier provinces benefiting from better school infrastructure and higher-quality educational supervision.

Furthermore, Türkiye's performance in various international assessments, such as PISA, PIRLS, TIMSS and ABIDE, reveals discrepancies depending on the studies and disciplines assessed. According to Aydın and Çilek (2024), Türkiye's performance in mathematics increased from 2012 to 2022 (+15.0). However, according to Sarıer (2020), in 2018, Türkiye reached its highest average scores in mathematics after a gradual increase since 2003, although a decline was observed in 2015. On the other hand, according to Suna and Özer (2021), more than 60% of the variation in mathematics scores in Türkiye is attributable to differences in achievement between schools—more than double the rate observed in OECD countries. These discrepancies show that, while some progress has been made, significant disparities persist, particularly between schools. It also appears that students' performance is strongly influenced by their access to educational resources, including the availability of qualified teachers, teaching materials and an environment conducive to learning (Polat et al., 2024).

Finally, educational inequalities in Türkiye are particularly visible in the PIRLS, TIMSS and PISA surveys. According to Yediyıldız and Ustun (2024), 64% of 15-year-old students in Türkiye are classified as socio-economically disadvantaged, placing the country among the most unequal in the OECD on this indicator. Furthermore, according to socio-economic status directly influences performance in math, science and reading. Other studies, such as those by Suna and Özer (2021), point out that socio-economic characteristics explain a significant proportion of the variance in school results. These findings show that improving results on international assessments cannot be separated from a broader reflection on equity and the redistribution of educational resources in Türkiye. According to Köseleci (2015), the performance gap between the most and least developed regions is exacerbated by the concentration of elite schools in large cities, accentuating inequalities between students.

All in all, Türkiye's results in international surveys show significant progress, particularly in TIMSS 2023, but also reveal potential problems with comparability of results over time and between countries, as well as major challenges in terms of equity and equal opportunities.

We thus propose to use a methodology to aggregate Türkiye's results in international assessments, from a dual perspective of measuring both Turkish educational performance and aspects of educational inequality. We use several indicators and various methodologies measuring both average quality and inequalities to analyze the state of knowledge and enhance the robustness of the results obtained. In doing so, we also seek to address the problems of measurement error inherent in international surveys.

While longitudinal analyses capture fixed effects and trace school career paths, cross-sectional approaches allow for a more comparative reading and, in turn, include many countries. With this in mind, we propose a hybrid, counterfactual approach. Using cross-sectional data spread over time, we analyze Türkiye's educational performance using a database of learning outcomes for nearly 130 countries between 1970 and 2020. In so doing, we combine the advantages of cross-sectional data (comparability with other education systems) with those of longitudinal analyses (the possibility of tracing the evolution of inequalities over time). We also use the double-difference method to correct exogenous effects similar to all developing countries and detect structural changes in the Turkish education system.[1]

In the remainder of this article, we first present the original data produced on the quality of education. The methodology used to construct the data is explained, followed by an analysis of Türkiye's performance. The latter focuses on a number of dimensions to confirm or refute the trends observed. Finally, we use an economic projection model to estimate the economic impact of a better education policy in Türkiye, using a historical macro-simulation model based on a counterfactual approach.

6.2 Data and Methodology

The originality of our work lies in the use of a database containing comparable scores in several areas of school competence, at different levels and over a period covering around five decades (1970–2020).[2] This database presents not only school performance scores, but also measures of performance in certain benchmarks and scores for sub-samples, enabling us to gain a better understanding of the equity of education systems, with a view to international comparison.

6.2.1 Assessments of Student Learning

Our assessment of the quality of education systems is based on the dimension of learning achievement, measured through an exercise that standardizes international surveys. The international database on student learning compiles results from various surveys (TIMSS, PIRLS and PISA).[3] Other assessments focus on adult skills (IALS, PIAAC[4]). We present these surveys very briefly. More information can be found in the respective reports for each assessment (Mullis et al., 2020, 2023; OECD, 2023b; Paccagnella, 2016).

---

[1] In a way, our approach can be seen as a natural, quasi-experimental experiment, with Türkiye as the control group and other developing countries as the control group.

[2] For a detailed description, see Altinok and Diebolt (2024).

[3] *Trends on International Mathematics and Science Study*, *Progress on International Reading Literacy Study* and *Programme for International Student Assessment*, respectively.

[4] Respectively *International Adult Literacy Survey* and *Programme for the International Assessment of Adult Competencies*.

The International Association for the Evaluation of Educational Achievement (IEA) was the first organization to conduct international surveys of student achievement. After a pilot survey in the 1960s (Foshay et al., 1962), several assessments tested primary and secondary school students in mathematics and science, but it was above all the TIMSS assessment that made its mark on the international community. This survey began in 1995 and focuses on mathematics and science. Since then, several waves of tests have been carried out every four years.[5] The IEA has also assessed students' reading skills since the 1970s, but it is undeniably the PIRLS survey that has highlighted young people's reading skills. In parallel with the IEA surveys, the PISA assessment has attracted a great deal of media attention, particularly in Germany (Waldow, 2009). PISA is an assessment developed by the OECD. Launched in 2000, it tests 15-year-old students in three skill areas (mathematics, science and reading). The PISA assessment has become the survey covering the most countries in the world. Organized every three years, eight different waves have been carried out up to 2022, with over 70 countries participating in the latest wave. Türkiye began participating in PISA in the second wave, in 2003.

Alongside assessments of student achievement, surveys of adult skills (IALS and PIAAC) can also be very useful for better assessing student skills. Using a specific methodology, some authors have, in fact, obtained panel data relating to the skill levels of young adults (Schwerdt & Wiederhold, 2019). All the surveys used to obtain the database can be found in Table 6.1.

6.2.2 *Methodology*

Our analysis includes several recently published original datasets measuring multiple dimensions derived from student achievement surveys (Altinok & Diebolt, 2024, 2025). In addition to traditional average scores from surveys such as PISA, we also use alternative measures such as the proportion of students reaching specific thresholds, differences between deciles, or even gaps between socio-economic levels. By mixing these dimensions with traditional measures used in education, it is possible to obtain indices of efficiency or equity.

6.2.2.1 Education Quality Database

Before preparing data on specific sub-samples or thresholds, it is essential to have an international database on the quality of education systems. The detailed methodology of this approach can be found in Altinok and Diebolt (2024). Below, we briefly

[5] The second wave dates back to 1999, then 2003, 2007. The latest wave with available data dates from 2019. Although TIMSS 2023 data have recently been released, they could not be included in our analyses.

Table 6.1 International surveys of student or adult learning achievement

No	Years	Organization	Abbrev	Material	Number of countries or regions	Grade
1	1959–1960	IEA	Pilot input	M,S,L	12	7/8
2	1964	IEA	FIMS	M	12	7/FS
3	1970–71	IEA	SSS-RC	L	15	4/8/FS
4	1970–72	IEA	FISS	S	19	4/8/FS
5	1980–82	IEA	SIMS	M	19	8/FS
6	1983–84	IEA	SISS	S	23	4/8/ FS
7	1990–91	IEA	RLS	L	32	3–4/ 7–8
8	1995–2019	IEA	TIMSS	M,S	45–38-26–48-66–65-64	3–4/ 7–8/ FS
9	1997–2019	UNESCO	LLECE	M,S,L	13–16-15–16	3–6
10	1999–2007	UNESCO	SACMEQ	M,L	7–15-16	6 6
11	2000–2019	CONFEMEN	PASEC	M,L	22–22-10–14	2/5 then 3–6
12	2001–2021	IEA	PIRLS	L	35–41-55–50-65	4
13	2000–2022	OECD	PISA	M,S,L	43–41-57–74-65–71-79–81	15 years
14	2010–2019	USAID/RTI	EGRA	L	29–40-5	1 to 6
15	2008–2019	ASER	ASER	L	2	1 to 6
16	2011–2017	OECD	PIAAC	L	39	Adults

Note IEA = "International Association for the Evaluation of Educational Achievement", NCES = "National Center for Education Statistics", CONFEMEN = "Conférence des Ministres de l'Education des Etats et Gouvernements de la Francophonie", OECD = "Organisation for Economic Co-operation and Development", USAID = "United States Agency for International Development", RTI = "Research Triangle Institute", ASER = "Australian Council for Educational Research", FIMSS = "First International Mathematics Study", SSS-RC = "Six Subject Survey: Reading Comprehension", FISS = "First International Science Study", SIMS = "Second International Mathematics Study", IAEP = "International Assessment of Educational Progress", RLS = "Reading Literacy Study", TIMSS = "Trends on International Mathematics and Science Study", LLECE = "Latin American Laboratory for Evaluation of the Quality of Education", SACMEQ = "The Southern and Eastern Africa Consortium for Monitoring Educational Quality", PASEC = "Programme d'Analyse des Systèmes Educatifs de la Confemen", PIRLS = "Progress in International Reading Literacy Study", PISA = "Programme of International Student Assessment", EGRA = "Early-Grade Reading Assessment", PIAAC = "Programme for International Assessment of Adult Competencies". Subjects: M = mathematics; S = science; L = reading. FS = "end of upper secondary" present the general approach to obtaining average scores before continuing with the dimension of educational inequalities.

Altinok and Diebolt (2024)'s approach is based on grouping the various international achievement tests (presented in the previous section) onto comparable scales. Since these surveys are diverse in nature, the authors developed a methodology for adjusting them to each other in order to avoid any potential bias. The surveys were adjusted to enable comparisons over time and space. The general idea behind this approach is to use the results of countries that have participated simultaneously in several surveys over the same period (Angrist et al., 2021).

In fact, by combining all the countries that have participated in several assessments, it is possible to calculate conversion rates, as one would for an exchange rate between currencies, for example. This method is used to adjust the scores of surveys carried out from the 1990s onwards and has already been implemented by previous research (Angrist et al., 2013, 2021; Gust et al., 2024). An additional approach was also implemented to anchor the surveys to each other over time, particularly before 1990. Following the pioneering approach of Hanushek and Kimko (2000), it is thus possible to anchor international survey data by referring to the U.S. results in the national survey of student achievement, namely the National Assessment of Educational Progress (NAEP).[6]

As for PISA and TIMSS, the calculation of a general conversion rate is sufficient to obtain a comparable database in terms of learning outcomes.[7] What is new, however, is the implementation of the multiple imputation method used in Lim et al. (2018). By using data that are highly correlated with educational attainment, Altinok and Diebolt (2024) explain that this approach makes it possible to extend both the period covered by attainment assessments and to predict scores for countries that have not participated in all these assessments.

This imputation procedure uses the "Amelia II" package (Honaker et al., 2011) and is useful for obtaining panel data for almost half a century (1970–2020).[8] Indeed, the database prepared by Angrist et al. (2021) only covers the period 2010–2020. The combination of multiple imputation and the earliest surveys, anchored through conversion rates and NAEP evaluation, allows Altinok and Diebolt (2024) to generate comparable scores for key OECD and developing countries from 1970 to 2020. This database will serve as the foundation for our analysis.

---

[6] Details of the methodology used to obtain a database of over 130 countries are presented in Altinok & Diebolt (2024). The present article focuses on the results for Türkiye, comparing this country with a sample of 20 developing countries with an economic level close to Türkiye's in 1970.

[7] Assuming that the average mathematics scores of countries participating in TIMSS 1999 and PISA 2000 are equal to 553 in TIMSS and 533 in PISA, then the conversion rate between PISA and TIMSS will be $553/533 = 1{,}0375$. PISA scores will thus be revised upwards by around 3.75%.

[8] Details of the multiple imputation procedure can be found in Altinok & Diebolt (2024). In contrast to Lim et al. (2018), we employ this multiple imputation method using different steps to minimize measurement error. Specifically, eight steps are implemented, ranging from predicting scores for countries with the most observations over a short period (between 1995 and 2020, step number 1) to countries with very little data on education quality and over a longer period (between 1970 and 2020, step number 8). This imputation procedure uses explanatory factors previously selected via multiple regressions and includes several explanatory variables.

Furthermore, in order to combine the quantity and quality of education, Altinok and Diebolt (2024) propose associating the average number of years of schooling with students' scores on achievement assessments. Filmer et al. (2020) were the first to perform such a conversion. This combination thus provides a relative measure of the quantity of education, taking into account the educational quality differential between countries. The main hypothesis is based on the idea that one year of education in a given country does not necessarily yield the same academic performance in terms of learning outcomes as in another country. Some countries prove to be more efficient than others, as highlighted by assessments such as PISA. With this in mind, the hybrid indicator we are implementing is the "Learning-Adjusted Years of Schooling" (Filmer et al., 2020). To calculate this relative indicator, the score obtained is divided by 700 (considered a theoretical ceiling), giving a value between 0 and 1. This ratio is then multiplied by the average number of years of schooling, taken from the database of Barro and Lee (2013). The new database thus obtained provides information about three complementary variables: the quality of education systems (via scores on various achievement surveys and performance thresholds), the quantity of education (via the average number of years of schooling), and the Learning-Adjusted Years of Schooling (LAYS).

6.2.2.2 Extending the Base to School Inequalities

The use of anchoring methods provides a panel database on the quality of education. In practical terms, data on the quality of education are spread over several school levels (primary, secondary) and skill areas (mathematics, reading, science) and are available between 1970 and 2020 for most OECD countries (including Türkiye), as well as a large number of developing countries.[9]

Analyzing the performance of an education system solely in terms of average scores can overlook the issue of equity. It is therefore appropriate to propose measures to assess the inequitable dimension of educational achievement. As school enrollment is not universal in all countries, we adjust inequality indicators based on school completion rates. This issue is more prevalent in developing countries like Türkiye.

Three main dimensions are used to analyze performance differences within countries. Firstly, we reproduce the data anchoring methodology almost identically, focusing on performance thresholds and scores across the different deciles. The approach used is very similar to that for average scores, with the difference that we prefer to use anchoring by the so-called equipercentile method instead of the "conversion rate" method in order to calibrate each performance threshold across countries and over time (Kolen & Brennan, 2014). The main advantage of this method is that it takes into account the distribution of scores within each database. In concrete terms,

[9] It should be noted that we use the term "panel" in the sense that the cross-sectional data are grouped together without longitudinal follow-up. However, as the data are statistically representative of the different countries included in the surveys, we can consider them as a panel for monitoring the performance of education systems.

instead of anchoring average scores with conversion rates, we anchor each percentile of a reference survey with the same percentile of another survey when calculating conversion coefficients. Around a hundred of these coefficients are calculated for a pair of surveys (each referring to a particular percentile). This allows us to take into account any differences in score distribution within each survey. Indeed, as we wish to calculate the proportions of students exceeding performance thresholds, it is important to take into account the distribution of scores within each assessment before anchoring the surveys to each other.

We calculate the proportions of students reaching different competency thresholds. More specifically, we are interested in two levels. The performance thresholds are based on those developed by the IEA, and these thresholds are also quite similar to those defined by the OECD in the PISA test. The first level refers to a "Minimum Proficiency Level" (MPL), whose main aim is to highlight the proportion of a population that achieves a certain level of competence, in order to obtain minimum skills for everyday activities. The Sustainable Development Goals explicitly refer to this minimum threshold (UNESCO Institute of Statistics, 2019). The minimum profi-cienct threshold refers to the IEA's minimum benchmark, the "Low International Benchmark", which corresponds to a threshold of 400 points. Students who reach this threshold have basic skills in mathematics, reading and science.[10] At primary level, they can perform basic arithmetic operations on one- and two-digit numbers as well as solve problems involving a small number of parameters. Students can handle fractions and common geometric shapes. Statistically, they can read and complete bar graphs and tables.

Alongside this minimum threshold, it is interesting to look at the proportion of students reaching the Advanced Proficiency Level (APL). The main purpose of this threshold is to measure the proportion of the population achieving a high level on tests of student achievement, and thus identify the proportion of elites within each country. We use the IEA's reference threshold, the Advanced International Benchmark, which is set at a level of 625 points.[11] At this level, primary school pupils can apply their knowledge and understanding in a variety of complex situations, and explain their reasoning rigorously. It is no longer a question of having basic knowledge, but rather of being able to use it in complex situations while knowing exactly which skills to mobilize, and mobilizing more sophisticated tools (such as the use of fractions or decimals). The use of multidimensional tools is essential to reach this advanced level. The set of skills acquired for each skill area and threshold is presented in more detail in OECD (2023b) and Mullis et al. (2020). In particular, we analyze the proportion of students achieving the Minimum Proficiency Level (MPL) against the proportion achieving the Advanced Proficiency Level (APL). A country that manages to get almost its entire population to reach the minimum threshold can be considered

[10] This threshold is very close to the level 2 defined in the PISA assessment (OECD, 2023b).

[11] It is important to note that this threshold is very close in secondary education to level 5 of the PISA study. The thresholds are close to 625 points for the 3 skill areas, bearing in mind that we use approximately the same threshold in reading. More precisely, the threshold is 607 points in mathematics, 633 points in science and 626 points in reading. See OECD (2023b), pages 92, 9–100 and 103 for the definition of thresholds according to the PISA assessment.

egalitarian. If the same country also manages to get a proportion of students to exceed the advanced skills threshold, it will be both egalitarian and successful.

In addition to average scores, we also calculate scores for each decile. The gap between deciles may prove to be a means of measuring educational inequality, following the approach developed by Piketty (2013) in the context of income inequality. In doing so, we calculate scores at deciles 1 and 9, i.e. D1 & D9, respectively, the average score of the lowest and highest performing 10%. An egalitarian country should logically obtain an interdecile ratio close to 1, meaning a very small gap in performance between the two extreme deciles. On the other hand, an unequal country that manages to get the best performers to do better, while neglecting the worst performers, will have a high interdecile ratio. Measuring the interdecile ratio will therefore enable us to assess the level of inequality in Türkiye in comparison with other countries.

An additional way of measuring educational inequalities concerns the potential differences in performance that may exist between populations with specific characteristics, such as whether or not they come from a family with high socio-economic capital. This brings us back to the classic analysis of inequalities in the sociology of education (Coleman, 1966). It is important to note that the initial anchoring is done on the scores of each sub-population, but the use of ratios is only carried out during the multiple imputation procedure (Altinok & Diebolt, 2025). The approach adopted here is to replicate the initial anchoring methods on sub-populations, then use ratios marking the absolute differences between sub-populations to perform data imputation.

Here, we use only the variability of scores relating to differences in socio-economic level. For this purpose, Altinok and Diebolt (2025) calculated socio-economic level scales within all surveys, using available data. It is impossible to have a standardized and similar scale for all surveys. However, as the authors use the interquartile range for each index (i.e. splitting the distribution of scores into four equal parts), comparison between different periods should not suffer from the lack of standardization of scales for this index between surveys. If students with the highest socio-economic levels have significantly higher scores than those from families without social and economic capital, the country can be considered unequal in terms of educational achievement. We use an index of socio-economic level, obtained from virtually all the assessments included in our database. As the measurement of this index is quite heterogeneous between achievement tests, it is primarily the absolute gap between quartiles that will be weighed in our analysis. The bottom quartile (Q1) will measure the average score of students from the 25% poorest families in terms of socio-economic status. We then measure the level of inequality by calculating the difference in performance between the top quartile (Q4) and the bottom quartile (Q1). The greater the difference, the greater the inequality.[12]

[12] It remains possible that if the structure of the population changes over time, such as the arrival of large numbers of poor immigrants in a country, the interquartile range may be modified exogenously.

6.2.2.3 Synthetic Performance Indices

The indicators presented above each measure a particular dimension and may relate to measures of effectiveness, efficiency, or equity. First, we propose to construct an indicator of educational effectiveness. This indicator is based on the assumption that a system can be considered efficient if it succeeds in getting all its students to reach the minimum performance threshold (MPL), without sacrificing those who could also reach the excellence threshold (APL). However, it is virtually impossible to have the entire population reach the threshold of excellence. This is why we weight the value relative to this threshold to obtain our efficiency index:

$$efficacy_{country,t} = \frac{(MPL + 2 \times APL)}{2} \times 10 \tag{6.1}$$

with MPL = Minimum Proficiency Level & APL = Advanced Proficiency Level

So let's assume a country A where 80% of the population reaches the minimum threshold and only 5% manage to reach the excellence threshold. Conversely, in country B, almost the entire population reaches the minimum threshold (95%), with almost a fifth reaching the excellence threshold (20%). The efficiency index is equal to 450 in country A compared to 675 for country B, which represents a difference of 50% in favor of the latter country.

Beyond efficiency, a system can also be measured by its degree of equity, i.e. the extent to which it enables everyone to succeed, regardless of their initial resources. The notion of equity is fairly subjective but often refers to the principle of equal opportunities to succeed, irrespective of individual characteristics. Equity does not imply perfect equality between all students, but rather equal access and success justified by factors independent of socio-economic characteristics or based on various dimensions (such as gender, immigrant status, or religion). It is impossible to combine all possible dimensions. The most commonly used one, given the ease of obtaining comparable data, refers to the socio-economic status of parents. However, the measure of socio-economic level is quite heterogeneous between the different assessments and may be interpreted differently depending on the economic level of the country. A more neutral measure refers to the analysis of deciles. More specifically, the gap between the bottom and top deciles can measure a degree of inequality, somewhat similar to the Gini index. We therefore propose to measure the equity of education systems by combining the extreme deciles in terms of student scores. The bottom 10% decile is calculated as the average score of students in the bottom 10%. In contrast, the top 10% score refers to the average score obtained by the top 10% of students. The greater the deviation from the median score, the more inequitable an education system is considered to be. More generally, the formula we use is as follows:

$$equity_{absolute,t} = \left(1 - \frac{Top_{10\%} - Bottom_{10\%}}{Median\_score}\right) \times 1000, \tag{6.2}$$

where $Bottom_{10\%}$ is the average score obtained by the bottom 10% of students, $Top_{10\%}$ is the average score obtained by the top 10% and *Median_score* is the median score.

This equity index thus represents the standardized score of the gap between the highest and lowest performers, relative to the median score. As Spaull (2018) points out, the incomplete schooling of a young population can call into question the interpretation of results within surveys such as PISA. If an education system is selective and does not include the entire school-age population, it is possible for the equity index to be biased. Let's take the example of a country where only half the population aged 15 actually attends school. In this case, the calculated index will tend to overestimate the level of equity in the country under the assumption that the population excluded from the education system would have performed less well if they had attended school. To take account of this exclusion bias, we calculate an adjusted equity index in which we include the school completion rate:

$$equity_{adjusted,t} = \left(1 - \frac{Top_{10\%} - Bottom_{10\%}}{Median\_score}\right) \times completion \times 1000, \qquad (6.3)$$

where *completion* represents the completion rate for the school level in question.

Descriptive statistics are presented in Table 6.2. Türkiye's position falls between the two groups of countries in terms of quality of education (respectively OECD and developing countries groups). However, the indicator relating to the number of years of schooling highlights the clear gap between developed countries and Türkiye. On average, OECD countries record around 10 years of schooling over the period 1970–2020, compared with 5.6 years for Türkiye. Even the group of developing countries has a higher level of schooling than Türkiye (6.9 years). This difference is confirmed by the hybrid indicator of years of schooling adjusted by the quality of education, which is around half as high in Türkiye as in OECD countries.

Although the equity index is relatively close between Türkiye and the group of OECD countries, once the completion rate is taken into account, adjusted equity is significantly lower in Türkiye. This disparity can be explained by the low enrollment of young people between 1970 and 2010. Finally, the efficiency index falls between the average for developing countries and that for OECD countries. Türkiye thus occupies a special position here, appearing to hold an average position among developing countries but lagging behind when OECD countries are used as a benchmark. It therefore seems important to compare Türkiye with similar countries, as the process of universal schooling was only implemented later in Türkiye, unlike in developed countries.

Table 6.2 Education database (1970–2020)

	Average	Standard deviation	Minimum	Maximum
Türkiye				
Quality of education	462.2	14.2	445.4	501.3
Years of schooling	5.6	1.9	2.6	8.1
Mixed indicator (LAYS)	3.7	1.3	1.7	5.8
Equity indicator	535.6	24.4	499.4	589.5
Adjusted equity indicator	394.2	102.0	284.2	537.5
Efficiency indicator	454.9	27.9	424.1	526.4
OECD-20				
Quality of education	499.2	37.6	379.7	599.2
Years of schooling	9.9	2.2	2.6	13.8
Mixed indicator (LAYS)	7.2	1.9	1.7	10.8
Equity indicator	537.4	43.9	340.4	633.6
Adjusted equity indicator	478.0	87.7	150.1	630.3
Efficiency indicator	534.7	84.7	288.9	754.9
Group of developing countries D20				
Quality of education	409.8	57.4	268.6	545.7
Years of schooling	6.9	2.7	1.6	13.0
Mixed indicator (LAYS)	4.1	2.0	0.6	9.8
Equity indicator	473.5	99.5	24.2	639.8
Adjusted equity indicator	338.3	142.3	21.1	597.7
Efficiency indicator	341.3	112.0	140.5	616.3

Notes The data include all observations available between 1970 and 2020 for a selection of 20 OECD countries, 20 developing countries and Türkiye. A total of 220 observations are available for the full sample of developing countries and 11 observations for Türkiye (data available every 5 years). Source: authors' calculations based on Altinok and Diebolt (2024, 2025)

6.2.3 *Analysis*

6.2.3.1 Double-Difference Analysis

In order to analyze the evolution of Türkiye's performance rigorously, we employ a counterfactual approach known as the double-difference method. It is possible that the recent increase in Türkiye's performance is mainly due to a catch-up effect with countries that were at the top in the 1970s. In this case, this evolution cannot be considered exceptional or as the result of educational policies specific to Türkiye. To test this hypothesis, we calculate the gap between Türkiye's performance and that of countries with roughly the same characteristics in the 1970s, i.e. a panel of 20 developing countries with roughly the same GDP per capita as Türkiye.[13]

We then calculate the performance gap between Türkiye and the selected countries in subsequent years, using the previously defined performance indicators. If the gap is significant, then we can deduce that the trajectory followed by Türkiye results from the country's own actions and is not the consequence of a simple catch-up phenomenon and/or of factors external to Türkiye.

Let's assume the following performance indicator (denoted *educ*) for Türkiye and a panel of countries similar to Türkiye, which we denote DEV_{20}:

$$edu_{TUR,1970} = Xetedu_{DEV20,1970} = Y. \tag{6.4}$$

We can calculate the variation in Türkiye's performance between two periods:

$$\Delta edu_{TUR,t\rightarrow t+10} = edu_{TUR,t+10} - edu_{TUR,t} \tag{6.5}$$

Similarly, it is possible to calculate the variation in performance for the control group (here the 20 developing countries in our panel, noted):

$$\Delta edu_{DEV20,t\rightarrow t+10} = edu_{DEV20,t+10} - edu_{DEV20,t}. \tag{6.6}$$

A significant effect of Türkiye's performance can be observed by calculating the difference between the variation in Türkiye's performance and that of the selected panel of countries (using the double-difference method):

$$\Delta edu_{TUR-net,t\rightarrow t+10} = \left(edu_{TUR,t+10} - edu_{TUR,t}\right) - \left(edu_{DEV20,t+10} - edu_{DEV20,t}\right). \tag{6.7}$$

The main drawback of this double-difference approach is the potential presence of measurement errors that could bias the net effect of the variation in Türkiye's performance. For example, if there were a measurement error that overestimated the indicator in a given year, then the variation calculated between two periods would mainly reflect this measurement error.

To partially mitigate this estimation bias, we propose two alternatives. First, we calculate the absolute deviation of Türkiye's performance relative to the panel considered for each period:

$$edu_{TUR-relative,t} = edu_{TUR-abs,t} - edu_{DEV20-abs,t}. \tag{6.8}$$

[13] We looked for countries with a GDP per capita close enough to Türkiye's in 1970 to form the control group sample. The countries in this group are as follows: Algeria, Brazil, Chile, Colombia, Costa Rica, Czech Republic, Ecuador, El Salvador, Guatemala, Iran, Malaysia, Mauritius, Mexico, Nicaragua, Peru, South Africa, Vietnam, Slovenia, Türkiye and Uganda.

Then, by calculating the average of these indicators, it is possible to determine whether the school performance observed in Türkiye significantly differs from that of other comparable countries:

$$edu_{mean,TUR-relative,t} = \frac{\sum_{t=1}^{n} edu_{TUR-relative,t}}{n}. \tag{6.9}$$

Another method is to extend the time intervals used to calculate the variation, to reduce potential estimation biases. Instead of using a 10-year interval, we could use intervals of 10, 15 or 20 years:

$$\Delta edu_{TUR-dif,t\rightarrow t+15} = \left(edu_{TUR,t+15} - edu_{TUR,t}\right) - \left(edu_{DEV20,t+15} - edu_{DEV20,t}\right). \tag{6.10}$$

6.2.3.2 Model for Projecting an Improvement in the Quality of Education

Furthermore, in order to assess the potential economic benefits of improving the quality of education in Türkiye, we use a forecasting model developed in several studies by economists such as Eric Hanushek and his co-authors (Gust et al., 2024; Hanushek & Woessmann, 2012; Hanushek et al., 2017a, 2017b).

In these forecasting models (the key features of which are presented in Appendix B), a macro-simulation of the impact of an educational reform is conducted using the results of growth models estimated in a previous study (Hanushek & Woessmann, 2012). We apply this model and attempt to measure the trajectory that Türkiye could experience if it implemented an effective policy to improve the quality of education.

Our first scenario estimates the economic benefits of a policy aimed at improving the test scores of the entire population by a quarter of a standard deviation, or around 25 points on the PISA-comparable scale. By simulating this increase, we can estimate the potential economic growth Türkiye could experience by 2100.

In these models, the skills of each cohort differ from those of the current workforce. We simulate a situation where an educational policy is introduced, gradually affecting the entire population over the period 2020–2100. Initially, the workforce maintains its pre-reform skill level. This workforce is then partially, and eventually fully, replaced by individuals who have experienced the reform. This transition takes several years, considering that the duration of working life is 40 years (W = 40). Thus, each year, 2.5% of Türkiye's total workforce comprises students who have experienced the educational reform.

We calculate the skill level of the workforce for each year between 2020 and 2100 by replacing the oldest workers with those from the new cohorts (i.e. $\overline{A}_t$) weighted as$1/W$, where W is the working life. In calculating the gain in cognitive skills from such a reform, we consider 4 different phases:

1. School reform ($t = 1, \ldots, R$): during the *R-term* reform, workers with an initial skill level are gradually replaced by more skilled workers.
2. Main replacement ($t = R + 1, \ldots, W$): workers with the initial skill level (i.e. pre-reform) are replaced by new workers for the next ($W - R$) years.
3. Quality reinforcement ($t = W + 1, \ldots, W + R$): for the following R years, some workers who have only partially experienced the reform are replaced by workers who have fully experienced the reform.
4. Population with complete reform ($t = W + R + 1, \ldots$): The entire workforce concerned has a skill level at the level of the desired reform.

In these models, a reform scenario assumes a linear progression path taking 15 years before the reform is fully operational (parameter R). This means that the educational levels of each of the first cohorts following the educational reform will have different (and better) levels of educational completion. For each year of the simulation, we calculate the GDP growth rate resulting from the educational reform as follows:

$$g_t^{reform} = p + \gamma \bar{A}_t, \tag{6.11}$$

GDP with or without the reform changes as follows:

$$GDP_t^{\Delta} = \left(1 + g_t^{\Delta}\right) \times GDP_t^{\Delta}, \tag{6.12}$$

where $\Delta \in$ (*reform*, *without reform*).

The total value of the reform is given by the sum of the discounted annual GDP differences:

$$\textit{Value of the reform} = \sum_{t=2020}^{t=2100} \left(GDP^t_{reform} - GDP^t_{without\ reform}\right) \times (1 + d)^{-(t-2020)}, \tag{6.13}$$

where d is the discount rate.

6.3 Results

We explore the overall performance of the Turkish education system by analyzing the evolution of the various indicators used in our study (Fig. 6.1). The quality of primary and secondary education appears to have fallen below the OECD average in the 1970s (i.e. set at around 500 points). However, an upward trend appears to have begun in the 2000s. The efficiency indicator of the education system, which combines the proportions of students reaching the two performance thresholds, seems to show an increase between 1970 and 1990, followed by a decline until the early 2000s. Thereafter, the index rises significantly, which can be explained by the educational

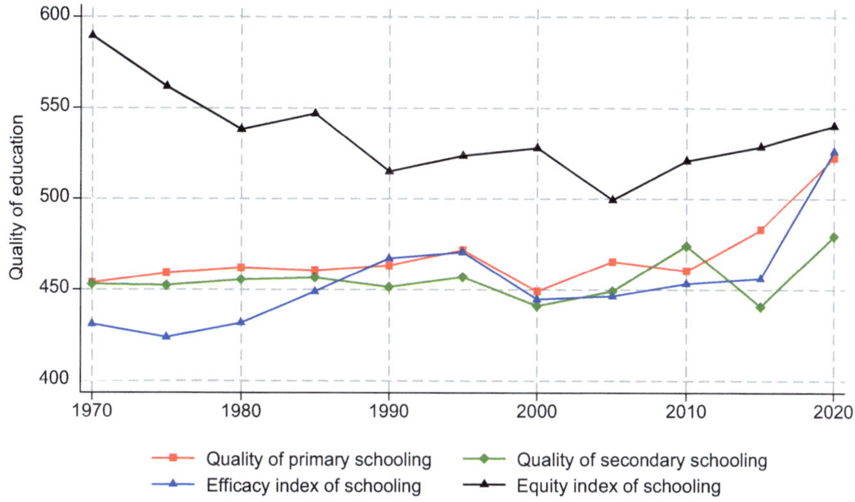

Fig. 6.1 Performance indicators for the Turkish education system (1970–2020). *Source* authors' calculations based on Altinok and Diebolt (2024, 2025)

policies outlined in the introduction. However, equity in Türkiye's education system seems to be eroding almost continuously, except during the last decade.

As indicated in the introduction to this article, the main innovation of our work lies in the availability of comparable data for the quality and equity of education over almost half a century (1970–2020). Restricting ourselves to a single country can conceal general trends and attribute exogenous improvements to one country. Our method is comparative and focuses here on countries similar to Türkiye, developing countries that we call DEV-20. One advantage of restricting ourselves to these countries is the availability of long-term data, and the fact that Türkiye is positioned among countries that have followed a similar trajectory in terms of school enrollment, particularly at the secondary level where enrollment was not universal in the 1970s. In this way, we can avoid comparing Türkiye with OECD countries where universal secondary schooling was achieved by the end of the 1970s, which would tend to overestimate Türkiye's performance in the various skill areas.[14] Looking at the quantitative dimension of education alone, we see a significant gap between Türkiye and OECD countries (Fig. 6.6). Secondary school completion rates are significantly lower in the developing countries in our sample than in OECD countries. At the same time, there has been very strong growth in student enrollment, especially since 1995. Beyond the quantitative dimension, a purely qualitative approach also highlights the dominance of OECD countries (Fig. 6.7). Indeed, the quality of education has always appeared superior for OECD countries, even if Türkiye seems to have caught up in the last decade. An analysis of our efficiency index confirms our approach of comparing

[14] By way of example, Spaull (2018) has shown that Türkiye's results in the PISA survey appeared to be overestimated in the early 2000s due to a lower enrollment of 15-year-olds than in other OECD countries.

Türkiye with developing countries. Although efficiency is higher in Türkiye than in developing countries, the country's singular position suggests that it should be placed at the level of emerging countries such as Argentina and Indonesia (Fig. 6.8). The equity of Türkiye's education system appeared quite high in the 1970s, especially in comparison with other developing countries (Fig. 6.9). However, it seems to have gradually declined over the years. It is therefore necessary to analyze all dimensions of education in order to gain a comparative perspective on Türkiye's performance.

6.3.1 High Performance Compared with Other Developing Countries

We begin by comparing the quality of education in Türkiye in a cross-section for the year 1970. The skill level we find for Türkiye is one of the highest among the developing countries in our panel—called *DEV-20*—for both grade levels, in reading and mathematics (Fig. 6.2). While Türkiye's average score is close to 500 points in mathematics at the primary level, its average level is only 360 points for the countries in our panel. Assuming that one year of achievement is equivalent to around 40 points for a developing country (Avvisati & Givord, 2023), this would mean that Türkiye was more than four years ahead of the other countries. It is worth noting that only Vietnam outperforms Türkiye, particularly at the secondary level, while Malaysia scores around 20 to 30 points lower than Türkiye. Moreover, in 2020,[15] Türkiye's position remains high, despite lower performance than countries such as Slovenia, the Czech Republic and Vietnam (Fig. 6.10). On the other hand, African countries such as South Africa and Uganda have significantly lower scores than the other countries in the sample.

Table 6.3 shows the evolution of performance for each skill area (mathematics, reading and science) and each school level analyzed (primary and secondary). The period studied spans 50 years, from 1970 to 2020. Based on an international average in 2000 of 500 and a standard deviation of 100, it appears that, since 1970, school performance in Türkiye has increased, even if it was below the OECD average in 2000. To assess the significance of the variation in performance, we calculated the measurement error for each mean score.[16] The reading level for primary school rose from 430 to 496 points between 1970 and 2020 (see Fig. 6.11). This represents an

[15] It should be noted that the 2020 data exclude the Covid-19 crisis because our projections stop at 2019 and we extrapolate the 2020 results by reproducing the trend observed over the last period (for example between 2015 and 2018 according to PISA or 2015–2019 according to TIMSS).

[16] The measurement error or "standard error" is calculated here in such a way as to encompass both the measurement error inherent in estimating *macro* performance from a *micro* survey, but also taking into account the measurement error arising from the multiple imputation method. Assuming that the two errors are independent, we can calculate the standard error as follows $error = measurementerror_{survey} + measurementerror_{imputation}$. The measurement error of the imputation is achieved through a *bootstrapping* method with 30 replications on the results from the imputation, which itself includes around 80 score predictions.

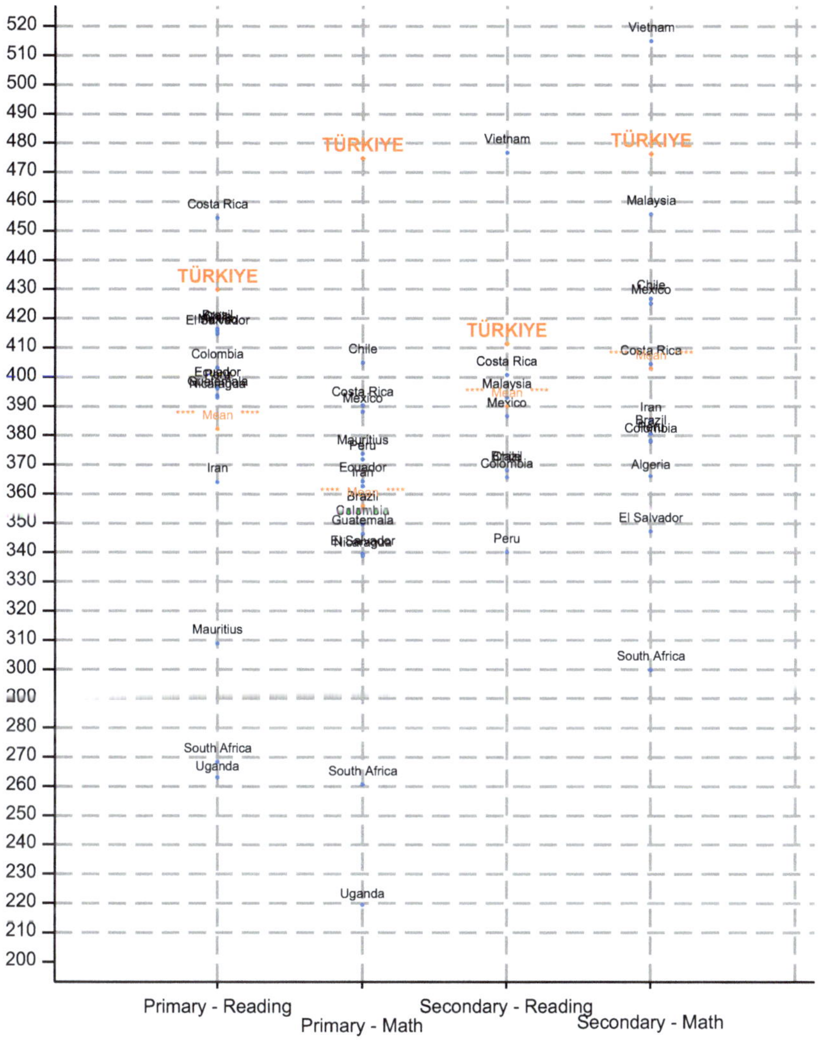

Fig. 6.2 Performance of DEV-20 countries in 1970. *Source* authors' calculations based on Altinok and Diebolt (2024, 2025)

increase of around 70 points, or 14 points per decade, which is the equivalent of two school years of learning over half a century. These variations are almost all significant in terms of the standard errors calculated.[17] If we look at the column relating to long-term standardized variation (column 8), the gains are all positive over the long term: the Turkish education system has therefore globally improved its ability to teach students since 1970. The average level in secondary education tended to fall between 1970 and 2000, while a clear rise was observed over the last two decades (see also Fig. 6.12).

In addition to the long-term analysis (50 years), we have also calculated short-term variations (over the last 20 years). Here, the results confirm and amplify the upward trend, highlighting an acceleration in performance in all areas and levels since 2000 (column 7). Performance in mathematics at primary level has risen by around 40 points per decade over the last 20 years, while at secondary level it has risen by around 13 points per decade (although the latter is not significant). If we relate this variation to the equivalence in terms of years of acquisition, the effects are quite significant. While, over the long term, Türkiye has gained the equivalent of more than a year's acquisition in reading (range between 1.6 and 2.4 school years), the increase is just as significant over the short term (range between 1.9 and 2.8 school years). The increase at primary level is double that at secondary level (3 years vs. 1.6 school years respectively).

We know that the level of school skills is closely linked to the economic level of nations (Hanushek & Woessmann, 2015). Even if the relationship is less clear-cut, we might therefore logically expect better results within schools that are better endowed with financial resources (Hanushek, 2019). Moreover, in order to test the extent to which Türkiye's performance is in line with what might be expected given its economic level or the scale of its education spending, we carry out various tests. First, we carry out a graphical analysis of the correlations between each skill area and educational level and the economic wealth indicator. More specifically, we establish a correlation between educational performance and GDP per capita in dollars, adjusted by the purchasing power parity method.

Figure 6.3 illustrates the significant gap between Türkiye and other countries for the quality indicator, obtained by grouping all subjects and all levels.[18] While the expected score would be around 375 points, the actual score is around 450 points, which is 75 points higher than the score predicted by a simple prediction based on GDP per capita. The same comparison for the year 2020 shows a stronger correlation between economic level and school performance (the correlation coefficient is

[17] Most short- and long-term variations are significant at the 5% level. To conduct the significance test, we combined the standard errors ("S.E.") and calculated the threshold using the following formula:$threshold = \sqrt{E.S._{France}^2 + E.S._{OCDE}^2} \times 1{,}96$. If the corresponding difference is greater than this value, we deduce that the difference is significantly different from 0 at the 5% threshold. Significant data are indicated with an asterisk (*).

[18] This analysis was carried out for each skill area and grade level. Additional results can be found in Figures A.8-A.11.

Table 6.3 Trends in education quality and productivity effects

	(1)		(2)		(3)		(4)		(5)		(6)	
	Mean performance in score points											
	1970		1980		1990		2000		2010		2020	
	Level	s.e	Level	s.e	Level	s.e	Level	s.e	Level	s.e	Level	s.e
Mean	454	(5.7)	459	(4.9)	458	(4.9)	445	(4.9)	468	(4.8)	501	(2.0)
Primary	454	(5.6)	462	(4.7)	464	(4.7)	449	(4.7)	461	(4.7)	523	(4.8)
Reading	430	(4.4)	452	(3.5)	456	(3.5)	445	(3.5)	472	(3.1)	496	(3.1)
Math	475	(6.2)	469	(4.8)	473	(4.7)	454	(4.8)	460	(4.7)	534	(4.8)
Science	457	(5.3)	466	(4.7)	461	(4.7)	450	(4.7)	451	(4.7)	538	(4.5)
Secondary	453	(5.7)	456	(4.9)	452	(4.9)	441	(4.9)	474	(4.8)	480	(2.0)
Reading	411	(6.5)	435	(5.8)	439	(5.8)	432	(5.8)	468	(3.7)	461	(2.0)
Math	476	(6.0)	463	(4.9)	454	(4.9)	452	(4.9)	471	(4.8)	478	(2.0)
Science	472	(5.2)	469	(4.6)	462	(4.6)	441	(4.5)	485	(3.9)	501	(2.1)

	(7)			(8)			(9)	(10)	(11)	(12)
	Trends over time						Productivity effects			
	Short term			Long Term			Short term		Long term	
	Var	s.e		Var	s.e		L.B	U.B	L.B	U.B
Mean	28	(2.6)	*	10	(1.2)	*	1.9	2.8	1.6	2.4
Primary	37	(3.4)	*	14	(1.5)	*	2.4	3.7	2.3	3.4
Reading	26	(2.4)	*	13	(1.1)	*	1.7	2.6	2.2	3.3
Math	40	(3.4)	*	12	(1.6)	*	2.7	4.0	2.0	3.0
Science	44	(3.2)	*	16	(1.4)	*	3.0	4.4	2.7	4.0
Secondary	19	(2.6)	*	5	(1.2)	*	1.3	1.9	0.9	1.3
Reading	15	(3.1)	*	10	(1.4)	*	1.0	1.5	1.6	2.5
Math	13	(2.6)	*	0	(1.3)		0.9	1.3	0.1	0.1
Science	30	(2.5)	*	6	(1.1)	*	2.0	3.0	1.0	1.4

Source authors' calculations based on Altinok and Diebolt (2024, 2025)

0.44), while Türkiye manages to perform better than expected if we consider a linear relationship between economic level and education quality (501 vs. 475).

To gain a better understanding of this potential performance gap, we regress performance on the economic level of each country. Beyond the coefficient associated with this last variable, it is the residual attached to each country that attracts our attention (Table 6.4).

In each regression, we associate a particular dimension of educational skills with GDP per capita. Since the data are panel data, this enables us to obtain country fixed effects that are not explained by the economic wealth indicator. Of the 20 countries included in the sample,[19] Türkiye's ranking is often in the top five, underlining its

[19] For some regressions, the number of countries is less than 20, due to missing values.

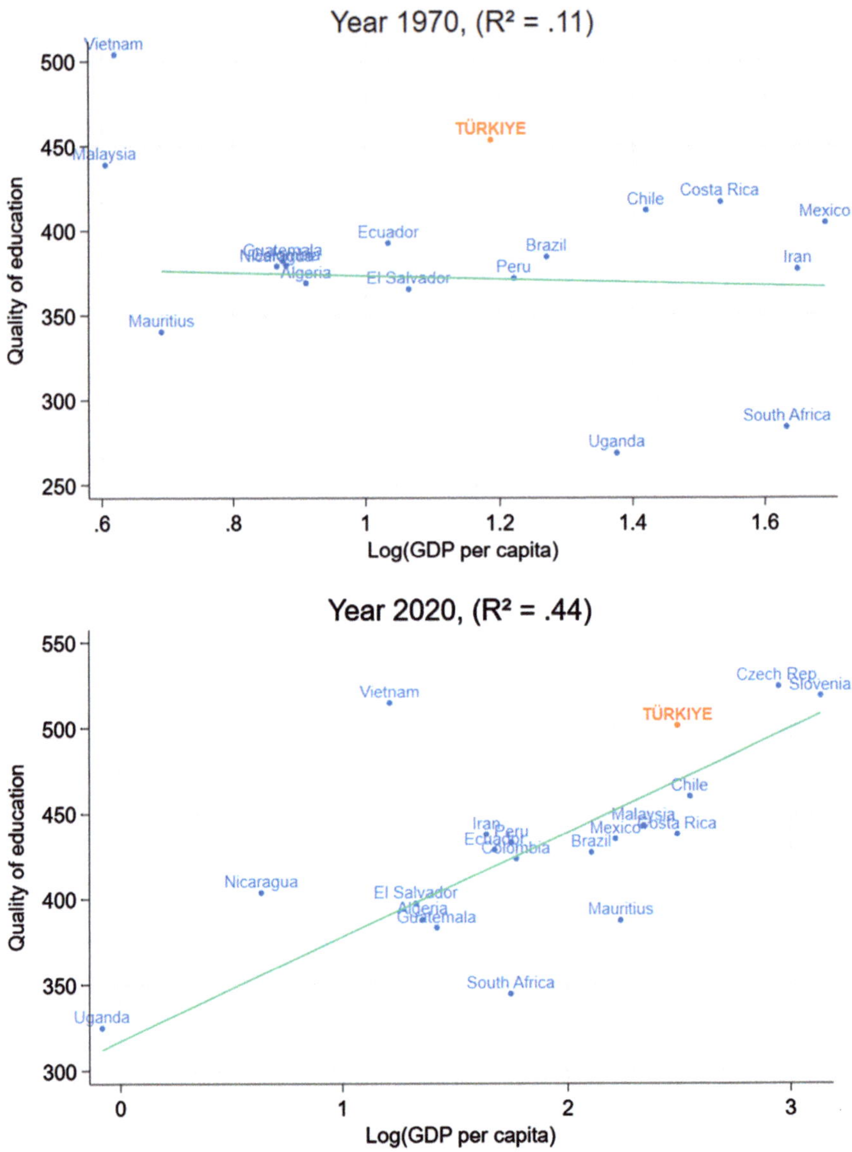

Fig. 6.3 Relationship between GDP per capita and quality of education. (DEV-20 countries). *Source* authors' calculations based on Altinok and Diebolt (2024, 2025)

Table 6.4 School performance and economic level of countries

	(1)	(2)	(3)	(4)	(5)	(6)	(7)	(8)	(9)
log(GDP pc)	50.232***	12.696**	36.279***	37.437***	28.401***	34.483***	99.190***	41.456***	77.492***
	(2.404)	(6.454)	(5.649)	(6.105)	(7.481)	(3.622)	(3.152)	(8.214)	(4.271)
Intercept	294.023***	383.119***	344.413***	317.415***	368.244***	328.309***	99.457***	94.317***	124.756***
	(8.770)	(12.309)	(12.475)	(13.285)	(11.745)	(7.596)	(16.608)	(28.489)	(15.541)
Level	Primary	Secondary	Both	Both	Both	Both	Primary (adj.)	Secondary (adj.)	Both (adj.)
Skill	All	All	Reading	Maths	Sciences	All	All	All	All
Adjusted	No	No	No	No	No	No	Yes	Yes	Yes
R-squared	0.53	0.10	0.31	0.31	0.22	0.30	0.68	0.45	0.56
Observations	502	433	293	337	305	935	502	427	929
Nb. countries	17	17	20	19	20	20	17	17	20
1970–2020									
Ranking	3	5	5	5	5	5	4	4	4
Residuals	−16.10	−19.82	−4.90	−28.89	−18.86	−17.99	39.17	123.97	81.50
Best ranked	Czech Rep	Czech Rep	Czech Rep	Czech Rep	Vietnam	Czech Rep	Uganda	Vietnam	Vietnam
2000–2020									
Ranking	2	4	4	4	4	4	6	4	3
Residuals	10.39	22.48	30.30	6.71	13.19	16.33	13.15	87.21	50.62
Best ranked	Czech Rep	Vietnam	Vietnam	Vietnam	Vietnam	Vietnam	Nicaragua	Vietnam	Vietnam

Source authors' calculations based on Altinok and Diebolt (2024, 2025)

higher score than would be expected if its economic level were taken into account. In fact, it should be remembered that the residual ranking allows us to measure what is not taken into account in the model, namely economic level.

In almost all regressions, the Czech Republic and Vietnam show the highest residuals. The latter country, which is often highlighted in PISA studies, performs much better than it should, taking into account its economic level (Boman, 2022; Parandekar & Sedmik, 2016; World Bank, 2011). For Türkiye, the ranking highlights a higher-than-expected performance in all cases over the short term, while a certain lag can be noted in the long-term data (see lines "Period 1970–2020" and "Period 2000–2020" for the long and short term, respectively). These results confirm those recently published for TIMSS 2023 (Polat et al., 2024) and PISA 2022 (OECD, 2023b). By way of illustration, the results of the regression between reading and economic level suggest an "over-performance" of around 30 points in the short term (column 3), once economic level is taken into account. As pointed out earlier (Avvisati & Givord, 2023), this difference is equivalent to a year of schooling gained for Türkiye. It should be noted, however, that even if Türkiye's "over-performance" appeared in the 2000s, it seems to go beyond a simple catch-up effect, since the residuals are all positive in the short term. Moreover, these differences in residuals are based on fixed effects and controlled for economic level. It therefore seems highly likely that the explanations for Türkiye's gap lie in structural rather than cyclical causes, and that they can be explained in particular by the educational reforms carried out since the early 2000s. Over the long term, however, the results are more mixed. Residuals are mostly negative (columns 1 to 6).

As previously mentioned, using the quality of education indicator alone can hide disparities in enrollment rates. A country may perform well on student achievement surveys mainly due to an educational policy aimed at selecting only the best students (Spaull, 2018). To circumvent this potential selection bias, we multiply the score in each domain and school level by the corresponding school completion rate. Thus, the average score at primary level is multiplied by the primary completion rate (column 7), while we use the total average score multiplied by the secondary completion rate thereafter (column 9). Türkiye's position among the residuals declines slightly, confirming our earlier findings of a certain lag in school completion (column 7). However, when all dimensions are taken into account, Türkiye's ranking returns to a rather good position (3rd place, column 9). This confirms that Türkiye's success is not solely due to a policy of selecting the best students and leaving the poorest out of the education system. The 2012 reform aimed at extending compulsory schooling to grade 12 may have had a strong impact on achieving universal enrollment. This reform restructured the Turkish education system into three stages of four years each: four years of primary education, four years of lower secondary education, and four years of upper secondary education (Köseleci, 2015).

A similar approach using an alternative indicator—educational expenditure as a percentage of GDP per capita—leads to similar conclusions (see Table 6.12). Indeed, when comparing countries according to their level of educational expenditure, Türkiye is ahead of other developing countries in the short term, while the opposite is true in the long term.

6.3.2 A Convergence of Educational Performance Achieved and Surpassed

The various results of international assessments all point to an increase in performance in mathematics and science over almost two decades (OECD, 2023a). In order to confirm or refute this trend, we have focused on the evolution of performance in the different skill areas and the two school levels since 1970, for countries with similar characteristics to Türkiye.

We note that a clear upward trend does indeed seem to have taken place in Türkiye since the early 2000s, whereas its ranking was average in earlier periods (see Table 6.3). Previously, we observed a long-term upward trend in school performance in Türkiye, but also an acceleration over the last two decades for all skill domains (Sect. 3.1). We feel it is important to compare these variations with other developing countries (Table 6.5). To do this, we calculate for each skill area, and for each year, the difference between Türkiye's performance and that of the average of the 20 developing countries included in our sample (i.e. DEV-20). The difference is standardized and expressed in terms of standard deviation. Since our database has a standard deviation of 100, the calculation for standardization is done by dividing the performance gap by 100. While Türkiye had a primary math score of 475 in 1970, compared with an average of 356 points for DEV-20, the performance gap is 119 points, or 1.19 standard deviations in Türkiye's favor. Almost always, Türkiye's performance is superior to that of the DEV-20 average (i.e. the coefficients in columns 1–3 are all positive). The significance of deviations from the mean can be approximated by estimating the threshold at which the deviation becomes significant. The threshold is calculated by adding the standard errors and weighting them by the 5% error threshold.[20] Thus, in Table 6.5, relative differences in performance that are significant at the 5% threshold are indicated in bold and followed by an asterisk (*).

We also calculate the variation in performance for the short (20 years) and long term (50 years). Columns 8–11 of Table 6.5 highlight that the variation in Turkish performance is fairly close to the DEV-20 country average over the long term (columns 10 and 11), even if progress is slightly higher for Türkiye. In the short term, however, the amplitude of the effects is different: while performance increases in almost all areas and school levels for the average DEV-20 country, the variation is more sustained in Türkiye. On average, primary school performance in DEV-20 countries improves by around 13 points per decade in the short term, while in Türkiye it rises by over 36 points. We note that Türkiye's performance gaps are greater at primary level than at secondary level. Explaining these differences by school level would require further research, which is beyond the scope of our study. However, it is possible to put forward a number of hypotheses that seem credible

[20] To conduct the significance test, we combined the standard errors ("S.E.") and calculated the threshold using the following formula: $hreshold = \sqrt{E.S._{Türkiye}^{2} + E.S._{DEV20}^{2}} \times 1{,}96$. If the difference between Türkiye and the DEV20 countries is greater than this value, we deduce that the difference is significantly different from 0 at the 5% threshold.

Table 6.5 Counterfactual analysis of Türkiye's performance on average education quality scores

	(1)		(2)		(3)		(4)		(5)		(6)		(7)	
	Standardized difference						1970				2020			
	1970		2000		2020		TUR	s.e	DEV	s.e	TUR	s.e	DEV	s.e
Mean	0.69	*	0.31	*	0.70	*	454	(5.7)	385	(4.8)	501	(2.0)	431	(2.4)
Primary	0.83	*	0.44	*	0.91	*	454	(5.6)	371	(4.6)	523	(4.8)	432	(2.5)
Reading	0.48	*	0.22	*	0.53	*	430	(4.4)	382	(4.7)	496	(3.1)	443	(2.4)
Math	1.19	*	0.68	*	1.13	*	475	(6.2)	356	(4.7)	534	(4.8)	421	(2.5)
Science	0.56	*	0.18	*	0.80	*	457	(5.3)	401	(4.9)	538	(4.5)	458	(2.4)
Secondary	0.58	*	0.16	*	0.45	*	453	(5.7)	395	(4.9)	480	(2.0)	435	(2.6)
Reading	0.21	*	0.04		0.22	*	411	(6.5)	390	(4.8)	461	(2.0)	439	(2.7)
Math	0.73	*	0.21	*	0.43	*	476	(6.0)	403	(4.9)	478	(2.0)	435	(2.6)
Science	0.63	*	0.01		0.49	*	472	(5.2)	409	(5.1)	501	(2.1)	452	(2.7)

	(8)			(9)			(10)			(11)			(12)			(13)		
	Short term trends						Long term trends						Short term			Long term		
	TUR	s.e		DEV	s.e		TUR	s.e		DEV	s.e		DinD	s.e		DinD	s.e	
Mean	28.0	(5.3)	*	8.2	(4.3)		9.5	(6.1)		9.2	(5.4)		19.8	(3.3)	*	0.3	(0.6)	
Primary	36.7	(6.8)	*	13.2	(4.2)	*	13.7	(7.4)		12.2	(5.2)	*	23.4	(3.9)	*	1.6	(0.7)	*
Reading	25.8	(4.7)	*	10.0	(4.4)	*	13.3	(5.4)	*	12.1	(5.3)	*	15.8	(3.1)	*	1.2	(0.6)	*
Math	39.9	(6.8)	*	17.6	(4.2)	*	11.8	(7.9)		13.0	(5.4)	*	22.3	(3.9)	*	–1.2	(0.7)	*
Science	44.4	(6.5)	*	13.2	(4.3)	*	16.2	(6.9)	*	11.3	(5.4)	*	31.2	(3.8)	*	4.9	(0.7)	*
Secondary	19.2	(5.3)	*	4.8	(4.5)		5.3	(6.0)		7.9	(5.5)		14.4	(3.4)	*	–2.6	(0.6)	*
Reading	14.6	(6.1)	*	6.0	(4.5)		9.9	(6.8)		9.8	(5.5)		8.7	(3.7)	*	0.1	(0.7)	
Math	13.3	(5.3)	*	2.3	(4.5)		0.3	(6.3)		6.3	(5.5)		11.0	(3.4)	*	–6.0	(0.7)	*
Science	29.8	(5.0)	*	6.1	(4.7)		5.8	(5.6)		8.5	(5.8)		23.7	(3.3)	*	–2.8	(0.6)	*

Source authors' calculations based on Altinok and Diebolt (2024, 2025)

to us, such as the fact that the primary education system performs better than the secondary level, a more optimal allocation of primary school teachers (particularly in the field of mathematics), but also a "survey" effect specific to the data available: as Türkiye participates more in the PISA surveys than in the IEA assessments, the smaller gap observed at secondary level would suggest the difference in approach used in the surveys. PISA focuses more on skills, while the IEA emphasizes knowledge based on common curricula (Wu, 2010). It is also possible that the selective nature of secondary education in Türkiye reinforces inequalities and lowers average performance (Alacacı & Erbaş, 2010; Dincer & Uysal, 2010; Özdemir, 2015; Sarıer, 2021).

The results of relative differences provide arguments in favor of an improvement in Türkiye's performance in almost all levels and skill areas. The analysis of double differences tempers these results, particularly over the long term, and reinforces the idea of a catch-up phenomenon in terms of educational quality (column 13), particularly at secondary level. In fact, the progress observed in Türkiye is lower than that observed in the DEV-20 countries at this level of education, while the level of performance is higher in Türkiye than in these countries. In the short term, however, convergence does not seem to be taking place: Türkiye seems to be breaking away from the group of developing countries with a clear increase in its performance at both school levels. Over the last two decades, Türkiye appears to be moving closer to the group of OECD average performers.

In Fig. 6.4, we refine the variation in school performance. We hypothesize that the countries in our sample with an initial competence deficit will have a more sustained rise in performance in subsequent decades. This convergence hypothesis can already be partially verified in Table 6.5, since Türkiye's relative lag is narrowing in most skill areas.[21] To verify this intuition, we cross-reference the initial level of educational measures with their variation in standardized form (i.e. expressed in standard deviations). The hypothesis of convergence is rather confirmed, as the slope of the regression line is negative in all quadrants. More specifically, we are testing the convergence of three education indicators: a quantitative education indicator, i.e. the secondary school completion rate; a learning achievement indicator; and a hybrid indicator combining education quality with the secondary school completion rate.

Although Türkiye initially lagged behind in terms of access to education (it was on the negative side of the x-axis for completion rate in 1970), its position has improved markedly since then, confirming the convergence hypothesis for this indicator (first dimension: "completion rate"). This convergence is confirmed and even exceeded in the short term (2000–2020). For example, Türkiye has been catching up with other countries in terms of completion since the 2000s, while this indicator seems to be increasing by around 0.5 standard deviations in Türkiye, if we take into account the average variation of the DEV-20 countries (Quadrant A). Quantitative performance

[21] This catching-up may initially be explained by a pure convergence effect, but other reasons could also explain it. The search for explanatory factors would require more detailed work on the variables involved in the educational production function, and the production of so-called multilevel models.

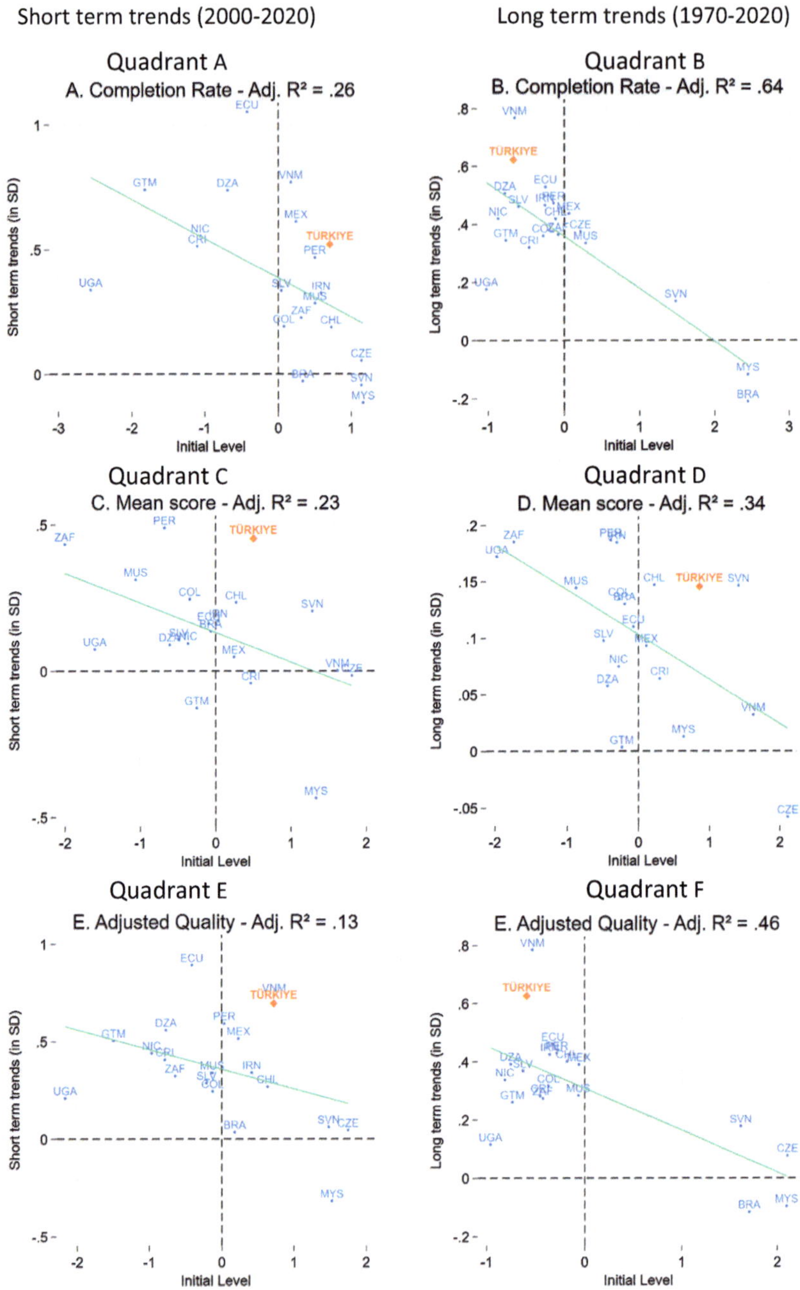

Fig. 6.4 Hypothesis of convergence of educational indicators in DEV-20 countries. *Source* authors' calculations based on Altinok and Diebolt (2024, 2025)

therefore appears to exceed that observed in other developing countries. Furthermore, the advance in learning achievement observed at the beginning of the period seems to be confirmed regardless of the period analyzed (positive ordinate values in Quadrants C & D. Moreover, this relative advance in educational attainment seems to have strengthened over time since the 2000s (positive ordinate in Quadrant C and a value close to 0.5 standard deviations). Our comparison between the initial level and variation on the hybrid quality-adjusted indicator reinforces these results: the low initial level tends to be reduced from the beginning of the twenty-first century (Quadrant F), and Türkiye's positive gap with other countries is clearly reinforced over the last two decades (Quadrant E).

6.3.3 Robustness Tests

The previous results point to a progression in educational performance in terms of quality in Türkiye, particularly over the last two decades, even after taking exogenous variations into account. In this section, we undertake calculations using the same methodology, but verifying the real potential progress of the Turkish education system across other dimensions.

Table 6.6 shows the trend in the proportion of Turkish pupils achieving the minimum and advanced proficiency levels (MPL and APL respectively).[22] The share of students reaching the minimum performance threshold rose from 72 to 89% on average between 1970 and 2020, i.e. a total increase of 17%, or an increase per decade of around 3%. This share accelerates in the short term, with the increase per decade rising from around 3% to an average of 4%. The results for the advanced skills threshold confirm those for the minimum skills threshold in terms of the acceleration observed. While average growth per decade is 0% over the long term, it has risen to 1.9% over the last two decades.

Beyond the performance thresholds, we also use the LAYS (learning-adjusted years of schooling) indicator, originally developed by Filmer et al. (2020). This indicator is calculated by combining the average education quality score and the number of years of schooling. The rise in the mixed indicator of school years adjusted by education quality shows a sharp increase since 1970: the average number of years has risen from 1.7 to 5.8 over the half-century studied. An additional measure concerns the school completion rate by level. The most significant change concerns the secondary school completion rate, which increased from 14% in 1970 to almost 100% in 2020. By crossing the completion rate and the average score, we obtain the adjusted measures of the quality of schooling. Adjusted quality thus rises from an average of 62 points to almost 501 points over the half-century.

[22] Only three dimensions of each measure are presented, in order to show the results of various indicators. However, these dimensions reflect averages and thus make it possible to synthesize the results obtained. The results for each dimension are available on request from the authors.

Table 6.6 Robustness analysis, part 1. Trends in performance thresholds and enrollment indicators

	(1)		(2)		(3)		(4)		(5)		(6)	
	Mean performance in score points											
	1970		1980		1990		2000		2010		2000	
	Level	s.e.	Level	s.e.	Level	s.e.	Level	s.e.	Level	s.e.	Level	s.e.
Minimum Prof. Level												
Mean	72	(5.0)	74	(4.9)	82	(4.9)	80	(4.9)	82	(4.8)	89	(2.0)
Primary	71	(4.9)	70	(4.7)	81	(4.7)	79	(4.7)	76	(4.7)	89	(4.8)
Secondary	74	(5.0)	79	(4.9)	84	(4.9)	81	(4.9)	88	(4.8)	88	(2.0)
Advanced Proficiency Level												
Mean	6.9	(4.9)	6.0	(4.9)	5.6	(4.9)	4.5	(4.9)	4.3	(4.8)	8.3	(2.0)
Primary	5.6	(4.7)	5.7	(4.7)	5.9	(4.7)	4.3	(4.7)	3.3	(4.7)	11.1	(4.8)
Secondary	8.2	(4.9)	6.4	(4.9)	5.2	(4.9)	4.7	(4.9)	5.4	(4.8)	5.4	(2.0)
School attainment												
Years of schooling	2.6	(0.0)	3.8	(0.0)	5.2	(0.0)	6.4	(0.0)	7.4	(0.0)	8.1	(0.0)
LAYS	1.7	(5.7)	2.5	(4.9)	3.4	(4.9)	4.1	(4.9)	5.0	(4.8)	5.8	(2.0)
Completion, pri.	91	(0.0)	88	(0.0)	95	(0.0)	97	(0.0)	99	(0.0)	99	(0.0)
Completion, sec.	14	(0.0)	24	(0.0)	35	(0.0)	79	(0.0)	100	(0.0)	100	(0.0)
Adjusted measures of quality of schooling												
Mean	62	(5.7)	108	(4.9)	162	(4.9)	354	(4.9)	468	(4.8)	501	(2.0)
Primary	414	(5.6)	408	(4.7)	440	(4.7)	435	(4.7)	456	(4.7)	517	(4.8)
Secondary	62	(5.7)	107	(4.9)	160	(4.9)	350	(4.9)	474	(4.8)	480	(2.0)

	(7)			(8)			(9)	(10)	(11)	(12)
	Trends over time						Productivity effects			
	Short term			Long term			Short term		Long term	
	Var	s.e.		Var	s.e.		L.B.	U.B.	L.B.	U.B.
Minimum prof. level										
Mean	4	(2.6)		3	(1.1)	*	0.3	0.4	0.5	0.8
Primary	5	(3.4)		4	(1.4)	*	0.3	0.5	0.6	0.9
Secondary	4	(2.6)		3	(1.1)	*	0.2	0.4	0.5	0.7
Advanced proficiency level										
Mean	1.9	(2.6)		0.3	(1.1)		0.1	0.2	0.0	0.1
Primary	3.4	(3.4)		1.1	(1.4)		0.2	0.3	0.2	0.3
Secondary	0.4	(2.6)		-0.6	(1.1)		0.0	0.0	-0.1	-0.1
School attainment										
Years of schooling	0.9	(0.0)	*	1.1	(0.0)	*	0.1	0.1	0.2	0.3
LAYS	0.9	(2.6)		0.8	(1.2)		0.1	0.1	0.1	0.2

(continued)

Table 6.6 (continued)

	(7)			(8)			(9)	(10)	(11)	(12)
	Trends over time						Productivity effects			
	Short term			Long term			Short term		Long term	
	Var	s.e.		Var	s.e.		L.B.	U.B.	L.B.	U.B.
Completion, pri.	1.1	(0.0)	*	1.6	(0.0)	*	0.1	0.1	0.3	0.4
Completion, sec.	10.3	(0.0)	*	17.2	(0.0)	*	0.7	1.0	2.9	4.3
Adjusted measures of quality of schooling										
Mean	74	(2.6)	*	88	(1.2)	*	4.9	7.4	14.6	21.9
Primary	41	(3.4)	*	21	(1.5)	*	2.7	4.1	3.5	5.2
Secondary	65	(2.6)	*	83	(1.2)	*	4.3	6.5	13.9	20.9

Source authors' calculations based on Altinok and Diebolt (2024, 2025)

It is now important to compare this trend with that observed in other developing countries (Table 6.7). The performance threshold indicators all point to higher performance in Türkiye. The double-difference method confirms these results, particularly in the short term. For example, the share of students reaching the minimum performance threshold increased more in secondary school in Türkiye than in the DEV-20 countries, by around 3.6% to Türkiye's advantage per decade. At the primary level, the increase observed in Türkiye is the same as that observed in the other countries (i.e. the double-difference variation is then equal to 0, see column 12 and the line on the minimum performance threshold at the primary level). As expected, the strong growth in the secondary school completion rate underlines Türkiye's strong performance, which is, however, not yet visible through the LAYS indicator, which uses the number of school years. Finally, the analysis of the quality indicator adjusted by the completion rate shows Türkiye's higher relative performance at all levels, even if it is stronger at the secondary level. For example, education quality adjusted by completion rate at the secondary level increases by 37.6 points more per decade in Türkiye than in the other developing countries in our sample.

It is possible to analyze the extent to which efficiency and equity have varied in Türkiye compared to other developing countries. Türkiye appears to be performing well on both dimensions in 2020 (Fig. 6.5). The efficiency of an education system is measured by combining the shares of students reaching the minimum and advanced proficiency thresholds (see Eq. 6.1). School efficiency increases by around 100 points in Türkiye over half a century, from 431 to 526 points (Table 6.8). The increase is more marked at the primary level (146 points) than at the secondary level (44 points). This rise seems to have accelerated over the last two decades (41 points per decade, column 7) compared with the long-term variation (19 points, column 8). The evolution of equity, measured by the gap relative to the median between the extreme deciles (see Eq. 6.2), highlights a decline in equity since 1970. Indeed, average equity fell from 589 to 540 points between 1970 and 2020. The decline is even more marked in secondary schools, where it falls from 628 to 547 points over

Table 6.7 Robustness analysis, part 2. Counterfactual analysis of performance thresholds and enrollment indicators

	(1)		(2)		(3)		(4)		(5)		(6)		(7)	
	Standardized difference						1970				2020			
	1970		2000		2020		TUR	s.e	DEV	s.e	TUR	s.e	DEV	s.e
Minimum Profiency Level														
Mean	0.19	*	0.17	*	0.21	*	72	(5.0)	53	(3.9)	89	(2.0)	68	(2.4)
Primary	0.30	*	0.25	*	0.25	*	71	(4.9)	41	(3.6)	89	(4.8)	64	(2.5)
Secondary	0.11		0.08		0.15	*	74	(5.0)	63	(4.2)	88	(2.0)	73	(2.6)
Advanced Proficiency Level														
Mean	0.03		0.01		0.05		7	(4.9)	4	(3.8)	8	(2.0)	3	(2.4)
Primary	0.04		0.02		0.09		6	(4.7)	1	(3.4)	11	(4.8)	2	(2.5)
Secondary	0.02		0.00		0.01		8	(4.9)	7	(4.1)	5	(2.0)	4	(2.6)
School attainment														
Years of sch	–0.02	*	–0.01	*	–0.01	*	2.6	(0.0)	4.1	(0.0)	8.1	(0.0)	9.4	(0.0)
LAYS	0.00		–0.01		0.00		1.7	(5.7)	2.0	(4.8)	5.8	(2.0)	5.9	(2.4)
Compl., pri	0.28	*	0.08	*	0.05	*	91	(0.0)	63	(0.0)	99	(0.0)	94	(0.0)
Compl., sec	–0.17	*	0.14	*	0.19	*	14	(0.0)	31	(0.0)	100	(0.0)	81	(0.0)
Adjusted measures of quality of schooling														
Mean	–0.56	*	0.77	*	1.48	*	62	(5.7)	119	(4.8)	501	(2.0)	353	(2.4)
Primary	1.80	*	0.73	*	1.09	*	414	(5.6)	234	(4.6)	517	(4.8)	408	(2.5)
Secondary	–0.78	*	0.39	*	1.14	*	62	(5.7)	141	(4.9)	480	(2.0)	366	(2.6)

(continued)

Table 6.7 (continued)

	(8)			(9)			(10)			(11)			(12)			(13)		
	Short term trends (S.T.)						Long term trends (L.T.)						Difference in difference					
	TUR	s.e		DEV	s.e		TUR	s.e		DEV	s.e		S.T	s.e		L.T	s.e	
Minimum Profiency Level																		
Mean	4.3	(2.6)		2.4	(2.1)		3.3	(1.1)	*	2.9	(0.9)	*	2.0	(1.7)		0.4	(0.3)	
Primary	5.1	(3.4)		5.1	(2.1)	*	3.6	(1.4)	*	4.6	(0.9)	*	0.0	(2.0)		–0.9	(0.3)	*
Secondary	3.6	(2.6)		0.0	(2.3)		2.9	(1.1)	*	2.0	(1.0)	*	3.6	(1.7)	*	0.9	(0.3)	*
Advanced Proficiency Level																		
Mean	1.9	(2.6)		0.0	(2.1)		0.3	(1.1)		–0.1	(0.9)		1.9	(1.7)		0.4	(0.3)	
Primary	3.4	(3.4)		0.3	(2.1)		1.1	(1.4)		0.2	(0.8)		3.1	(2.0)		0.9	(0.3)	*
Secondary	0.4	(2.6)		–0.3	(2.3)		–0.6	(1.1)		–0.5	(1.0)		0.7	(1.7)		–0.1	(0.3)	
School attainment																		
Years of sch	0.9	(0.0)	*	0.9	(0.0)	*	1.1	(0.0)	*	1.1	(0.0)	*	0.0	(0.0)	*	0.0	(0.0)	*
LAYS	0.9	(2.6)		0.6	(2.2)		0.8	(1.2)		0.8	(1.1)		0.2	(1.7)		0.0	(0.3)	
Compl., pri	1.1	(0.0)	*	2.3	(0.0)	*	1.6	(0.0)	*	6.1	(0.0)	*	–1.2	(0.0)	*	–4.5	(0.0)	*
Compl., sec	10.3	(0.0)	*	7.6	(0.0)	*	17.2	(0.0)	*	10.0	(0.0)	*	2.7	(0.0)	*	7.3	(0.0)	*
Adjusted measures of quality of schooling																		
Mean	73.8	(2.6)	*	38.2	(2.2)	=	87.8	(1.2)	*	47.0	(1.1)	*	35.6	(1.7)	*	40.8	(0.3)	*
Primary	41.1	(3.4)	*	22.8	(2.1)	=	20.7	(1.5)	*	34.8	(1.0)	*	18.3	(2.0)	*	–14.1	(0.4)	*
Secondary	64.7	(2.6)	*	27.1	(2.3)	=	83.5	(1.2)	*	45.0	(1.1)	*	37.6	(1.7)	*	38.5	(0.3)	*

Source authors' calculations based on Altinok and Diebolt (2024, 2025)

the same period. This can be explained by the rise in school enrollment rates among the least affluent populations. The democratization of education has increased school enrollment among the poorest and could therefore explain the rise in the gap between the extreme deciles. To test this, we adjust the equity indicator to take into account the school completion rate (Eq. 6.3). We then see that the adjusted equity index increases significantly in both educational levels. The increase is more marked over the recent period for the secondary level. It is possible that the rise in enrollment rates explains the increase in the gap between the extreme deciles.

We compare these variations with those observed in the other countries in our sample (Table 6.9). Almost all the coefficients are positive in the first three columns, suggesting that the variations observed in Türkiye are stronger than those in other developing countries. For example, while efficiency is equal to 526 points in Türkiye in 2020, it is only 371 points in the DEV-20 panel of countries. While for each decade, school efficiency increases by 40.7 points in Türkiye between 2000 and 2020, it is only 12 points for the DEV-20 countries, leading to a positive result for the double-difference method (+28.7%). The results for equity suggest a weaker performance for Türkiye if we disregard enrollment levels, particularly in secondary education (-36.7% gap in the short term). Once enrollment levels are taken into account (adjusted equity indicator), the gap remains negative, but its amplitude is divided by three (-11.7% versus -36.7%). This means that the issue of inequality in the Turkish education system is not solely due to mass schooling, but also to other factors specific to Türkiye, such as a policy of segregation between schools (Dincer & Uysal, 2010).

6.3.4 Projection Model

In Sect. 2.3.2, we presented the projection model initially developed by Hanushek and Woessmann (2012) and then updated in Gust et al. (2024).[23] We use this model to predict the growth Türkiye would experience if it succeeded in meeting targets for improving its education system. The parameters we use are those developed in Gust et al. (2024). We consider the gains obtained from an education policy over a period of 80 years (S), which leads to the year 2100. This period is roughly equivalent to the life expectancy of a child born in Türkiye at the start of the reform. The discount rate in our base model is set at 3%, a standard value in long-term projection models (see, for example, Borsch-Supan (2000)).

We first assume a growth in education quality of the order of 50 points, or 0.50 standard deviations (scenario 1). According to our estimates, and adopting the parameters presented in Table 6.10, we find that such a policy to improve the quality of Türkiye's education system should increase its GDP by 68% by 2100 (see Table 6.11). The gain from educational reform would thus be 736% of Türkiye's current GDP (i.e.

[23] We would like to thank S. Gust, E. Hanushek and L. Woessmann for providing us with the Stata codes to replicate and adjust the projection model.

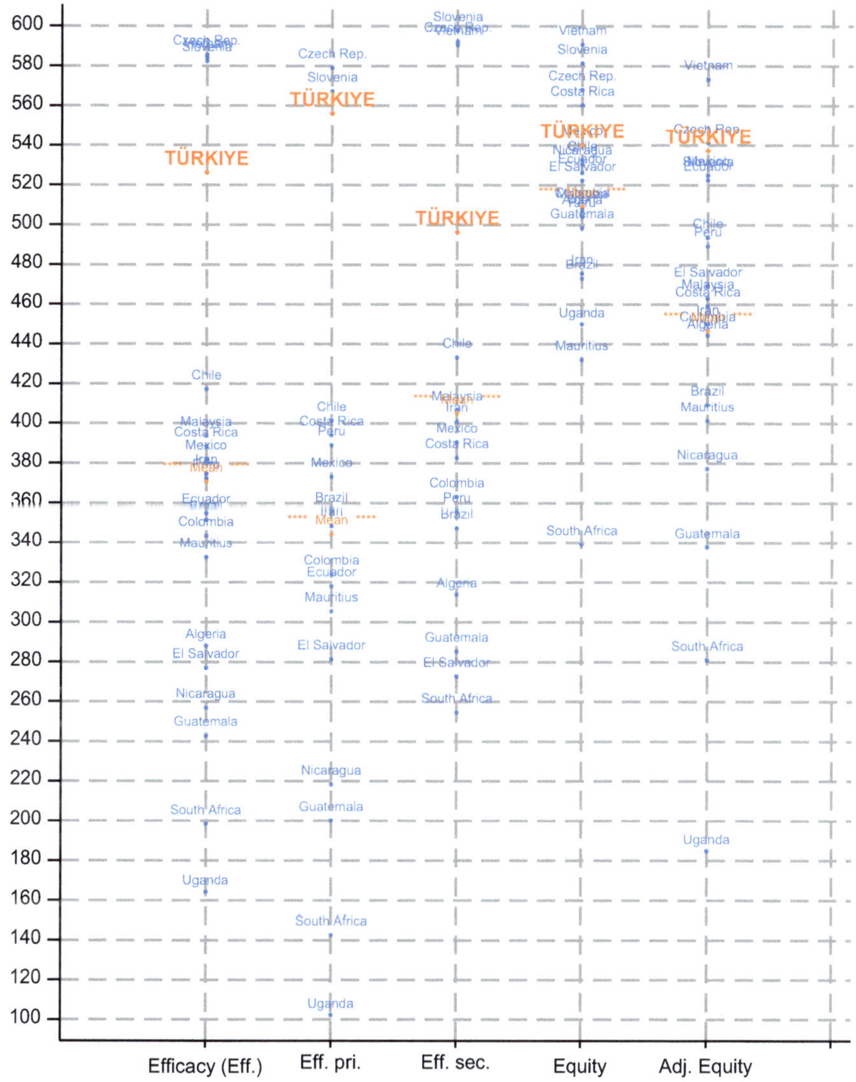

Fig. 6.5 Efficiency and equity in Türkiye's education systems and DEV-20 countries in 2020. *Source* authors' calculations based on Altinok and Diebolt (2024, 2025). "Eff." = Efficacy, "pri." = primary; "sec." = secondary, "Adj." = Adjusted

Table 6.8 Robustness analysis, part 3. Trends in education system efficiency and equity indices

	(1)		(2)		(3)		(4)		(5)		(6)		(7)			(8)			(9)	(10)	(11)	(12)
	Performance in score points												Trends over time						Productivity effects			
	1970		1980		1990		2000		2010		2020		Short term			Long Term			Short term		Long term	
	Level	s.e	Level	s.e	Level	s.e	Level	s.e	Level	s.e	Level	s.e	Var	s.e		Var	s.e		L.B	U.B	L.B	U.B
Efficacy																						
Both levels	431	(0.0)	432	(0.0)	468	(0.0)	445	(0.0)	454	(0.0)	526	(0.0)	41	(0.0)	*	19	(0.0)	*	2.7	4.1	3.2	4.8
Primary	410	(0.0)	406	(0.0)	463	(0.0)	437	(0.0)	414	(0.0)	556	(0.0)	60	(0.0)	*	29	(0.0)	*	4.0	6.0	4.9	7.3
Secondary	453	(0.0)	458	(0.0)	472	(0.0)	453	(0.0)	493	(0.0)	497	(0.0)	22	(0.0)	*	9	(0.0)	*	1.4	2.2	1.5	2.2
Equity																						
Both levels	589	(0.0)	538	(0.0)	515	(0.0)	528	(0.0)	521	(0.0)	540	(0.0)	6	(0.0)	*	–10	(0.0)	*	0.4	0.6	–1.6	–2.5
Primary	551	(0.0)	498	(0.0)	479	(0.0)	460	(0.0)	491	(0.0)	533	(0.0)	37	(0.0)	*	–4	(0.0)	*	2.4	3.7	–0.6	–0.9
Secondary	628	(0.0)	578	(0.0)	551	(0.0)	596	(0.0)	551	(0.0)	547	(0.0)	–24	(0.0)	*	–16	(0.0)	*	–1.6	–2.4	–2.7	–4.1
Equity (adjusted)																						
Both levels	294	(0.0)	288	(0.0)	325	(0.0)	459	(0.0)	518	(0.0)	538	(0.0)	39	(0.0)	*	49	(0.0)	*	2.6	3.9	8.1	12.2
Primary	502	(0.0)	440	(0.0)	454	(0.0)	445	(0.0)	486	(0.0)	528	(0.0)	41	(0.0)	*	5	(0.0)	*	2.8	4.1	0.9	1.3
Secondary	87	(0.0)	136	(0.0)	195	(0.0)	473	(0.0)	551	(0.0)	547	(0.0)	37	(0.0)	*	92	(0.0)	*	2.5	3.7	15.4	23.0

Source authors' calculations based on Altinok and Diebolt (2024, 2025)

Table 6.9 Robustness analysis, part 4. Counterfactual analysis of education system efficiency and equity indices

	(1)		(2)		(3)		(4)		(5)		(6)		(7)	
	Standardized difference						1970				2020			
	1970		2000		2020		TUR	s.e	DEV	s.e	TUR	s.e	DEV	s.e
Efficacy														
Both levels	1.27	*	0.98	*	1.55	*	431	(0.0)	305	(0.0)	526	(0.0)	371	(0.0)
Primary	1.89	*	1.49	*	2.12	*	410	(0.0)	221	(0.0)	556	(0.0)	345	(0.0)
Secondary	0.72	*	0.41	*	0.91	*	453	(0.0)	381	(0.0)	497	(0.0)	405	(0.0)
Equity														
Both levels	1.42	*	0.56	*	0.31	*	589	(0.0)	447	(0.0)	540	(0.0)	510	(0.0)
Primary	1.26	*	0.08	*	0.31	*	551	(0.0)	425	(0.0)	533	(0.0)	502	(0.0)
Secondary	1.59	*	1.04	*	0.30	*	628	(0.0)	469	(0.0)	547	(0.0)	517	(0.0)
Equity (adjusted)														
Both levels	0.94	*	0.95	*	0.91	*	294	(0.0)	200	(0.0)	538	(0.0)	447	(0.0)
Primary	2.42	*	0.38	*	0.53	*	502	(0.0)	259	(0.0)	528	(0.0)	475	(0.0)
Secondary	-0.55	*	1.52	*	1.29	*	87	(0.0)	141	(0.0)	547	(0.0)	419	(0.0)

	(8)			(9)			(10)			(11)			(12)			(13)		
	Short term trends						Long term trends						Short term			Long term		
	TUR	s.e		DEV	s.e		TUR	s.e		DEV	s.e		DinD	s.e		DinD	s.e	
Efficacy																		
Both levels	40.7	(0.0)	*	12.0	(0.0)	*	19.0	(0.0)	*	13.3	(0.0)	*	28.7	(0.0)	*	5.7	(0.0)	*
Primary	59.8	(0.0)	*	28.2	(0.0)	*	29.3	(0.0)	*	24.8	(0.0)	*	31.5	(0.0)	*	4.5	(0.0)	*
Secondary	21.7	(0.0)	*	-3.2	(0.0)	*	8.8	(0.0)	*	4.9	(0.0)	*	24.9	(0.0)	*	3.8	(0.0)	*

(continued)

Table 6.9 (continued)

	(8)			(9)			(10)			(11)			(12)			(13)		
	Short term trends						Long term trends						Short term			Long term		
	TUR	s.e		DEV	s.e		TUR	s.e		DEV	s.e		DinD	s.e		DinD	s.e	
Equity																		
Both levels	6.2	(0.0)	*	18.9	(0.0)	*	-9.9	(0.0)	*	12.5	(0.0)	*	-12.7	(0.0)	*	-22.3	(0.0)	*
Primary	36.7	(0.0)	*	25.4	(0.0)	*	-3.5	(0.0)	*	15.4	(0.0)	*	11.3	(0.0)	*	-18.9	(0.0)	*
Secondary	-24.4	(0.0)	*	12.4	(0.0)	*	-16.2	(0.0)	*	9.5	(0.0)	*	-36.7	(0.0)	*	-25.7	(0.0)	*
Equity (adjusted)																		
Both levels	39.1	(0.0)	*	41.2	(0.0)	*	48.7	(0.0)	*	49.2	(0.0)	*	-2.0	(0.0)	*	-0.6	(0.0)	*
Primary	41.3	(0.0)	*	33.6	(0.0)	*	5.2	(0.0)	*	43.0	(0.0)	*	7.6	(0.0)	*	-37.9	(0.0)	*
Secondary	37.0	(0.0)	*	48.7	(0.0)	*	92.1	(0.0)	*	55.4	(0.0)	*	-11.7	(0.0)	*	36.7	(0.0)	*

Source authors' calculations based on Altinok and Diebolt (2024, 2025)

Table 6.10 Projection model parameters

Parameter	Definition	Baseline value
R	Reform period	15
W	Length of work life	40
S	Simulation period (years)	80
d	Discount rate	3%
p	Status quo growth rate	1,5%
μ	Growth coefficient due to the reform	1,98%
A*	Scores from achievement tests	500

Table 6.11 Estimated gains from improving Türkiye's education system

	Scenario 1: Increasing the quality of education	Scenario 2: Reducing inequalities	Scenario 3: Combining quality and inequality
Value of reform (bn USD)	16,500	6,638	25,569
In % of current GDP	736%	296%	1,140.7%
In % of discounted future GDP	15.7%	6.3%	24.4%
GDP increase in year 2100	68.1%	25.8%	111.0%

Notes Methodology adapted from Gust et al. (2024). Discounted value of future increases in GDP until 2100 due to the reform scenario, expressed in billion USD, as a percentage of current GDP, and as a percentage of discounted future GDP

around $16,500 billion over the entire 2020–2100 period). Even if such a scenario proves optimistic,[24] it shows the extent to which an improvement in the quality of the education system can raise the economic level of a developing country like Türkiye.

Other scenarios are conceivable, in particular those that could focus more on school inequalities. For example, a so-called positive discrimination policy could aim to raise the performance of students with the lowest socio-economic capital to the level of students with the highest socio-economic capital (i.e. the average score of the poorest quartile would equal that of the richest quartile). This policy amounts to increasing the performance of a quarter of the population by 87 points. Thus, the total effect on the population is 22 points (obtained by dividing the targeted 87-point effect by four), i.e. a growth of 0.22 standard deviations. The total effect on GDP by

[24] It is possible to draw up other, more realistic scenarios and compare the respective gains, but as the aim of our work is not to carry out simulations, we prefer to present only this policy for combating inequality. For example, in a recent publication, Gust et al (2024) show that a reform aimed at bringing the entire population up to at least the basic skills threshold would bring Türkiye $5,846 billion, or 261% of current GDP (see table A.6 on page 24). This reform would therefore be three times less effective in terms of growth than one aimed at intensively boosting the quality of Türkiye's education system.

Table 6.12 Schooling level performance and expenditures in education

	(1)	(2)	(3)	(4)	(5)	(6)	(7)	(8)	(9)
Log(GDP pc)	42.448***	7.003	23.141***	14.922**	11.415	17.604***	64.504***	29.115***	46.769***
	(3.563)	(4.660)	(7.589)	(7.052)	(7.164)	(4.282)	(5.041)	(8.712)	(5.596)
Expenditures on education	–25.859***	63.702***	–16.151*	–3.345	25.981***	–0.968	–1.294	88.833***	22.285***
	(5.183)	(8.378)	(8.687)	(7.443)	(6.566)	(4.682)	(6.596)	(14.146)	(6.126)
Intercept	316.453***	370.781***	418.567***	405.307***	398.803***	400.304***	179.644***	84.066***	200.381***
	(20.598)	(18.595)	(30.607)	(26.601)	(24.282)	(16.392)	(30.386)	(31.762)	(25.118)
Level	Primary	Secondary	Both	Both	Both	Both	Primary (adj.)	Secondary (adj.)	Both (adj.)
Skill	All	All	Reading	Maths	Sciences	All	All	All	All
Adjusted	No	No	No	No	No	No	Yes	Yes	Yes
R–squared	0.593	0.488	0.382	0.498	0.452	0.420	0.709	0.632	0.643
Observations	502	433	293	337	305	935	502	427	929
Nb. countries	17	17	20	19	20	20	17	17	20
1970–2020									
Ranking	3	5	4	4	5	5	1	2	2
Residuals	–20.5	–40.4	–10.6	–33.3	–18.8	–22.1	64.8	129.6	116.1
Best ranked	Czech Rep	Czech Rep	Brazil	Czech Rep	Vietnam	Czech Rep	Turkey	Vietnam	Vietnam
2000–2020									
Ranking	1	3	2	3	2	2	1	3	2
Residuals	9.2	–2.9	24.5	2.8	12.2	11.8	49.5	88.2	87.1
Best ranked	Turkey	Vietnam	Vietnam	Vietnam	Vietnam	Vietnam	Turkey	Vietnam	Vietnam

Source authors' calculations based on Altinok and Diebolt (2024, 2025)

2100 would be an increase of 296% (or $6,638 billion discounted to 2020 dollars), with an average annual growth rate increasing by 1.42%, and a gain of 25.8% if the amounts are discounted.

A final scenario would aim to combine a policy of general improvement in the quality of education with one targeting pupils with the least socio-economic capital (a mix between scenario 1 and scenario 2). Thus, by raising the level of the entire population by 0.5 standard deviations, while at the same time boosting the performance of the poorest pupils (by making them converge toward that of the richest pupils), the total effect in terms of raising the quality of education is 72 points (i.e. 0.72 standard deviations, obtained by combining 50 points from scenario 1 and 22 points from scenario 2). The cumulative effect on GDP in 2100 would be a discounted increase of 111%. In the end, the cumulative gain from this reform would be $25,569 billion (or 1,141% of discounted 2020 GDP).

6.4 Conclusion

Türkiye is a country that has simultaneously seen an increase in its results in international surveys of student achievement and a rise in access to education. This rather exceptional feature merits analysis. We have tried to understand whether these simultaneous trends can be explained by exogenous factors. Using a counterfactual analysis, we found that the progress observed in Türkiye over the last two decades is not mirrored in other countries with similar characteristics.

For example, while the average progression in terms of the quality of education has been 28 points per decade over the recent period, it is only 8.2 points for economically close countries. This suggests that Türkiye's progress is 20 points higher than that of developing countries with an economic level close to Türkiye's in the 1970s. This improvement is more marked at the primary level than the secondary level, although it remains significant at both levels.

In order to gain a better understanding of the performance of education systems, two indices have been calculated. The first refers to the efficiency of education systems and groups together the two indicators relating to performance thresholds. A system is said to be highly effective if it succeeds in bringing the entire population up to the minimum competency threshold while ensuring that a certain number can reach the threshold of excellence. The efficacy indices for Türkiye reinforce the idea that the Turkish education system is improving more than those of other developing countries. Recent efforts by the Turkish government to extend compulsory schooling to the age of 16 appear not to have hampered the quality of the education system (Çelik & Gür, 2013; Köseleci, 2015; Özdemir, 2015). However, fears of rising inequality seem to be present, particularly at the secondary level. This issue seems to be the central problem of the Turkish education system (Alacacı & Erbaş, 2010; Sarıer, 2021; Yediyıldız & Ustun, 2024).

Indeed, equity at this level seems to have regressed since 1970 and especially since 2000. Using the double-difference method, we find that Türkiye has diverged in terms of equity. The other countries have improved their equity more than Türkiye, raising fears of a rise in inequality in this country. Further work is needed to understand the origins of these inequalities. Indeed, there appears to be a high degree of segregation between schools within the Turkish education system.

For example, the OECD has calculated a school inclusion index, which can be interpreted as a measure of the degree of equity and uniformity of educational outcomes between different schools in an education system. A low index suggests significant heterogeneity, where the quality of education and student achievement vary considerably from school to school. A low index of school inclusion, such as that implicitly suggested by the disparities observed in the Turkish education system, points to notable heterogeneity with significant differences in academic achievement between schools (T. Aydın & Çilek, 2024). This heterogeneity means that some schools achieve better results than others, which can be attributed to a combination of factors such as available resources, teacher quality and students' socio-economic status (A. Aydın et al., 2012; Dolu, 2020; Sarıer, 2020).

In addition to inequalities between schools, there are also significant differences between Turkish provinces. Significant inequalities in educational achievement between Turkish provinces are evident in data from international assessments such as PISA and TIMSS. Uysal and Gelbal (2018), analyzing PISA data from 2009, 2012 and 2015, found significant differences between regions in math, science and reading scores for all years studied, identifying Southeast and East-Central Anatolia as generally having the lowest scores. Other authors confirm these differences between Turkish provinces (Alacacı & Erbaş, 2010; Dinçer & Oral, 2013; Dolu, 2020; Köseleci, 2015). Drawing on PISA 2012 data, Köseleci (2015) points out that the percentage of 15-year-old students scoring below Level 2 varied considerably from region to region, ranging from 29% in Central Anatolia to 62% in Southeastern Anatolia region.

This shows that a policy aimed at improving the quality of education should also be accompanied by action to reduce educational inequalities. We show that such a mixed policy scenario could significantly improve Türkiye's economic performance. This acceleration in growth could then enable Türkiye to double its GDP by 2100 (+111%, see Table 6.11), in discounted terms. This growth could then undoubtedly lift Türkiye out of the developing country trap (Yilmaz, 2015) and into the status of a developed country.

The question remains, however, regarding the educational policies needed to achieve these objectives, and the sources of funding. Surveys of students' skills enable us to accurately measure the evolution of countries' school performance. However, the experiences of some countries cited as examples—such as Vietnam or the Netherlands—are difficult to replicate in other countries, and even more difficult in a country like Türkiye. Each country will have to find its own ways of targeting an effective education policy. A detailed analysis of the actions implemented in the past in Türkiye can help develop an effective policy.

In the context of this article, our research into the evolution of learning achievement in Türkiye has produced new evidence spanning half a century and in comparison with most emerging countries, leading to the conclusion that educational performance in reading and mathematics is declining, with average scores being significantly low. We have also shown that Türkiye's trajectory in terms of educational achievement tends to diverge from that of other developing countries. Generally speaking, our results enrich the conclusions drawn from national surveys, while providing new historical and comparative insights. Finally, they invite us to look beyond considerations centered on purely quantitative indicators and consider the major importance of the qualitative dimension of education.

Appendix A

See Figs. 6.6, 6.7, 6.8, 6.9, 6.10, 6.11, 6.12, 6.13, 6.14, 6.15, 6.16.

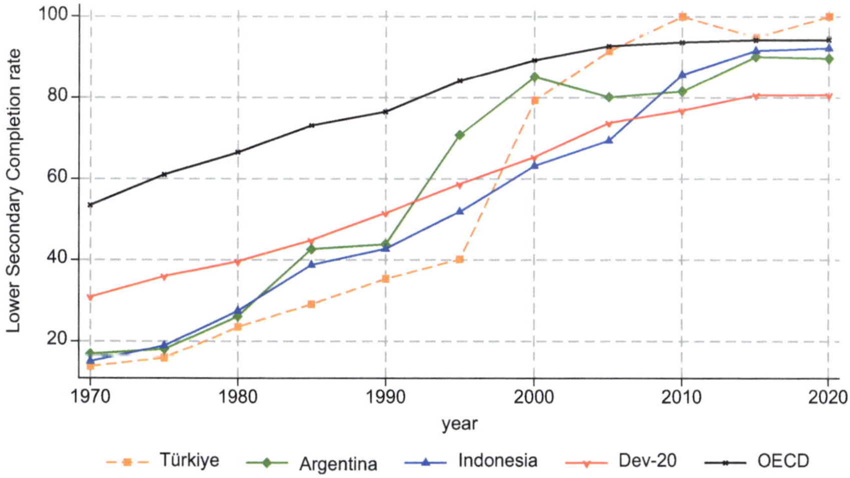

Fig. 6.6 Lower Secondary Completion Rate across different countries and regions (1970–2020). *Source* authors, based on Altinok and Diebolt (2024, 2025)

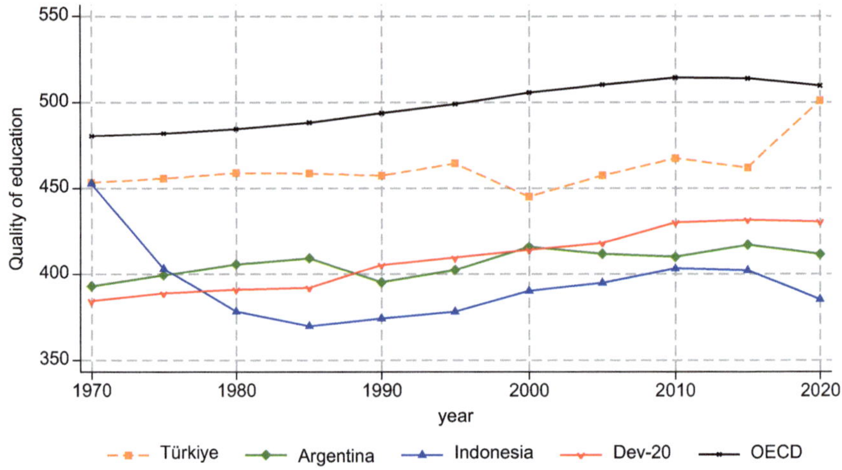

Fig. 6.7 Quality of schooling across different countries and regions (1970–2020). *Source* authors, based on Altinok and Diebolt (2024, 2025)

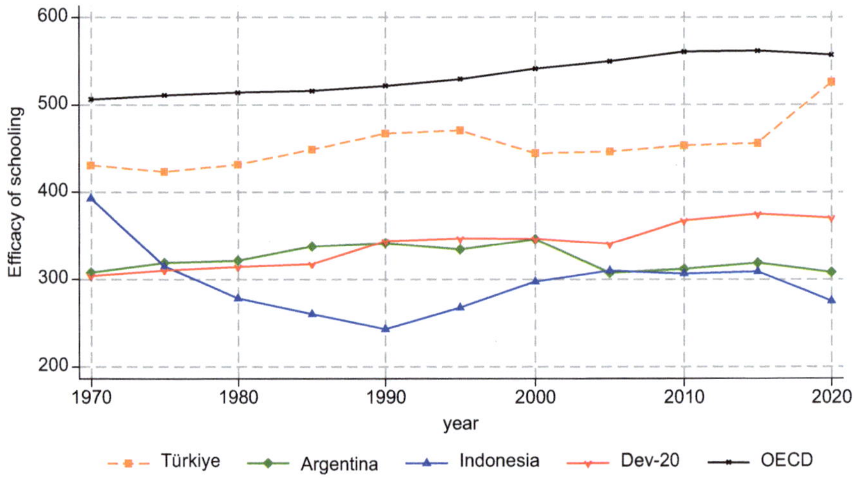

Fig. 6.8 Efficacy index of schooling across different countries and regions (1970–2020). *Source* authors, based on Altinok and Diebolt (2024, 2025)

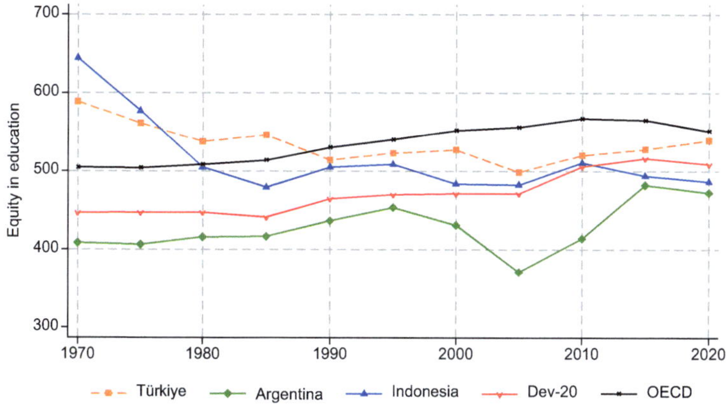

Fig. 6.9 Equity index of schooling across different countries and regions (1970–2020). *Source* authors, based on Altinok and Diebolt (2024, 2025)

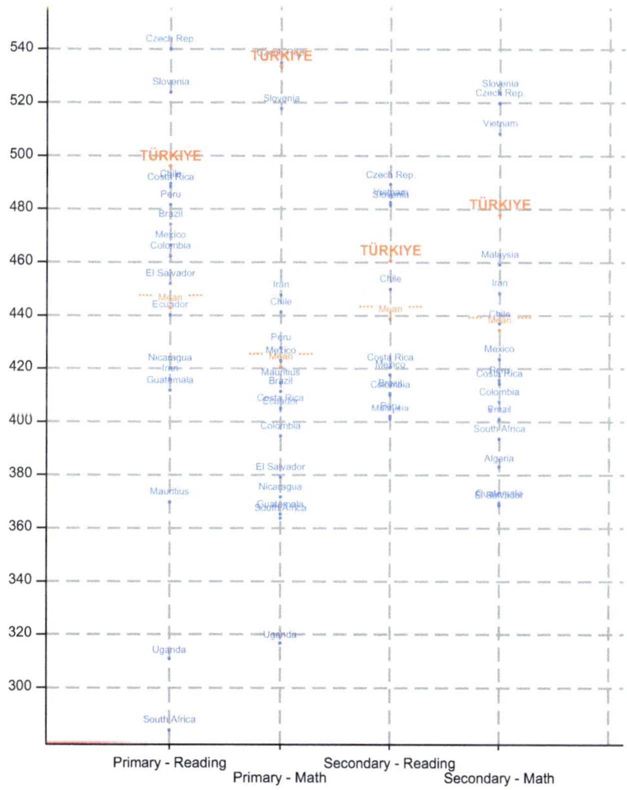

Fig. 6.10 Performance of Türkiye compared to similar countries in 2020. *Source* authors' calculations based on Altinok and Diebolt (2024, 2025)

Fig. 6.11 Trends on school performance in mathematics, primary education. *Source* authors' calculations based on Altinok and Diebolt (2024, 2025)

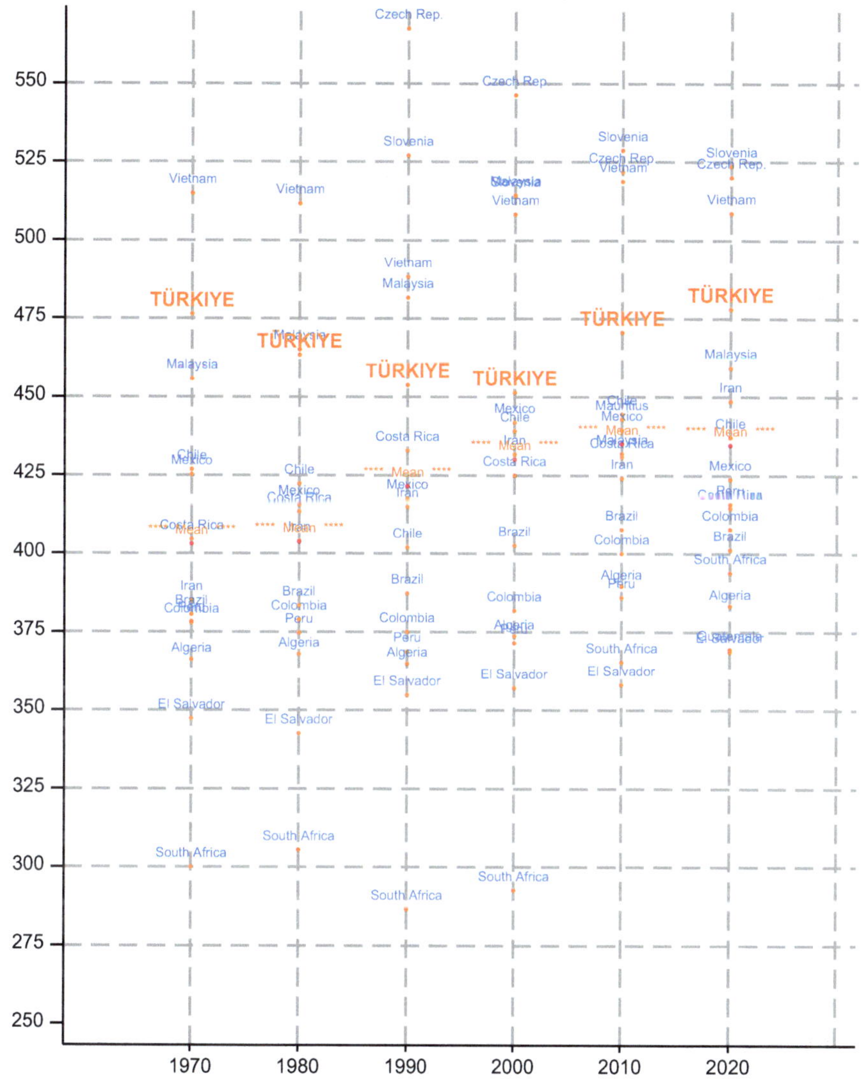

Fig. 6.12 Trends on school performance in mathematics, secondary education. Source authors' calculations based on Altinok and Diebolt (2024, 2025)

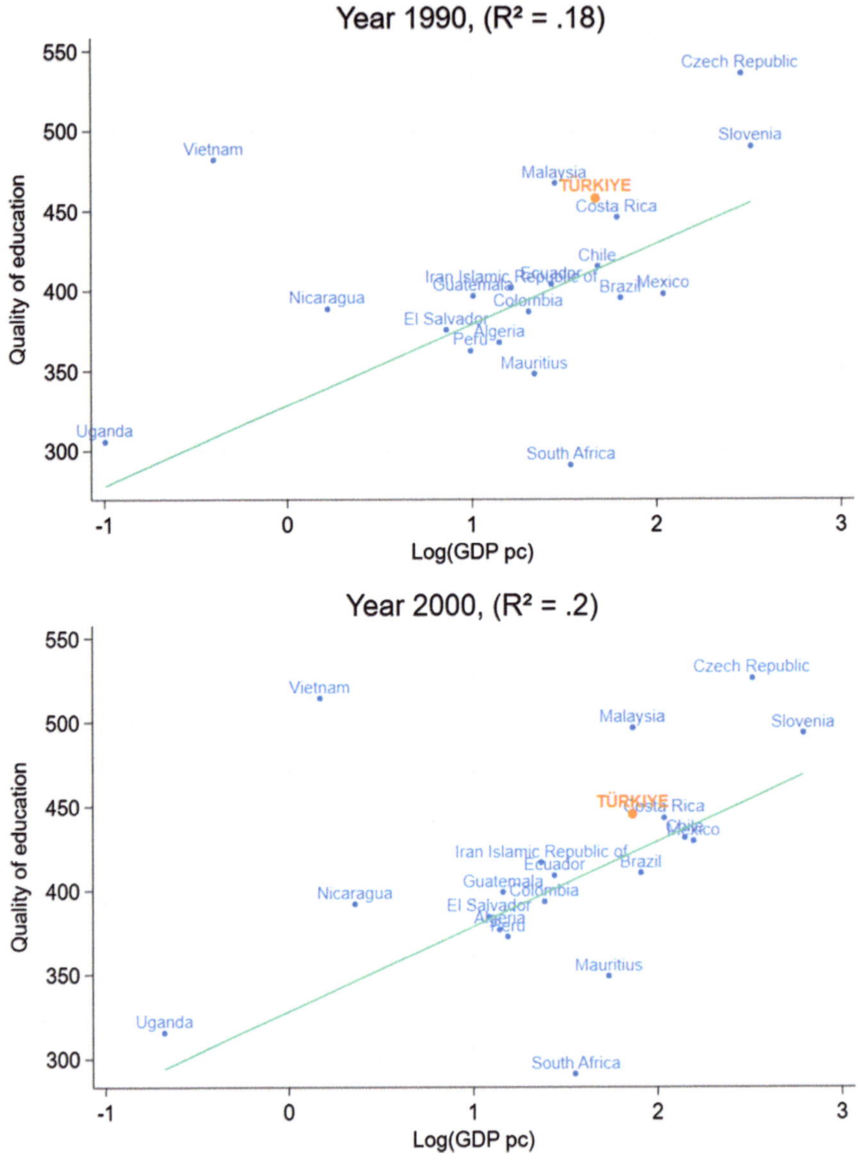

Fig. 6.13 Relationship between GDP per capita and quality of education (1990 & 2000). Source authors' calculations based on Altinok and Diebolt (2024, 2025)

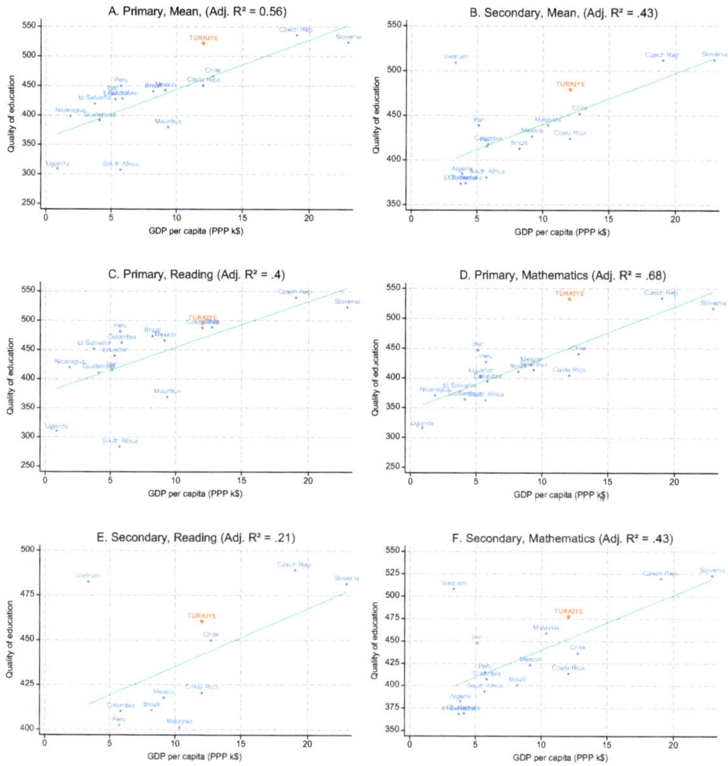

Fig. 6.14 Relationship between performance in each skill and level and GDP per capita. *Source* authors' calculations based on Altinok and Diebolt (2024, 2025)

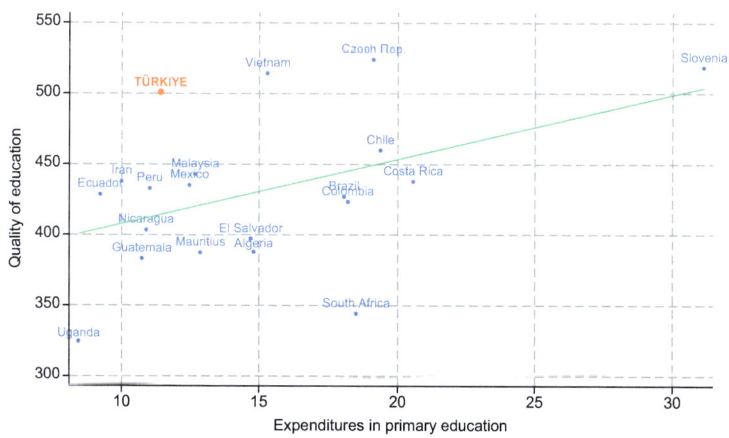

Fig. 6.15 Expenditures on education and quality of education in 2020 (Adj $R^2 = 0{,}15$). *Source* authors' calculations based on Altinok and Diebolt (2024, 2025)

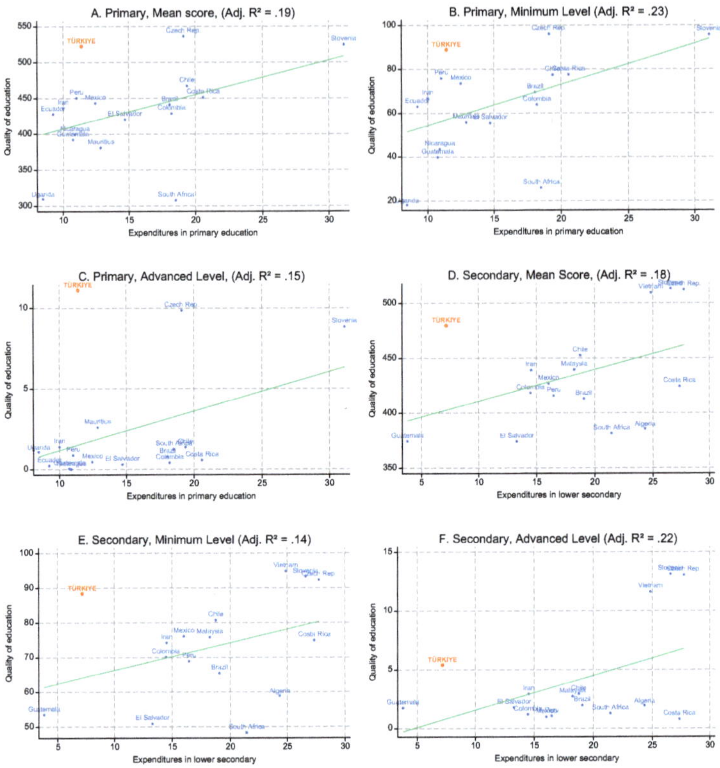

Fig. 6.16 Expenditures in education and quality of education (2020). *Source* authors' calculations based on Altinok and Diebolt (2024, 2025)

Appendix B

This appendix is adapted from Hanushek and Woessmann (2011) and Hanushek et al. (2017a). For more information, see Hanushek and Woessmann (2011).

The projection model is based on four different phases. First, we introduce the reform (Phase A), where the effect of the quality of education is passed on over a 10-year period. In the next phase (Phase B), older workers are replaced by reform workers (i.e. young people affected by the reform and having graduated enter the labor market). This means that the reform only becomes fully effective over a period of 30 years. Third, workers who were only partially affected by the reform are replaced (Phase C). Finally, all workers affected by the reform are replaced, and the effect of the reform comes to an end (Phase D).

Phase A (2020–2030): Introduction of Reform.

During the first 10 years of the educational reform, the additional growth in GDP per capita due to the reform for year *t* is given by:

$$\Delta^{t}_{growth} = growth\,coeff. \times \Delta Scores \times \frac{1}{Working\ life} \times \frac{t-2020}{10} + \Delta^{t-1}_{growth}, \tag{6.14}$$

where the *growth coefficient* represents the effect of the one standard-deviation increase in test scores obtained in the growth models of Hanushek and Woessmann (2012) and Δ *Scores* is the change in educational performance due to the reform analyzed. Each year, only part of the workforce is replaced by new workers who have received a better education (i.e. the one related to the reform). We take this lag into account with $\frac{1}{Working\ life}$, with a working life of 40 years. The $\frac{t-2020}{10}$ term shows that it takes 10 years for the reform to be fully effective.[25]

Phase B (2031–2060): Replacement of Older Workers by New Ones Who Have Benefited from Reform.

The educational reform is now fully effective, and the academic quality of all students remains stable at this new level. However, given that the working life is assumed to be 40 years, there are still workers with previous levels of schooling who will be replaced by new workers with a higher level of quality. Thus, over the next 30 years, additional growth should follow the following path:

$$\Delta^{t}_{growth} = growth\,coeff. \times \Delta\,Scores \times \frac{1}{Working\ life} + \Delta^{t-1}_{growth}. \tag{6.15}$$

Phase C (2061–2070): Replacement of Workers Who Have Received Part of the Reform with a Higher-Quality Product.

---

[25] In the first version of their projection model (Hanushek & Woessmann 2011) assumed that the reform would only be fully effective after 20 years; we have used the latest version of their model, in which this period is reduced to 10 years. However, the results change little if this period is reduced to 20 years.

After 40 years, all workers who have not experienced educational reform have been replaced by new workers. At the same time, the cohorts of the first 10 years were only partially affected by the educational reform. During this phase, these workers are replaced by cohorts who have received all the educational reform. The additional growth for the following 10 years is thus:

$$\Delta_{growth}^{t} = growth\,coeff. \times \Delta\,Scores \times \frac{1}{Working\ life} - \left(\Delta_{growth}^{t-40} - \Delta_{growth}^{t-41}\right) + \Delta_{growth}^{t-1}. \tag{6.16}$$

Phase D (after 2070): Educational Reform for All Workers.

The entire workforce has been exposed to the reform via the renovated education system. Additional economic growth is now at a constant long-term level:

$$\Delta_{growth}^{t} = growth\,coeff. \times \Delta\,Scores. \tag{6.17}$$

The cumulative effect of the reform can be assessed by calculating various indicators. The total value of the reform can be obtained by calculating the present difference between GDP with and without the reform. We therefore calculate the gain from improving the education system over a period of 80 years, using the discount rate (d) which is similar to that used in Hanushek et al. (2017a) and set at 3%:

$$Value\ of\ reform = \sum_{t=2020}^{t=2100} \left(GDP_{reform}^{t} - GDP_{without\ reform}^{t}\right) \times (1+d)^{-(t-2020)}. \tag{6.18}$$

Expressed as a percentage of current GDP, the total value of the reform is obtained using the following equation:

$$Value\ of\ reform_{\%\ of\ current\ GDP} = \frac{Value\ of\ reform}{GDP_{without\ reform}^{2020}} \times 100. \tag{6.19}$$

Other indicators can also be obtained, such as the ratio between the total value of the reform and the discounted GDP obtained over the entire duration of the reform (Eq. 6.19):

$$Value\ of\ reform_{of\ discounted\ future\ GDP} = \frac{Value\ of\ reform}{\sum_{t=2020}^{t=2100} GDP_{without\ reform}^{t} \times (1+d)^{-(t-2020)}} \times 100. \tag{6.20}$$

Furthermore, we can also calculate how much additional GDP growth the reform could generate for any year, such as 2090, using Eq. 6.21:

$$GDP_{Increase\ in\ 2090\ (\%)} = \frac{GDP^{2090}_{reform} - GDP^{2090}_{without\ reform}}{GDP^{2090}_{without\ reform}} \times 100. \quad (6.21)$$

References

Alacacı, C., & Erbaş, A. K. (2010). Unpacking the inequality among Turkish schools: Findings from PISA 2006. *International Journal of Educational Development, 30*(2), 182–192.

Altinok, N., & Diebolt, C. (2024). Cliometrics of learning-adjusted years of schooling: Evidence from a new dataset. *Cliometrica, 18*(3), 691–764. https://doi.org/10.1007/s11698-023-00276-x

Altinok, N., & Diebolt, C. (2025). Mapping educational inequality worldwide: A new dataset (1970–2020). Mimeo, January 2025.

Angrist, N., Djankov, S., Goldberg, P. K., & Patrinos, H. A. (2021). Measuring human capital using global learning data. *Nature, 592*(7854), 403–408.

Angrist, N., Patrinos, H. A., & Schlotter, M. (2013). An expansion of a global data set on educational quality: A focus on achievement in developing countries. *The World Bank: Policy Research Working Papers*. https://doi.org/10.1596/1813-9450-6536

Avvisati, F., & Givord, P. (2023). The learning gain over one school year among 15-year-olds: An international comparison based on PISA. *Labour Economics, 84*, Article 102365.

Aydın, A., Sarıer, Y., & Uysal, Ş. (2012). Sosyoekonomik ve sosyokültürel değişkenler açısından PISA matematik sonuçlarının karşılaştırılması. *Eğitim ve Bilim, 37*(164).

Aydın, T., & Çilek, A. (2024). PISA 2022 Sınav Sonuçları Bağlamında Türk Eğitim Sisteminin Genel Görünümü. *Abant İzzet Baysal Üniversitesi Eğitim Fakültesi Dergisi, 24*(4), 2361–2378.

Barro, R. J., & Lee, J.-W. (2013). A new data set of educational attainment in the world, 1950–2010. *Journal of Development Economics, 104*, 184–198.

Boman, B. (2022). Vietnam's exceptional educational achievement: A thematic review of the emerging literature. *Discover Education, 1*(1), 14. https://doi.org/10.1007/s44217-022-00014-x

Borsch-Supan, A. (2000). A model under Siege: A case study of the German retirement insurance system. *The Economic Journal, 110*(461), F24–F45. https://doi.org/10.1111/1468-0297.00506

Çelik, Z., & Gür, B. S. (2013). Turkey's education policy during the AK party era (2002–2013). *Insight Turkey, 15*(4), 151.

Coleman, J. S. (1966). *Equality of educational opportunity* (Vol. 1). US Department of Health, Education, and Welfare, Office of Education.

Dinçer, M. A., & Oral, I. (2013). Türkiye'de devlet liselerinde akademik dirençlilik profili. *İstanbul: Eğitim Reformu Girişimi Yayınları.*

Dincer, M. A., & Uysal, G. (2010). The determinants of student achievement in Turkey. *International Journal of Educational Development, 30*(6), 592–598.

Dolu, A. (2020). Sosyoekonomik Faktörlerin Eğitim Performansi Üzerine Etkisi: Pisa 2015 Türkiye Örneği. *Journal of Management and Economics Research, 18*(2), 41–58.

Filmer, D., Rogers, H., Angrist, N., & Sabarwal, S. (2020). Learning-adjusted years of schooling (LAYS): Defining a new macro measure of education. *Economics of Education Review, 77*, Article 101971.

Foshay, A. W., Thorndike, R. L., Hotyat, F., Pidgeon, D. A., & Walker, D. A. (1962). *Educational achievements of thirteen-year olds in twelve countries: Results of an international research project, 1959–61* (Vol. 4). Unesco.

Gust, S., Hanushek, E. A., & Woessmann, L. (2024). Global universal basic skills: Current deficits and implications for world development. *Journal of Development Economics, 166*, 103–205.

Hanushek, E. A. (2019). *Addressing cross-national generalizability in educational impact evaluation.* National Bureau of Economic Research.

Hanushek, E. A., & Kimko, D. D. (2000). Schooling, labor-force quality, and the growth of nations. *The American Economic Review, 90*(5), 1184.

Hanushek, E. A., Ruhose, J., & Woessmann, L. (2017a). Economic gains from educational reform by US States. *Journal of Human Capital, 11*(4), 447–486.

Hanushek, E. A., Ruhose, J., & Woessmann, L. (2017b). Knowledge capital and aggregate income differences: Development accounting for US States. *American Economic Journal: Macroeconomics, 9*(4), 184–224.

Hanushek, E. A., & Woessmann, L. (2011). How much do educational outcomes matter in OECD countries? *Economic Policy, 26*(67), 427–491.

Hanushek, E. A., & Woessmann, L. (2012). Do better schools lead to more growth? Cognitive skills, economic outcomes, and causation. *Journal of Economic Growth, 17*(4), 267–321. https://doi.org/10.1007/s10887-012-9081-x

Hanushek, E. A., & Woessmann, L. (2015). *The knowledge capital of nations: Education and the economics of growth.* MIT Press.

Honaker, J., King, G., & Blackwell, M. (2011). Amelia II: A program for missing data. *Journal of Statistical Software, 45*(1), 1–47.

Koca, H., Yakar, A., Dev, F., & Şen, G. (2024). TIMSS ve PISA verileri üzerinden Türkiye'nin eğitim performansının gelişiminin analizi. *Ulusal Eğitim Dergisi, 4*(2), 644–660.

Kolen, M. J., & Brennan, R. L. (2014). *Test equating, scaling, and linking: Methods and practices.* Springer Science & Business Media.

Köseleci, N. (2015). Progress towards good-quality education for all in Turkey: A qualified success? *Comparative Education, 51*(4), 555–574.

Lim, S. S., Updike, R. L., Kaldjian, A. S., Barber, R. M., Cowling, K., York, H., Friedman, J., Xu, R., Whisnant, J. L., & Taylor, H. J. (2018). Measuring human capital: A systematic analysis of 195 countries and territories, 1990–2016. *The Lancet, 392*(10154), 1217–1234.

MEB. (2018). *Turkey's Education Vision 2023.* https://planipolis.iiep.unesco.org/sites/default/files/ressources/turkey_education_vision_2023.pdf

Mullis, I., Martin, M. O., Foy, P., Kelly, D. L., & Fishbein, B. (2020). TIMSS 2019 international results in mathematics and science. In *Retrieved from Boston College, TIMSS & PIRLS International Study Center website:* https://www.timssandpirls.bc.edu/timss2019/international-results. https://timss2019.org/reports/wp-content/themes/timssandpirls/download-center/TIMSS-2019-International-Results-in-Mathematics-and-Science.pdf

Mullis, I., von Davier, M., Foy, P., Fishbein, B., Reynolds, K., & Wry, E. (2023). *PIRLS 2021 International Results in Reading.* https://doi.org/10.6017/lse.tpisc.tr2103.kb5342

OECD. (2021). *OECD economic surveys: Turkey 2021.* OECD Publishing. https://doi.org/10.1787/2cd09ab1-en

OECD. (2023a). *OECD Economic Surveys: Türkiye 2023.* OCDE. https://doi.org/10.1787/864ab2ba-en

OECD. (2023b). *PISA 2022 Results (Volume I).* OECD. https://doi.org/10.1787/53f23881-en

Özdemir, C. (2015). *Relationship between equity and excellence in education: multilevel analysis of international student assessment data with a focus on turkey.*

Paccagnella, M. (2016). Literacy and numeracy proficiency in IALS, ALL and PIAAC. *OECD Education Working Papers, 142.* https://doi.org/10.1787/5jlpq7qglx5g-en

Parandekar, S., & Sedmik, E. (2016). *Unraveling a secret: Vietnam's outstanding performance on the PISA test.*

Piketty, T. (2013). Le capital au XXIe siècle. In *Les Livres du nouveau monde.* Seuil.

Polat, M., Karabiyik, T., & Kartal, G. (2024). *TIMSS 2023: National Report Türkiye.*

Sarıer, Y. (2020). TIMSS uygulamalarında Türkiye'nin performansı ve akademik başarıyı yordayan değişkenler. *Temel Eğitim, 2*(2), 6–27.

Sarıer, Y. (2021). Pisa Uygulamalarinda Türkiye'nin Performansi Ve Öğrenci Başarisini Yordayan Değişkenler. *Türkiye Sosyal Araştırmalar Dergisi, 25*(3), 905–926.

Schwerdt, G., & Wiederhold, S. (2019). A macroeconomic analysis of literacy and economic performance. *Mimeo.* https://www.dataangel.ca/docs/A%20Macroeconomic%20Analysis%20of%20Literacy_February2019.pdf

Spaull, N. (2018). Who makes it into PISA? Understanding the impact of PISA sample eligibility using Turkey as a case study (PISA 2003–PISA 2012). *Assessment in Education: Principles, Policy & Practice*, 1–25.

Suna, H. E., & Özer, M. (2021). Türkiye'de sosyoekonomik düzey ve okullar arası başarı farklarının akademik başarı ile ilişkisi. *Eğitimde Ve Psikolojide Ölçme Ve Değerlendirme Dergisi, 12*(1), 54–70.

UNESCO Institute of Statistics. (2019). Costs and benefits of different approaches to measuring the learning proficiency of students. *UIS Information Paper, 53.* http://uis.unesco.org/sites/default/files/documents/ip53-costs-benefits-approaches-measuring-proficiency-2019-en.pdf

Uysal, N. K., & Gelbal, S. (2018). Inequality in education in Turkey in the scope of PISA and TSI. *Kastamonu Education Journal, 26*(4), 1187.

Waldow, F. (2009). What PISA did and did not do: Germany after the 'PISA-shock.' *European Educational Research Journal, 8*(3), 476–483. https://doi.org/10.2304/eerj.2009.8.3.476

World Bank, T. (2011). *Vietnam: High quality education for all by 2020.* World Bank. https://openknowledge.worldbank.org/handle/10986/27450

Wu, M. (2010). Comparing the similarities and differences of PISA 2003 and TIMSS. *OECD Education Working Papers, 32,* 0_1.

Yediyıldız, B., & Ustun, U. (2024). Deciphering socioeconomic inequality in science literacy: Evidence from PISA 2015 in Türkiye. *International Journal of Educational Development, 111*, Article 103173.

Yilmaz, G. (2015). Turkish middle income trap and less skilled human capital. *Iktisat Isletme Ve Finans, 30*(346), 9–36.

Chapter 7
Conclusion—What Edumetrics Still Has to Teach Us

Abstract This chapter positions edumetrics as a framework to understand how education drives long-term prosperity, emphasizing that it is not years of schooling but learning outcomes that matter. Beyond technical skills, the true mission of education is to instill from the earliest age both the mastery of fundamentals and the capacity to "learn how to learn". Each student who drops out represents not only a personal loss but also a collective erosion of economic potential and civic vitality. By linking measurement to action, edumetrics reframes education as a foundation for adaptability, equity and resilience in a rapidly changing world. Ultimately, it offers both a diagnostic tool and a strategic compass for building human capital in the twenty-first century.

In the words of Lord Kelvin, "If you cannot measure it, you cannot improve it". This conviction lies at the heart of Edumetrics and frames the central message of this book: education is the single most important driver of long-term prosperity. Our findings demonstrate that differences in sustained economic growth rates across countries can be largely explained by their educational contexts. Crucially, it is not the number of years spent in school that matters most, but rather what is actually learned during those years—hence our focus on measuring the quality of education worldwide.

While educational failure is often most visible in deficits in foundational skills—reading, writing, mathematics and the natural sciences—it is equally vital to consider lifelong learning and continuous training. The digital revolution is a compelling reminder that the skills required for success evolve rapidly and that learning cannot be confined to the early years of life. Simply spending more on education will not suffice; what matters is investing more wisely. This requires a collective effort by all stakeholders in the system—teachers first and foremost, but also unions, governments, the private sector and civil society—to cut through the Gordian knot of persistent educational challenges.

Supplementary Information The online version contains supplementary material available at https://doi.org/10.1007/978-3-032-13277-2_7.

N. Altinok and C. Diebolt, *Edumetrics*, Population Economics,
https://doi.org/10.1007/978-3-032-13277-2_7

We remain skeptical of piecemeal strategies and quick fixes. Too many reforms, poorly coordinated and constantly changing, can undermine the very progress they seek to achieve. In our view, the path forward lies in a return to fundamentals: ensuring that every learner can read, write and count. The rest will follow in due course—there is wisdom in allowing time for learning to mature, even if this runs counter to the present Zeitgeist of acceleration. Moreover, we must recognize the distinction between written and oral skills, both of which merit deliberate cultivation.

We must also recognize that beyond the acquisition of technical skills, the true mission of education is to cultivate from the earliest years both the desire and the ability to *learn how to learn*. This disposition is not merely an academic virtue; it is a survival skill for individuals and societies navigating an era defined by technological acceleration, ecological transition and geopolitical uncertainty. The capacity to learn continuously, to adapt and to reinvent oneself is what allows knowledge to remain alive, relevant and transformative. At its core, this lifelong disposition rests on a secure foundation: the mastery of the fundamentals—reading, writing and numeracy. Without these, the edifice of human capital cannot be built, for all higher-order skills, whether digital literacy, scientific reasoning, or intercultural communication, are predicated upon this essential triad.

Yet the importance of fundamentals should not be interpreted as narrow utilitarianism. To read is to access worlds beyond one's own; to write is to shape thought and communication; to count is to model, measure and make sense of the world's complexity. In this sense, the basics are not merely practical tools—they are the gateways to autonomy, creativity and critical judgment. They also serve as the scaffolding that enables students to cultivate the metacognitive habits of self-questioning, reflection and persistence that "learning how to learn" requires.

The challenge is that every student who disengages from this process, who leaves school without these basic skills or without the desire to continue learning, represents not just an individual tragedy but a collective loss. Each dropout erodes our shared reservoir of economic potential, but also our civic fabric. A society where significant portions of the population lack the tools to participate fully in knowledge economies and democratic life is one that condemns itself to fragility, division and stagnation. The invisible cost of disengagement is borne not only in lost productivity but also in diminished civic participation, weakened trust, and reduced capacity for collective problem-solving.

From this perspective, ensuring that no learner is left behind is not simply a moral imperative rooted in ideals of fairness and equity; it is also a profoundly strategic choice. Investing in every child's capacity to master the basics and to carry forward the disposition to keep learning is the surest guarantee of sustainable prosperity. It is also the most powerful insurance against the risks of polarization, alienation and exclusion that increasingly threaten the cohesion of our societies.

Moreover, cultivating the will and capacity to learn is inseparable from fostering resilience. In a world where automation can render skills obsolete within a decade, and where global shocks—whether pandemics, financial crises or climate-related disasters—can reshape labor markets overnight, the ability to relearn and adapt becomes the ultimate comparative advantage. What edumetrics teaches us is that these capacities can and must be measured, nurtured and valued as central outcomes of education systems, alongside traditional indicators of attainment and performance. Learning also presupposes the right to err. Just as a child learns to walk by falling, knowledge progresses through trial, error, and correction. Error is not a failure of learning; it is its very condition. To deny learners the possibility of making mistakes is to deprive them of the most powerful engine of intellectual growth. This principle applies not only to schooling, but to life itself—and to science. Scientific progress has never advanced along a straight line; it is built upon conjectures, refutations, revisions, and the humility to recognize what we do not yet know. In education systems, however, error is too often stigmatized, sanctioned, or concealed, rather than understood, analyzed, and transformed into learning. Such a culture discourages risk-taking, curiosity, and intellectual courage. Yet, without the freedom to make mistakes, there can be no genuine learning, no creativity, and no innovation. Encouraging learners to take the risk of being wrong—without blame, humiliation, or exclusion—is not an act of pedagogical indulgence; it is a condition for progress. From this perspective, valuing error is neither utopian nor naive. It is a profound shift in how we conceive knowledge transmission and human development. To learn is to experiment; to experiment is to err; and to err is to advance. Edumetrics, by focusing on learning trajectories rather than static outcomes, invites us to rethink education not as the avoidance of error, but as the disciplined and constructive engagement with it—just as science itself has always done.

This focus also reframes the role of teachers. They are not only transmitters of knowledge but architects of curiosity, builders of confidence and guides in the lifelong journey of learning. Their task is to awaken the appetite for discovery, to provide the tools to navigate complexity and to model the intellectual humility that true learning requires. Policies that neglect this role in favor of narrowly technocratic reforms risk missing the very essence of what makes education transformative.

In the end, to foster "learning how to learn" is to recognize that education is not a finite project with a terminal point, but an ongoing process that sustains human flourishing across the life course. It is to understand that the dropout rate is not merely an administrative statistic but a mirror reflecting the extent to which we are wasting human potential. And it is to affirm that the fundamentals are not antiquated relics of an old pedagogy, but the living roots from which all future growth must spring.

Finally, we hold a personal conviction: school is about instruction; education is the domain of families. The two are complementary, not interchangeable. Whatever challenges our societies face, we are convinced that the root cause of our difficulties is not the school—it is, in fact, the solution. Our collective future depends on the strength of our education systems and the quality of instruction they provide.

What Edumetrics Still Has to Teach Us for Human Capital in the 21st Century is that measuring learning is not a purely technical exercise—it is an act of societal self-reflection and strategic foresight. By rigorously quantifying both the cognitive and non-cognitive dimensions of learning, edumetrics enables policymakers, educators and citizens to distinguish between the illusion of progress and its reality. It teaches us that human capital is not built simply by increasing formal years of schooling, but by ensuring that those years translate into deep, transferable skills that empower individuals to adapt, innovate and collaborate in a rapidly changing world.

Edumetrics also reminds us that quality matters more than quantity, and that learning outcomes must be contextualized within broader social, cultural and economic environments. It pushes us to look beyond averages to examine inequalities in educational achievement, for the distribution of skills within a population is as decisive for a nation's prosperity as the overall level. In doing so, it reframes education policy not as a race to expand systems, but as a mission to enhance their effectiveness and equity.

Moreover, edumetrics challenges us to integrate lifelong learning into our conception of human capital. In an age where technological disruption, climate change, migration and demographic shifts redefine the skills needed for participation in the economy and civic life, initial schooling can no longer be the endpoint of educational policy. The capacity to reskill and upskill—whether in response to automation, artificial intelligence, ecological transition, or global competition—becomes a core dimension of economic resilience.

Here, the parallel with cliometrics becomes especially illuminating. Just as cliometrics revolutionized economic history by combining theory, quantitative data and rigorous empirical analysis to reinterpret the past, edumetrics aspires to do the same for the future of education. Where cliometrics provided a scientific framework for understanding long-term economic and demographic dynamics, edumetrics seeks to provide a comparable framework for the study of learning, skills and human capital across time and space. Both approaches share the conviction that only through measurement, anchored in theory and guided by empirical rigor, can we transform narratives into knowledge and knowledge into policy.

This prospective vision also highlights new frontiers where edumetrics can play a decisive role. The transition to a green economy will demand not only new technologies but also new skills in sustainability, systems thinking and collective problem-solving. The expansion of artificial intelligence will transform the labor market in ways we cannot yet fully anticipate, underscoring the importance of fostering adaptability, creativity and ethical reasoning. Migration flows will continue to reshape the educational and cultural fabric of nations, calling for better tools to measure and bridge linguistic and intercultural competencies. In each of these domains, edumetrics can provide the evidence base for policies that are proactive rather than reactive, strategic rather than fragmented.

Finally, edumetrics teaches humility. Measurement is indispensable, but it is not an end in itself. Metrics should illuminate the path forward, not become an idol that blinds us to the complex, human realities of learning. Data can guide strategy, but wisdom must shape vision. In this sense, edumetrics is not merely a tool for assessment; it is a framework for rethinking the purpose of education itself: to cultivate capable, adaptable and thoughtful citizens who can build and sustain prosperity in the twenty-first century.

If Lord Kelvin was right that improvement begins with measurement, edumetrics adds that meaningful measurement must be tied to action—action that is informed by evidence, guided by values and sustained by a shared commitment to the human potential that education unlocks. This, above all, is what edumetrics still has to teach us.

MIX
Papier aus verantwortungsvollen Quellen
Paper from responsible sources
FSC® C105338

If you have any concerns about our products,
you can contact us on
ProductSafety@springernature.com

In case Publisher is established outside the EU,
the EU authorized representative is:
Springer Nature Customer Service Center GmbH
Europaplatz 3, 69115 Heidelberg, Germany

Printed by Libri Plureos GmbH
in Hamburg, Germany